CINEMA AND URBAN CULTURE

IN SHANGHAI, 1922-1943

Edited and with an Introduction by

Yingjin Zhang

Cinema and Urban Culture in Shanghai, 1922-1943

STANFORD UNIVERSITY PRESS

STANFORD, CALIFORNIA 1999

Stanford University Press

Stanford, California

© 1999 by the Board of Trustees of the

Leland Stanford Junior University

Printed in the United States of America

CIP data appear at the end of the book

 *For Su, Mimi, and Alex*

Contents

Illustrations

Acknowledgments

The idea for this project was conceived in the summer of 1994, when I began organizing two back-to-back panels, "Watching Electric Shadows: Cinema and Urban Culture in Republican China," for the annual meeting of the Association for Asian Studies (AAS) convened in Washington, D.C., April 6–9, 1995. The panels attracted a large audience, and all panelists agreed to contribute to a volume that I proposed to edit. In the following months, I solicited more contributions in an attempt to achieve better coverage.

The editing of the volume and the writing of the introduction took place in 1995–96, while I held a postdoctoral fellowship with the Center for Chinese Studies at the University of Michigan. In addition to the Michigan Center, I am indebted to Indiana University for two summer faculty fellowships, a research leave supplement, a short-term faculty exchange with Nankai University, China, several departmental, college, and graduate school research and conference travel grants, and an Outstanding Junior Faculty Award, all during 1995–97. My research also benefited from the library travel grants from several institutions in 1995: the Center for East Asian Studies at the University of Chicago, the Center for Chinese Studies at the University of Michigan, and the Center for East Asian Studies at Stanford University.

I thank Ted Huters and Leo Ou-fan Lee for serving as chairs and discussants at the 1995 AAS meeting. For different reasons, the panelists Poshek Fu, Paul Pickowicz, and Randolph Trumbull were unable to contribute their papers, but I appreciated their initial support nonetheless. I am grateful to all contributors to this volume for their patience and cooperation; to Dudley Andrew for introducing me to film studies at the University of Iowa in the late 1980s; to Cheng Jihua and Wang Renyin of Beijing for their encouragement; to An Jingfu for locating videotapes of early films; to Zhiwei Xiao for typing an early draft of the Character List; to Sarah Stevens, Paola Voci, and Stephanie DeBoer for their assistance in preparing the Select Bibliography and Index; to John Ziemer for his unfading support for my numerous projects; and to Helen Tartar and the staff of Stanford University Press for their assistance in the final production of the book. The Chinese faculty at Michigan, especially Yi-tsi Mei Feuerwerker, Shuenfu Lin, and David Rolston, provided collegiality during my fellowship year there, and so did the "Hoosiers" back home in Bloomington—Michael Robinson, Sue Tuohy, Jeffrey Wasserstrom, and George Wilson in particular. Finally, I owe all I achieved in the year on leave to my wife, Su, who took the extra burden of taking care of Mimi and Alex while I commuted between Bloomington and Ann Arbor. This book is dedicated to my family, for sharing my interest in watching "electric shadows."

Y.Z.

Note on Romanization

With the exception of personal names and bibliographical data, the pinyin system of romanization is used throughout the book. In the case of personal names, especially those used in Hong Kong or Taiwan, the pinyin equivalents follow the first mention of the name, in parentheses.

Contributors

MICHAEL G. CHANG is a Ph.D. candidate in East Asian history at the University of California–San Diego. He is currently writing a dissertation on imperial touring in the Qing imperium during the seventeenth and eighteenth centuries.

ANDREW D. FIELD is a Ph.D. candidate in the Department of East Asian Languages and Cultures at Columbia University. He is currently writing a dissertation on Shanghai's cabaret culture and its connections with urban cultural politics during the Republican era.

KRISTINE HARRIS is assistant professor of history at the State University of New York in New Paltz. Her work has appeared in *Republican China* and has been anthologized in *Transnational Chinese Cinemas* (University of Hawaii Press, 1997). She is completing a book manuscript, *Silent Speech: Envisioning the Nation in Early Chinese Cinema*.

LEO OU-FAN LEE is professor of Chinese literature at Harvard University. He is the author of *The Romantic Generation of Modern Chinese Writers* (Harvard University Press, 1973), *Voices From the Iron House: A Study of Lu Xun* (Indiana University Press, 1987), and other books in Chinese; the editor of *Lu Xun and His Legacy* (University of California Press, 1986); co-editor of *Modern Chinese Stories and Novellas* (Columbia University Press, 1981) and *Land Without Ghosts: Chinese Impressions of America from the Mid-Nineteenth Century to the Present* (University of California Press, 1989). His articles have appeared in numerous journals and anthologies in Chinese and English, and his new book, *Shanghai Modern*, is forthcoming from Harvard University Press.

SHELLEY STEPHENSON is a Ph.D. candidate in the Department of East Asian Languages and Civilizations at the University of Chicago. She is writing a dissertation on Chinese film spectatorship and the star system in occupied Shanghai.

SUE TUOHY is assistant professor of folklore, ethnomusicology, and East Asian languages and cultures at Indiana University. She is the co-editor of the Indiana East Asian Working Papers series on Language and Politics in Modern

China and has published in *Asian Folklore Studies* and *Zhongguo yinyue*. Her current projects include a book manuscript, *In the Sea of Songs: Musical Performance, Genre, and Ethnography in Northwest China.*

ZHIWEI XIAO is assistant professor of history at California State University–San Marcos. He co-authored *Encyclopedia of Chinese Film* (Routledge, 1998) and contributed to *Transnational Chinese Cinemas* (University of Hawaii Press, 1997). He is completing a book manuscript on film censorship in Republican China.

YINGJIN ZHANG is associate professor of Chinese, comparative literature, and film studies at Indiana University–Bloomington. He is the author of *The City in Modern Chinese Literature and Film: Configurations of Space, Time, and Gender* (Stanford University Press, 1996); co-author and editor of *Encyclopedia of Chinese Film* (Routledge, 1998); editor of *China in a Polycentric World: Essays in Chinese Comparative Literature* (Stanford University Press, 1998) and two other anthologies in Chinese. He has published articles in numerous journals and anthologies in Chinese and English, and is currently writing a history of Chinese cinema for Routledge's national cinemas series.

ZHEN ZHANG is assistant professor of cinema studies at New York University. In 1998–99 she was a Mellon Postdoctoral Fellow in the Humanities and a visiting assistant professor of Chinese at Stanford University. She is a noted poet as well. Her critical and creative work has appeared in *Asian Cinema, Chinese Women Traversing Diaspora* (Garland, 1998), and *Spaces of Their Own* (University of Minnesota Press, 1998). She is completing a book on early Chinese film culture and the vernacular experience, *An Amorous History of the Silver Screen.*

CINEMA AND URBAN CULTURE

IN SHANGHAI, 1922-1943

Chapter One

Introduction: Cinema and Urban Culture in Republican Shanghai

YINGJIN ZHANG

Cinema and the Archaeology of Knowledge

The international success of China's "Fifth Generation" of filmmakers, represented by Chen Kaige (b. 1952) and Zhang Yimou (b. 1950), since the mid-1980s has suddenly made Chinese film studies a worthy academic subject in the West.[1] In 1993–95 alone, noted film scholars published five books on the subject, all of them focusing on the 1980s–1990s.[2] By contrast, considerably less attention was paid to Chinese cinema before 1949.[3] This imbalance in academic production is striking not only in terms of a long history of filmmaking in China in the first half of the twentieth century, but also because early Chinese cinema exerted considerable influence on post-1949 film productions. One immediate objective of the present volume is to redress this imbalance by directing scholarly attention to Chinese cinema of the 1920s–1940s. A sustained investigation of early Chinese cinema in its urban cultural context in the Republican era contributes a much-needed historical perspective in Chinese film studies in the West.

Beyond its emphasis on historical investigation, the present volume also strives toward a second objective: to construct cinema as a significant cultural force in Republican China and to link film scholarship to the increasing number of recent publications on the cultural history of Shanghai.[4] Several essays in this volume disclose certain previously concealed or neglected aspects of cultural production, such as the composition of bilingual film plot sheets (*dianying shuoming shu*) for distribution by movie theaters,[5] or the circulation and containment of sexual imagination in urban institutions such as cinema, press, or censorship; others unravel hitherto untouched topics, such as the functions of film music on and off screen, or stardom prior to and during the Japanese occupation. Overall, this volume demonstrates that film culture, when defined in a specific sociopolitical context, provides a rich and fascinating site for an archeology of knowledge in modern China.

I evoke the Foucauldian notion of the "archaeology of knowledge" here for several reasons.[6] First, popular film culture in the Republican period—rather than during the sway of political ideologies that may have influenced film production and film criticism—has not been adequately explored in China studies. A great deal of archival research awaits film and history scholars in this area. Second, because many original films, especially those of the 1910s–1920s, were lost and their scripts never published, an exploration of early Chinese cinema resembles an archeology in that it must seek to unearth the traces of lost artifacts. It must describe, on the basis of information pieced together from miscellaneous sources—advertisements, fan magazines, film plot sheets, posters, reviews, personal memoirs—the discursive formations and functions of these artifacts in their earlier historical context. Third, because the "archive cannot be described in its totality,"[7] the knowledge uncovered from such archaeological research is subject to further adjustment, refinement, or even revision. New archival sources will surface to challenge previous and current hypotheses regarding a system of ordered procedures for the production, regulation, distribution, circulation, and operation of certain artifacts. With these considerations in mind, the study of early Chinese cinema in this volume might be said to relate itself methodologically to an archeology of knowledge, a pursuit of a specific type of knowledge acquired through the systematic description of rich artifacts and archives otherwise buried or glossed over by standard sociopolitical histories of modern China.

In what follows in this introduction, I will first sketch a few scenes in the history and historiography of Chinese cinema and highlight the different approaches adopted by scholars in mainland China, Hong Kong, and Taiwan over the past decades. I will then briefly summarize individual essays and place them in three thematic clusters—institutions and innovations (Part One), representations and practices (Part Two), and construction and contestation (Part Three). Finally, I will move to a larger picture of the cultural history of Republican China by identifying the subjects awaiting further research and by briefly describing some archival resources pertaining to these new subjects. The extensive notes to this introduction will serve as a preliminary bibliographic guide to further studies of cinema and urban culture in Republican China.

Cinema in Republican China: History and Historiography

It has become a familiar story by now that, after its debut in December 1895, cinema traveled to China for the first time in its exotic form of "electric shadows" (*dianying*). These were the Lumière films screened at Xu Garden (Xuyuan), a popular entertainment quarter in Shanghai, on August 11, 1896. The years 1995–96 were thus marked as an occasion for a centennial celebration, making a critical reflection on Chinese cinema all the more appropriate.[8] As the story goes, *Dingjun shan* (Dingjun mountain, 1905), a short film featuring the Peking opera star Tan Xinpei (1846–1917) and produced by Fengtai Photographic Studio in Beijing, came to be the first Chinese attempt at filmmaking. It was followed years later by *Nanfu nanqi* (The difficult couple, 1913), the first Chinese short feature produced by Zheng Zhengqiu (1888–1935) and Zhang Shichuan (1889–1953) in Shanghai. But the 1910s was a decade when film did not function as a major player in the urban entertainment industry. In the early 1920s, Ren Pengnian's (1894–1968) *Yan Ruisheng* (Yan Ruisheng, 1921), the first feature-length Chinese film, based on a sensational real-life murder case, became a huge box-office success, and many investors began to try their luck in this new industry.[9] The ensuing years, one of the most fascinating periods in the history of Chinese cinema, constitute the central object of scholarly inquiry for the present volume.

Before going into detail on accounts of the development of Chinese cinema in the 1920s–1940s, I want to give a few hints as to how Chinese film was perceived in the early Republican period. On the positive side, Shen Suyue asserted that by the mid-1920s Chinese cinema had passed "the initial stage" (*mengya shidai*) and had entered "the era of progress" (*jianjin shidai*) or that of "early flourishing" (*chusheng shidai*). His two-page article, "Zhongguo dianying zhi shide guannian" (A historical view of Chinese cinema), appeared in a publication of Da Zhonghua Baihe (Great China/Lily) Film Company in 1926 and seemed to predict, based on an evolutionary model, a brighter future for Chinese cinema.[10] On the negative side, filmmaking continued to be seen as a lowly trade by Chinese cultural elites. When the famous dramatist Hong Shen (1894–1955), educated in the United States and chair of the Drama Department of Fudan University, accepted Zhang Shichuan's invitation to assist Mingxing (Star) Film Company, the act was deplored by his colleagues and students as one that would degrade his decent professorial status or even lead to the "prostitution of art."[11] This kind of persistent contempt for the filmmakers explains why very few scholars would pay serious attention to Chinese film studies in the 1920s. Indeed, from 1926 to 1931, the market was inundated by the first wave of commercial films: costume drama (*guzhuang pian*), martial arts (*wuxia pian*), and films treating immortals and monsters (*shenguai pian*).[12]

The situation changed dramatically in the early 1930s, especially after the Japanese invasion of Shanghai in January 1932, which had inflicted heavy damage to the film industry. As more and more Chinese filmmakers turned to patriotic themes and contemporary issues, film criticism soon became a serious business in itself, and several influential Shanghai newspapers carried regular film supplements. The leftist (or, as it is normally called, "left-wing") influence was generally acknowledged for its success in reinforcing film's educational function and its social responsibility in the 1930s. A narrative of the concerted effort to fashion a type of film criticism ideologically akin to the newly established underground Communist film team, headed by Xia Yan (1900–1995), was retrospectively reconstructed.[13] The actual scene of the early 1930s, however, was much more complicated. As one insider pointed out 60 years later, the "doctrinaire tendency," "sectarian" politics, and utter intolerance in much of leftist criticism of the time had not only alienated liberal writers, filmmakers, and readers, but had also given up important ground to the right-wing writers supported by Pan Gongzhan (1895–1975), a Nationalist (KMT) cultural leader in Shanghai.[14] "Soft film" (*ruanxing dianying*), a concept formulated by Huang Jiamo, Liu Na'ou (1900–1940), and Mu Shiying (1912–40), first emerged as a reaction to the leftist proclivity of mechanically attaching ready-made ideological labels to domestic and foreign films alike. It championed film's entertainment function and its aesthetic effect. Following this soft model, Huang Jiamo and Liu Na'ou involved themselves in commercial filmmaking. For instance, the light comedy *Huashen guniang* (The disguised girl, episodes I–II, 1936; episodes III–IV, 1939) proved to be a crowd-pleaser and was remade in Hong Kong as late as 1956.[15] Nevertheless, since the mid-1930s, soft film was largely forgotten; it existed only as a target of ideological criticism in mainland China.[16]

As far as current research indicates, the Republican period saw very few major publications on Chinese film history. Numerous short articles on the topic were scattered in film magazines or yearbooks and were usually written in a survey fashion. The 1927 film yearbook entry by Cheng Shuren (S. J. Benjamin Cheng), "Zhonghua yingye shi" (The history of the motion picture industry in China), for example, devotes most of its limited space to the origins of *yingxi* (shadowplay) in China, which were traceable to Emperor Wu of the Han dynasty (140–88 B.C.) (see fig. 1). Jiang Gubai's 1933 article, "Zhongguo yingye guoqu xianzai yu jianglai" (The past, present, and future of the Chinese film industry), is another example of this kind of short survey.[17] There are, however, two significant exceptions: first, "Zhongguo dianying fada shi" (A history of the development of Chinese cinema), written by Gu Jianchen (b. 1896), Dean of the Mingxing Film School, and published in the 1934 *Yearbook of Chinese Cinema*; and, second, Zheng Junli's (1911–69) full-length contribution in 1936, "Xiandai Zhongguo dianying shilüe" (A concise history of modern Chinese film), which

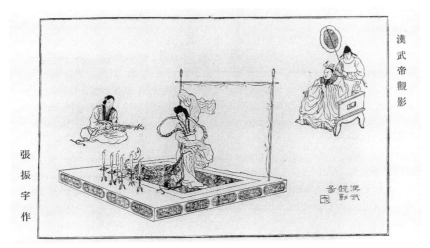

張
振
宇
作

漢
武
帝
觀
影

1. Emperor Wu of the Han dynasty watching a shadowplay; a 1927 drawing by Zhang Zhenyu (Gan Yazi et al.).

was miraculously "rediscovered" in the late 1980s.[18] A brief analysis of these two works here will pave the way for our survey of Chinese film historiography in the post-1949 era.

Gu Jiancheng's history starts with the invention of cinema and details its technological development. He traces the introduction of cinema to China, the early periods of filmmaking, and the transition to sound. What distinguishes Gu's history from other early writings on Chinese film history is its inclusion of by now hard-to-find primary materials. Gu quotes directly and extensively from early film publications, provides detailed information (e.g., lists of early film companies, producers, and titles, or statistics showing Mingxing's revenues and deficits in 1926–30), and occasionally offers his own opinions (as on the rise of costume drama). Like Gu, Zheng Junli also includes a rich source of primary materials in his history and pays special attention to the technical aspects of filmmaking. Unlike Gu, however, Zheng is more analytical than descriptive. For one thing, he divides early Chinese cinema into four major periods: (1) the budding period of 1909–21, with its dominant genres of newsreel, documentary, and comedy; (2) the flowering period of 1921–26, with its dominant genres of social education, romance, and war; (3) the decaying period of 1926–30, with its dominant genres of historical drama, martial arts, and detective; and (4) the reviving period since 1930. For another, Zheng subscribes to leftist discourse and employs ideological terms such as "capitalism" and "imperialism" in his analysis. His documentation of early film exhibition and filmmaking is of great value to our present research, and so are his observations on generic and thematic features of early Chinese film. What is most unusual in Zheng's history is his open acknowledgment of U.S. influence on the development of Chinese cinema. He often lists original English names and titles and furnishes supporting bibliographic sources. Indeed, so far as documentation is concerned, Zheng's history is more reliable than many film histories published in subsequent decades. A noted film actor in the early 1930s, Zheng had proved himself a perceptive film scholar with this substantial contribution to Chinese film history.

Since the 1950s, publications on the history of Chinese cinema began to appear and their number has increased dramatically since the 1980s. To highlight their different methodological approaches and thematic focuses, I classify them in three broad categories: history of film politics, history of film art, and history of film culture. The most influential history of film politics is the two-volume *Zhongguo dianying fazhan shi* (A history of the development of Chinese cinema) written by Cheng Jihua (b. 1921), Li Shaobai (b. 1931), and Xing Zuwen (b. 1922) and first published in Beijing in 1963. As Chen Huangmei (b. 1913) reveals in his Foreword to the second edition (issued in 1981), Cheng's history of pre-1950 Chinese cinema was a product of a decade-long research project and had been approved by Xia Yan, Cai Chusheng (1906–68), and others before its publication. After the Cultural Revolution in 1967–77, which had caused the deaths of many veteran filmmakers, Chen Huangmei was more than happy to acknowledge a "revolutionary Red line" (*geming hongxian*) in Chinese cinema that ran from the 1930s through the 1970s.[19] Indeed, Cheng's history is fundamentally a history of the leftist film movement because all historical and textual materials are arranged according to this ideological orientation. Film politics are present everywhere in Cheng's history: in his selection of political events, discussion of film studios in terms of their political leanings, and evaluation of individual films by whether or not they reflect the correct political ideology. With such exclusive political standards, Cheng's history is one-sided in its treatment of non-leftist films. For instance, it dismisses Fei Mu's artistic feature, *Xiaocheng zhichun* (Spring in a small town, 1948), as merely a "passive film" (*xiaoji dianying*), which supposedly "served to paralyze people's will-power" at a time of popular movements during "the Liberation War."[20] In spite of its obvious ideological preference, however, Cheng's history remains the most comprehensive guide thanks to its catalogues of all film productions in Republican China, and the easiest to use thanks to its indexes to film titles and people. It is little wonder that it has shaped the subsequent attempts at film historiography, especially those in mainland China and in the West.[21]

An ideological counterpart to Cheng's history is found in Du Yunzhi's two-volume *Zhonghua minguo dianying shi* (A history of film in the Republic of China), published in Taibei in 1988 by the Culture Committee of the Nationalist government's Administration Council (*xingzhengyuan*).[22] To strengthen his political affiliation, Du surveyed Taiwan and Hong Kong film industries from 1950 to 1983 and kept his earlier resolution that "the [post-1949 mainland] film activities should not be included in the main body of Chinese film history."[23] In terms of narrative structure, Du's history bears close resemblance to an earlier book by Zhong Lei, *Wushinian laide Zhongguo dianying* (Chinese cinema in the past fifty years), which came out in Taibei in 1965 and devoted three chapters to Taiwan and Hong Kong during the 1950s.[24] Unlike Zhong, who was content with an outline sketch, Du Yunzhi offered a detailed political classification of leftist and non-leftist filmmakers. He recounts the infiltration of the leftists into three major studios (Mingxing, Lianhua, and Yihua) and the Nationalists' counterattack in the 1930s. He classifies Bu Wancang (1903–74) and Sun Yu (1900–1990) among the "established directors"; Wu Yonggang (1907–82) and Tang Xiaodan (b. 1910) among the "emerging directors"; and Shen Xiling (1904–40), Cheng Bugao (1898–1966), Cai Chusheng, and Shi Dongshan (1902–55) among the "leftist directors."[25]

In spite of the equally obvious ideological preferences in Du Yunzhi and in Cheng Jihua, Du is generally less discerning than Cheng when it comes to film politics. In Cheng's history, the 1930s was still an unsettled period, where one director might produce a film to be praised as "progressive" (Sun Yu's *Dalu* [Big road, 1934] or Wu Yonggang's *Shennü* [Goddess, 1934]) and another to be condemned as "regressive" (Sun's *Dao ziran qu* [Back to nature, 1936]) or even as "absurd" and "reactionary" (Wu's *Lang taosha* [The desert island, 1936]).[26] The differences in Cheng's and Du's classifications of the leftist filmmakers and their individual works point to the slippage of the term "leftist" and its inadequacy as an overarching concept for the history of Chinese cinema.

To get away from political constraints and to probe beneath the ideological surface of Chinese films, a number of scholars shifted their attention to film's aesthetic effect, narrative structure, and thematic concerns from the mid-1980s on, and the result is what I call the history of film art.[27] Zhou Xiaoming's two-volume *Zhongguo xiandai dianying wenxue shi* (A history of film literature in modern China) takes screenplays as an entry point and distinguishes various schools of scriptwriting in the Republican era. Zhou follows conventional wisdom by celebrating officially sanctioned "realism" as a central thread running from "the old school" (Zheng Zhengqiu, Bao Tianxiao [1876–1973], and others) through "the new school" (Hong Shen, Ouyang Yuqian [1889–1962], and others) to "the leftist groups" (a term radically loosened up to include not only Sun Yu and Wu Yonggang but also Yao Sufeng and Ma-Xu Weibang [1905–61]). But Zhou installs new perspectives by concentrating on the representations of peasants, bourgeoisie, proletariat, petty urbanites, women, and intellectuals, and by identifying the aesthetic and narrative features of the leftist groups.[28]

While Zhou Xiaoming primarily dwells on screenwriters, other scholars have chosen film directors or film texts as narrative focuses in their accounts of Chinese film history. *Zhongguo dianying yishu shigang* (An outline history of Chinese film art) is a substantial single volume that surveys Chinese film from the beginning to the 1980s. Feng Min and his associates observe the historiographic convention of "sandwiching" historical background, biographic information, and textual analysis in each period, but they foreground the contribution of individual directors (rather than screenwriters, as in Cheng Jihua's history) by discussing select films in detail. Moreover, Feng Min pays special attention to the development of film technique and film art in the early period, special effects like "flying knight-errants" (an actor attached by a wire hanging from the roof) in *Huoshao honglian si* (Burning of the Red Lotus Temple, 1928), "separate identities" (two roles played by the same actress, Hu Die [1907–89]) in *Zimei hua* (Twin sisters, 1934), and a 540-inch long take (*chang jingtou*) in *Xiao Lingzi* (Little Lingzi, 1936), a rare experiment dated twenty years before its European counterpart.[29]

Zhong Dafeng goes a step further than Feng Min. In a co-authored textbook of Chinese film history designed for use in the Beijing Film Academy, Zhong pays extra attention not only to directorial styles—like realism, romanticism, and aestheticism—and film genres, but also to the questions of traditional and foreign influences.[30] In his account of the 1930s, for instance, Cai Chusheng emerges as an artist influenced by the *yingxi* tradition, who emphasizes dramatic tension and intriguing plot lines; Sun Yu as an artist influenced by the Hollywood tradition, who favors fresh visual images and a smooth narrative flow; and Shen Xiling as an artist influenced by the Soviet tradition, who makes extensive use of montage to highlight striking social contrasts. As for the 1940s, Zhong praises Fei Mu's *Spring in a Small Town* as an exceptional case in which a "non-mainstream film" (*fei zhuliu dianying*) achieves excellence outside the time-honored *yingxi* tradition.

With an exclusive focus on early Chinese cinema, *Zhongguo wusheng dianying shi* (A history of Chinese silent film), co-authored by Li Suyuan and Hu Jubin, spends a great deal of time analyzing topics such as genre development, narrative mode, thematic concerns, camera work, and art design. Adopting a scheme similar to that of Zheng Junli's 1936 periodization, although adding one brief chapter to pre-cinema and another to the fall of silent film, Li and Hu attempt a composite picture of Chinese film art in the early decades by reading through a huge number of primary materials, most of them scattered in early newspapers and magazines. For example, they discuss the significance of the nonprofessional cast in *Yan Ruisheng*; the use of close-up, medium, and point-of-view shots in Zhang Shichuan's comic short *Laogong zhi aiqing* (Laborer's love, 1922); the first attempt at underwater photography in Dan Duyu's (1897–1972) soft-porn *Pansi dong* (The spider queen, 1927); as well as the high-angle shot and other camera "tricks" in Hou Yao's (1900–1945) costume drama, *Xixiang ji* (The romance of the western chamber, 1927).[31] As a result of sustained scholarly attention to film art found in Zhou Xiaoming, Feng Min, Zhong Dafeng, Li Suyuan, and Hu Jubin, Chinese film history has gradually acquired a dimension previously obscured or overshadowed by exclusively ideological standards.[32]

The third approach to film historiography, one that emphasizes film culture, was actually adopted earlier than the previous two categories and had a longer tradition in Chinese film circles. Yang Cun's *Zhongguo dianying sanshinian* (Thirty years of Chinese cinema), published in Hong Kong in 1954, consists of numerous journalistic accounts of film activities in Republican China. Organized in chronological order, Yang's accounts relish stories and anecdotes about film producers and actresses, as well as highlights of film productions and exhibitions. Completed in a span of six months, Yang's history foregrounds film's entertainment character but fails—as he himself anticipated in the book's preface—to provide a historical vision.[33] This failure aside, Yang's book had an influence in that its use of biographic structure was carried over by Gongsun Lu in the latter's two-volume *Zhongguo dianying shihua* (A history of Chinese cinema), first published in small installments in *Tiantian ribao* (Daily news) in Hong Kong from November 1, 1960, to December 31, 1961. Gongsun Lu based his research on extensive interviews with veteran film people, such as Ren Pengnian, Bu Wancang, Luo Mingyou (1900–1967), Dong Keyi (1906–73), Hu Die, and Yan Jun (1917–80), as well as rare materials from private collections and old publications. His book offers first-person narratives and often presents multiple perspectives on certain events. His command of original materials impressed the Hong Kong media so much that his history was hailed as a "miracle" when issued in book form.[34]

It seems that biographic structure and anecdotal form were among the most effective narrative means by which to get closer to the ambience of film culture in the "good old days."[35] In this respect, a pictorial history, *Yong yanjing kan de Zhongguo dianying shi* (A history of Chinese cinema seen through the eyes), published in Taibei by Longjiang Cultural Enterprises in 1979, is worth mentioning. Sandwiched between pages of large photographs (some in color), the history of Chinese cinema is narrated with ample references to individual filmmakers and actresses. For instance, the book tells of how Dan Duyu, an eccentric, self-taught artist, started a family business called Shanghai Film Company in 1920 and made his wife Yin Mingzhu (Pearl Ing, b. 1904) the first female lead on the Chinese screen. It goes to explain how she came to set the trend for "foreign fashion" in Shanghai and earned the nickname of "Miss F F," a name resonant with "Miss A A" (Fu Wenhao), a famous socialite-turned-actress in Dan's company.[36]

Many points overlap among the three types of film historiography briefly reviewed in the preceding pages, and a particular book may choose to emphasize film politics in one part and film art or film culture in another. One such example is Wang Zilong's *Zhongguo yingju shi* (A history of Chinese film theater), published in Taibei in 1960. While combining the history of Chinese film and theater in one book, Wang manages to discuss political issues such as censorship and film education, new art forms such as cartoons, and other topics such as Hu Die's crowning as "Movie Queen" and Wang Renmei's (1914–87) popular songs.[37] But on the whole, the three categories adopted in this section give the reader a picture of dominant practices in Chinese film historiography.

Once a historical perspective is developed for Chinese film studies, we can view the objects of inquiry in this volume as pertaining to a fascinating part of a general cultural history of Shanghai, and to approach Shanghai cinema and urban culture as specific conjunctures of space and time, of text and context, of image and sound, of discourses and practices. As we shall see from the following essays, film has evolved as a cultural force in modern China from an exotic shadowplay (*yingxi*) to a respected art form. Its setting has shifted from the noisy, old-fashioned teahouse to the air-conditioned, modern theater, and its appeal has extended from mere comic acting to narrative sophistication and spectacular visualization. The complex process of this evolution gave rise to a number of intriguing stories, most remarkable among which are those of screening romance, of imaging sexuality, and of constructing identity.

Cinema and Urban Culture: Institutions and Innovations

Individual essays in this volume are arranged in three parts. Part One, "Screening Romance: Teahouse, Cinema, Spectator," focuses on family romance as a main attraction for urban film audiences in the 1910s–1930s. Zhen Zhang's "Teahouse, Shadowplay, Bricolage: *Laborer's Love* and the Question of Early Chinese Cinema" concentrates on a 1922 short feature, reputedly the earliest extant Chinese film, scripted by Zheng Zhengqiu. She discusses the ways the strong influence of traditional Chinese theater (such as leather-puppet shadowplays, *wenming xi*, and variety shows) gradually yielded to cinematic and narrative concerns in Chinese films of the 1920s. By way of reconstructing the ambience of the teahouse culture, she demonstrates that the shift of attention from theatrical exteriority (for instance, farcical acting) to narrativized interiority (psychological motivation, for example) left numerous textual tensions requiring interpretations in terms of class and gender, and that the whole issue of early Chinese cinema calls for a reexamination from a global perspective in the 1990s.

From the perspective of an institutional history, the origins of the Chinese film industry can be traced back earlier to the 1910s, not just to traditional teahouse culture as described by Zhen Zhang, but also to *wenming xi* (civilized play), a new type of Chinese spoken drama. According to Zhong Dafeng, an advocate of a distinctively Chinese *yingxi* film tradition, Zheng Zhengqiu displayed in his early works of drama and film a tendency to fashion *yingxi* on the model of *wenming xi*, a genre that had drastically changed from a politically sensitive play in the late Qing period to an ethical family melodrama in the 1910s. For Zhong, Zheng Zhengqiu's *wenming xi* tradition, especially its renewed attention to the changing urban ethos and popular tastes, was carried on by subsequent film investors and producers; it was therefore instrumental in forming and shaping the Shanghai film audience and film industry in the 1920s.[38]

In fact, the relationship between Chinese theater and film might be more intimate than one initially suspects. For a short time in the 1910s, a new effort was made to assist the Chinese audience to get accustomed to watching films in a public place. In addition to featuring alternate film showings and stage performances that tell different stories, several *lianhuan xi* (chained-sequence plays), such as *Lingbo xianzi* (Fairy maiden) and *Hong meigui* (Red rose), were jointly produced in 1924 by Shanghai's Xin wutai (New stage) and Kaixing (Happy) Film Company, the latter headed by Xu Zhuodai (1881–1958) and Wang Zhongxian.[39] Modeled after their Japanese counterparts, these plays consisted of a sequence of interrelated stories narrated in both film and live performance by stage actors. Visually fascinating but technically and financially difficult to handle (for the same actors have to appear in both films and stage performances), chained-sequence plays were quickly abandoned. However, the influence of traditional theater on Chinese film continued in the subsequent decades, even up to the 1990s, and the ever-looming "electrical shadow" has followed the Chinese filmmakers everywhere in the domestic and international markets alike.[40] It is no exaggeration to claim that the tradition of *xiren dianying* (film produced by theater people) that characterized the first generation of Chinese filmmakers is still functional in contemporary Chinese cinema.[41]

Returning to early Chinese cinema in a fashion similar to Zhen Zhang, Kristine Harris's "*The Romance of the Western Chamber* and the Classical Subject Film in 1920s Shanghai" explores issues facing Chinese filmmakers in the 1920s. Her close reading of the 1927 film adaptation of a classic Chinese narrative reveals a complex nexus of intertextual (literature-theater-drama-film) and intercontextual forces (Shanghai-Europe-Hollywood) at work in the Chinese film industry in the late 1920s, as well as the rich visual and psychological subtexts created in the film by then cutting-edge techniques and special effects. Rather than dismissing it as escapism or atavism, Harris contends that popular costume drama was a new film genre that sought to shed the nickelodeon's image of vulgarity, to attract the emerging middle-class audience with its "authentic" representation of the national past, and to secure steady box-office returns that would make it possible for the Chinese film industry to survive the dominance of Hollywood.

Leo Ou-fan Lee's "The Urban Milieu of Shanghai Cinema, 1930–40: Some Explorations of Film Audience, Film Culture, and Narrative Conventions" presents a picture of the cultural and historical conditions in which Chinese cinema came to prominence in the 1930s. He examines the ways in which urban venues (movie theaters, popular magazines, and city guidebooks) promoted moviegoing as an indispensable item of modern urban lifestyles, and he demonstrates that the viewing habits of Shanghai audiences at the time might have been shaped by print culture to an extent greater than we previously anticipated. After briefly comparing the narrative modes of Hollywood and Chinese films, he reasons that the Chinese aesthetic of the long take might be a product not so much of originality as of "stylistic hybridity," marked as it were by slow tempo and theatrical acting on the one hand, and innovative film techniques on the other. Hybrid or not, the emergent film culture contributed its share to the fashioning of a distinct modern sensibility in 1930s Shanghai.

The intricate linkages between film and print culture in Republican Shanghai deserve more attention. Indeed, if examined from the perspective of urban culture, the "intrusion"—or rather recruitment—of the school of "mandarin ducks and butterflies" (*yuanyang hudie pai*) into Chinese cinema in the 1920s may have been another strategic step taken by the Shanghai film industry to help Chinese audiences adapt to or "domesticate" the alien entertainment form (that is, Western shadowplay). Not only were most film plot sheets of domestic and foreign features rendered in literary Chinese to appeal to the conservative reading habits of the literati and the general reading public in a transitional period, but many "butterfly" writers, such as Bao Tianxiao and Zhou Shoujuan (1894–1968), wrote screenplays and promoted films through popular magazines, many of which they edited.[42] As Lee points out, during the 1930s some magazines even issued monthly graded "film guides" (*guanying zhinan*) to assist the audience in selecting films to watch, and the grades given to individual films were rarely inflated. To cite an example different from Lee's, not a single "A" was given to the films listed in a 1937 issue of the movie weekly *Diansheng* (Movietone): *Three Smart Girls* (1936, translated as "Manting fang") was rated B+; *Yeban gesheng* (Singing at midnight, 1936), Ma-Xu Weibang's much publicized horror film, B–; *Tanxing nüer* (A flexible girl, 1937), a mediocre Yihua production, C; and *Polo Joe* (1936, translated as "Maqiu dawang") D–.[43]

Apart from film magazines and other popular periodicals, which are subject to critical reading by several contributors to this volume, city guidebooks provide information closely related to cinema and urban culture: a 1919 Shanghai guidebook describes various movie theaters, which collected tickets priced from

10 cents to one yuan; a 1935 guidebook includes a similar account with ticket prices ranging from 10 cents at some theaters in the southern district to six times as much or higher at Carlton Theater (Ka'erdeng) and others.[44] Reports on movie theaters in major Chinese cities appeared from time to time in film magazines and other urban publications.[45] For instance, in 1939 *Qingqing dianying* (The chin-chin screen) instructed its readers on how to get the best deal in the second-run theaters in Shanghai, and a study of the development of movie theaters in Shanghai had already appeared a year before in a Shanghai research volume.[46] To say the least, the movie theater in Republican Shanghai simultaneously functioned as an icon of modern culture, through which the fashionable lifestyle of the emerging bourgeoisie was displayed and imitated, and as an institution of the entertainment industry, where domestic and foreign film studios competed for market shares.

Cinema and Erotic Imagination:
Representations and Practices

Moving from the level of institution to that of representation, the essays in Part Two, "Imaging Sexuality: Cabaret Girl, Movie Star, Prostitute," study public discourse on the sexuality of three interrelated groups of famous or infamous urban women, and the circulation and manipulation of their on- and off-screen images in Shanghai. Andrew Field's "Selling Souls in Sin City: Shanghai Singing and Dancing Hostesses in Print, Film, and Politics, 1920–49" traces the public perception of cabaret girls in city guidebooks and magazines and analyzes various modes of representation (including literary and cinematic) that gradually took shape in Shanghai during the period. His rich sources demonstrate that, although functioning in many ways as modern surrogates for the courtesans of the late Qing and early Republican periods, cabaret girls were not merely a new icon fixed in the cultural imaginary of Shanghai but were also deeply enmeshed in the political economy of the industrial city.

The public image of the sexualized cabaret girls was widely circulated in contemporary cinematic and literary representations. Cai Chusheng's *Xin nüxing* (New woman, 1934), for example, features an elaborate sequence in which the female protagonist is shocked to see her date relishing exotic performances in a dance hall. A memoir by a seasoned Shanghai adventurer, Chen Dingshan, describes in lurid detail how, back in the 1930s, several midnight shows at Carlton Dance Hall captivated their audiences: a "fairy dance" (*yuxian wu*) in which some revealing moments were glimpsed when the fairies fluttered their wings; a "black-out dance" (*heideng wu*) in which a black dancer spun around the tables in the hall kissing customers while displaying her rounded breasts which were barely covered by two golden leaves; and, finally, a 30-minute musical "bedroom show" in which a blonde, wearing only a bikini, acted out her sexual frustration on a dimly lit stage: languishingly reading in bed, anxiously waiting by the door, and eventually masturbating on a chair with her naked back to the audience.[47] Needless to say, to portray Shanghai dancers, foreign as well as Chinese, in this "corporeal" fashion was to capture the urban erotic imagination. In this sense, Chen Dingshan's written description participates in a typical representation of the 1930s: the "modern woman" as urban secrecy, the revelation of which provides the male adventurer with a great deal of erotic and intellectual pleasure.[48] This explains why dancing hostesses received regular coverage in many pictorials and fan magazines, such as *Beiyang huapao* (The pei-yang pictorial news) and *Diansheng*, in the Republican period.[49]

The connection between dancing hostesses and movie stars is also investigated in Michael Chang's "The Good, the Bad, and the Beautiful: Movie Actresses and Public Discourse in Shanghai, 1920s–1930s." Through his depiction of the emergence of China's earliest three "generations" of movie stars, Chang unravels not only the discursive processes through which the actresses were elevated to stardom but also the issues of class and gender involved in the processes. A noticeable difference surfaces from Chang's investigation: whereas in the 1920s a negative discourse attempted to delegitimize upwardly mobile actresses and to make notoriety the sibling of celebrity, in the 1930s a positive discourse promoted actresses according to its standards of "true character" (*bense*), "good girl," and professional training. Chang observes, however, as far as public discourses are concerned, one sees both promotion and containment at work in the Republican period. A similar discursive strategy was employed in the late Qing representation of courtesans, the literati's "ideal" companion whose seductive sexual images strengthened the erotic attraction of cabaret girls and movie stars for the general public in the 1920s–1930s.

Yingjin Zhang's "Prostitution and Urban Imagination: Negotiating the Public and the Private in Chinese Films of the 1930s" carries the investigation further along the line of sexuality and morality. It contends that prostitution used to be a focal point of the urban imagination, as demonstrated in Chinese film and literature of the early twentieth century. The public presentation of the otherwise "unpresentable" (that is, the ill-reputed and ill-fated prostitutes) furnished Chinese filmmakers with a highly contested space where, for instance, the ethico-moral legitimacy claimed by elite intellectuals confronted and sometimes yielded to the epicurean or voyeuristic tendency in mass audiences. With reference to recent Chinese films, Zhang detects a trend in cinematic representation that moved from a sympathetic account of the streetwalker's miserable life in the 1920s–1940s to an ingenious reinvention of the courtesan's glamorous fashion in the 1980s–1990s.

Cinema and National Identity: Construction and Contestation

Female sexuality was a sensitive but intriguing issue in Republican China, not just to filmmakers and audiences but to government censors as well. In Part Three, "Constructing Identity: Nationalism, Metropolitanism, Pan-Asianism," the contributors explore the question of control in terms of what types of identity the filmmakers and government regulators sought to construct in the period. Zhiwei Xiao's "Constructing a New National Culture: Film Censorship and the Issues of Cantonese Dialect, Superstition, and Sex in the Nanjing Decade" examines the role of the Nationalist film censorship in constructing a new national culture. He investigates the ways the new Chinese "national" identity was measured against and prioritized over the "regional" (as represented by Cantonese-dialect films), the "international" (as evident in Hollywood sex scenes), and the "traditional" (as reflected in age-old Chinese superstition). All these categories were highly contested in the realm of censorship where the government and local interest groups negotiated their deals. Although the Nationalist censorship did not succeed in enforcing all of its rules and regulations, Xiao concludes, it nevertheless shaped the film culture that would emerge in the Republican era by promoting the national language (*guoyu*) and encouraging the production of wholesome screen images.

Unlike dialects and images, music proved harder to control. As Sue Tuohy shows in "Metropolitan Sounds: Music in Chinese Films of the 1930s," music in Chinese films constituted a heterogeneous space marked by a metropolitan, if not cosmopolitan, quality that often paralleled music performed in Shanghai outside the films. In this pioneering study of music in early Chinese film, Tuohy looks at the role of music in contemporary artistic and intellectual discourse and debate. She locates in film music of the time a range of diverse ideas and models (for instance, Chinese folk songs and Hollywood musicals) and provides an entry point for us to understand film music and culture in the context of individual films, many of them later labeled "leftist." Significantly, some musical compositions—many of them also later labeled "leftist"—entered a wider circulation as sheet music and patriotic songs in larger sociopolitical contexts (e.g., a public rally or demonstration).

From Tuohy's study one realizes even more clearly how problematic such terms as "leftist cinema" or "leftist music" would become in ensuing decades. It is true that many songs in these "leftist" films became and continued to be immensely popular, yet what people from the 1950s on considered to be most "leftist" in these songs ("March of the Volunteers," for instance) were substantially revised versions of these earlier incarnations. In addition, some of those 1930s composers labeled as "leftist" composed what were considered nonleftist songs. For example, He Luting's (b. 1903) "Qiushui yiren" (A beauty set against autumn waters) was composed for *Guta qi'an* (The strange case of the ancient tower, 1937) and was popular for decades due to its "soft" melody and its sentimental lyrics. An unlikely product from an acclaimed "leftist" composer, this song fits the picture of Shanghai's "corrupt" bourgeois society and, in this sense, might be appropriate for an eroticization of old Shanghai in films such as Josef von Sternberg's *The Shanghai Gesture* (1941) and, more recently, Zhang Yimou's *Yao a yao, yao dao waipo qiao* (Shanghai triad, 1995).

Back in the late 1930s and the early 1940s, the distinction between the leftist and the nonleftist became insignificant because the outbreak of the Sino-Japanese war soon redrew the political map of the Chinese film industry and divided it into the Japanese-occupied areas (Manchuria, Shanghai, and Hong Kong) and the Nationalist-controlled hinterland. Many veteran filmmakers, such as Bu Wancang, Fei Mu, Ma-Xu Weibang, Wu Yonggang, and Zhang Shichuan, stayed in Shanghai and produced commercial genres, especially costume dramas and theater pieces. Most other filmmakers, such as Shen Xiling, Shi Dongshan, Sun Yu, and Ying Yunwei, moved to Chongqing, the wartime capital; due to the limited film stock, they only directed a small number of patriotic titles for the newly established Nationalist-owned film studios. Some others, such as Cai Chusheng and Situ Huimin, traveled to Hong Kong first and made a couple of Mandarin films before leaving for the hinterland. Yet others, such as Chen Boer (1907–51) and Yuan Muzhi, traveled to Yan'an and started documentary filmmaking in the Communist headquarters.

In the early 1940s, Shanghai film culture was very much politicized, and who appeared in what films became an intriguing topic subject to close public scrutiny from all sides. It is against the backdrop of this unstable urban milieu that an actress suddenly rose to fame with her beautiful theme songs. Her name was Li Xianglan, a mysterious figure whose national identity became a sensitive political secret for both the Japanese rulers and the Chinese press. Shelley Stephenson's "'Her Traces Are Found Everywhere': Shanghai, Li Xianglan, and the 'Greater East Asia Film Sphere'" analyzes the press coverage of this Manchurian-born, Chinese-educated Japanese film star who concealed her identity and passed as Chinese. Stephenson demonstrates that the textual strategies promoting Li Xianglan in some Shanghai fan magazines closely parallel the discursive function of the ever-absent, ever-moving entity of the ideology of the "Greater East Asia Co-Prosperity Sphere" (*Dadongya gongrong quan*). The discourse of stardom in this case worked for the politics of Pan-Asianism, a Japanese colonialist construct that found a perfect embodiment in Li Xianglan.

All three essays in Part Three clearly illustrate that the identity issue is enmeshed in the categories of nation, region, tradition, and related terms such as foreign, Western, metropolitan, and Pan-Asian. Xiao discusses these categories in relation to regional dialect, public morality, and film censorship; Tuohy points out a variety of methods by which the Chinese negotiated these categories in filmmaking and music composition; and Stephenson looks at the ways in which these categories combined to shape an individual's multiple identities. In these cases of contested national, cultural, and personal identities, the meanings of the categories were never fixed but rather worked out in a particular context—cinema and urban culture in Republican Shanghai. This context is of special significance because it is in Shanghai more than any other cities in China that the categories of nation, national culture, and national identity became most dubious and most problematic. The multiracial, multiregional components of the Shanghai population, the transnational business firms in the international settlement of the treaty port, and the crosscultural exchanges between Shanghai on the one hand and Hollywood, the Soviet Union, Japan, Hong Kong, and Southeast Asia on the other—all this makes the identity issue in Chinese cinema all the more conspicuous and all the more complicated.[50]

Cinema, Cultural History, and the 'histoires des mentalités'

It is evident from the preceding summary of individual essays that this volume would not be able to cover all important topics concerning cinema and urban culture in Republican Shanghai. As Stephenson's research shows, the Chinese occupation-era film industry has just started to draw serious attention, and more efforts are needed to sort out the complex situation of both wartime and postwar Shanghai film productions.[51] Another key element in a cultural history of Shanghai that has not been adequately researched is Hollywood's dominance of the Chinese film market,[52] although there is no lack of archival materials for scholarly work in this area. To cite a few examples, several 1923 issues of *Xiaoshuo shijie* (The story world), edited by Ye Jingfeng, carried regular coverage of Hollywood films, complete with film synopses in Chinese (of *My American Wife, Second Fiddle,* and *The Girl I Love,* for instance) and photos of famous stars (Lillian Gish, Anita Steward, Pearl White, Harold Lloyd, and Rudolph Valentino).[53] From August 1933 to July 1937, the Tianjin-based *Beiyang huabao* published 107 weekly issues of "The World of the Screen" (Dianying zhuankan), which frequently contained news of Western films.[54] In the mid-1930s, the Nationalist Film Censorship Committee issued a report listing all films (most of them Hollywood productions) approved for public screening in addition to about 60 domestic features banned during 1931–34.[55] In the early 1940s, popular magazines like *Shanghai shenghuo* (Shanghai guide), edited by Gu Lengguan, would carry articles enumerating screen adaptations of Broadway shows and Hollywood's production plans for 1941–42.[56] In the late 1940s, the semi-monthly *Dianying zazhi* (Picture news) devoted most of its space to Hollywood news, publishing special columns such as "Translated Names of Foreign Stars" (Yingxing biaozhun yiming) and "Foreign Films in Shanghai," a listing of both English and Chinese titles of Hollywood films arranged by major studios (such as Columbia, M.G.M., and Paramount).[57]

The Soviet influence on Chinese cinema may not have been as direct as that of Hollywood and thus it proves more difficult to assess.[58] However, its effect was clearly felt in film criticism of the 1930s, as translations of Soviet film theory came to inform young critics of the time.[59] More information regarding Shanghai film circles in the Republican period can be gathered from dozens of memoirs by famous directors, screenwriters, actors, and actresses, which often recount anecdotes, episodes, or personal experiences excluded in standard film historiography.[60] If one consults official publications alone, *1927 Zhonghua yingye nianjian* (1927 China cinema yearbook) is perhaps the earliest comprehensive guide, which covers all conceivable aspects of the Chinese film industry and contains perhaps more information than one would expect.[61] To continue enumerating subjects relevant to cinema and urban culture in Republican Shanghai, one should recognize the important roles played by other influential cultural forces: photography, pictorials, comics (*manhua*), or illustrated press in general, as well as newspapers, radio, and other institutions of the mass media.[62]

It must be obvious by now that the relationship between film and print culture constitutes one of the central focuses in this volume. In most cases, our aim is to probe beneath the surface of printed materials or behind the moving images on the silver screen and to reach down to a level where political statements, public perceptions, and private fantasies commingle and conglomerate, in spite of their mutual differences, into a relatively stable structure invisible from the surface. At the beginning of this introduction, I evoked the notion of an "archaeology of knowledge" to describe our searches for archival sources pertaining to cinema and urban culture in this volume and our analyses of their discursive formations and functions in the context of Republican Shanghai. In this concluding section, I will connect our endeavors to current research practices in cultural history.[63]

Roger Chartier proposes two ways to look at cultural history: first, "it must be conceived as the analysis of the process of representation," and second, it "must also be understood as the study of the processes by which meaning is constructed."[64] Employing representation, practice, and appropriation as three key concepts in his research, Chartier recommends "a cultural history of the social realm that has as its goal the comprehension of configurations and motifs —of representations of the social sphere—that give unconscious expression to the positions and the interests of social agents as they interact, and that serve to describe society as those social agents thought it was or wished it to be."[65] A new cultural history, accordingly, must seek to reach the level of the *unconscious* in the social realm (or the collective unconscious), a level far beyond or beneath the surface of multifarious social phenomena. In light of this recommendation, what emerges as significant in historical research may no longer be individual representations (that is, what various social agents think society is or should be), but rather specific configurations and motifs that cohere around a system of thought or belief and persist through political and economic changes.

Jacques Le Goff uses the notion of *mentalité* to "refer to a kind of historical beyond"; for him, *mentalité* is itself a structure "which escapes historical individuals because it reveals the impersonal content of their thought."[66] To unravel such *mentalités*, Le Goff specifies two stages in historical research: first, "the identification of different strata and fragments of what . . . we may call 'archaeo-psychology'"; second, the determination of "these psychic systems of organization" responsible for ordering artifacts or archival sources in certain ways.[67] Although he claims that the "specificity of the *histoire des mentalités* lies rather in the approach than in the material," he nonetheless names several outstanding sources, among them literary and artistic sources (because they are "concerned not so much with 'objective' phenomena as with the representation of these phenomena"), the mass media (because they are "the primary vehicles for the expression and ordering of *mentalités*"), and "those marginal or paroxysmal aspects of a society's attitudes and behavior from which we can, indirectly, learn much about the common, central *mentalité* of a period."[68]

Chartier's and Le Goff's propositions dovetail with Siegfried Kracauer's earlier reflection on film historiography: "What films reflect are not so much explicit credos as psychological dispositions—those deep layers of collective mentality which extend more or less below the dimension of consciousness."[69] Observations like these by cultural historians offer a new way to situate our current research.[70] Judged from the vantage point of social, economic, or political histories of modern China, most of the information from the archival sources presented in this volume might appear trivial, insignificant, or at least marginal. Instead of monumental historical events such as the May Fourth movement or the Japanese invasion, these sources are preoccupied with aspects of attitudes and behavior in Shanghai society in the Republican era, which point not to any historical progress fashioned by a model of social evolution, but to "the arcane, rarely directly stated and often unconscious world of *mentalités*, the world of belief, symbol, and cultural patterns."[71] To cite one such example, the late Qing literati *mentalité*, characterized by its sensualist propensity and its moral self-righteousness, has not only informed the representations of movie stars, dancing hostesses, and prostitutes in film and print culture (as demonstrated in Part II), but has also contributed to the rise of ethical family melodrama as a viable genre in both *wenming xi* and early cinema (as illustrated in Part I). The remnants of such a *mentalité* are visible even in the 1930s works of the acclaimed leftists—for instance, in a sequence of *Chuanjia nü* (Boatman's daughter, 1935) where the modern-day literatis' *jouissance* in gazing at the eroticized body of a female model is greatly enhanced by their mimicking of the decadent style of French artists.[72] Cases like these abound in cinematic, literary, and pictorial representations in Republican Shanghai; if viewed together, as parts of a whole, they might point to certain patterns of behavior, certain systems of thought, certain structures of *mentalités* that are typical to the modern city of Shanghai.[73]

Moreover, what is remarkable about the *histoire des mentalités* is that, set against the long duration (*longue durée*) of history, one may be able to comprehend better the persistent nature of certain types of *mentalités*. Indeed, as stated earlier in this introduction, the revisiting of cinema and urban culture in Republican Shanghai in this volume encourages a rethinking of China's changing film culture in the new *fin de siècle*. In the 1990s, as the new, "Shanghai-type" commercial culture, buttressed by Hong Kong, Taiwan, and overseas capital, is producing ever-renewed fashions of urban entertainment (ballroom dances, KTVs, mini-bars, rock concerts, soap operas, soft-porn magazines), certain old Shanghai *mentalités* have reemerged, and their impact has reached far beyond the original geographic boundary.[74]

What is more interesting in this connection is that this sweeping commercial tide has practically inundated the ivory tower of Chinese film studies (which was still proud of its pursuit of film art and film language merely a decade ago) and has substantially altered the direction of contemporary film theory. By the mid-1990s, it has already become possible for a senior Chinese film scholar to proclaim, in unambiguous words, that "film is primarily an industry and only secondarily an art form"—a proclamation followed by several corollary theses, such as "film art cannot be an individualized art" or "filmmaking involves no contradiction between commercialization and artistic creation."[75] Not surprisingly, this kind of outright surrender to the commercial pressure from the film industry has its echoes in the history of Chinese cinema, especially in the commercial trends of costume dramas and martial arts films in the late 1920s and during the Japanese occupation period. After reviewing the antagonistic world of film criticism in the 1930s, one veteran critic refers to this urgent plea by the Shanghai Film Distribution and Exhibition Company in the early 1990s—"returning film to its original status as an entertainment commodity (*yule shangpin*)." He gives his article an ironic title, "Dianying de 'lunhui'" (The cycles of cinema), implying that Chinese cinema, in spite of much glorified ideological victories won by the leftist films of the 1930s–1940s and the socialist realism of the 1950s–1960s, has come full cycle and returned to its humble starting point in the 1910s–1920s.[76] Indeed, the almost uncanny resemblance between 1990s China and 1920s–1930s Shanghai will inevitably haunt the historian of modern Chinese culture for some time to come. In this sense, the essays collected in this volume serve as a double invitation: to go back to a rich chapter in the cultural history of modern China, and to look ahead to future issues that are bound to arise in our research in the next millennium.[77]

PART **ONE** SCREENING ROMANCE: TEAHOUSE,
CINEMA, SPECTATOR

Teahouse, Shadowplay, Bricolage: 'Laborer's Love' and the Question of Early Chinese Cinema

ZHEN ZHANG

Laogong zhi aiqing (Laborer's love, 1922) is allegedly the earliest extant complete Chinese film. A silent film with *original* bilingual intertitles (Chinese and English), this approximately thirty-minute short comedy is one of over a hundred films made by two pioneers of Chinese cinema: Zhang Shichuan (the "director") and Zheng Zhengqiu (the "screenwriter").[1] A plebeian story about how a carpenter turned fruit vendor wins the hand of an old doctor's daughter, the film was among the few short comic films made by the Mingxing (Star) Company created by Zhang and Zheng in 1922. These shorts reportedly failed to become box office hits, which subsequently impelled the company to manufacture more "serious long moral dramas" (*changpian zhengju*) in order to make up the loss.[2] It is surprising that such a noncanonical film, deemed "frivolous or vulgar,"[3] should have survived the ravages of history and stand now as the "beginning" of Chinese cinema. It has toured around the world as the "earliest extant Chinese narrative film," placed at the beginning of retrospective shows.[4] To what extent can this accidental residue or leftover of Chinese film history help critics today to reimagine the cultural "chronotope" of early Chinese cinema?[5] And how can we situate the genesis of this particular cinema—or, to be more modest and realistic, this particular film—in the discursive field of early cinema as a cultural as well as critical category? Finally, why is the fascination with and ambivalence toward early Chinese cinema so crucially linked to the success of the contemporary Chinese new cinema and the rise of a theoretical consciousness of the cinematic apparatus? I do not intend to use *Laborer's Love* here as an all-purpose text to answer these large historical and theoretical questions, which are inevitably interrelated. The film serves rather as an intersection traveled by a number of contextual meanings, which collide there; the singularity of the film text acts upon film history even though it was long relegated to oblivion. And perhaps, precisely as the film is not an "ideal" text or a milestone in mainstream Chinese film history, when we are confronted with it, its vivid textual details and particular cultural context may actually offer us a compelling glimpse of early Chinese cinema and its complexity. In what follows, I would like to discuss this complexity with regard to the dimensions outlined in the questions above, and how they actively converge in *Laborer's Love*. While trying to be sensitive to historical and textual specificity, I will also employ theoretical categories derived from significant studies on early cinema as a whole in order to raise some conceptual issues regarding the nature of early Chinese cinema, and its situatedness in modernity, including its relationship to cinema as a global mass medium.

Early Chinese Cinema: Hybrid Text and Messy History

The topic of early Chinese cinema has been until recently either neglected or else depicted in derogatory or dismissive terms in scholarship on Chinese cinema, which has largely been informed by an evolutionist model of history. For instance, the official mainland publication, *A History of the Development of Chinese Cinema*, portrays film practice during the first two and a half decades (ca. 1905–31, which roughly coincides with the silent period), before the "left-wing" (*zuoyi*) Communist group entered the film world in Shanghai, as mostly "immature" and "chaotic."[6] Jay Leyda's *Dianying / Electric Shadows: An Account of Films and the Film Audience in China* is one of the earliest works on Chinese cinema in English, and devotes a considerable portion to the Republican period. Its attention to film reception as a vital part of film culture illustrates to some extent the excitement as well as ambivalence expressed by Chinese people in their encounter with an entirely modern medium.[7] The value of Leyda's work as an ambitious exercise in film history is, however, undermined by its many empirical errors as well as its lack of a critically informed methodology. In the few other existing chronologically organized studies in English on Chinese cinema, this period is either conspicuously missing or underrepresented. Paul Clark's *Chinese Cinema: Culture and Politics since 1949* contains a brief sketch of the pre-Liberation period, as a prelude.[8] *Perspectives on Chinese Cinema*, an anthology edited by Chris Berry, consists of a number of essays on Chinese cinema from different angles, particularly on the New Chinese Cinema that emerged in the 1980s. Again, the question of early Chinese cinema is hardly touched upon except for a tentative discussion of films of the 1930s and the late 1940s in Leo Ou-fan Lee's article on the literary roots of Chinese cinema.[9]

Until recently, before Zhang Yimou and Chen Kaige garnered glittering prizes at Cannes, Berlin, Venice, and Tokyo, many film scholars of the West who have an eye on non-Western cinemas have been particularly enamored with Japanese cinema. A central concern fueling this passion seems to be the possibility that a non-Western cinema, in this case the Japanese one, could offer a counter-Hollywood or alternative cinematic discourse. Noël Burch's *To the Distant Observer: Form and Meaning in the Japanese Cinema* is typical of how Japan becomes the vehicle for this academic radicalism. The main aim of the study by this "distant observer" is to identify prewar Japanese cinema as the "only national cinema to derive fundamentally from a non-European culture"; hence it distinctly and "radically" differs from the "standard 'Hollywood style' of shooting and editing adopted by the industries of Europe and the US, as well as by colonized nations."[10] In other words, Japan simply becomes a convenient metaphor in his political project of challenging the hegemony of Hollywood cinema. The second related reason, according to Burch, for the "originality" or purity of the Japanese text is located in Japan's avoidance of the "colonial stage" in the late nineteenth century. On the contrary, Burch laments, the former great civilizations, such as India, China, and Egypt, colonized or infiltrated by Western powers, have failed to fully develop indigenous original modes of filmic representation, and have produced no "masterpieces" as Japan has. Burch apparently does not like the muddiness of hybridity, as it cannot be radically different from Hollywood cinema, and it complicates his clean-cut program of buttressing Western theory by means of non-Hollywood practice. Quoting some figures from Leyda's book, Burch finds early Chinese cinema precisely such a hybrid text enslaved by American cinema—from film stock and cameramen to visual style.[11] In other words, the formative period of Chinese cinema is characterized by infantile dependence and mimicry.

It is, however, precisely the problematic of hybridity that provides a possible entry point to early Chinese cinema. Homi Bhabha in his seminal essay "Signs Taken for Wonders: Questions of Ambivalence and Authority under a Tree Outside Delhi, May 1817" finds hybridity encapsulated in an ambivalent staging or *Entstellung* of the intention and "effect" of a colonial text (in that case, the Bible).[12] Hybridity, argues Bhabha, "is not a third term that resolves the tension between two cultures . . . in the dialectical play of recognition." Rather, "it is always the split screen of the self and its doubling, the hybrid." He elaborates further:

> The colonial hybridity is not a *problem* of genealogy or identity between two *different* cultures which can then be resolved as an issue of cultural relativism. Hybridity is a *problematic* of colonial representation and individuation that reverses the effects of the colonialist disavowal, so that other "denied" knowledges enter upon the dominant discourse and estrange the basis of authority—its rules of recognition.[13]

Although the Indian experience of colonialism is arguably very different from the Chinese encounter with the West in the nineteenth and the early twentieth centuries, the concept of hybridity allows an interpretive access to early Chinese cinema, which was largely produced and consumed in the semicolonial yet highly cosmopolitan city of Shanghai in the early decades of this century. It complicates the trajectory of authority in knowledge distribution (here in the form of cinema as an exemplary modern technology) and obviates any exclusive claim to modernity on the part of the West.

Seen in this light, Burch seems all too hasty in drawing his pessimistic conclusion on early Chinese cinema based on some statistical figures found in Leyda's study. If American films comprised 90 percent of the films shown in China in 1929, that does not mean that China did not have a film industry of its own. Nor can one conclude that before and after this low ebb in the late 1920s, due to the onslaught of American sound cinema, Chinese film production failed to attract a Chinese audience. In fact, the 1920s was an enormously lively and complex period in Chinese film history, a period marked by the consolidation of the Chinese film industry, the transformation from a "cinema of attractions,"[14] which consisted mostly of short films, to longer narrative features in the early part of the decade and the difficult transition to sound at the threshold of the 1930s. Although only a handful of the films from that period are still extant, over 500 films were produced in the 1920s.[15] The number of registered small or large film companies around 1925 was 175, out of which 141 were in Shanghai.[16] Though many quickly went out of business, some 40 companies actually produced films, and many others were in some ways presumably involved in film distribution and exhibition.[17] The wide variety of films produced in this period may be glimpsed through the titles of some box-office successes: ranging from Zhang and Zheng's moral tale *Guer jiuzu ji* (The orphan rescues grandfather, Mingxing, 1923), Ren Pengnian's gory crime story *Yan Ruishen* (Zhongguo yingxi [China Shadowplay], 1921), Hou Yao's *Qifu* (The abandoned wife, Changcheng [Great Wall], 1924) advocating women's rights, to Wen Yimin's martial arts film *Hongxia* (The red heroine, Youlian, 1929) featuring a female protagonist. The success of these films reveals an interesting aspect of early Chinese cinema: the thematic and stylistic obsession with traditional arts and the propensity for theatrical adaptations along with the tendency to address certain modern issues. If the film stock and cameras used to produce these films were imported from Europe or America, and the majority of film production was concentrated in semicolonial Shanghai, these films were undoubtedly Chinese productions preoccupied with attracting an urban and to some extent also rural audience which was still largely immersed in the traditional and theatrical performative arts. Far from being thoroughly Westernized or colonized, early Chinese cinema lingered long in a different mode of perception and (re)presentation while strenuously trying to accommodate an entirely new visual apparatus imported from the West.

It would, however, be erroneous to draw the conclusion that Chinese cinema, being deeply in debt to indigenous forms of presentation and representation, was also "essentially" or "radically" different from the Hollywood style. Given the particular semicolonial historical context, the unevenness of development within China, the international nature of the film medium, and the diverse styles of individual filmmakers, there was certainly no such thing as an "original" Chinese cinema. At the same time, to conceive early Chinese cinema in terms of total dependence and mimicry (as opposed to the "autonomy" of the Japanese case in about the same period) is even more removed from the complex cultural context to which *Laborer's Love* now stands as a compelling, albeit "silent," witness. Situated at a crucial point of an early Chinese cinematic venture, the short comedy has a fairly long story to tell.

A re-visit to this "beginning" of Chinese cinema can provide some insights to a highly syncretic and urbanized Chinese film culture. However, the risk of generalization is certainly constant in such a re-vision of an obscure(d) and "chaotic" historical period in Chinese film history, whose earliest residue is a brief slapstick comedy. My challenge here concerns the status of the individual text in any theoretical and historical analysis of cultural production. Tom Gunning in his article "Film History and Film Analysis: The Individual Film in the Course of Time" attempts to rescue film history from the tyranny of theory in film studies during the past decades (in particular, that of film theory rooted in linguistic structuralism and Lacanian/Althusserian theory of subject positioning). Yet he also cautions against any confusion of a historical approach with a naive (mis)conception of history as a "chaos of facts drawn out in an endless chain and the endless round of predictable recycling."[18] Analysis of the individual film, argues Gunning, "provides a sort of laboratory for testing the relation between history and theory," as the individual text often reveals the "stress points in each as they attempt to deal with the scandal of the actuality of a single work as opposed to the rationality of a system." Certain "transitional texts" that "contain a conflict between older and more recent modes of address" are instances that manifest the interplay and interpenetration between the "synchronic slice" and the "diachronic axis" in a given textual situation.[19]

My analysis of *Laborer's Love* as such a transitional text will be an exercise in historical textual analysis, the aim of which is to reveal the "complex transaction that takes place between text and context, so that one never simply functions as an allegory of the other."[20] I will try to demonstrate how some historical data may be mobilized as part of a larger textual field, rather than being relegated to a "historical background" or prehistory of the more established narrative cinema in various versions of the social history of Chinese film. In such a textual field, a confluence of cinematic experiences of production, exhibition, and spectatorship is woven into the individual text, while the latter is seen treading the tightrope between different aesthetic and cultural norms, transforming spectatorial expectations. My reading of the film will thus be situated in a particular spectatorial space, the "teahouse culture"; its hybridity and transformation in the early decades of the Chinese cinematic experience are crucial to our interpretation of early Chinese cinema as a product of a vibrant but also tension-ridden modern urban mass culture.

The Teahouse: From "Shadowplay" to 'Laborer's Love'

Cinema arrived in China only months after the Lumière brothers' show in the basement of the Grand Café in Paris on December 28, 1895. It quickly settled into the Chinese urban space. On August 11, 1896, the first projection by some French showmen took place in the Xu Yuan teahouse in Shanghai, an entertainment venue for variety shows that usually featured traditional operas, magicians, firecrackers, and acrobats. The film program was integrated into the live shows and attracted a large audience. In the next few years, a number of European and American showmen entered the trading port, which by then was already divided into many foreign (or Western) concessions in addition to the old city area, to exhibit films mostly in teahouses such as Tianhua, Tongqing, and Shengping.[21] This peculiar mode of exhibition, that is, the coexistence of the "foreign shadowplay" (*xiyang yingxi*) and indigenous popular performances in a popular entertainment venue (a sort of vaudeville), continued well beyond 1908 when a Spanish showman named Antonio Ramos built the first film theater, Hongkew (Hongkou daxiyuan), a simple sheet-iron structure boasting 250 seats, at the intersection of Haining Road and Zhapu Road in central Shanghai.[22]

The teahouse is a significant spatial trope in Chinese urban mass culture around the turn of the century, and figures strongly in the history of early Chinese cinema. It should not be perceived, as in typical exotic imagination and representation, as a place where Chinese scholars in long gowns discourse on intellectual matters over a cup of green tea. In many cases, at least for a long time in Shanghai, teahouse (*chayuan*) and theater-house (*xiyuan*) were interchangeable terms for entertainment establishments where traditional opera pieces and other popular variety shows were offered, along with tea, snacks, and cold towels. Many multifunctional gardens such as Zhang Yuan, Xi Yuan, and Yu Yuan, as well as entertainment centers like The Great World (Dashijie) and The New World (Xinshijie), were also major venues for a wide selection of traditional and modern forms of mass entertainment, including the "foreign shadowplay."[23]

Some larger establishments such as the Qinglian Ge (Blue lotus pavilion) on Fourth Avenue (now Fuzhou Road), where Ramos made his projection debut in a rented booth, were also notorious sites for gambling, prostitution, and gangster activities.[24] Even a more refined teahouse such as Wenming Yaji (literally, the civilized and elegant gathering place) on Second Avenue (now Jiujiang Road), where calligraphers and painters used to gather, once featured a wax figure show and a simulated train ride / show accompanied by landscape films.[25]

One of the earliest illustrated Chinese newspapers, *Tuhua ribao* (The illustrated daily), which began to publish in 1908, often carried news and portrayals of the Shanghai "teahouse culture" with vivid and visual details. The seventh issue of August 1908 reported and illustrated "The Noisy Shadowplays on Fourth Avenue" as a particular social phenomenon in Shanghai. The writer of the story appears to be amazed at the use of trumpets and even Chinese gongs and drums in front of the teahouse to advertise for the supposedly Western silent films. The performances depicted in other illustrations range from Peking opera and puppet plays to storytelling. Fireworks, magic shows, and "foreign shadowplay" were reportedly the main attractions of Xi Yuan, which was brightly lit with hundreds of electric bulbs at night. The clientele of this teahouse culture consisted mostly of urban commoners of varying means who patronized venues appropriate to the depth of their pockets. Both men and women attended shows, though the seating was sometimes segregated. The audience members were usually seated around tables; waiters with big trays carried teapots, cups, and snacks to the customers. Fanning themselves, women chatted and gossiped. The space was often depicted as a hotbed of women's freedom and sexual desire, and hence a constant subject for public anxiety. For instance, the phenomenon of summer night gardens (*ye huayuan*) allegedly provided a haven for romantic rendezvous, and the illicit liaisons formed in certain theater houses between female spectators and actors scandalized the public.[26]

Significantly, before and even after the arrival of cinema in China, the teahouse also served as a venue for the traditional shadowplay. A leather-puppet show behind a screen illuminated by gaslight where there was still no electricity, this indigenous art form has generally been considered by Chinese film historians to be the bedrock of the Chinese cinematic (un)conscious. The age of the shadowplay has been the subject of controversial speculation,[27] though most accounts cite as the earliest record a Song dynasty source about Emperor Han Wudi's experience of a staged shadowplay to meet the soul of his deceased wife. While one should be mindful of the risk involved in any such attempt to fix an originary moment of a cultural category, the overlap of the puppet shadowplay and "foreign shadowplay" in the late Qing and the early Republican period nevertheless deserves critical attention, if one considers cinema as at once an international and contested modern cultural practice.

Most existing accounts describe the two-dimensional puppet as made of donkey skin painted with vivid colors. The performance consisted of a white cloth screen dividing the spectators and the puppeteers, who narrated and sang while manipulating the puppets. Usually there was also a Chinese orchestra accompanying the show.[28] Although themes and styles differed according to genealogical as well as geographical particularities, the common repertoire consisted of popularized versions of classical tales, vernacular stories, religious legends, and adaptations from various local operas. The shows also varied from a group of unrelated short scenarios to serialized long dramas. While some puppeteers relied on scripts, others resorted to memory and improvisation. Beijing alone had two major schools. One, which used scripts, dominated the eastern part of the city (Dongcheng); the other, which did not use scripts, flourished in the western part (Xicheng).[29] Leather-puppet shadowplay also flourished in Shanghai in the late Qing and early Republican periods.[30] In the mid-1930s, some entertainment establishments still had shadowplay as a staple program.

Until the early 1930s, cinema in Chinese was called "shadowplay" (*yingxi*) before the term gradually changed to "electric shadows" (*dianying*), indicating its umbilical tie to the puppet show and other old and new theatrical arts—in particular, the modern stage drama from the West via Japan. The emphasis on "play" rather than "shadow"—in other words, the "play" as the end and "shadow" as means—has, according to the film historian Zhong Dafeng, been the kernel of Chinese cinematic experience.[31] As the pioneers of Chinese cinema were deeply immersed in traditional Chinese theater while also enthusiastically espousing the transplanted modern spoken drama called *wenmingxi* (literally, the "civilized drama"),[32] the notion of "play" became, if unconsciously, the guiding principle in their film practice. That some of the earliest Chinese films are "recordings" of Peking opera performance and adaptations from *wenmingxi* pieces indicates not only a thematic predilection for the ready-at-hand "play," but also attests to the shooting style that foregrounds the frontal, tableau effect of stage performance. Such a visual style is certainly congenial with the aesthetic of early cinema before Hollywood as a whole, that is, before the onset of a more narratively integrated and diegetically absorbed cinema. The persistence of the "cinema of theater people" (*xiren dianying*) in China and its attendant stylistic strategies (including the prevalence of medium-long shot, nonperspectival spatial relations) requires, however, a consideration of its cultural texture at a given historical moment.[33] It has to be pointed out that this theatrical proclivity is by no means a signifier for "tradition" in a rigid sense; in other words, early Chinese cinema cannot be simply seen as a process of Westernization of Chinese culture or sinicization of Western technology. The modern spoken drama played a significant part in negotiating "play" and "shadow" in a hybrid urban space like Shanghai. The first successful commercial films such as *Heiji yuanhun* (Wronged souls in an opium den, 1916) and *Yan Ruisheng* (1921) were adapted from sensational *wenmingxi* plays. Yet an awareness of the film camera as a visual apparatus, and cinema as a far more complex modern commercial practice, also impelled the early filmmakers to explore the potential of the "shadowy" side of film.

Laborer's Love is very much a product of the teahouse culture, and of a confluence of discourses and practices on shadowplay in Shanghai in the early decades of this century. The makers of the film, Zhang Shichuan and Zheng Zhengqiu, before they established the Mingxing company in 1921, had collaborated eight years earlier to make some Chinese films for their Yaxiya (Asia) Company, a small joint venture between two American businessmen and the two enterprising Chinese. Zhang and Zheng had been directly involved with other forms of popular culture before their accidental encounter with cinema in 1913, that is, shortly after the Chinese national revolution that abolished the Manchu imperial system. A relative to the wife of an entertainment business tycoon, Zhang was for a while a sectional chief of the enormous entertainment complex New World located at the heart of the city.[34] Zheng, on the other hand, was already making a name for himself in news supplements as a Peking-opera *feuilletoniste*, and was well connected in theater circles. The two embraced the new medium simply "out of curiosity." Zhang recalled later, "because it is about shooting shadow-'play,' I naturally thought of old Chinese theatrical 'plays.' "[35] The two signs in front of their rather shabby "studio"—one "Asian Shadowplay Co.," the other "Xinmin New Theater Research Society"—signify a marriage of the "Western shadow" and the "Chinese play."[36] Their first film, *Nanfu nanqi* (The difficult couple, 1913), a parody of feudal arranged marriage, was "scripted" by Zheng and "directed" by Zhang with all the enthusiasm of innovation. With stage actors of their acquaintance playing the roles, and a static camera running until the end of the reel, the four-reel film with a discernible narrative (but hardly a narrative structure) has nevertheless been hailed as the beginning of China's narrative cinema (see fig. 2).

After this film Zheng left the company to form his own *wenmingxi* troupe while Zhang continued to film a number of short subjects, mostly comedies with neither coherent narrative nor didactic concerns. A cursory survey of some of the titles reveals that it was a very different kind of cinema from what Zheng wanted to create with *The Difficult Couple*: *Huo Wuchang* (A living Wuchang), *Wufu linmen* (Five blessings at the threshold), *Erbaiwu baixiang chenghuang-miao* (The blockhead roams round the temple of the town god), *Da chenghuang* (Beating the town god), and so on, all made between 1913–14. Mainstream Chinese film history tends to dismiss these films as frivolous, vulgar, and in bad taste, and points to the fact that they were shown as interludes at drama performances as evidence of their shoddy and nonprogressive quality. Zhang had to cease filming when the First World War cut off the supply of film stock from

2. A static camera shooting a scene in the Asia studio, courtesy of the China Film Archive.

Germany. But after a new source of film stock from the United States was secured, Zhang's new film company Huanxian (Dream Fairy) and some other companies turned out a wide range of short and long films: *actualities*, scenics, comedies, educational films, films of Peking opera or adaptations of opera for film, and detective films based on real crime cases. Most of them were all-Chinese productions and with them Chinese cinema as a national culture industry seemed to have come of age.

The early 1920s saw an unprecedented cinema craze in China. After a stock market crash, many speculators turned to investing in the nascent film industry. It was also a blooming era for Chinese journalism and popular literature, which had great impact on film production. In particular, the popular romance genre called "mandarin ducks and butterflies" (*Yuanyang hudie*), which was mostly serialized in literary supplements and magazines, provided ready-made stories for the screen. Although originally derived from traditional vernacular fiction sentimentalizing romantic love of, usually, a poor young scholar and a beauty who is willing to sacrifice her wealth or family name for love, the "mandarin ducks and butterflies" literature in the early twentieth century was more diversified, and included detective stories, muckraking reportage, martial arts romance, and some ghost fiction.[37] The popularity of this literary phenomenon reached its heyday in the 1920s and had a definitive impact on the emergence of a narrative cinema in the same period. Many popular fiction writers, seeing the potential of the new medium, also began to write "shadowplay" scripts. But the link between popular fiction and cinema, as Zhong Dafeng points out, was largely filtered through *wenmingxi*, which first adapted successful "mandarin ducks and butterflies" literature for the stage, often with major "editorial" changes.[38]

Such a mediation through drama enhanced theatrical effect at the expense of narrative closure.

It was in this sizzling ambience that Zhang and Zheng began their second, now all-Chinese, collaborative venture, this time with a larger budget and greater ambition. Instead of the open-air, mud-floored tiny studio in which they filmed *The Difficult Couple* in 1913, with rudimentary filmic control but an immense curiosity, the new company, now named Mingxing (Star), was housed in Zhang's former stock market company building and had a sizable staff. From the very start, it also established the "Mingxing Shadowplay School" to train professional actors and actresses.[39] The company was no longer just an amateur artisan workshop experimenting with rendering stage drama into "shadowplay." It was a business serious about its ability to produce profitable films. With fancy movie houses mushrooming in the city, and under pressure to compete with foreign films, the demand for long, integrated narratives also grew.

What was happening to Mingxing in particular and the Chinese film industry in general at that time may be conceived in terms of a gradual and tension-ridden transition from what Tom Gunning calls the "cinema of attractions" to that of "narrative integration," characterized by changing dynamics of spectatorial pleasure. Gunning argues that early cinema, in "its ability to *show* something," is an "exhibitionist" cinema, contrasted to the voyeuristic tendency in later narrative cinema.[40] The institutional ambition of Mingxing and its growing narrative impulse stemmed from a similar epistemological shift in cinematic perception. An increasing awareness of the apparatus behind the "shadowplay" and its commercial power, coupled with the consolidation of a drastically different mode of exhibition and spectatorship, forced Chinese film production to be conscious of a more varied audience and a less predictable market. No longer confined to the customers of Shanghai teahouses or drama theaters, the film industry had to consider the potential (and far larger) audiences patronizing the more sophisticated but also less noisy and spontaneous film theaters, in addition to the audiences in the interior cities, rural areas, and overseas Chinese communities.

This transformation, however, was less apparent and more gradual than any retroactive concept of it tends to suggest. The Mingxing company retained many vestiges of the earlier cottage industry; it took nearly a decade to establish a full-fledged studio when it produced the first Chinese sound film in 1931. In fact, its first four productions of 1922, *Laborer's Love* among them, carried over much of the spirit of Zhang's earlier "attractions." Two other comedies featured "Chaplin" (played by a British resident of Shanghai, who worked at the New World entertainment center): *Huaji dawang you hua ji* (The king of comedy visits China), *Danao guai juchang* (Disturbance at a peculiar theater). Another film, *Zhang Xinsheng*, was based on an actual crime story first adapted to theater, complete with gory and shocking details. In addition, Mingxing produced five newsreels on sports events as well as public ceremonies, including a funeral. These films are largely products of Zhang's production philosophy, which centered on "experiment" (changshi), entertainment, and instant mass appeal: "Always pursue the current attractions and tastes, in order to bring out merry laughter from the people" (chuchu wei xinqu shishang, yiji boren yican).[41] But these short films of "attractions and tastes" failed to produce large returns for the company. Mingxing soon found itself following Zheng's line of thought to make more "serious long moral dramas" (changpian zhengju), which answered the market demand in a timely fashion.

Laborer's Love, the only extant film of these early Mingxing productions, is a peculiar film in that it combines presentational and representational impulses. Its stylistic features tend to oscillate between those of a "cinema of attractions" and a "cinema of narrative integration." If the latter is often marked by a certain representational closure, or, in Thomas Elsaesser's term, "interiorization,"[42] Laborer's Love still shows its stubborn exaltation of theatrical or performative exteriority while flirting with narrativized interiority. By "interiorization," Elsaesser refers to the shift from the diverse practice of early cinema to narrative cinema in the West in the late 1910s, and the emergence of an increasingly institutionalized (and isolated) spectatorship in the wake of the establishment of picture palaces and other fixed exhibition outlets. He writes: "For the very pressure towards longer narratives coming from the exhibition sector meant that the struggle for control once more shifted away from the mode of presentation to the mode of representation, though defined by the new commodity-form embodied in the multi-reel film, which required self-sufficient fictional narratives." In other words, the stress on "interiority" and the segregation of audiences of the picture palaces are linked to new forms of closure and the "interiorization of the narrative instance" in film production.

The narrative trajectory of Laborer's Love is clear, but the film is less concerned with the internal psychology of the characters than with their actions, which often amounts to a show that disrupts any incipient diegetic absorption. While the film is rather skillful in cross-cutting and temporal continuity so as to render narrative representation coherent, the emphasis on mechanical movement and optical experiment often foreground the cinematic apparatus, betraying the sustained fascination with the medium which first brought Zhang and Zheng to cinema nearly a decade before. This obsession with movement and optical play is thematized or inscribed in the seemingly harmless story of a romance between a fruit vendor and a doctor's daughter. The story is in fact a "frivolous" commentary on the question of social mobility, implicitly mocking the feudal and patriarchal codes regulating marriage and family. In the following pages, I will show how the film serves as a metacommentary on the teahouse culture and early Chinese cinema, and its implication for a transforming cinematic perception.

Space, Vision, and the Bricoleur from Nanyang

Laborer's Love is staged between two kinds of spaces: the exterior and the interior, the theatrical and the cinematic. Moreover, its setting evokes an unmistakable but changing milieu. The three-reel film can be divided into three parts. The first part establishes the basic pattern for a narrative "exchange": the vendor desires the doctor's daughter and proposes a marriage. The second part describes how the vendor arrives at the idea of turning the clients of a nightclub into the doctor's patients. The last part is simply the execution of this idea, which leads to the predictable "happy ending."

The first part, with exclusively exterior, frontal tableau shots, weaves the dynamics of desire between the fruit shop, the doctor's shop, and the hot-water shop (hereafter referred to as a teashop).[43] The first shot of the film—an introductory intertitle—tells the audience that Carpenter Zheng returned from overseas (Nanyang, or the South Seas—referring to Southeast Asia), and changed his profession, becoming a fruit vendor. The following tableau shot shows the fruit vendor cutting melons and peeling sugarcanes with his carpentry tools. Next to his stand is the teashop where some local hooligans hang out. The old doctor (played by the screenwriter Zheng Zhengqiu), clad in his long robe and very nearsighted, practices traditional Chinese medicine in his shop located opposite the fruit shop and the teashop. The mise-en-scène of the doctor's open shopfront, which consists of a Chinese calligraphic couplet and antique furniture, is clearly established as a stage of spectacle, framing his young daughter as object of desire for the vendor as well as for the hooligans at the teashop. We are told the doctor is in dire financial straits, with no patients visiting his shop. His daughter mends his gown in public, betraying the deteriorating situation of a traditionally elite class.

The vendor's business, however, is booming. He gazes at the daughter doing embroidery in her corner of the shop, and sends her fruits placed in a carpenter's ink marker (as a container) with a rope, a *mechanical* maneuver attributable to his carpentry skill. This "sending over" (through alternating shots) links the two "opposite" shop spaces, injecting a pleasurable movement (of desire) into an otherwise static frontal framing. By using a string, the movement also invokes a classical Chinese motif for love and marriage, hence the other name of the film, *Zhiguoyuan*, literally, "fruit-throwing love connection," a title derived from folklore. One of the hooligans at the teashop gets jealous and walks across the street to tease the daughter. She quickly sends back the ink marker, alerting the vendor to her situation. The vendor throws an apple at the hooligan. He moans and the doctor mistakes the hooligan for a patient, as all those exchanges have escaped his nearsighted notice.

The same movement of desire in relation to vision is repeated when the doctor tries to find an auspicious date in the fortune-telling calendar to pray for his dwindling business. He takes off his spectacles and unwittingly puts them in the ink marker, sent by the vendor for the second time. Unaware of this, the daughter sends back the box along with a handkerchief (again, a classical motif for "expressing love through an object," or *yiwu chuanqing*) and the spectacles. The vendor delightedly smells the kerchief but is confounded by the spectacles. As he puts them on, a point-of-view shot masked in the form of the spectacles reveals an unfocused world. The vendor's altered vision ceases to relay any voyeuristic desire; and the smoothness of the narrative is suddenly halted: there is nothing to see but the *frame* of the spectacle(s). The doctor, on the other side of the street, deprived of his visual aid, also becomes confused and disoriented. Thus, in her unwittingly mischievous gesture, the daughter momentarily disarms the visual pleasure of both men in the film, and of the spectator as well.

In the remaining half of the first part of the film, the pattern of desire moves from staging to acting out. After the "denial" of male vision, the daughter takes the initiative of movement. She crosses the street to buy hot water from the teashop. The hooligan once again tries to make advances, but she walks instead to the fruit shop to chat with the vendor. By intruding upon both sites of male desire and showing her preference for the vendor, she asserts her role as a subject of desire rather than simply remaining a desirable living prop in her father's shop. The vendor shyly proposes to her and she advises him to go talk to the doctor—she still has to observe the time-honored patriarchal codes regarding matrimony. The vendor brings melons and sugarcanes over to her father to make a proposal. Here the mockery of traditional arranged marriage could not be more obvious. The Chinese educated elite has always harbored a deep contempt for the mercantile class. That a petty vendor with only fresh fruits as gifts goes to propose to a doctor's daughter would have been unthinkable in a previous time, when social hierarchy was more rigorously observed. But the poor doctor is desperate as his *vision* is failing him and traditional medicine seems increasingly out of fashion. He will allow the marriage only if the vendor will make his business prosper. At first dejected, the vendor closes his shop and goes inside to rest.

The second part of the film shifts the narrative into a primarily interior space, coupled with more sophisticated filmic control. If the treatment of space in the first segment remains largely theatrical, characterized by frontal framing and presentational performances, this part, shot mostly in the vendor's bedroom and the nightclub upstairs, experiments with some particular cinematic techniques, such as superimposition, cross-cutting, and editing (for instance, between close-ups and long shots) to articulate narrative logic, movement, and development. First we find the vendor in his room again in a frontal shot, drinking water and smelling the girl's handkerchief. But quickly the film surprises the viewer with two "dream-balloon" shots showing the vendor's daydream of the girl and the doctor's stern face. The vendor's "interiority," or subjectivity, is thus contained within the narrative frame. In the next shot, the vendor looks at the table clock; a following point-of-view shot shows the clock at 9:47. The vendor yawns and goes to bed. This sequence is intercut with the staircase outside leading to the club. The cross-cutting thus links temporal and spatial movement, the interior and exterior space.

The nightclub is the interior extension and elaboration of the open teashop (see fig. 3). Unlike its "primitive" form, which serves merely hot water, tea, and a view of the street, the "All-Night Club" (Quanye julebu) signifies an interior-ized spatial figure of modern urban entertainment life, particularly in the more sophisticated large film theaters that thrived on (narrative) closure. The transi-tion from the vendor's bedroom to the interior of the club is accomplished by a mini-sequence of the mahjong game. A close-up of the mahjong table with hands mixing the tiles signals the emergence of a different space. The following long shot brings the club into full view. Two subsequent medium and close-up shots refocus the attention of both the diegetic and filmic viewer onto the mahjong game: someone wins, everyone in the room stretches to see. There fol-lows a fight between two hooligans over a seat next to a girl—a session of slap-stick—which wakes the vendor downstairs. Another point-of-view shot of the clock: 2:56 A.M. The elliptical editing here is smooth and convincing. Hearing some clients descend the staircase, the annoyed vendor gets an idea. But he puts a finger on his lips, gesturing to the camera—that is, the spectator—to keep the secret for him! As a whole this segment demonstrates a clean and cinematic handling of narrative progression. The interiorized narrative and subjective space becomes subtly analogous with a cinematic space. Yet, as my analysis has noted, a number of theatrical elements persisted: the fight, in a slapstick vein, resonates with the earlier fight at the teashop; the final shot of the vendor ges-turing at the spectator breaks the fairly tight diegetic space cultivated up until that point.

The two kinds of spaces are juxtaposed and integrated in the last part of the film. The morning after the sleepless night, the vendor visits the doctor's shop and strikes a deal with the latter: the doctor will have many patients, and the vendor will marry the daughter. While customers keep ascending the staircase to the club, the vendor, resuming his carpenter identity for the time being, makes a trick staircase to replace the original one. In the next exterior shot, he fixes every step in the staircase onto his device underneath and tests its efficiency. By

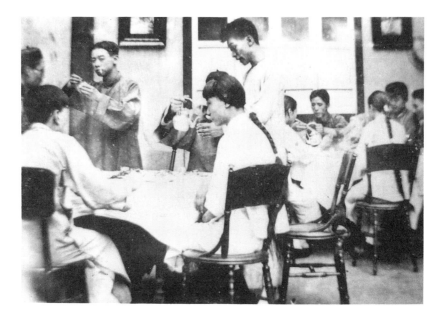

3. The interior: a teahouse party in *Laborer's Love* (1922), courtesy of the China Film Archive.

pulling the device, he can turn it into a slide. When pushed, the slide will reappear as a stair. Meanwhile, a reconciliatory banquet goes on upstairs, presided over by an old man who admonishes the young playboys/hooligans against infighting. He exits, only to become the first victim of the trick stairs. As the banquet reaches its end, more people make their "fall." In this sequence, the editing alternates between the interior of the club and the exterior street scene, between long shots of the entire scenario of the "sliding" and medium shots of the moaning victims at the bottom of the staircase. The long shots of the scene clearly retain the virtuosity of a theatrical space: with the "magic" staircase diagonally dividing the screen, the vendor on the left side of and under the stair is kept "invisible" to the victims on the right side of the frame. As some Chinese critics point out, such a "hypothetical plane space" renders the causality of action visible to the viewer by placing both cause and effect within a single frame.[44] This treatment of space effects a kind of internal cutting within the same frame; the exposure of cause and effect *at once* renders linear progression redundant. The vendor's secret is truly an open one, since the audience is in on his trick (see fig. 4).

This scene is also crucial to my view of the film as a celebration of social mobility as well as a metacommentary on a transitional cinema. On the one hand, the film satirizes through the literal "fall" or "sliding" of the "leisure class" the thriving but also often chaotic "teahouse culture" in modern urban space.[45] The "fall" of his victims in turn becomes the stepping-stone leading to the vendor's climbing the social ladder.[46] The old man who first slides down the staircase can be seen as a double of the doctor whose social and physical decline places him at the same level as that of the vendor; what the viewer witnesses here is thus also a *dramatic* transformation of the existing social hierarchy. After being "mobilized" by the carpenter-vendor's mechanical intervention, the magic stair turns static steps into a smooth slide. This play with movement, based on the erasure of the fixed repetition of steps, paradoxically precipitates the multiplication of bodies. The vendor repeats the act of pulling the steps into a slide many times, so that finally the entire crowd from the nightclub is turned into a mass of injured bodies on the street.

The excess of the vendor's (and our) "perverse" pleasure becomes as overwhelming as the excess of movement caused by the loss of equilibrium—the downward sliding proves far more dizzying than the theatrical horizontal crossing in the first part of the film. Hence the acceleration or intensification of movement at the end of the film. The injured crowd, now the potential clientele of the doctor and thus endowed with an exchange value, swarms to the doctor's shop for treatment. Silver coins are one after another piled into the money tray

4. The exterior: the mobile ladder in *Laborer's Love* (1922), courtesy of the China Film Archive.

in close-up shots, as the patients fill the shop only to receive cursory mechanical treatment for their wounds. The doctor handles the bodies in a fashion similar to the way the vendor handles the fruit and the stair. Seeing the doctor overloaded with work, the vendor comes over and volunteers to help, and thus literally joins the social rank of the doctor. In a frenzied acceleration of screen action the two "doctors" twist heads and limbs, knock chests and spines as if on an assembly line. The identities of the patients are blurred and the whole scene spins out of control. This optical confusion recalls the previous loss of sight triggered by the displacement of the spectacles, only now the blurriness is saturated with an overinvestment of *head-spinning* movement and a polymorphous perverse pleasure rather than the male pleasure centered around the body of the daughter.

Both instances exemplify, hyperbolically, the kind of fascination and ambivalence with which the earliest generation of Chinese filmmakers regarded cinema as a modern perceptual and communicative medium. The character of the carpenter-vendor may be viewed as an on-screen representative figure of this emerging "cinematic *bricoleur*,"[47] a term Thomas Elsaesser employs to describe the makers of the Weimar cinema of the 1920s, who are said to be preoccupied with the "Edisonian imaginary," or a realization of the technological and epistemological potential and risk the cinema brings. Elsaesser locates the "Edisonian imaginary" in the "'defective' narratives of the Weimar cinema, their undecidability, their peculiar articulation of time and space, and their resulting problematic relation to visual pleasure and the look, all [of which] point to a form of perception that is neither altogether voyeuristic-fetishist nor an imitation of 'normal vision.'"[48] His overevaluation of the status of the "auteur" (though of a more composite form than a single director) over the "spectator" in discussing the historical and perceptual genesis of the Weimar cinema is certainly problematic. The concept of the "cinematic *bricoleur*" is, however, useful to the understanding of *Laborer's Love* and other films produced in the early 1920s by Zhang Shichuan and Zheng Zhengqiu. They still treated cinema as a curious, if not "Edisonian," imaginary, before they launched longer narrative moral dramas under the pressure of an increasingly interiorized film exhibition practice and the competition of foreign cinema.

The problematization, albeit with a jocular overtone, of narrative and visual pleasure in *Laborer's Love* is anchored in the specific cultural milieu of early Chinese cinema. The oscillation between and the imbrication of the theatrical and cinematic spaces in the film, its hesitancy to inscribe voyeuristic-fetishist pleasure on the *body* of and in the film or to embrace "an imitation of 'normal vision,'" have to be understood in relation to the "undecidable" position of the first generation of Chinese filmmakers. The carpenter-vendor in *Laborer's Love* is in a sense a bricoleur par excellence. The magic staircase is his quintessential mise-en-scène, linking the theatrical and the cinematic, exterior and interior spaces. The professional as well as the social status of this bricoleur remains ambiguous throughout the film. The fruit vendor is consistently called by his previous profession, "Carpenter Zheng." (As Zheng is the last name of both male actors, and one of them is the "screenwriter," this self-referentiality underscores the identification between the carpenter-vendor and the "cinematic *bricoleur*.")[49] Yet he is no longer practicing traditional artisanship, especially after his return from the "South Seas" (Nanyang).[50]

The allusion to Nanyang is significant, as it obliquely underscores the importance of this possibly biggest market for Chinese films during that time.[51] Historically, but more stereotypically, overseas Chinese of Nanyang have always been associated with commercial skills in the colonial or semicolonial Southeast Asian countries. Carpenter Zheng is presented as a worldly-wise man who returns to his hometown to become a businessman, engaging in exchange rather than production. But instead of abandoning his past altogether, he adapts his carpentry skills to vending fruit (an allusion to the tropical Nanyang, of course). And when his desire is at stake, this skill is also utilized in courting and "bridging" a social gap between his fruit shop and the doctor's place. In other words, he "transcends" the old mechanical role of carpenter, and becomes rather the master of both production and exchange at once. And while the vendor sells flawed "bodies" to the doctor in exchange for the daughter, the cinematic bricoleur manufactures and mobilizes an incipient narrative of desire.

This narrative economy, however, remains "defective" or complicated in two respects. The first has to do with the bricoleur's ambivalence in relation to cinematic interiority. He never enters the interior of the club where we have observed the most cinematic moment (in the classical sense) of the film, in the mahjong play. Although he is granted a couple of point-of-view shots of the clock and two "dream-balloon" shots of his interior desire, the film is at pains to perform his secret desire and his carpentry magic in the theatrical open space. *Laborer's Love* is thus very much a "last echo of an early cinema," at once embodying and challenging Zhang Shichuan's faith in "attractions and tastes."[52] The second "defectiveness" is related to the displacement or blurring of visual pleasure discussed above. The gendered configurations of vision and desire in the film are resonant with what Miriam Hansen said about the spectatorship in/of early cinema in relation to a gendered public sphere:

> The polymorphously perverse energies that animated the cinema of attractions were not yet channeled into the regime of the keyhole, the one-way street of classical voyeurism which has led feminist theorists to describe the place of the female spectator as a "locus of impossibility."[53]

In the film, before the doctor's daughter denies the male vision in the scene of the spectacles, she had already glanced directly into the camera in her first appearance. Facing the street working on her embroidery, she is a spectator of, as well as a participant in, public life. The desire that motivates the narrative as well as gender *performance* is hardly a "one-way street"; she crosses the street to express her equal infatuation with the vendor, and tacitly agrees to be the future proprietress of the fruit shop. This "exchange" underscores not so much the theme of social mobility as a simple reversal of social hierarchy as a more fluid or democratized distribution of labor and social and gender relations, a mobility that thus also includes demographic and spatial movement such as trade, migration, and immigration.

The insistence on the double identity of the carpenter-vendor is very much an insistence on bricolage. While the film delights in an incipient form of filmic narration, it also passionately adheres to the formal conventions and themes derived from traditional and modern theater, popular literature, and folklore. Momentarily flirting with the "Edisonian imaginary," *Laborer's Love* nevertheless refuses to be absorbed completely by the magic power of the apparatus. The first word and the final one are given to the human heart and hand, as indicated in the calligraphic couplet hung in the doctor's shop: "A virtuous heart saves the world / A magic hand can bring back spring" (*Renxin zai jishi, miaoshou ke huichun*). The cliché has been relentlessly satirized but is given new meaning at the end of the film.

The film as a whole frankly acknowledges the presence of film technology and the impact that mechanical reproduction had on traditional cultural practices (for example, Chinese medicine and calligraphy). The humorous image of the bricoleur as a versatile filmmaker, who uses his hands as much as his entrepreneurial skills, however, represents the desire of the first generation of Chinese filmmakers to reconcile art with profit, craftsmanship with technology.

Epilogue: Early Cinema in a New Era

In a curious way, the return of early Chinese cinema in Chinese critical discourse is concomitant with the rise of the Chinese New Cinema, and the search for a new concept of film in the context of the renewed project of Chinese modernity. The Chinese New Cinema has in the past decade surprised and enthralled the world with a number of award-winning films, such as *Huang tudi* (Yellow earth, 1984), *Hong gaoliang* (Red sorghum, 1988), *Dahong denglong gaogao gua* (Raise the red lantern, 1991), and *Bawang bieji* (Farewell my concubine, 1993). Elaborate cinematography, lavish colors, exotic landscapes, state-of-the-art post-production, and the rise of Gong Li as the vedette of this new oriental cinematic reverie have ushered Chinese cinema into the spotlight of the international film scene.[54]

The success of this new cinema is a well-known story and I will not reiterate it here. What is of interest to the present inquiry is the status of early Chinese cinema in the emergence of a renewed cinematic consciousness in the latest drive for modernization. In the early eighties, as many filmmakers and actors who were active in the thirties and forties were rehabilitated, some of their films that had survived the perils of history were also reexhibited after decades of wasting away in archives. But they are mainly the "left-wing" films (*zuoyi dianying*) such as *Chuncan* (Spring silkworms, 1933), *Yuguang qu* (Song of the fishermen, 1934), *Dalu* (Big road, 1935), and *Malu tianshi* (Street angel, 1937).[55] The film industry during the Republican period as a whole remained a sensitive subject, and relevant materials were only available to a few researchers. The 1982 reexhibition of some more "progressive" early films, made mostly in the Shanghai studios before the Communist takeover in 1949, nevertheless had considerable impact on the rebuilding of a national cinema after the hiatus of the Cultural Revolution.[56] It also inadvertently stimulated a cultural nostalgia for a cinematic past which was not dictated by a single ideological and formal orthodoxy. In their reassessment of Chinese film history, however, the filmmakers and critics of the 1980s voiced their ambivalence toward the Chinese cinematic tradition as a whole. Its deep roots in the theatrical and literary traditions are singled out as the main obstacle for developing a truly modern cinema. The advocates and practitioners of the New Cinema assumed a mission to rid Chinese cinema of the "walking stick of drama" and to aim for the "modernization of film language."[57] The Chinese critical discourse on film in the 1980s, marked by a resuscitated interest in Bazin's film theory, signaled a shift of critical focus from the previous preoccupation with political (truth-)content to an "unprecedented self-consciousness of the cinematic medium, the belated awakening of a cinema as cinema."[58] The early phase of the post–Cultural Revolution period saw desperate gestures made by directors old and young to catch up with the "world" (that is, the West). This is manifest in an unreflective "cinematic" frenzy as depicted by Leo Ou-fan Lee:

> Gone are the old "normal ways" of spatial realism and slow relaxed tempo. Instead, one finds a splurge of fancy techniques: fast zooms, close-ups, split screens, fast cutting, superimposed images—as if the Chinese filmmakers were determined to catch up with the technical progress of the West and to show the outside world that the Chinese are capable of performing all the advanced "tricks" with the camera.[59]

The failure of many films produced in this "modernization" drive, or indeed Hollywoodification, have led film critics and filmmakers to search for an indigenous or "national form" (*minzu xingshi*) for Chinese cinema. The shift to the question of national culture and form is not unrelated to the emergence of the so-called Fifth Generation cinema, which inadvertently and ironically became an international legend. As a unified group, the Fifth Generation hardly exists. Individual directors and cinematographers differ widely in visual style and thematic approach. Trained by the prestigious Beijing Film Academy after the Cultural Revolution, the Fifth Generation directors have little or no background in theater or literature (not to mention the entertainment business), as did the generation of Zhang Shichuan and Zheng Zhengqiu. Having spent many years in the countryside as *zhiqing* (educated youth) during the Cultural Revolution, their cameras (re)turned to the peripheral rural landscape, or the "past," as an imaginary yet visually palpable space. The old hybrid urban Shanghai culture that fostered China's early cinema definitely did not provide the "cultural roots" for this new generation of filmmakers until very recently.

A closer look at some of the successful films of this New Cinema, however, reveals a curious kinship with early cinema that may not be visible at the outset. Although the connection to spoken drama is clearly absent, many such films are hardly pure filmic events. For one thing, many of this group of films are literary adaptations (*Yellow Earth, Red Sorghum, Raise the Red Lantern, Farewell My Concubine, Huozhe* [To live, 1994]). The many references to traditional Chinese performing arts and rituals in these films, such as folk song, folk dance, Peking opera, funerals or weddings, often constitute the films' most spectacular moments, which erupt into or out of the narrative economy. Zhang Yimou's *To Live*, which is explicitly structured around the vicissitudes of the traditional "leather puppet play" (shadowplay) in twentieth-century China, invites further pondering on the intricate relationship between early cinema and contemporary cinema.[60]

Toward the end of the 1980s, with the booming of mass media culture, the focus of critical debate in film criticism began to shift to the "entertainment film."[61] Film historians scrambled to rearticulate an even earlier cinema before the "left-wing" cinema, whose melodramas were thought to be too didactic and formally too much influenced by Hollywood.[62] A great deal of scholarly attention was paid to "shadowplay" as an aesthetic and historical category in the study of the genesis of Chinese cinema.[63] The emphasis on "plays" is also manifest in studies on short comedies of "perverse pleasures," spectacular and transgressive martial arts films, and films based on "mandarin ducks and butterflies" popular fiction and drama.[64] Unlike previous mainstream scholarship, which has trivialized or infantilized this cinema by accusing it of being "vulgar" in content and "primitive" in form, Ma Junxiang's study, for example, insightfully identifies this cinema as a "compensation" for the absence of avant-garde and genre film in the Chinese context. Ma argues that the martial arts film, which was a great success in domestic as well as overseas (mainly Southeast Asian) markets, carried over the emphasis on optical techniques from the short comics or "attractions," and was "avant-garde" in integrating traditional narrative art and modern visual media to create a powerful but hardly pure "national form."[65] Beyond the ontology of film, and viewing early cinema as a complex cultural and economic practice, the noted film historian and theorist Li Shaobai called for a critical investigation of film market and spectatorship in a broad historical framework.[66] Such an approach to early Chinese cinema tends to view the cinematic experience it yielded as a complex process involving internal as well as external influences, popular as well as experimental aspirations, artistic as well as commercial concerns. The critical value of this historical revision of a neglected part of early Chinese cinema is not to be underestimated, although its tendency to rechannel early cinema into a new discourse of "national form" has to be carefully examined. Moreover, the prevalent emphasis in this scholarship on narrative integration as a yardstick for a "mature" cinema still betrays an evolutionist influence and an unwitting subscription to Hollywood cinematic codes in the (re)writing of film history.

The theoretical explorations in early cinema paralleled the resurgent interest in martial arts and popular urban literature and film at a time when rapid modernization has spurred an explosion of media culture in China. The urban space once again provides a hotbed for this proliferation of mass media. Chinese cinema finds itself encountering a new yet not entirely strange spectatorship. The "teahouse culture" seems to have returned, accompanied by new variants such as large-screen video projection theaters and karaoke bars. In Shanghai, while many unprofitable cinemas have been turned into "teahouses" or nightclubs, some have rebaptized themselves with the famous names used in old Shanghai and remodeled their theaters into entertainment centers. Some renovated luxurious viewing rooms (or *mini ting*) are complete with coffee tables, cocktails, and discreet loveseats ("mandarin ducks seats," *yuanyang zuo*) or family seats. Cheaper all-night shows also attract restless youth and homeless migrant souls. Serial TV dramas and films based on the life of old Shanghai are the latest fad in visual production. And it is not surprising that Chen Kaige, with his *Fengyue* (Temptress moon, 1995) and Zhang Yimou, with his *Yao a yao, yao dao waipo qiao* (Shanghai Triad, 1995), are leading the vogue once again. Filmmakers find themselves increasingly divided not only between "serious" and "commercial" films but also between cinema and television production, and some have even taken up advertisement work. But more ambitious film directors, including Zhang Yimou and Chen Kaige, are aiming to produce a sort of commercial avant-garde film with enormous (foreign) budgets, for domestic and international audiences alike, but certainly at the expense of the kind of cultural radicalism that made them famous.

In a sense, Chinese cinema and media culture at large have finally managed to "march into the world," leaving traumatic memories and the current unevenness of development "behind," while hastily leaping into a globalizing postmodern world order. To install a contemporary perspective on the issue of early Chinese cinema at this juncture can be helpful to the understanding of the symptomatic crisis of perceptual consciousness brought by rapid modernization and advanced televisual communication technologies in China today, now inundated by pagers, mobile phones, fax machines, pirated videotapes, and even laser or digital film disks.[67] A longer view of Chinese film history is not so much to see early cinema as an object of nostalgia for the contemporary Chinese cinema, its critics and spectators, as to shed some light on how a historically neglected film like *Laborer's Love* may prove to be more than a significant textual instance, because it embodies in itself many issues that have haunted Chinese filmmakers and critics for decades. The sustained recourse to indigenous art forms—in particular, the traditional theater—and their modes of address, on the one hand, and a fascination with cinema as an international mass medium on the other, constitute a dynamic cultural nexus that engenders the making and reception of Chinese cinema now and decades ago. *Laborer's Love* is a random and hybrid beginning that has become the inevitable starting point for this inquiry. The brevity of this silent story and its jocular overtone have a long echo that we are only beginning to hear.

'The Romance of the Western Chamber' and the Classical Subject Film in 1920s Shanghai

KRISTINE HARRIS

In 1927, Minxin Film Company (a.k.a. China Sun) brought the classic *Xixiang ji* (The romance of the western chamber) to twentieth-century film audiences in urban China—and beyond, to Western Europe. This cinematic incarnation emerged from a lineage of texts beginning in the ninth century. Reconstituted for the visual medium of silent film, the narrative's striking swordplay and psychological dream sequences were accentuated by self-conscious references to the act of looking and moments of direct confrontation of the spectator. These moments recall what Tom Gunning has termed "the aesthetic of attractions" of late nineteenth-century Europe and the United States, where cinema "displays its visibility, willing to rupture a self-enclosed fictional world for a chance to solicit the attention of the spectator."[1] Shadowing the social and political anxieties of early twentieth-century China, *The Romance of the Western Chamber* operates along the compelling juncture of richly descriptive literary texts and silent modern technology.

The many classical renditions of *The Romance* exemplified a genre of storytelling known as the scholar-meets-beauty romance (*caizi jiaren*). Early versions of *The Romance* date back to the Tang dynasty, with a *chuanqi* tale called *Yingying zhuan* (Story of Yingying) by Yuan Zhen (779–831) and spin-off songs like *Yingying benshi ge* (The ballad of the true story of Yingying) by Li Shen (d. 846). By the twelfth century, the tale began resurfacing in new forms: first, as a *zhugongdiao*, or performance combining recited narration and song, by Master Dong Jieyuan (fl. 1189–1208), and then as a Yuan drama by Wang Shifu (late thirteenth century). Dong Jieyuan's version provides the most interesting basis for comparison with the 1927 screen rendition, since the *zhugongdiao*'s alternating method of narration comes closest to a silent film's alternation of images and intertitles. As it happened, *The Romance* is the sole extant complete work in the *zhugongdiao* form, attracting the fresh attention of scholars in China's literary world during the early 1910s.[2]

New emphases emerged each time *The Romance* was cast in a new form, but the various retellings generally adhere to the following plot. An aspiring young scholar named Zhang Gong,[3] en route to the capital for the civil service examination, makes an overnight stop at the scenic Pujiu Si (Temple of universal salvation) in Puzhou. There he spots the enigmatic young beauty Cui Yingying sequestered in mourning for her deceased father, a minister of state. Scholar Zhang is instantly enamored of Yingying's beauty, but finds he must win the favor of her strict mother. In the face of numerous obstacles, the young couple initiates a passionate love affair aided solely by Yingying's maid Hongniang. Only when Zhang saves Yingying's life does her mother finally permit them to unite in marriage.[4]

The film's narrative, point of view, and gender stereotypes developed from this genealogy of antecedents. Demonstrating love's ability to transcend social restrictions, *The Romance* possessed a timeless appeal, but it acquired a special currency and pliability during the early decades of the twentieth century when "feudal" attitudes towards marriage were being reassessed. The late Qing satirist Wu Jianren (1867–1910) spearheaded a revival of *The Romance* with his vernacular novelization of the Yuan drama, published posthumously in October 1921.[5] In a later modern variation of 1936, famed Peking opera actor Xun Huisheng (1900–1985) created a showcase for his mastery of the female role in *Hongniang*, named for Yingying's personal maid.[6] Other notable reinterpretations included a 1927 movie called *Hongniang xianxing ji* (Hongniang reveals her true colors), a wartime film made by Zhang Shichuan in 1940, and Tian Han's stage drama of 1958.

What distinguished the 1927 Minxin film rendition from all these other versions? First of all, converting dialogue, song, and theatrical space to the silent screen called for significant departures from earlier redactions. Most versions of *The Romance* were rich in visual description that could suggest ready translation into the moving image; yet the solutions to problems of cinematic perspective and silence were very much the work of modern authors: scenarist and director Hou Yao (1900–1945) and title writer Pu Shunqing (1902–?). To understand their self-referential composition of expressive camera angles, intertitles, and locations—culminating in a revelatory dream sequence—our analysis must begin by placing Hou Yao and Pu Shunqing in their literary context. While adapting a classical romance may have appeared something of a withdrawal from Hou's contemporary social dramas for the stage, the resulting picture did convey a certain resonance with the historical and literary moment of late 1927. The point of view Hou Yao constructed for the besieged scholar figure, Zhang Gong, evokes the apprehensive vision of a post–May Fourth literatus poised at the threshold between war and a precarious national unity.

Mediating between Hou Yao, Pu Shunqing, and their predecessors were the demands of a booming genre and a particular studio style. Chinese cinematic adaptations of traditional legends and dramas flourished in the mid- to late 1920s, and their success largely depended on swordplay action and special effects. Minxin's founder, filmmaker Li Minwei (1892–1953), drastically recut the film at least once before its formal Shanghai release, and possibly again for export. The extant five-reel film (said to be only half its prior length) is devoted mainly to extended swordplay and dream sequences. Therefore, in terms of its overall structure, rhythm, and special effects, *The Romance* needs to be understood also as the product of collaborative effort. A synergy of forces came together in *The Romance*—individual filmmakers, a popular genre, the literary and political climate in 1927, and the process of adapting musical theater to the silent screen.

The Romance gives us insight into the position of classical culture, and even film culture, in Republican-period politics. The nostalgia, spectacle, and commodification of the classical subject films made them targets of charged political criticism from both the left and the right. Whether these imaginative, fictional films were subversive or conservative in their internal ideology, they claimed to create faithful visual representations of Chinese culture. Their commanding—if unlikely—attempt to ally spectacle and authenticity contended with political orthodoxy for the attention of a national populace.

The Authors' Early Work in Theater and Film

The playwrights Hou Yao and Pu Shunqing were initiated into film work during the early 1920s at Changcheng (Great Wall Film Company). This company had a patriotic yet cosmopolitan flavor, formed by a group of young Chinese who had recently returned from New York City eager to produce pictures for the domestic market. Hou Yao served as Great Wall's principal scriptwriter for three years before going on to write and direct for Minxin. Pu Shunqing was married to Hou Yao, and participated in a variety of film production activities alongside him at both companies during the same period.[7]

Minxin was Hong Kong's first Chinese-owned and -operated motion picture company, with a new base in Shanghai. Its founder and manager Li Minwei was, like Hou Yao, a Cantonese theater man. Li had run a drama club during the 1910s before acquiring American equipment and funding for a prototype filmmaking venture. The short-lived Huamei (Sino-American) Film Company dissolved after making a single film in 1913, but Li's interests expanded into newsreel and documentary work. He opened Minxin Company for this purpose in 1922, and branched out into narrative film production four years later with dramatists Ouyang Yuqian (1889–1962), Bu Wancang (1903–74), and Hou Yao. Minxin later merged with three other studios in 1930 to form Lianhua (United China Film Company, a.k.a. United Photoplay), which functioned as a key gathering point for left-wing filmmakers until 1937.

Minxin shared Great Wall's aim to create stylish locally made films that would compete with Hollywood products. Hou Yao's own training also typified this fusion of national consciousness, social justice, and middle-class commercial entertainment, establishing a commitment to produce social dramas within the context of a contemporary brand of aesthetic idealism. Hou and Pu had been educated at the relatively conservative Southeastern University in Nanjing between 1920 and 1924,[8] but Hou was also associated with the Shanghai offshoot of the influential May Fourth group, the Wenxue Yanjiu Hui (Society for literary research, a.k.a. The literary association).

The Literary Association had been founded in Beijing in November 1920 by a group of twelve veterans from the May Fourth enlightenment magazine *Xinchao* (New tide, a.k.a. The Renaissance); over the course of its twelve-year existence the loosely knit membership grew to over 170.[9] By the spring of 1921 a Shanghai branch had emerged around the Shangwu yinshuguan (Commercial press) journal *Xiaoshuo yuebao* (Fiction monthly, a.k.a. Short story magazine) with Shen Yanbing (Mao Dun, 1896–1981) at its helm. The self-appointed mission of this group of young authors and literary scholars was *rensheng yishu* (art for life's sake). Their "humane realist" stance would soon be challenged by the romantic *chun yishu* (pure art for art's sake) approach suggested by poet Guo Moruo (1892–1978), playwright Tian Han, and fiction writer Yu Dafu (1896–1945) in the Chuangzao she (Creation society) between 1922 and 1927.[10] In advocating "new literature," the Literary Association also set itself apart from "middlebrow" authors of semiclassical, serialized fiction in the so-called Yuanyang hudie pai (School of mandarin ducks and butterflies).

True to these aims of humane realism, Hou Yao and Pu Shunqing specialized in "social problem dramas" and "home dramas" first for the stage and then the screen. Hou became the leading member of the Association to be seriously engaged in writing for film during this period. The group's approach to foreign literature was particularly influential on Hou's early work. Mao Dun had advocated selective translation of Western literary works that would introduce "the world's modern thought" while excluding, for economy's sake, the aestheticist and the antiquated.[11] Accordingly, Hou named Henrik Ibsen and Guy de Maupassant as inspiration for plays such as *Yichuan zhenzhu* (A string of pearls, 1925), *Zhaixing zhi nü* (The woman who plucked stars, 1925), and *Fuhuo de meigui* (Revived rose, 1927).

Hou Yao's many plays about women's issues contributed to a dynamic colloquy about the possibilities for women and the limits of social change during the early 1920s. An outstanding example is his 1922 theatrical script for *Qifu* (The abandoned wife), later adapted for film at Great Wall Studios in 1924. Hou Yao created a *Doll's House*–like story of a twenty-three-year-old woman, Wu Zhifang, who takes leave of her debauched husband and tyrannical mother-in-law, joins the women's rights movement, and aspires to earn an independent living. In a bleak twist (more evocative of Maupassant than of Ibsen), Zhifang never becomes the "beacon for this dark society" as she had hoped, but rather is driven insane by "this dark world."[12] Performed in women's normal schools and art schools in Nanjing and Wuhu (in Anhui province) between 1922 and 1924, and also reprinted numerous times in the Commercial Press series Tongsu Xiju Congshu (Popular drama collection), this proto-feminist dramaturgy would have striking impact on later left-wing film narratives such as *Shennü* (Goddess, 1934) and *Xin nüxing* (New woman, 1935).

Pu Shunqing may have been China's earliest female playwright to enter the world of cinema. Most of her known film work was done in collaboration with her husband, and the couple shared an interest in bringing women's issues to the stage and screen. She began working at Great Wall when Hou Yao did, in 1924, performing in his film *The Abandoned Wife* opposite China's leading actress of the time, Wang Hanlun. Pu also adapted her own stage play, *Aishen de wan'ou* [God of love doll], into a film scenario for Great Wall that year. When Hou Yao moved to Minxin, Pu participated in the writing and location shooting of several films directed by Hou Yao, and was credited with composing the intertitles for *The Romance*. Intertitles, of course, were inserted after the filming was complete, and as we shall see, the narrative exposition of this particular film depends less on titles than on the director's visual narration.

When Shanghai student protesters were killed in the May Thirtieth Incident of 1925, Hou Yao adapted for Great Wall and Minxin a series of his own stage plays about the human costs of violence and civil war. These films included *Chungui mengli ren* (The person in the spring boudoir dream, 1925), *Heping zhi shen* (Spirit of peace, 1926), and *Haijiao shiren* (The poet at the end of the seas, 1927). When they were originally produced for the stage in the early 1920s, plays like *The Person in the Spring Boudoir Dream*—which dramatized the civil war through the eyes of a young soldier torn from the women in his life—had been praised by key members of the Literary Association as "art for life's sake."[13]

In August of 1927 Minxin Company presented *The Romance* for a test screening, and the film played a successful run at Shanghai theaters like the Hangzhou Shadowplay House and the Palace Theater (Zhongyang Daxiyuan) that autumn.[14] By then, though, the Nationalist Party had already abandoned its "United Front" with the Chinese Communist Party and orchestrated a brutal massacre of Shanghai workers. Literary debates became newly charged with calls for proletarian "revolutionary literature." This turn of events appeared to cast Hou Yao's revival of a classic tale of amorous courtship in a politically dimmer light. Minxin's costume dramas and Hou's film work after 1925 seemed to elude the paradigms of "revolutionary literature."[15]

Adapting Classical Subjects for Modern Films

Classical subjects tracked an erratic and even controversial course in early twentieth-century Chinese filmmaking. They had been a staple of early experiments with cinema ever since the Fengtai photography shop began filming Tan Xinpei's opera scenes in 1905. But in 1921, they were being eclipsed by modern detective stories, comedies, and Western-style *wenming xi* or "civilized" dramas. So when Chinese studios intensively resurrected swordplays and costume dramas *en masse* between 1925 and 1931, the move struck many—most vocally, the politicians—as a withdrawal into the past. Qu Qiubai (1899–1935), head of the Chinese Communist Party from 1927 to 1928, declared war on the "reactionary" arts still enjoyed by the masses, urging instead a "mass art for the proletarian revolution" that would "raise" the standard from

> cartoons, the lowest class of legends and stories ... , big shows (*daxi*), shadow-play/films (*yingxi*), slapstick shows (*mutouren xi*), peep-shows (*xiyang jing*), story-tellers (*shuoshu*), Suzhou opera (*tanhuang*), Buddhist readers (*xuanjuan*) and so on, like *Huoshao honglian si* (Burning of the Red Lotus Temple). Their ideology is full of black smoke, miasmas of feudal demons, and a "vegetable market morality"—the "pay or starve" mentality of the capitalist class.[16]

Aside from the economic determinants, the same bleak view of popular culture as backward and unprogressive was shared by China's nation-builders in the KMT—though, of course, for opposite ends. For a Nationalist Government concerned with stability and control, the problem was not that these films were insufficiently revolutionary, but rather that they were *too rebellious*. Through numerous incarnations from 1929 onwards, the government's Censorship Board reacted to the upsurge in mystical swordplay films by including provisions that outlawed any films that "harm public order" (namely, those that featured "pirates and bandits" or the "improper actions of individual and group struggle") and any films that "encourage superstition" (whether through the representation of "spirits, immortals, ghosts, omens, religion, or magic" or even of "histori-cally recorded odd happenings and social lore of the strange and unusual").[17]

The two main surveys of Chinese cinema echo these official mandates: from the mainland Chinese perspective *The Romance* is relegated to the realm of "feu-dal remnants" and "bourgeois intellectual backwardness," and in the Taiwan historiography, it is called "regressive" (*tuibu*) and "escapist" (*taobi xianshi*).[18] Certainly the scholar-beauty romance apparatus appeared nostalgic when fa-miliar "high culture" notions of gender were being forcefully challenged in the early twentieth century. The official route to success for men—scholarship and a civil service position—eroded with the abolition of the national examination system in 1905. The presumed authority of a father's, husband's, or son's house-hold was fractured by vocal reformers including Kang Youwei (1858–1927) and missionary groups, who issued challenges to the norms of arranged marriage, filial piety, and footbinding.

In the context of these radical social changes and ideals of progress, it was al-most inevitable that the traditional romance genre would be charged with atavism. But whether it was cultural anxiety or a new independence that led filmmakers like Hou Yao to rely on China's cultural resources, their recourse to preexisting narratives was an important factor in the development of the local film industry. A comparison with similar practices in the United States illumi-nates the significance of this factor. During the 1910s, U.S. film producers and exhibitors had also relied on faithful adaptations of tried-and-true successes from fiction and the theater, such as *Ben-Hur* (1907), *Les Miserables* (1909), *A Tale of Two Cities* (1911), *Faust* (1911), *Dante's Inferno* (1911), and *Homer's Odys-sey* (1912). Dovetailing neatly with the highbrow cast of classic theater produc-tions, these sources provided sustained narratives for the latest breed of longer, multiple-reel films and justified higher ticket prices. The goal was to shed the nickelodeon's image of vulgarity and attract the middle-class theatergoer into movie houses.[19]

In China of the late 1920s, the long narrative film and a middle-class audi-ence for foreign imports were already established, but the challenge remained to create a domestic product that would appeal to a broader local urban con-stituency. With the benefit of hindsight on trends abroad, Chinese film compa-nies speculated—accurately—that familiar subjects could augment box-office returns. In their case, there were three particular advantages to filming an adap-tation. First, it offered a readily available, preexisting scenario which eliminated the time, expense, and uncertainties of producing an entirely original script. Second, this popular material possessed distinctive content and visual textures which could be commodified as a clear alternative to Hollywood products in the China market, and which spoke to the many Chinese viewers who felt excluded by the foreign intertitles and extraterritorial settings of the ubiquitous import film culture. Finally, a well-known, dependable title could reassure apprehensive exhibitors of ticket sales.

To fit the bill, studios—particularly those of Cantonese extraction such as Li Minwei's Minxin, the Shaw Brothers' Tianyi, and Da Zhonghua-Baihe, along with the smaller companies Fudan and Da Zhongguo—mobilized episodes drawn from legends, serial novels, and poetic *zaju* opera dramas set to music. In 1927 *Sanguo zhi* (Romance of the three kingdoms), *Xiyou ji* (Journey to the west), *Tieshan gongzhu* (Princess iron fan), *Honglou meng* (Dream of the red chamber), and *Burning of the Red Lotus Temple* were all released. According to some sources, there were more than a hundred small film companies in China by 1925, and they produced at least 644 films between 1921 and 1930. During the late 1920s, the majority of this output fell into the broad category of martial arts swordsman legends (*wuxia pian*), period costume dramas (*shidai xi / guzhuang xi*), or "fantasy" films.[20]

The Romance is an important example in this robust genre of classical-subject adaptations.[21] The careful art direction for these films included research in period costumes and settings. As one example from 1927 shows, reviews and articles commented on this factor in Da Zhonghua-Baihe's popular two-part costume drama film, *Meiren ji* (Beauty's strategy, a portion of the epic classic *Romance of the Three Kingdoms*), and advance studio publicity touted its accurate representation of Chinese culture:

> The Chinese theater filmed by Westerners is so disgraceful it makes one's eyes burst with anger. It dishonors our past and makes us the laughingstock of nations. . . . But we refuse to be discouraged. Instead we've rolled up our sleeves to denounce those immense ventures and are filming our own pure ancient costume drama, *Beauty's Strategy*. The costumes and locations are all scrupulously researched; the actors are hand-picked for excellence. A full year of preparation has gone into the making of this picture.[22]

Emphasis on loyalty to the original was also common in U.S. publicity for film adaptations, but in China the contemporary rhetoric of national self-representation added another lofty layer to the cinematic use of native legends and classics. Ironically, the film industry's claim to authentic representation of the national past may have been an important, if unspoken, reason why politicians so vocally criticized the classical subject films. As unorthodox sources of "true" national consciousness, these fiction films were stealing the show—diluting or detracting from the Communist and Nationalist competition to represent China.

While very few of the classical-subject films are extant, *The Romance* provides evidence that in terms of cinematic innovation alone they could be more than stalwart period pieces. Often they were at the cutting edge of technical expertise in China's moving picture world, combining acrobatic stunts with special effects (such as superimposition and animation) to recreate the flying tricks and elaborate pyrotechnic displays of famous martial arts legends.[23] *Burning of the Red Lotus Temple* was a prime example of the scale and popularity of this genre: Mingxing (Star Film Company) used 400 extras and allocated a quarter of its budget to the construction of elaborate temple sets. The film sold out for 23 days straight, convincing Zhang Shichuan to develop it into an eighteen-part serial. Overall, the spectacle of the classical-subject film brought commercial success that fortified stronger companies like Mingxing with the financial means to compete with Hollywood productions in the 1930s.[24] The genre also allowed many smaller, more vulnerable studios such as Tianyi and Minxin to stay afloat. It is no surprise, then, to see a film adaptation of *The Romance* built around two swordplay-style segments that were so popular at the time. Minor elements of *The Romance*'s plot were abridged in trimming the classic down to a 55-minute picture, and a disproportionately long time—two-thirds of the film—was given over to swordfighting scenes where local marauders attack the monastery to capture Cui Yingying and her mother.[25]

Theatricality and Spectacle

There were many practical obstacles for a dramatist crossing over to the new medium of cinema, particularly when presenting traditional theatrical material. Some audiences had first experienced Peking opera on the silent screen through Mei Lanfang's (1894–1961) cameos of select roles filmed by the Commercial Press during the early 1920s. As Mei himself emphasized, the team made an effort to choose segments of operas that were sufficiently spectacular to stand without sound.[26] He commented, however, that the actor's sense of continuity was disrupted by the constant struggle to transform the large, three-dimensional ground of stage performance into a static movie camera's two-dimensional frame:

> Film space was level and flat, so I couldn't move through the entire stage space. Even though we'd rehearsed a number of times, when it got to the actual filming so many unavoidable problems cropped up. Whether it was the wrong angle, or I'd moved out of the frame, the cameraman would call out, "That shot won't do!" And we'd have to go along with him for yet another take.[27]

Furthermore, the translation of three-dimensional stylized stage space onto a new "realist" flat screen would have posed additional difficulties for any artist accustomed to the spatial conventions of China's long screen-painting tradition—conventions radically different from the Renaissance principles of fixed-point perspective and foreshortening that had produced the camera lens.[28]

By 1927, narrative filmmaking conditions in China were slightly more flexible, but Hou Yao was still constricted by a static camera. In an effort to overcome the limitations of filming theatrical space, he shot numerous exterior scenes on location in Suzhou and Hangzhou in natural settings. At this time, location shooting beyond the Shanghai vicinity was still a fairly new ingredient in Chinese narrative cinema, and so the film's ability to transport the viewer to another place was a major attraction—not only for local audiences, but for viewers abroad as well.

The Romance was one of the first Chinese films to gain wide exposure in the European market, touring Paris, London's Chinatown, Geneva, and Berlin. Its success there might be partly attributed to the fascination with "oriental" motifs in 1920s European and American design and cinema, as the film's interiors were copiously ornate.[29] For these audiences *The Romance*'s classic Hangzhou waterside vistas may have added another exotic aspect to this "new spectacle," as the Paris newspaper *Le Temps* described it.[30] Ostensibly, for Chinese audiences abroad, the film's locales served more as a nostalgic reminder. In sum, the authenticity and naturalism of the film's landscapes presented a sort of travelogue which allowed the viewer to transcend geographic and internal distance (an ideal the film also shared with classical Chinese painting).

Taking full advantage of the outdoor location, Hou Yao shot the battle between "Flying Tiger" Sun and "White Horse General" Du as an extravaganza of broad, long distance shots of the large-scale scrimmage between sword-wielding cavalry and infantry—for which the studio had hired a large number of extras. To multiply their numbers even further, footage of "100,000" soldiers emerging from their respective stations (a bandit cave and the Puguan garrison) was duplicated and spliced together sequentially. Without the benefit of a mobile camera, the film manages to achieve an engaging rhythm through rapid edits, overhead shots, and stylized, superimposed close-ups of clashing weapons. *The Romance* advanced a wide array of montage techniques from Chinese swordsman films which complemented its lavish interiors and the magnificent scale of its outdoor location (see fig. 5).

Cinematic Gazes

The 1927 film reproduced the explicit references to visions and gazing that had been a mainstay of *The Romance* as it was transmitted from the Song period on. In the written and theatrical precedents that were available to Hou Yao and Li Minwei, Zhang and Yingying's fateful initial meeting consists of an al-

5. Film poster for *The Romance of the Western Chamber* (1927), courtesy of the China Film Archive.

most cinematic pattern of moving images, changing views, and exchanged glances. In fact, the plot can almost be reduced to a sequence of moments of vision. These excerpts from the first chapter of Dong Jieyuan's version, for example, read like directions in a film scenario:

> Suddenly something caught his *eye*;
> He stood *transfixed*, as if his soul had left him. . . .
>
> Catching this *glimpse*, he was startled, almost deranged. . . .
>
> What did Zhang *see* just then? What did he *see*? He came face to face with his predestined lover. . . .
>
> The vermilion gate opened;
> He caught a *glimpse* of her face fair as a flower.
>
> Ignoring Zhang's *stare*,
> She twisted a blossoming twig between her fingers. . . .
>
> "This *sharp pair of eyes*
> Have had to *look* at a myriad of abominable faces
> And never before *seen* such a perfect countenance."
>
> Brighter than autumn water are her *eyes*. . . .
>
> The moment he *saw* her
> He yearned for her. . . .
>
> Her intelligent, lively, *eyes*
> Were exquisite and refined.
> Though she feigned haughtiness, she did *glance* furtively at Zhang,
> Who was stricken—
> Stricken with overpowering passion. . . .
>
> He *gazed* at her demeanor
> And decided that she was unmarried. . . .
>
> He had never *seen* her before.
> He had never talked with her. . . .
>
> When the young lady *saw* Zhang, she retired shyly. . . .
>
> What Zhang had *seen*
> Had left him completely *dazed*.
> He thought to himself: "Who has ever *seen* such a beauty!"[31]

Much of the gazing in the various original texts occurs without a word being spoken, and the filmmakers conveyed the lovers' interaction in the silent film visually, through camera and editing techniques—principally, extreme close-ups on facial gestures and shot/reverse-shot structures—rather than through expository intertitles.

Throughout the film, the intertitular written word is secondary to visual expression, following the texts' rich description and sparse dialogue. At many

6. Cui Yingying (right), with the servant girl Hongniang, burns incense at Pujiu temple in *The Romance of the Western Chamber* (1927), courtesy of the China Film Archive.

points, the young scholar's vision virtually "narrates" the film. In tension with that visual authority, Hou Yao also emphasizes the way Zhang's sight of Yingying is obstructed. The tension helps drive the plot forward. For example, in the film, after Yingying and Hongniang shuffle silently past Zhang hiding their eyes, Yingying turns and looks back: an extreme close-up on her eyes emphasizes her defiance of that feigned modesty. She then interrupts her own brief look and quickly returns to her quarters. The maid shuts a round "moon gate" behind them. The monastery's abbot assists her in blocking Zhang's furtive visual pursuit, which only intensifies Zhang's frustration. Only now do intertitles appear, as Zhang voices his protest. These titles continue the references to sight and gazing, and are taken almost directly from the Dong Jieyuan text, which reads:

> "This compound is private, Sir. Please go elsewhere." Zhang
> retorted: "I intend to *see all the sights* in this temple. Why can I
> not go in there?". . . .

Facong soothed him:
"Honestly,
There's *nothing worth seeing* inside. . . ."
Zhang said: "What nonsense!
There must be *rare and precious sights*. . . .
How is it that just now
Guanyin herself *appeared before me?*"

The abbot then attempts to demystify what he terms Zhang's "vain imagining":

" . . . Should a servant be called to the [Cui family's] inner
court, he knows better than *to raise his eyes* and look
around. . . ."
Facong repeatedly exhorted Zhang:
"Cease your vain imagining, sir,
And listen to me.
Surely I wouldn't lie to you.
The beauty you just *saw*
Is the daughter of Minister Cui.
She must be sixteen or seventeen.
Her name is Yingying.
In no manner did you *witness the apparition* of Guanyin."

The monastery, in a sense, is a barrier to Zhang's vision: it is a place of abstinence and ritual propriety whose fortifications sequester the chaste heiress for mourning. At the same time, the courtyards' open latticework and the balustered passageways between prayer halls make for a permeability within the monastery which allows Zhang to observe and eventually meet the young lady. In numerous "peeping" scenes, the camera is aligned with Zhang's angle of vision—for example, as he surreptitiously watches Yingying's prayer ritual through a fretted temple wall. Such scenes emphasize the plot's progression from concealment to visual revelation.

Eventually the monk introduces Zhang to Yingying and her mother. In the film, their eyes meet in a series of alternating shots. This time, Yingying hides her face behind a fan in deference to conventional modesty (since, unlike the first encounter with Zhang, her mother is now present). An extreme close-up on Zhang's darting, anxious glance and suggestively raised eyebrow emphasizes the physical language of gestures and looks so central to *The Romance*; yet in cinematic terms, this shot also establishes a relationship between the spectator and an almost comical young man whose vain attempts to catch Yingying's eye are constantly thwarted. Even after the women have retreated into the temple, the performer playing Zhang (Ge Cijiang) faces the camera as if interacting with an audience present to him. This partially carries over from the earlier versions of *The Romance* (such as Dong Jieyuan's *Zhugongdiao*), where the narrator frequently addressed the listener in asides, offering commentary and creating dramatic suspense. Yet, in the film, close-ups on fervent glances and a pair of eyebrows oscillating between eager and perturbed also enact the same kind of "recurring look at the camera by actors" that characterized the early "cinema of attractions" in the United States and Europe.[32] Stepping outside the narrative for a brief moment to address the camera and spectator *directly* with this "look," the performer calls attention to how the film formally represents its protagonist's vision. This is yet another reminder that Zhang's desiring gaze, and the obstructions to that gaze, are what shape the cinematic narrative.

Through the camera's lens, Zhang's pursuit of the object escaping his vision also duplicates the cinematic spectator's *own* gaze at moving pictures that are similarly concealed and revealed over the passage of time. Laura Mulvey's essay "Visual Pleasure and Narrative Cinema" is concerned primarily with Hollywood conventions, but her description of the cinematic gaze can be equally relevant to this early example of Chinese cinema:

> At first glance, the cinema would seem to be remote from the undercover world of the surreptitious observation of an unknowing and unwilling victim. What is seen on the screen is so manifestly shown. But the mass of mainstream film, and the conventions within which it has consciously evolved, portray a hermetically sealed world which unwinds magically, indifferent to the presence of the audience, producing for them a sense of separation and playing on their voyeuristic fantasy. Moreover the extreme contrast between the darkness in the auditorium (which also isolates the spectators from one another) and the brilliance of the shifting patterns of light and shade on the screen helps to promote the illusion of voyeuristic separation. Although the film is really being shown, is there to be seen, conditions of screening and narrative conventions give the spectator an illusion of looking in on a private world.[33]

While this passage is part of Mulvey's broader attempt to define the "visual pleasure" of cinema within the Freudian and Lacanian psychoanalytic framework of scopophilia and narcissism, it can encourage us to begin thinking about how *The Romance* constructs its own spectator. So far, we have examined the male lead's various looks in relation to the camera: on the one hand, he briefly acknowledges "the presence of an audience" outside the film; on the other hand, his "surreptitious observation of" the female protagonist gives him (and the film spectator) an "illusion of voyeuristic separation." Both the monastery and the cinema are liminal places set between the outside world and the private family home, where a secret liaison of looks or fantasies is possible.[34]

There is a noteworthy correlation between that theoretical spectator constructed by the film, and the audiences described in Shanghai newspapers of the late 1920s. To cite one example, the following arts editorial entitled "The Movies and Young Men and Women" appeared in the newspaper *Shenbao*, during the same week that *The Romance* opened in Shanghai:

The movies are sometimes called a tool for social education, especially a tool for the social education of young men and women. . . . Japan's Diet recently raised the case of a young boy and girl under the age of fifteen who broke the law prohibiting them from going to the movies. According to Japanese surveys, there is a daily increase in crimes committed by young men and women under the influence of the darkness of the movie theater. Supposedly, the movies cause two types of afflictions: one is biological and hygiene-related, and the other is psychological and moral. In the first, old movies are harmful to your vision and that the air in movie theaters is dirty and hazardous to your health. In the second, the reductiveness of movies will make people go out and commit crimes and become susceptible to evil influences.[35]

Although this particular writer went on to argue that movie theaters were harmless, he or she was responding to the litany of proscriptions in the popular press which regularly commented on the ostensible connections linking the "darkness of the auditorium," clandestine interaction of the sexes, and even criminality.

In a technical allusion to this "voyeuristic separation" in the darkened movie theater, *The Romance* dramatizes Zhang Gong's secret desire for Yingying through the prominent use of a circular black mask "iris shot." This emphatic technique isolates a subject by obscuring its surroundings, similar to the way a cinematic light image is itself surrounded by darkness.[36] In *The Romance*, these iris shots produce a keyhole or telescoped target effect, suggesting clandestine surveillance from a distance.[37] The film begins with a dilating "iris in" on a piece of embroidery, and opens out to show the nearly motionless Yingying working at it. This dissolves to introductory close-ups of her maid and her mother, and then cuts to Zhang galloping into Puzhou on horseback. As he asks "What is the most picturesque area?" (*you shen xiqi jingwu*)—promising, in the film, a spectacle (*jingwu*) of rare scenic locations, Zhang spots in a telescopic iris the monastery's turret rising in the distance. This effectively completes the opening iris shot of Yingying embroidering: it unites the young man's vision of a monastery he is about to visit, and a woman he is about to meet.

More than eighty percent of the film's static iris shots represent the exclusive vision of Zhang and the monks. Cumulatively, this point-of-view editing cues the visual perspective to a predominantly male gaze within the film. The "male gaze" in *The Romance* works along the lines of classical Hollywood narrative conventions, as feminist film theorists have understood them—conventions which construct the agent of the look as masculine, and the object of that look as feminine.[38] Not surprisingly, Yingying's point of view and even her return of a look are only represented in occasional isolated moments (for instance, in a single iris shot, or in the close-up on her eyes mentioned earlier).[39] The male protagonist's optical range generally determines the focus and action of the story: in collaboration with a sympathetic skilled army, the young scholar fights to defend Yingying against unrefined military invaders (or *wu*) who battle for control over the same object of desire.

A rare shot from the female protagonist's point of view intersects a scene where Yingying embroiders a design on cloth. When her own view of this handiwork is shown in a close-up, a miniature likeness of Zhang appears superimposed at the center of a cluster of plum blossoms, so that she seems to have stitched both images together. For an audience familiar with the significance of the plum flower—its tenacity, as the first flower of spring blooming in snow; and its political connotation, as the young Republic's national symbol—the needlework composition evokes the aesthetic patterns of civil culture (*wen*) and the efflorescence (*hua*) of China, and metaphorically associates the characters of Yingying and Zhang with a version of a culture that is opposed to the *wu* of military invasion. (The film's export title, *La Rose de Pu-chui*, designates a flower with equally powerful symbolism for European cultures.) In the 1927 context, such an allegory could be understood in terms of the national (resistance to imperialism), domestic politics (civil war), and cultural (the tension between traditional refinement and the rush of modernity). The allegorical reference is brief, but it is an important antecedent to the subtle depiction of national consciousness in later films.[40]

The generally passive figure of Yingying seems incongruous with Hou Yao's and Pu Shunqing's earlier theatrical scripts, which were peopled by activist women and liberated female protagonists. Of course, the May Fourth approach to the "love question" was not always so far off from *caizi jiaren* or Mandarin duck and butterfly romances. As was common in many works of May Fourth fiction, particularly those by male writers, the film's visual representation of its female protagonist reproduces a voyeuristic male desire.[41] As we have seen, the film always frames the possibility of "free love" between Zhang and Yingying, and her "liberation" from a parentally arranged marriage, within the male protagonist's perspective. To translate the drama's original spoken and sung language into silent cinematic images, special effects were marshalled to create an authoritative vision for scholar Zhang. This authority was further reinforced by intertitles in his "voice" and even a letter written in his hand. By contrast, the few voices of female characters that had been present in earlier renditions were jettisoned, and there are almost no spoken dialogue titles for the female characters in the film.[42]

The Minxin production proceeds into a finale that is perhaps the most conservative of all renditions. The couple's two-way physical desire found in earlier versions gets sublimated into Zhang's one-way visual pleasure for the 1927 film, and he admires the chaste Yingying from a distance rather than physically consummating this desire before marriage.[43] In the context of uncertainty over relationships and morality during the late 1920s, this film seems to aim for the middle ground. It revives a classic of the *caizi jiaren* genre in which the female protagonist is elevated in beauty and status,[44] while making added efforts to assert the centrality of the male scholar protagonist.

The Scholar's Brush

At the center of the film, however, Hou Yao concocts a surreal dream sequence that stands out from the film's overall narrative. Since the strange imagery in this sequence is not present in the original, we might ask why Hou invented these cinematic flourishes for his film. The dream magnifies to absurd proportions the film's conventionalized roles for the scholar-hero and eligible young beauty. But then for a brief and unsettling moment, it overturns these conventions. As we recall, the young scholar had written a letter summoning General Du's assistance to ensure the women's safety from bandits in the monastery. Exhausted after the fight, he takes up his books and brush-pen and prepares to study for his examinations but instead falls asleep. In a dream, Zhang reenacts his rescue of the damsel, but this time singlehandedly, and with astonishing results. The ensuing symbolic imagery and disarming special effects merit a detailed description, since they accentuate the psychic significance of this fantastic battle for the scholar.

Above Zhang's dozing head, a miniature superimposed apparition of Yingying "floats" onto the screen. This dissolves into a full shot of Yingying physically entering Zhang's study, signaling a movement into the world of dreams. Zhang seems to "awaken" from his desk-side slumber and gazes into Yingying's eyes. At this moment the bandit Sun intrudes and abducts the young woman. His terrifying face lunges at the camera, in a rudimentary zoom-in effect that forces the audience to identify with Yingying's and Zhang's fear. Sun carries her away and Zhang once again "awakens," empty-handed but for his ineffectual brush-pen.

The dream sequence already contains two ambiguous awakenings, but it has not really ended. Zhang shakes his brush-pen in frustration, and "magically" the object grows to an enormous size in his hands (a trick achieved with stop-motion photography). Through one brilliant stroke, the brush immediately accrues three other connotations: weapon, vehicle, virility. Alone in his study, Zhang wields this pen like a sword, facing the camera directly and forcing it at the viewer. The film cuts to a double-exposed shot of him mounted on the huge "brush-pen," "flying" against an artificial backdrop of clouds and hills that resembles a painted landscape scroll. This "flight," intercut with shots of Sun galloping away with Yingying, creates a supernatural chase scene.

Zhang intercepts just as Sun is about to rape Yingying, and a point-of-view shot unites the film's spectator with our male protagonist. Through Zhang's eyes, we watch the enormous tip of his spear/brush poke at a close-up of the sword-bearing brigand. The defeated, contorted Sun rolls on the grass, his face covered in blood/ink beside Zhang's sword/brush. As if Zhang's phallic grip of the sword/brush—mounted between his legs as he rides it tip-forward through the heavens—were not an obvious enough reference to the male libido, this out-pouring of blood/ink from his weapon figuratively asserts his sexual potency. The emphasis on gender difference is also key to the scene's tempo. Close or me-dium shots of the two men's dueling action are rapidly cut into contrasting long shots of Yingying passively watching in fear from behind a distant tree. This tension terminates in the dream (as in the film's larger scheme) when scholar and beauty are reunited and the screen fades to black.

The surreal, Méliès-style enlargement of the brush-pen and all its attendant meanings were Hou Yao's own innovations for *The Romance*. In prior dramatic and poetic renditions, Zhang's dream was a fairly straightforward recapitula-tion of his overflowing first-person interior monologues about Yingying and numerous sexual trysts. The silent film, on the other hand, conveyed sexual ten-sion and anxiety through expressive, psychological images contained within a hallucinatory dream sequence.

Setting the film even farther apart from previous versions of *The Romance* is a coda to the psychological dream sequence. The volatile sexual imagery that agitated Zhang's climactic dream swordplay with Sun persists into the young scholar's waking world. He awakes to find himself passionately embracing not Yingying, but his faithful servant boy. The scholar notices that his hands are bathed in his own ink, and with a bawdy aside then notices his servant boy's face covered in the same ink (as was the impaled Sun's). Zhang has been so aroused by his victory that, in the absence of his dreamed object of desire, his passion has been displaced onto a passive sleeping figure (his inferior in both age and social status).

Why did Hou Yao add this comic incongruity to the film? It certainly conveys a sense of confusion and masculine unease, and undermines the carefully me-diated structure of gender codes and visual "authority" in the film's conclusion. By undercutting the gender stereotypes adopted from *The Romance* and the simple assertion of Zhang's triumph in battle and sexual potency, Hou Yao gelds the upwardly mobile scholar's heroic fantasy. This brief moment in the film reminds us of all the anxieties of twentieth-century historical change for the male writer: the uneasy role of the scholar gentleman in the absence of the traditional examination system, and amid a country of warlords, a new visibil-ity of women in society, and a new endorsement of free love and romance.

The dream sequence was more than just a retreat into the fantasy world of a movie character. It was a powerful metaphor that offered an oblique glimpse of

Hou Yao's own precarious status as a man of letters and culture in a postdynastic age of warlords. Certainly the film built on previous versions of the tale which contrasted the civil arts of peace and the weapons of warriors. For example, Master Dong's *Zhugongdiao* had opened with a wry comment on the placid surface that is about to be disturbed by an attack on the monastery:

> Happily, we now enjoy peace and leisure.
> Weapons are put away, armor is untouched;
> Living at a time like this
> Why shouldn't we be merry?[45]

Some audiences of the film might have been familiar enough with Wang Shifu's play to know that "a time like this" would soon be "out of joint"—much as their own time was. As Zhang sings in the beginning:

> A highly cultured (person finds it) impossible to adapt himself to the
>   merely vulgar.
> When the times are out of joint, a man cannot fulfill his highest
>   aspirations.

They might also recall the moralizing phrases at the close of the play, after Zhang emerges victorious over both the military challenge and Yingying's arranged fiancé Zheng Heng:

> [This] shows the high literary man of determination was bound to
>   succeed,
> As the ill-fated Zheng Heng was doomed to failure.[46]

The film is more tentative about the triumph of literary merit, but ultimately Zhang is still rewarded with success. This general ideal—the power of the pen over the opponent's sword—is consonant with Hou Yao's other pacifist heroes who deplored physical violence.

Familiar gender binaries are reinscribed in the film's brief denouement. Zhang's solitary nocturnal divagations give way to social convention. The couple undergoes an elaborate "backstage" ritual grooming by their servants in anticipation of the celebratory betrothal dinner proposed by Madame Cui. The film cuts rhythmically back and forth, five or six times, between Zhang and Yingying sitting before their respective altarlike vanity mirrors in separate parts of the monastery. On a symbolic level, the reiteration of these conventions serves to legitimate the couple's relationship. Moreover, this purposive rehearsal for a performance of social order calls to mind the whole process by which gender identity is socially constructed—as Judith Butler has suggested:

> As in other ritual social dramas, the action of gender requires a performance that is *repeated*. This repetition is at once a reenactment and reexperiencing of a set of meanings already socially established; and it is the mundane and ritualized form of their

legitimation. . . . The effect of gender is produced through the stylization of the body and, hence, must be understood as the mundane way in which bodily gestures, movements, and styles of various kinds constitute the illusion of an abiding gendered self.[47]

We might recall that such repetitions have occurred elsewhere in the film: the dream sequence, for instance, repeats the monastery battle from Zhang's perspective.

The Romance appropriately concludes in a very cinematic ritual. When Zhang returns from his examinations, he and Yingying are reunited in an embrace. Hou Yao presents this "happy ending" in silhouette through a white paper window screen, self-consciously suggesting a leather-puppet shadowplay—and, by extension, the cinematic screen itself. As if to heighten the theatrical artifice, the playful servant girl Hongniang watches this tableau along with us, the film spectators, while the image is gently irised out to black. A stylized closing shot to Hou Yao's film brings this narrative performance of gender to its predetermined resolution, but the dream and its disquieting repercussions persist in reminding us of the intrusions of a less stable world.

"Silvery Dreams" and the Popular Cinema

Analyzing the social values embedded in *The Romance*'s dream sequence befits filmmaking discourse about the power of the "dreamlike" cinematic image in 1927. At that time, Chinese writers for theater and film were less interested in the polarities of literary manifestoes on revolution or aesthetics. Instead they were more inclined to mingle notions of populism and democracy with the transcendent, transformative possibilities of "new heroism" and "silvery dreams." In one important piece published contemporaneously with the making of *The Romance*, the dramatist Tian Han explored—as did many of his contemporaries in China, the United States, and Japan—the "dreamlike" and "democratic" quality of cinematic art. Tian Han explicitly allied himself with Tanizaki Jun'ichiro's optimism about the future of cinema, deferring to the general populace as the significant audience for art in the twentieth century:

> The arts have no hierarchy; those whose forms suit the times will flourish, and those which go against the times will naturally make no progress. Today is the era of "Democracy," and the scope for elitist art is narrowing. Much more populist than theater, film is truly the art which most suits our time; it has much room for development and reform.[48]

Tian's editor, the film critic Lu Mengshu, went even further in defining the progressive possibility of the popular cinema. Only a few months later, in January

1928, Lu was praising "new romanticism" in the cinema for "striking a sympathetic chord in the hearts of the audience, who undergo a kind of transformation." Far from conjuring idle daydreams, the artist employing "new heroism" is able to "renew this old decayed China's lease on life, and create a new national people—a national people in action."[49] The constant references to the "new" underscore Lu's desire to convey a sense of novelty, change, and progress.

The concepts of "new heroism" and "new romanticism" were similar to the "new idealism," an idea promoted by such magazines as *Dongfang zazhi* (Eastern miscellany). One article on cultural developments stated that:

> The idealism of the laboring class is not like the idealism of the aristocracy, which is so entirely lost in fantastic dreams. The idealism of the laboring class does not stand apart from everyday reality; yet neither is it imprisoned by everyday reality. It strikes a *blow* at everyday reality, and serves to reconstruct that reality.[50]

The construction of "laboring class idealism" and its dreams as confrontational rather than fantastic was of course itself an idealism on the part of these authors. The championing of labor and democracy may have sounded new, but the underlying didacticism and the imperative of popular salvation were customary stances for Chinese intellectuals of the time. This populism was halfway between Tanizaki's belief in the power of a daydreamlike "pure film" and Qu Qiubai's enlightenment approach to mass taste.[51]

From this earlier period Tian Han and other playwrights and directors retained a faith in film as a "populist art" and in the "idealism of the laboring class," which carried through into their statements about proletarian art during the 1930s. But they recast their prior forays into aesthetic idealism, announcing that "the morning light" of revolutionary realism had "awakened" them from what they now saw as romantic "dreams."[52] As far as we know, Hou Yao made no such disavowal. *The Romance* is a testament to the self-styled progressives of Chinese cinema and drama in the late 1920s and 1930s who sought to create aesthetically compelling images and entertaining narratives.

Adaptation of classical subjects for film cannot be dismissed as pure escapism or atavism. The popular costume drama film set in a bygone era may appear to be a comforting nostalgic escape from the changes of modern urban life, but in developing this distinctive genre, studios like Minxin, Tianyi, and Mingxing addressed local audiences and forwarded the independent domestic film industry. They publicized these productions as spectacular images of an authentic Chinese culture, and their claims to authoritative representation soon collided with the agendas of political modernizers and advocates of revolutionary literature.

Hou Yao, Pu Shuqing, and Li Minwei were filmmakers who took up the challenge of cinematically reinventing familiar narratives from theater and literature. Amid multiple layers of "silvery dreams," scholarly civility and romantic desire transcend military obstacles and filial obligation. The film also contains moments that recall the aesthetic of attractions, calling attention to the cinema as spectacle. All in all, *The Romance of the Western Chamber* is clearly marked by the concerns of contemporary dramatists working in a new visual medium. The cinematic gaze reinforces some scholar-beauty conventions, while capsizing others—as in the unsettling coda to the scholar's dream. Coming from authors like Hou Yao and Pu Shuqing, very much engaged in presenting "women's issues" on stage, this coda reveals the psychological underside to the tale in its contemporary context. In Shanghai of the late 1920s, classical subjects for film accommodated powerful experiments with the meaning of individual and cinematic vision.

The Urban Milieu of Shanghai Cinema, 1930-40: Some Explorations of Film Audience, Film Culture, and Narrative Conventions

LEO OU-FAN LEE

Studies of modern Chinese cinema in American academia have largely been concerned with textual readings of individual films. The necessity of knowing its cultural context is invariably acknowledged, but that context is seldom explored. In this essay I would like to begin from an "extrinsic" approach; I will attempt to depict the urban milieu of Shanghai of the 1930s. Early Chinese films were first produced in this milieu partly as a result of, I would argue, the demand for leisure and entertainment (rather than an extension of the May Fourth project of intellectual enlightenment). The construction of new movie theaters, the increasing popularity of going to the cinema as a new urban lifestyle, and the viewing habits evolved in part from print culture provided the background against which the aesthetics of early Chinese cinema must be measured. In short, my argument—or at least hypothesis—is that the development of modern Chinese cinema was closely connected with this urban setting in which cinema figured prominently as both a new commodity and a new item in the modern lifestyle of leisure and entertainment. The dominance of Hollywood movies served as both a model and a foil for native filmmakers, regardless of their intellectual backgrounds and ideological persuasions. When we approach the study of films from this "external" angle, we are compelled to wrestle with a different set of questions: What can we say about the relationship between the film text and the context of urban culture? What did the moviegoing experience mean in the everyday lives of Shanghai urbanites? In what ways did their film-viewing habits have an effect on their lifestyle—and vice versa? What were their mental expectations in watching a Hollywood film as opposed to watching a Chinese film? Did such expectations in turn have an impact on the narrative structures of the Chinese films themselves? Did Chinese filmmakers consciously cater to such film-viewing habits in order to manipulate them and inject a different set of messages into their consciousness? These are not easy questions, and much research remains to be done on them. But I would nevertheless attempt to explore *some* of the implications under the premise that there is some validity to these questions.

Movie Theaters and Movie Magazines

By 1930, movie theaters had definitely become a new addition to the architectural landscape of Shanghai, especially in the foreign concessions, which had been marked by British colonial buildings on the Bund, multistoried modern hotels and apartment mansions, and the private residences of the foreign *nouveau-riche* in the French Concession built in a variety of Western styles.[1] The renovation and construction of movie theaters began in the 1920s and reached a peak in the early 1930s with the opening of the newly renovated, air-conditioned Grand Theater (Daguangming) in 1933, designed by the famous Czech architect Ladislaus Hudec, complete with 2,000 sofa-seats (and equipped since 1940 with earphones or *yiyifon* for simultaneous interpretation), a spacious lobby done in art deco style, three fountains, a huge neon-lit marquee, and toilets painted in light green.[2] Before that, there had been about a dozen western cinemas—with such names as Carlton (Ka'erdeng), Odeon (Aodi'an), Empire (Enpaiya), Embassy (formerly Olympic), Palace (Zhongyang), Victoria (Xin zhongyang), and Paris (Bali)—showing first-run Hollywood movies and, since 1926, another half-dozen theaters showing first-run Chinese films (see fig. 7). The eight Hollywood companies all had their branch offices and designated cinemas in Shanghai. In August 1926, the world's first "talkie" film was premiered in Hollywood; in the next year, Shanghai's first-run movie theaters began to show sound films; in 1931, the first Chinese sound film was made.[3] Chinese audiences thronged into the cinemas with the same zest with which they greeted the opening of foreign parks.[4] By the end of the decade, there were 32 to 36 movie theaters in Shanghai, which led one movie pictorial (*Diantong huabao*) to put the photos of all these theaters on a map of Shanghai with a splashy announcement: "the houses which devour a million people every day!"[5] The thriving business of the new movie houses contrasted sharply with the decline of the amusement halls since 1931.[6]

Most of the deluxe movie houses showed first-run Hollywood movies; those showing Chinese films were often second-run houses of lesser grandeur. The situation was somewhat ameliorated by some enterprising moves by Chinese film companies to purchase first-run theaters or to form a chain of theaters to

7. The interior of the Odeon Theater (Gan Yazi et al.).

show their own films—a move in direct imitation of the Hollywood distribution system.[7] A campaign was launched in the early 1930s to make more serious good-quality Chinese films in order to counter Hollywood products. Lianhua took the lead in this direction, followed by Mingxing and other companies. After the January 28 bombing of Shanghai by Japanese warplanes in 1932, some film columns in journals or newspapers also began to promote native Chinese films (*guochan dianying*), which coincided with the movements to promote native goods (*guohuo*). The annual numbers of Chinese films produced increased.[8] Thus it was not until the 1930s that a notable Chinese film scene (*yingtan*) was established.

The popularity of movies went hand in hand with the popularity of movie magazines and special columns and issues about movies in the regular magazines. According to recent research by a team of Chinese scholars based in Shanghai, their appearance in print could be traced to 1921, when the Shanghai newspaper *Shenbao* published its *Yingxi congbao*; around the same time, the first independent film magazine, *Yingxi zazhi* (note the use of the compound *yingxi* or "film-and-play") was published. A listing of film magazines published in the period 1921–49 has a total of 206 titles (film monthlies, weeklies, and special issues).[9] Some were publications by the film companies: the *Dianying yuebao* (Film monthly) was a prime example of a "trade journal" of the six Chinese film companies.[10] More journals, however, were published by the other book companies. One of the largest and most enterprising was the Liangyou (Young companion) Publishing Company, which in addition to featuring photographs of famous movie stars in its best-selling flag magazine, *Liangyou* (The young companion pictorial), also published a special film issue in 1934 and inaugurated another magazine devoted entirely to the movies, *Yinxing* (Silver star), edited by Lu Mengzhu. A book of essays on film and literature edited by Lu included contributions by such famous writers as Tian Han, Zhang Ruogu, and Fu Yanchang. The journal *Yinxing* was later combined with *Tiyu shijie* (Athletic world) into a monthly that received equal billing with the company's two other journals: *Zhongguo xuesheng* (Chinese students) and *Jindai funü* (Modern women). It became increasingly common practice to feature news and photos about movies and movie stars in the mushrooming journals for women. In this newly constructed "modern lady" image and lifestyle, an interest in the movies was definitely *de rigueur*. The trend was promoted in many other women's magazines and pictorial journals (which also tried to boost their sales by providing gift photos of Chinese and Western movie stars to their subscribers).

To take one rare, though by no means atypical, example, I have located a women's weekly in a mini-format, *Linglong funü tuhua zazhi* (with its own English title, *Lin Loon Lady's Magazine*; or literally "Petite: a pictorial magazine for women") edited by a woman, Chen Zhenling, and featuring numerous photos of young women.[11] But the most inventive feature is that its back pages become a movie supplement, which has an English title, "Movies," sandwiched by its Shanghai-accented Chinese translation, *mu-vie* (*muwei* in Mandarin, literally "screen flavor"), which conveys the obvious pun of a "taste" (*wei*) for movies. It is billed as "the only movie weekly in the nation." Aside from displaying glamorous photos of Hollywood stars, each issue also includes a rating sheet of current films shown in Shanghai, taken from another newspaper, *Funü ribao* (Women's daily). For instance, a 1933 issue features on its back cover (i.e., the front cover for the "movies" supplement) the famous star Ruan Lingyu (1910–35, who committed suicide two years later) in a chic long gown (*qipao*). Amid advertisements for "Cutex," "Canidrome" (a dog-racing place), and "Koda Verichrome Film Pack," as well as tidbits about Greta Garbo, Al Jolson, and Hitler recalling all German stars from abroad, is the following list of "Ratings of Chinese and Western new films in the past two weeks":[12]

1. *One Sunday Afternoon*   B–
2. *The Great Decision*   C+
3. *Golden Harvest*   B
4. *42nd Street*   B
5. *Sweepings*   B–
6. *Torch Singer*   B

7. *Xiangcao meiren* (Flowers and beauty),
   a Chinese film   B–
8. *Modern Womanhood*   B
9. *Beauty for Sale*   B
10. *Her Highness Commands*   B

Evidently, there is only one Chinese film, which receives a low rating, in this group of ten films. Interestingly, seldom did any film receive an "A" rating, which was given only to two films in the entire year: *My Weakness* (a film chosen for the premiere showing of the newly opened Grand Theater), and *Don Quixote*. In the later issues, only a listing of "average or above average" films without rating was included—perhaps an indication of a Chinese attitude toward the quality of mass-produced movies from the burgeoning big company system in Hollywood.

At the same time, however, considerable space in each issue is devoted to Hollywood movie stars. Vol. 4, no. 5 (Jan. 31, 1934) is a special issue devoted entirely to Hollywood movie stars, with both front and back covers plus eleven pages devoted to photos of Katherine Hepburn, Marlene Dietrich, Helen Hayes, Janet Gaynor, Claudette Colbert, Kay Francis, Myrna Loy, Dolores Del Rio, and the ubiquitous Greta Garbo. This massive influx of glamorous photos of Hollywood stars may have been the result of publicity by the Shanghai branch offices of Hollywood's "big eight" companies. But more likely they were reproduced from the many movie magazines in America. Aside from the Chinese ratings of films, *Linglong* also quoted from ratings by American reviewers in such journals as *Film Classics* and *Film Mirror*. As in the case of Chinese reception of Western literature, the major source of information came from American popular journals, to which there was easy access through several Western bookstores—particularly Kelly & Walsh—and libraries (including the foreign books library of the Commercial Press) and even through direct subscription.

To what extent did this new genre of popular print culture shape the viewing habits of film spectators? How do we gauge such viewing habits? A vivid testimony of the moviegoing experience can be found in a popular Chinese guidebook to the city, *Shanghai menjing*, published in 1932. The section on cinema has the following introductory statement:

> Cinema originally was a foreign medium. After it was imported into China, it was taken not only as entertainment but was found to have true artistic worth, and it could be an effective instrument to aid social education. So the intellectuals were among the first to welcome it. . . . Now, the average man and woman have had considerable knowledge about cinema, and "going to the movies" has become a modern slogan. Young boys and girls in schools do it; even old people are patronizing movie theaters. Although native film industry has not prospered in recent years, movie the-

aters are still in demand by the general public. More than twenty movie theaters have been built. [Cinema] is in a thriving state and threatens to wipe out the stage and the amusement hall.[13]

The author, Wang Dingjiu, admitted from the outset that "going to the cinema does not mean catering to the foreign, but Chinese movies are really not as good as foreign movies. This is undeniable in industrially backward China. . . . If a Chinese film costs two or three hundred thousand yuan, it is called a big production. But in America's Hollywood, the headquarters of world film-making, frequently a film would cost tens of thousands and even millions of dollars. With such discrepancy in capital, the distance in achievement is likewise large."[14] The author listed a total of eighteen "modern cinemas" and gave brief evaluations of each of them—singling out such theaters as Carlton, Grand, Nanking, and Odeon for special praise. But then the ticket prices in these cinemas were too costly—ranging from one to two yuan, almost ten times higher than the matinee price of the cheapest second- or third-run theaters. Thus the author cautions moviegoers to choose good films well in advance, to base their decision on obtaining enough information about the fame and ability of the movies' stars, and the past record of their directors and screenplay writers. He also gives such tips as buying snacks outside the theater (to avoid the high price inside), bringing a newspaper or book to read before the showing, and sitting upstairs if one brings a date. Above all, he urges the patrons to keep the bilingual plot sheets (*shuoming shu*) and read them in the English original (for those who can), because the translations often lose meaning; "if you keep all the sheets of all the movies you have seen, together they become a marvelous collection of fiction."[15]

This source has given us an intriguing glimpse into one crucial facet in the kaleidoscopic world of living and leisure in Shanghai. (The guidebook also contains "how-to" chapters on food, clothing, lodging, shopping, and entertainment, with guides to restaurants, amusement halls, local opera theaters, department stores, hotels, and even houses of prostitution.) The nature of the guidebook dictates that whoever the author may be, he must have been an insider whose familiarity with details of Shanghai life lent both authority and authenticity to his work. He is clearly enamored with Hollywood movies shown in first-run theaters, to which Chinese movies were in his opinion clearly inferior. His advice on how to behave in movie theaters provides a clue to a new form of social etiquette. His point about keeping the bilingual plot sheets as "fiction" reminds us of a possible link with popular fiction of the time—not of the New Literature variety but of the novels of the Saturday School of "mandarin ducks and butterflies." In fact, some of its authors—Zhou Shoujuan, for instance—also wrote movie columns in their own journals or even served as advertising advisors to movie theaters. More research would show that the kind of "traditional" aesthetic that informs "butterfly" fiction also had an impact on the language of the plot sheets and translated titles of Hollywood movies.[16] A large majority of such titles were rendered in a classical vein, often with four Chinese characters with obvious references to traditional Chinese poetry and fiction. For instance, from the above list: *Liangyuan qiaohe* for *One Sunday Afternoon, Jinyuan chunnong* for *Her Highness Commands*—and interestingly, *Gewu shengping*, a most appropriate title for the Busby Berkeley musical, *The Gold Diggers of 1933*. The novelty of a foreign film is thus "familiarized" by virtue of this pseudo-literary inscription in Chinese. In the case of Hollywood movies based on Western fiction that had been already translated into Chinese by the likes of Lin Shu or Zhou Shoujuan, this fortuitous connection would be even more welcome (as, for example, in the Sherlock Holmes stories or romantic novels such as *La Dame au Camelias* by Dumas *fils*, rendered by Lin Shu for all posterity as *Chahuanü*). Thus for a native filmgoer of the time, spending a few hours watching a Hollywood movie seemed to provide a double pleasure: of losing oneself in an exotic world of fantasy while still finding one's own reading habits enriched by this new visual medium.

Another, less traditional, source of information about the close relationship between film and print comes from the new-style writers in the 1930s. Moviegoing was the predominant leisure habit for many Shanghai writers—from Lu Xun, who favored Soviet films, to Shi Zhicun (b. 1905), Xu Chi, Liu Na'ou, Mu Shiying, Zhang Ruogu, and Ye Lingfeng (1904–75), in addition to leftists like Tian Han, Hong Shen, and Xia Yan. The poet Xu Chi told me that he saw practically every Western film shown in Shanghai.[17] Shi Zhicun wrote an erotic story with the Paris Cinema as its setting. In my interviews with them both writers frequently mentioned deluxe cinema houses like the Grand Theater, Metropole (Da Shanghai), Cathay (Guotai), Majestic (Meiqi), and Carlton, the last being also a theater for spoken drama. Their favorite pastime was going to the cinema, the bookstores, and coffeehouses. For Liu Na'ou and Mu Shiying, however, the cinema and the dance hall were almost interchangeable as their favorite hangout in both fiction and real life. In particular Liu Na'ou, who imported the Japanese New Perceptionist School (*Shin kangaku kai*) of fiction, became a film devotee and wrote a large number of film reviews and articles on film aesthetics in such journals as *Furen huabao* (Women's pictorial) and *Xiandai dianying* (Modern cinema), with topics ranging from discussions of film writing, film rhythm, and camera angles to an appreciation of Greta Garbo's and Joan Crawford's facial beauty.[18] He also became actively involved in filmmaking during the late 1930s.

Liu's writings on film show a surprisingly modern sensibility. In a revealing essay bearing the original French title "Escranesque," Liu defined cinema as "a motion art that combines the feeling of art and the rationality of science. As architecture embodies the purest form of rationality of the 'mechanical civiliza-tion' (*jiqi wenming*), so the art form that most characteristically depicts the so-cial environment of this mechanical civilization is the cinema."[19] The basic source of this new civilization, for Liu, lies in motion; "the changes of its speed, direction, and energy thus generate its rhythm." Liu's rather ecstatic panegyric to the cinema had a lot to do with his obsession with the hallmark of Western modernity—time and speed—which he considered to be the true essence of modern life. This in turn led him to an aesthetic position which is at the heart of his brand of New Perceptionism: that modern art aims to capture and describe the tumultuous effect on the human senses and feelings caused by speed—the *jouissance* (Liu's term is *kuaigan*) that one experiences while driving a "Road-ster" automobile or watching a movie. In film, as in all the arts, "it's the Form that counts" (Liu wrote the sentence in English). "A work of art becomes a work of art because of form. Content is but an appearance of form; artistic content exists only within artistic form."[20]

Several of Liu's stories, as well as those by Mu Shiying, are clearly indebted for their language and form to the foreign movies their authors watched.[21] Thus written literature and print culture—particularly popular journalism and fic-tion—not only lent a helping hand to the new visual medium of film, but to-gether they became the main instruments for the creation of a new popular cul-tural "imaginary" of urban modernity.[22] I have dealt with the role of print cul-ture in the construction of a Chinese modernity in another paper, in which I reconstructed the contours of such an imaginary through studying advertise-ments and front covers of two best-selling journals, *Dongfang zazhi* (Eastern miscellany) and *Liangyou*.[23] In that paper I argued that these visual materials (photographs, drawings, clothes design, and pictures in advertisements, etc.) helped create the image of a modern (transliterated in Chinese as *modeng*) every-day lifestyle centered around the tropes of domesticity, family hygiene, seasonal fashion, leisure and consumption. Moviegoing thus easily fit into this new lifestyle, just as movie theaters became a visible institution—together with cof-feehouses, dance halls, and department stores—in the new urban space of leisure and consumption. What remains to be explored is the complex problem of how this new urban film spectatorship figured in the construction of such a modern imaginary—and in the "making" of native Chinese cinema.

Popular Tastes, Film Scholarship, and Narrative Convention

In recent American film studies there have been some notable works that attempt to theorize from the angle of film spectatorship. In her analysis of American spectators during the era of the silent film, Miriam Hansen has argued that cinema "offered the possibility of a new, different kind of public sphere, a chance to close the gap . . . between a genteel literary culture and the encroachment of commercialism."[24] In creating such a public sphere the Hollywood film industry catered specially to the female consumer by way of a "discursive apparatus surrounding the film rather than the text itself, as for instance fan magazines devoted to the purportedly female obsession with stars, glamour, gossip and fashionability."[25] The female stars had a special appeal to female audience for they "served to instruct the female viewer on how to become *correctly* modern, . . . to train the female audience in fashionable femininity."[26] In my own research on urban popular journalism, I have also found a similar orientation toward female consumers, for whom a whole series of modern goods for domestic use were advertised. In this new world of the modern woman, clothes and fashion occupy a central place, and Chinese female film stars looked to be the very embodiment of modernity.

At the same time, however, we must be aware that the emergent world of consumerism and commodification in Shanghai, in which film played a part, did not entirely replicate the American culture of high capitalism. One significant sign of difference is that "fashionable femininity" as exhibited in the Chinese movie magazine photos does *not* convey the same kind of strident sexuality as did Hollywood stars. From my samples drawn from the *Linglong* magazine, the glossy photos of Hollywood stars invariably convey a rampant body fetishism—the face glamorously made up, a half-revealed torso, or most frequently a pair of exposed legs. By contrast, photos of famous Chinese stars like Hu Die and Ruan Lingyu show them wearing Chinese long gowns that cover their entire bodies except for their bare arms. This elementary difference betrays nevertheless a different aesthetic of the feminine—an aesthetic derived from the women's portraits and photos on magazine covers since the turn of the century. This aesthetic was perpetuated in the numerous calendar posters, to which these star photos bore a striking "intergeneric" resemblance.[27] Instead of—or in addition to—serving as objects of the male gaze in a patriarchal society, these cover photos also helped to project a new persona for Chinese women—a "modern" woman in possession of certain new qualities who is not ashamed to display her personality in public. As a revealing article published in the *Linglong* magazine commented, such a modern woman should not be known merely by her chic appearance: "a permanent-wave hairdo or a powdered face" is not enough; a true "modern" woman must also possess such qualities as "rich knowledge, lofty thinking, and strong will"—all derived from reading and studying.[28] In other words, behind their bodies was instilled a certain spiritual essence, which made them "virtuous." One could, of course, consider all this written rationale as the purposeful imposition of a "false consciousness" by the producers of this new commercial culture of modernity. But a reading of the visual evidence tells a similar story. When we peruse the various photos of Ruan Lingyu, for instance, we find a traditional-looking woman touched with sadness: this is not merely due to her traditional dress (the *qipao* could be "sexy" too) or to our knowledge that she later committed suicide. Rather, a more plausible reason may be that the public image of Ruan Lingyu was closely connected, in the popular mind, with the roles she played, of which the most famous was that of a virtuous prostitute in *Shennü* (Goddess). In fact, I find a close similarity of dress and look between photos of Chinese movie stars in magazines and portraits of women in commercial calendars. In one such calendar portrait, a woman who bears a striking resemblance to Ruan Lingyu is set against a landscape from a traditional Chinese painting, in which a pair of swans swim in a pond. The Chinese caption, written in four archaic characters, has the classic phrase "Qiushui yiren" (A beauty set against autumn waters), thus evoking a lyrical mood. I have found the figures in this landscape not only familiarly traditional but bearing a cross-generic relationship to the popular fiction of "mandarin ducks and butterflies." This is but another link between print culture and film which provides a precondition for the taste and viewing habits of the popular audience.

The eminent film historian Jay Leyda has remarked on "the Chinese spectator's love of tradition, with all the security and serenity that tradition represents."[29] By this he meant the old popular sources of "Peking opera, fairy tales, myths, and folklore," from which Chinese films of the 1920s drew for their adaptive material. Leyda acknowledged that "these 'old subjects' were so extremely popular with film audiences then that we are forced to look beneath the 'escapist' surface and beyond the ticket-buyer's wish to forget for a couple of hours the huge political issues and the prospect of disturbing change that were coming down upon Shanghai."[30] Perhaps the ticket-buyer's wish was more than mere escapism. The question nevertheless remains: why were audiences drawn to such formulaic plots? A Chinese film scholar has argued that this is precisely the "national characteristic" traceable to the traditional aesthetic taste in narrative art. Such a narrative mode emphasizes the "story quality" (*gushixing*) and tends to impart a "romantic" or legendary (*chuanqi*) spell—the term, which harks back to Ming drama if not to Tang fiction, is further defined as being a pronounced formal feature of traditional Chinese fiction and drama, which "excels by the richness, novelty, and copious twists and turns of plot."[31] Such plot structures easily incorporate coincidences and chance encounters in which certain "contradictions" are unfolded or uncovered. One could venture even further by speculating on the popularity of certain foreign films over others on account of their narrative affinities to such formulaic plot twists from traditional fiction—for instance, *The Perils of Pauline*. The story of a virtuous hero or heroine of feeling who is made to suffer through hardships or to struggle against forces beyond her control has been a recurring feature in late Qing fiction and translations (for instance, Wu Woyao's *Henhai* [The sea of sorrows] and Lin Shu's translation of *Uncle Tom's Cabin*, from which a play was adapted focusing only on a few scenes of the heroine's escapade). Such narrative affinities would appeal to a native audience especially in the case of silent films, because the plot is necessarily "written up" on the screen to "simulate" the reading experience of popular fiction. I have some evidence to indicate that such linkage between film and print may have been made consciously through the plot summary sheets, which were apparently distributed to the audience as they entered the theater. In a few cases, the plot summary was even shown on the screen. An article in the Butterfly School magazine, *Banyue* (The half moon journal), complains that the theater showing a Hollywood film, *Hongfen kulou* (literally "Skull of a Beauty") shows on screen a plot summary at the very beginning, thus ruining the audience's pleasure of enjoying all the unexpected twists and turns of the plot.[32]

What I have suggested is that the Chinese audience's tastes and viewing habits may have been to a large extent shaped by print culture—particularly popular fiction. To this factor of native cultural predisposition must be added the enormous popularity of Hollywood movies demonstrated above, which must have exerted a powerful impact on both the Chinese film audience and the filmmakers. In this connection, the issues become even more complex. We must first understand the basic features of the Hollywood film before we can tackle its possible influence.

In her book cited earlier, Miriam Hansen argues that there was a paradigmatic shift from early to classical American cinema during the decade of 1907–17, which is "defined by the elaboration of a mode of narration that makes it possible to anticipate a viewer through particular textual strategies, and thus to standardize empirically diverse and to some extent unpredictable acts of reception." Hansen stops short of saying whether such "empirically diverse acts of reception" can be extended to other cultures and countries. But she does define this dominant Hollywood mode of narration as based on a new "American hieroglyphics," which was "troped in the ambiguous celebration of film as a new universal language."[33] What are the rules of this "new universal language" that presumably would apply to the viewing habits of empirically diverse audiences everywhere? To begin with, Hansen notes "the industry's increasing focus on the dynamic of character, individual psychology, and the personality of the star," since "the star system had been flourishing since 1910, and by 1916 the cultivation of stars was more than an established publicity device."[34] From this was developed a mode of narration that became the hallmark of classical Hollywood cinema: "the interweaving of multiple strands of action moving toward resolution and closure, a web of thorough motivation centering on psychology of individual characters, and the concomitant effect of an autonomous fictional world offered to the spectator from an ideal vantage point."[35]

In what ways did this narrative mode exert a direct or indirect impact on classical Chinese cinema (by which I mean films produced in the 1930s–40s, both silent and sound)? On the one hand, as Paul Pickowicz has shown, "films by such recognized masters as D. W. Griffith and Charlie Chaplin were well known in China by the early twenties,"[36] and presumably Chinese filmmakers learned much from watching them and other Hollywood films. On the other hand, we must be aware that the same Chinese practitioners also came from a *Chinese* background. Recent film scholars from Hong Kong have depicted such a background in two categories: *wenren dianying*, or films made by those with a background in May Fourth literature such as Tian Han, Xia Yan, Hong Shen, and other leftist writers who had "penetrated" into the film world in the 1930s; and *xiren dianying*, or films made by those craftsman-directors who derived their aesthetics from the conventions of traditional Chinese theater, particularly the *wenming xi* or "civilized plays"—a hybrid form of popular drama with some modern content.[37] The established view among Chinese Communist film historians is that the former began to dominate the film scene beginning in the early 1930s, thereby effecting a total transformation of the latter as well as raising the quality of Chinese cinema from frivolous entertainment into serious art of social criticism that served to advance the cause of revolution.[38] To some extent, and from the Party's own point of view, this thesis sounds plausible. On the basis of a number of popular magazines from this period, I have found that there was increasing attention paid to native Chinese cinema. For example, a journal called *Xin Shanghai* (New Shanghai) featured a column on cinema in its inaugural issue in 1933, in which the editor proclaimed that this column would be devoted only to Chinese cinema, which had survived the onslaught of Hollywood films chiefly through the efforts of a couple of native film companies (presumably Lianhua and Mingxing).[39] One article lauded the entry into the film world of such central literary figures as Tian Han, Lu Xun, and Mao Dun (a partial mistake, because the latter two did not become personally involved) for "injecting a shot of morphine" (meaning a new stimulus): "I can state emphatically that the success of Lianhua films is due not so much to directors . . . cameraman and actors but to the contribution of members from the literary circles who entered into the film world. They [directors and others] merely helped a bit with their specialized film knowledge."[40] The director Cheng Bugao was singled out as the most hopeful and progressive director of the Mingxing company who had connections with the literary circles. Another article praised Lianhua for ushering in the new subject of the "suffering masses of laborers" by such directors as Fei Mu, Bu Wancang, and Cai Chusheng (but neither Fei nor Bu was a leftist). It also praised Mingxing, not for its enlightened ideology but for its clever marketing move to withhold the premiere showing of its prized films such as *Xiangcao meiren* (which eventually received a B– rating from the journal *Linglong*) and *Chuncan* (Spring silkworms; based on Mao Dun's famous story) in the non-air-conditioned Palace Theater in summer until the weather turned cooler in the fall.[41]

On the other hand, Pickowicz has questioned this leftist thesis: he charges that most Chinese film historians on the Mainland have failed "to acknowledge the close connection between the 'May Fourth' films of the thirties and the popular melodramas of the twenties."[42] In fact he (re)defines the nature of leftist filmmaking as "marriage between classic melodrama and elementary Marxism."[43] By elementary Marxism is meant the new subject of the laboring masses and the focused sympathy for it. But the source of emotional force comes from "classic melodrama," which the film theorist Nick Browne considers "the most complex and compelling popular form that embodies the negotiation between the traditional ethical system and the new state ideology, one that articulates the range and force of the emotional contradictions between them."[44] Browne defines melodrama as, among others, a "theater of social misfortune in which personal virtue is contested, hidden, misrecognized, or subverted, a form of theater that seeks within the confining and largely recalcitrant parameters of the old society to restore and recenter the ethical imperatives required of the bourgeois age."[45] Following Browne, Pickowicz finds in modern Chinese cinema a tradition of melodramatic representation characterized by "rhetorical excess, extravagant representation, and intensity of moral claim"; its purpose "is not to deal with the monotony of everyday life. Rather, it seeks to put an insecure and troubled mass audience in touch with the essential conflict between good and evil that is being played out just below the surface of daily life." Hence "melodramatic representation was appealing to low-brow, nonintellectual consumers of urban popular culture in the troubled early Republican period because it provided clear answers to nagging questions."[46] This is indeed a much needed corrective of a longstanding ideological interpretation.

My own argument is closer to Pickowicz's, though I hesitate to use the term "melodrama" to characterize the kind of materials I have presented above. In my opinion, while Chinese cinema had indeed improved its quality in the 1930s, thus establishing a firmer foothold among urban audiences and becoming more competitive with Western films, it certainly did not owe its popularity entirely to the influence of the leftist literary movement. From Xia Yan's recent memoirs we learn that he was in fact *invited* by the manager of the Mingxing Film Company to be one of the "script advisors" through mutual friends.[47] The manager and the veteran film directors at Mingxing—Zhang Shichuan and Zheng Zhengqiu —realized that Japanese aggression in Manchuria and the bombing of Shanghai had created a changed mood among Shanghai audiences, whose new patriotism

made them lose interest in sword flicks and ethical-sentimental films. This patriotic feeling made it possible for the leftist intellectuals to gain a foothold in
the film world. But they made their inroads initially through journalism—that
is to say, by publishing a massive amount of film criticism in the film supplement pages of all the leading newspapers—before their own written scripts began to make any headway. In other words, they were able to manipulate consciously the existing structure of the urban "print public sphere" in the same
way that other journalists and publicists had done to help promote and shape
audience interest. This linkage of the two media—print and film—definitely
worked to their advantage, however, because the major figures—Xia Yan, Tian
Han, Yang Hansheng—were all writers and dramatists from the *huaju* (spoken
drama) background. Their initial advising role was, in fact, to "write up" the
rather rudimentary "scenarios" (*mubiao*) used by directors into more elaborate
scene-by-scene scripts.[48] Besides, according to Xia Yan's memoirs, the leftist
script writers *refrained from* imposing their own ideological opinion on the directors they worked with. Rather they were quite respectful of the directors' intentions when they wrote up the scripts, and gradually developed friendships
while working together. This is how the director Cheng Bugao became gradually
"progressive" in his thinking. The directors in turn were delighted by the "higher
quality" of the stories themselves, in which some leftist ideas—"elementary
Marxism" in Pickowicz's words—managed to "seep in" without their notice.[49]
Thus, it can be said that the leftist scriptwriters managed to tap the anxieties of
the Chinese audience not by injecting any blatant political ideology (due to censorship) but by bringing a new narrative mode at the story level—the depiction
of the petty city dwellers living in limited urban space as a mirror of social hierarchy and the thematic trope of city and country as contrasting worlds of evil
and good. In this new narrative structure, the city—a projection of Shanghai—
took on increasingly darkened colors and negative tones, whereas the countryside became the idealized "other" to this urban mode of cinematic self-
reflexivity. In short, the film stories begin to incorporate and to foreground the
experiences of the small men and women of rural origin or character who are
increasingly victimized in the urban environment.

As we read the published scripts, naturally they read like short stories: the
literary quality seems obvious. I have argued in an earlier article that the descriptive verbiage of these film scripts is "rich on plot and characterization but
rather sparing in what might be construed as montage sequences."[50] While the
script provides a film's content, it is the "montage sequences" and other formal
qualities that constitute the *visual* style of the film itself. Here I would like to argue that regardless of their ideological background, most Chinese film directors, with a few notable exceptions, came to share a basic technical "language"
of Chinese filmmaking that had evolved through both imitation and innova-

tion. What, then, constitutes this basic cinematic language and what is its relationship to the viewing habits of the film audience? Once we enter into such a discourse, the issues are complicated indeed. The following remarks are made in the spirit of a preliminary exploration.

The Making of a Native Tradition

A film theorist from Hong Kong, the late Lin Niantong, has characterized this native film language as a combination of two separate principles of film aesthetics—the "montage" and the "long take"—the former from Soviet traditions of filmmaking, the latter from French and American ones. According to Lin, the principle of the long take tends to emphasize continuous sequentiality of time and contiguity of space, whereas the montage is a principle of composition built on discontinuous and noncontiguous shots, thus emphasizing conflict and tension. The technique of "long take, deep focus" is often composed of medium and long shots that encompass greater space and longer temporal duration, so that on the one hand it can put human beings in a larger environment and form a unity between them and, on the other hand, manifest their "contradictions" in the same time and space.[51] In an earlier article, I have considered this cinematic technique as used in Chinese filmmaking as "a direct transposition from the convention of spoken drama" to "serve as its cinematic equivalent."[52] I now realize that this assertion is too simplistic and needs further negotiation.

In her book *Babel and Babylon*, Miriam Hansen argues that the shift from primitive to classical cinema involves a shift in modes of narration centering on "diegesis": "classical cinema offered its viewer an ideal vantage point from which to witness a scene, unseen by anyone belonging to the fictional world of the film." In spite of its claim to reflect "reality," the Hollywood feature film creates a self-contained world, an *illusion of reality*, which exerts a spell on the audience in the duration of its showing. Toward that goal, "the resources of cinematic discourse, of framing, editing, and mise-en-scène, were increasingly integrated with the task of narration."[53] This "diegetic" process is intended to achieve the desired effect of naturalness: "The camera must be made to see, as with the eyes of the spectators . . . all that takes place, but that which the camera sees and records should appear truthful and natural and should not bear on its face the stamp of counterfeit."[54] In light of the above, it seems that this was precisely the "realistic" effect that Chinese film writers and directors, particularly leftists, wished to achieve. At the same time, however, compared to Hollywood products since Griffith, the Chinese films fell far short of achieving a total diegetic effect, due to obvious institutional reasons. For one thing, classic Hollywood cinema cannot be said to stem from the long-take tradition alone;[55] Noel Burch has remarked that its "diegetic" effect centers around the basic principle of "shot-counter-shot: the absence/presence of the spectator at the very center of the diegetic process" whereby "the spectator becomes the invisible mediator between two gazes, two discourses which envelop him/her, positioned thus as the ideal, invisible voyeur."[56] Extending from the basic shot-counter-shot unit is a large number of camera shots—long and medium shots and close-ups—in order to manipulate audience reaction. In this regard, Chinese filmmakers simply could not afford to produce such an elaborate film footage, due to their limited budget. Still, when we look at Chinese films made in the 1930s, it is difficult *not* to see ample traces of Hollywood influence, since Hollywood films predominated the film market in Shanghai, and Chinese filmmakers (especially from the *xiren* background) had nowhere else to go for inspiration. They simply imitated the acting styles, lighting design, as well as camera movements of Hollywood movies. Even some of the stories of their films were adaptations of foreign films. At the same time, however, some recent Chinese film scholars, following Lin Niantong, have taken great pains to establish the theoretical claim that Chinese filmmakers had developed their own tradition beyond or despite Hollywood influence. In a learned essay the Hong Kong film scholar Huang Ailing has argued forcefully that the Hollywood-style "diegetic" effect—in which by putting the audience's gaze "at the ideal vantage point within narrative space" the camera becomes in fact concealed—was *not* what Chinese filmmakers wanted to achieve. In her opinion, the Chinese directors' penchant for the "long-take, deep focus" shots derives essentially from the traditional Chinese aesthetic principle (for instance in classical painting) which does not place the viewer in any ideal vantage point but rather gives a prominent role to space itself. Hence "Chinese filmmakers have a strong desire to maintain the distance between the audience and the drama [inside the film], and to destroy the illusion of reality represented on the screen."[57] Following Lin Niantong, she further points out that Chinese filmmakers were quite aware of the Soviet theory of montage; in fact, Tian Han had premiered the showing of Eisenstein's film *Battleship Potemkin* in 1926 and Xia Yan and Zheng Boqi had translated essays by V. I. Pudovkin. They considered this theory progressive, but still they preferred to use long takes to maintain a sense of spatial and temporal continuity. Thus they tried to achieve their montage effect through other means within a general frame of contiguity.[58]

This is indeed a powerful "nationalistic" thesis. In my view, however, Huang seems to have given too much credit to the ingenuity and originality of Chinese film directors, as if they knew exactly what their choices were aesthetically and technically. She does not seek to explain why montage sequences are used so sparingly within the slow, even leisurely, rhythm of the film's narrative. Nor does she say anything about film acting, perhaps because it is not crucial to any consideration of film aesthetics. In my view, the narrative weight of Chinese films is carried for a large part by acting and other aspects that film theorists tend to dismiss as irrelevant to its formal quality.

By far the most insightful study of leftist filmmaking is by the Mainland film scholar Ma Ning, whose article "The Textual and Critical Difference of Being Radical: Reconstructing Chinese Leftist Films of the 1930s" itself gives a "radical" argument against previous interpretations. Through a close reading of the film *Malu tianshi* (Street angel, 1937), Ma argues that the leftist mode of filmmaking is influenced by Hollywood melodrama but goes beyond it, as it contains "extra-diegetic intrusions and explicit social references."[59] Moreover, it incorporates two different discourses, what Ma calls the "journalistic" and the "popular":

> The journalistic discourse in these films in the form of news items such as newspaper headlines and historical footage, because of its quasi-objective nature and its emphasis on individual rights and the supremacy of law, can be identified as that of the Chinese bourgeoisie. On the other hand, popular discourse manifests itself in such cultural forms as folk songs, shadow plays, wordplays and magic shows that can be seen as proletarian because of its collective nature and its appeal to radical actions.[60]

It is these native, extrinsic elements that, in Ma's view, transform the Hollywood conventions and help provide "a larger system of intelligibility that gives the text its allegorical structure." In one sense, one could make a class distinction between "bourgeois" and "proletarian" tastes. But these native tastes were often mixed up in the lifestyle of the urban spectators of the period. In my view, Ma's argument could be seen as confirming the linkage between the genres of written, oral, and film culture, which combined to condition popular tastes. In particular, the insertion of newspaper headlines into the film narrative, as in the case of *Street Angel*, further betrays the leftist filmmaker's previous background in print culture. (Lu Xun plays a similar game of distrust of news reporting in his many *zawen* written at the time.) At the same time, it must be noted that for all the brilliance of cinematic technique, Chinese films of the 1930s—leftist or not—continued to emphasize the development of plot, a feature that they share with popular fiction of the time. What Ma calls the "proletarian" elements—folk singing and other forms of folk performance—further reinforce the impression that certain scenes are "staged." Hence the emphasis on acting.

The primary text for Ma's argument is *Street Angel*, directed by Yuan Muzhi, which was based on an American film of the same name (1928).[61] Leyda also gives high praise to this film classic: "Regardless of its source, Yuan made the film in his own style, with sharply incised characters, spare dialogue, an always alert use of sound, and story points indicated in gesture or camera movement; the film opens with a long camera movement, from the highest roofs of Shanghai to the cluttered surfaces of a canal."[62] The film, in fact, begins with a very fast-paced montage sequence of the city with shots of the Shanghai skyscrapers from extreme angles, crowded streets with automobiles and streetcars, and flashes of the neon signs of entertainment quarters, especially cafes and dance halls. Moreover, for this brilliant sequence, Ma counts a total of 52 shots, of which 36 contain onlookers who are seen as passive, a reminder of Lu Xun's famous critique of the Chinese crowd. On the other hand, the actor-characters, in Ma's view, are given privileged visions that entitle the spectator to embrace this sequence of the urban spectacle as "a metaphorically forced coupling of Chinese feudalism and foreign powers."[63] Still, however brilliant these beginning shots may be, when the main story unfolds the film shifts to a totally different "realistic" mode, consisting of a series of largely interior sequences in which episodes of comic and sentimental encounters followed by hardship, victimization, and suffering are played out, leading to the final denouement. Interestingly, the narrative tempo slows down considerably and drags its sentimental plot to a close.

Of course, as latter-day spectators used to speedier rhythms, we cannot fully replicate the viewing habits of contemporary spectators, who may well have been drawn to the story's sentimental plot precisely by its slow tempo. On the other hand, it would be intriguing to compare the narrative devices and rhythms of *Street Angel* with the original Hollywood version on which it was based. Does the Hollywood version contain a comparable amount of singing? And while singing, dancing, and comedy had become integral components of the Hollywood musical, Chinese films of that period featured very few elaborate dance sequences. Rather, singing had become quite popular not only in Shanghai nightclubs but also in the burgeoning radio programs. The Chinese sound film, therefore, incorporated this popular practice and created the singing actresses Zhou Xuan and Bai Guang as well as the convention of film songs, one of which, "March of the Volunteers," composed by Nie Er and used in the film *Fengyun ernü* (Children of troubled times, 1935), has since become the national anthem of the People's Republic. In *Street Angel*, the plot progression literally stops when Zhou Xuan is singing—a practice also found in countless Hollywood musicals —but generically the film is not a musical, nor a comedy, but a social-ethical drama with comic touches provided mainly by Zhao Dan and the ensemble acting of other players. Thus the Chinese film does not follow strictly the established conventions of the Hollywood genre film (the musical, the slapstick comedy, the Western, film noir) but rather uses some of its generic devices for its own purposes. In so doing, it may also have resisted audience expectations. Barring further research, we can speculate that contemporary Chinese audiences may not have expected from the Chinese films the same kind of smooth, natural rhythm of diegesis characteristic of Hollywood movies. The narrative tempo fluctuates precisely because the Chinese film is made to contain diverse elements from different film and cultural genres.

The slow tempo also marks the speech pattern of the actors and actresses, some of whom enunciate their words in imperfect Mandarin. In present-day standards, their acting style seems rather "overdone"—with exaggerated facial expressions and gestures reminiscent of Hollywood stars of the silent film era. I would still like to maintain that such an acting style shows traces of spoken drama. But another source of inspiration may have come from foreign silent films, including works of German expressionism such as Fritz Lang's *Metropolis*, which were shown in Shanghai. One of the clear debts to German expressionism can be found in the facial close-ups lit from below, often to punctuate a character or an act of villainy.

When we look at another film, *Taoli jie* (The plunder of peach and plum, 1934), in which Yuan Muzhi, who wrote the screenplay, collaborated with director Ying Yunwei, another former actor, the acting seems to carry the weight of the film. This may not be the best film produced in the 1930s, but it is representative in many ways in terms of its thematic content (the story of a well-educated intellectual couple forced by the urban environment into poverty and theft). Interestingly, we find a contemporary evaluation of Ying Yunwei's directorial style by a pair of western critics, W. H. Auden and Christopher Isherwood, who traveled to Hankow in 1938 and saw the rushes of a war film directed by Ying: "The producer (Ying Yun-wei) had an astonishingly subtle feeling for grouping; his weakness lay in the direction of the actors themselves—he had indulged too often the Chinese talent for making faces. All these grimaces of passion, anger, or sorrow, seemed a mere mimicry of the West. One day a director of genius will evolve a style of acting which is more truly national—a style based upon the beauty and dignity of the Chinese face in repose."[64] It is a pity that Auden and Isherwood never saw the work of Fei Mu, particularly his masterpiece, *Xiaocheng zhichun* (Spring in a small town, 1948).[65] Still, their comment on acting is relevant, for Ying Yunwei's directorial style is by no means idiosyncratic but quite characteristic of other directors as well. Whether or not directly influenced by spoken drama, Chinese cinema always foregrounds acting, especially performances by big-name stars with acting talent such as Ruan Lingyu, Zhao Dan (1915–80), Shi Hui (1915–57), and others. Since the 1930s Mingxing and other big companies of the Chinese film industry had gladly adopted the Hollywood star system.[66]

Approaching the film from a technical angle, Huang Ailing argues that the "tragic power" of this film is derived from "camera movement and the long-take shots in which (the camera) steadily stares at the actors."[67] Why does the camera "stare at" the actors all the time? Huang's theory gives exclusive attention to the role of the camera in its "relentless siege of the downtrodden characters." At the beginning of the film, the camera in a "marvelous long take" introduces the protagonist as it follows the school principal and the three prison guards to locate him at a corner in his cell, with his back facing the camera. Thus begins the story, told in flashback. Huang also discusses a crucial scene where the protagonist's wife, physically weak after childbirth, carries a bucket of water and walks up the stairs. She walks up toward the camera, her face looking distorted as she comes near, and tension builds until suddenly she falls from the stairs and faints. Throughout the whole sequence, the camera remains immobile.[68] But throughout her discussion Huang does not comment at all on the acting by Yuan Muzhi, who plays the intellectual protagonist, and Chen Bo'er, who plays his wife. When seen in isolation—that is, without following the story—the acting, though expressive, confirms Auden and Isherwood's impression, but it takes on an emotional force precisely because, especially in the stairway episode, it is one of the high points of the story—and the lowest point in the life of this couple. In narrative terms, therefore, it seems that Ying Yunwei wants to play up those moments of suffering with cinematic flourish in order to accentuate these key points of the film's plot and to heighten the emotional impact on the viewer. Interestingly, because of the emphasis on this melodramatic moment, the film's portraiture of the two protagonists may have departed from the original intention of the script. At least according to one contemporary reviewer, the honest character of the male protagonist, who should have been the central focus but is not effectively delineated in the film, becomes displaced by the suffering wife, whose death is seen by "the innocent audience" as a sacrifice for the stubborn self-righteousness of her husband.[69]

In fact, in the contemporary writings about Chinese cinema we find constant references to audience and its important role in governing the choices—sometimes compromises—of the filmmakers. I would like to give two samples from an extensive collection of archival material. First, a confession by Cai Chusheng, director of *Yuguang qu* (Song of the fishermen, 1934; now generally acknowledged to be a masterpiece) shortly after the film's first showing:

> Having seen a few films which did not achieve their desired good results, I believe even more firmly that the most fundamental condition of a good film is to make the audience interested. Why is it that some films produced did not achieve perfect results despite the correctness of their ideological tendency? Because they are too boring to draw the audience's interest. Accordingly, in order to make the audience accept the intentions of the author more easily, we cannot but put on a sugar coating over correct ideology. . . . Regrettably, few workers and peasants at present have the opportunity to go to the movies, and the vast majority of the audience consist of urban residents of the cities.[70]

He apologizes for the film's happily coincidental ending because of his concern for "dramatic quality" and for the fact that "the general audience love more plot (twists)." Secondly, Song Zhidi, another famous leftist scriptwriter, wrote an article on "Film Appreciation and Audience Psychology" in 1935 in which he argued, from an audience's point of view, that a director before making a film must give careful thought to both the choice of subject matter and the method of expression:

> The eyes of an average member of the audience are rather opaque. We can only see the general contour of an event, and a contour is not very exciting and can hardly get our response. Therefore, what a film shows to us should and must be those parts with the most sharpness hidden within the core of a phenomenon. The director considers, analyzes, organizes, and then uses them in order to stimulate and move us. We are not wooden puppets. A direct application of subject material would be a waste. The organization of shots and the editing of "cuts" should be simple, clear and lively, [which sets] an emotional rhythm that links up the whole drama and that controls the pulse of the drama. Paying attention only to the emotional linkage between contiguous shots would still be considered a waste. What is necessary is not only to sustain the dramatic emotion of the entire film but to make it pour out like the torrent of a big river.[71]

What does Song mean by "those parts with the most sharpness"? And what does he mean by a sustained "emotional rhythm" that pours out like a river's torrent? The awkwardness of his wording certainly does not make it easier to translate his meaning into the language of present-day film theory. He could be talking about the necessity for montage, which is supposed to sharpen a film's emotional impact; more likely, however, he was talking about a Hollywood type of diegesis—a "dramatic" rhythm achieved by a judicious application of film "craftsmanship" (*jiqiao*), which he carefully differentiates from "technique" (*jishu*), the mechanical condition. When we read Song's statement together with Cai Chusheng's apologia about the necessity of "dramatic quality" and the audience's love of "more plot," it becomes clear that for both directors film technique (in the nonmechanical sense) is made to serve the dramatic, even melodramatic, twists of plot. To the extent that narrativity—the telling of a story—is still foregrounded in modern Chinese cinema, I would argue that the slow rhythm is maintained precisely to highlight the dramatic moment and to accommodate the audience's demand for "more plot"—to create, in other words, a Chinese-style diegetic effect. It is perhaps in this sense that we can agree with Lin Niantong that Chinese films combine both the montage and long-take traditions. But does this mean that they represent a case of pure native originality? Instead of originality, I would rather opt for a position of stylistic "hybridity" for the following reasons.

First, we must consider the physical condition of filmmaking in the 1930s. There was moving testimony about the crude condition of filmmaking. Shen Xiling, director of *Shizi jietou* (Crossroads, 1937), made the following lament:

In Chinese cinema there is neither adequate equipment nor sufficient capital, and the entire condition of filmmaking has reached a state of utmost poverty. [Background] music and dialogue cannot be synchronized with each other; to record the sound of a shot you cannot but put several cotton quilts (to muffle the sound of the recording machine). To make movies in such difficult conditions, we cannot but admit that we really have suffered enough hardship. But even more painful than this is the creative freedom which is denied us. In this treaty-port, we cannot utter a single word about recovering the lost territory; we cannot hang a map of Northeast . . . We . . . I cannot go on; we can only swallow our tears.[72]

Contemporary and latter-day viewers of *Crossroads* may well marvel at the clever way in which the social and patriotic messages are sneaked into the film via the use of print culture—shots of newspaper headlines. At the same time, the film tells a story with a romantic plot twist about how two poor urbanites living in the same rented room divided by a thin wall finally meet each other and fall in love.[73] At the beginning of the film, the credits are superimposed on a montage sequence of slanting Shanghai skyscrapers shot from extreme low angles and linked by "wipes." This sequence is subdued in comparison with the beginning of *Street Angel*, which is a more surrealistic evocation of the speed, energy, and decadence of this foreign-flavored metropolitan city.[74] (How the city is always evoked in a similar fashion at the beginning of so many films of this period!) Then follow a few stunning exterior shots and close-ups of a man about to jump into the river—as if lifted from a silent film by Eisenstein. But then the story settles down to a typical slow narrative rhythm, compounded by technical problems that fully confirm the director's complaint about nonsynchronicity of dialogue and background music (mostly arbitrary chunks of symphonies by Sibelius, Tchaikovsky, and Berlioz, followed by some badly played cello music, etc.). These crudities are compensated for, however, by the inventive use of lighting. Still, the film's dream sequences of the girl on a swing are clearly borrowed from Hollywood musicals. Needless to say, the acting is in the usual style of exaggeration.

If it is necessary to emphasize formal inventions, the evidence must be found in films by mostly nonleftist directors, some of whom in fact reached unexpected artistic heights in some of their works. For instance, Wu Yonggang's silent film *Goddess* is truly a masterpiece,[75] not only due to Ruan Lingyu's remarkable performance but as a result of the director's creation of a sustained lyrical mood which reminds this viewer of the works of the French master Robert Bresson. Even more unusual is Wu's sound film, the first produced by Lianhua Film Company, *Langtaosha* (The desert island, 1936), which succeeds in conjuring up within its humanistic plot about a criminal and a policeman an existential plight near the end of the film, where both men are caught on a deserted island. (We must remind ourselves again that Wu Yonggang came from a *xiren* background.) The artistic worth of his work has only recently been given its due by film scholars outside of China, in particular Chen Huiyang, who views the film's beginning sequence—a virtuoso display of framed montage composed of a series of scroll shots—as a kind of formal metaphysics based on traditional Chinese aesthetics and philosophy.[76] Another exceptional example is Ma-Xu Weibang's *Yeban gesheng* (Singing at midnight, 1936), now acknowledged as "the first Chinese film which was overtly influenced by expressionism."[77] Its first half-hour, which encases a plot derived from "Phantom of the Opera," is a masterful adaptation of German expressionist cinema. We can be sure that the film's success at the box office does not lie in its implausible and forced political message of patriotism (in some ways an addition by Tian Han) but rather in the director's unique cinematic vision and craftsmanship as the first "master of the horror film."[78] Neither Wu Yonggang nor Ma-Xu Weibang is included in Leyda's list of "Contributors to the Art and History of Chinese Films" as appended to his book, *Dianying: An Account of Films and the Film Audience in China*. As one might expect, both men received scathing ideological criticism in Cheng Jihua's *Zhongguo dianying fazhan shi* (A history of the development of Chinese cinema).[79]

These unusual products from the burgeoning film industry of the 1930s have given a dimension of stylistic variety to the legacy of Chinese cinema as they enrich its subject matter and content. Whether or not they also appealed to the contemporary audience in the same way is of course a moot point, despite their box-office records. It has not been my intention to equate artistic innovation with popular receptivity. On the contrary, I believe that cinema is definitely an art form whose artistic aura is subject to "mechanical reproduction" for a mass audience. But one should nevertheless be wary of applying Walter Benjamin's insight or the Frankfurt School argument in a Chinese setting without further cultural mediation. To what extent can we consider the urban audience of Chinese films as a "mass audience" and how do we gauge its sensibilities to this new medium? I have tried to show that such an audience was already nurtured by native print culture, by their reading of popular literature and drama. I have also argued that such an audience was further exposed to the modern culture of Hollywood cinema; and in spite of the obvious differences between traditional Chinese popular literature and the new foreign medium, one could nevertheless establish some narrative affinities between them. The construction of a Chinese modernity, to which film and filmgoing definitely contributed a share, has been a mixed phenomenon of both the old and the new, which nevertheless galvanized the enthusiasm and imagination of a sizable segment of the Chinese population. Since ideologically predisposed Chinese film historians influenced by both leftist and May Fourth discourses have given us only a biased and partial picture, much work remains to be done to uncover the richness of both the texts and contexts of Chinese film culture of this early period.

PART **TWO**   IMAGING SEXUALITY: CABARET GIRL,

MOVIE STAR, PROSTITUTE

$\int$ elling Souls in Sin City: Shanghai Singing and Dancing Hostesses in Print, Film, and Politics, 1920-49

ANDREW D. FIELD

One of the signal activities of the fashionable urbanite in Republican-era China was Western-style social dancing. Imported from Europe and America after the First World War and popularized during the Nanjing era (1927–37), ballroom, jazz, and other modern dance forms took Chinese urban areas by storm. Deemed an exotic practice in the 1920s, by the 1930s dancing was a favorite pastime among Chinese elite city dwellers along the eastern coast, particularly in the cosmopolitan and semicolonial city of Shanghai. This essay will explore Shanghai's dance culture, particularly its "cabaret girls," professional singers and dancers important in the emerging mass media of film and print, who became intimately associated with the city itself. We will see that in many ways cabaret girls were modern surrogates for courtesans of the late Qing and earlier periods. Yet though they inherited many elements of the courtesan legacy, Shanghai cabarets and their women workers were deeply enmeshed in the political economy of a modern industrial city.[1] A study of these urban spaces, these women, their stories, and their connections with the political life of the era thus gives us a fascinating window into the transformation of urban culture and values in China's most cosmopolitan city during the first half of this century.

Social dancing entered China primarily through the Western concessions of Shanghai, Tianjin, Qingdao and other cities with large concentrations of European and American expatriates. As in the West, upon its introduction into China dancing took on multiple institutional forms, including tea dances, charity balls, professional song-and-dance troupes (*gewutuan*), ballet dancing, dancing schools, and social gatherings for student associations, government, military, and professional organizations. Yet it was in the urban space of the cabaret that dance had its greatest impact on both the cultural life of the city and the mythology associated with the name of Shanghai.[2] By the early twenties, Shanghai had acquired the reputation of "Paris of the Orient" for its numerous cabarets.[3] White Russian immigration following the Russian Revolution—by one account "one of the strangest streams of human history, and certainly one of the most romantic elements of Shanghai"[4]—brought a host of entertainers, musicians, ballet dancers, and cabaret artists into the foreign settlements of China's treaty port cities. These men and women made their living as dancing partners, performers, musicians, and bouncers in the cabarets that dotted settlement roads, particularly around the race course and on the main drags of Shanghai's International Settlement.[5] By the thirties a multitude of businessmen, politicians, sailors, soldiers, adventurers, gamblers, gangsters, and ne'er-do-wells from all over the world had crowded into the "Paradise of Adventurers" to earn their livings. Hundreds of cabarets featuring an equal variety of female entertainers sprouted up all over the city to cater to their nighttime dreams and fantasies.

Eventually Chinese society adopted these foreign institutions and practices as its own, leading by the 1930s to an abundance of cabarets run and staffed by Chinese people. Part and parcel of the cabaret industry were its women workers, who served as barmaids, waitresses, performing artists, and, of course, dancing partners. These women, though few in number compared to those in the industrial labor force, nevertheless came to occupy a central place in Shanghai's popular lore, appearing regularly in numerous dailies, novels, films, and tourist accounts of the city and its vices. As we shall see shortly, their presence in the collective urban imagination filled a space that the courtesans of the late Qing and early Republic were vacating.

From Sing-Song Girls to Singing Hostesses: A Disappearing Breed

In order to provide the necessary context for the emergence of Shanghai's cabaret culture, we must go back to earlier times, when courtesans were the dominant female entertainers in the city's elite leisure culture. Shanghai had been famous for its courtesans, or "sing-song girls" as they were known in contemporary Western literature, since the late Qing. These women served as both social and sexual companions for the city's elite, particularly the scholar class, who dedicated numerous poems, guidebooks, and novelettes to courtesans and their culture. A number of important literary works from the late Qing period, notably Han Bangqing's (1856–94) *Haishang hua liezhuan* (Sing-song girls of Shanghai, 1892–94), attest to the popularity of Shanghai courtesans as urban narrative subjects, while describing their culture in great detail.[6] In the early 1900s, the city's first "mosquito" journals (*xiaobao*)—gossipy, tabloid-like newspapers—praised and appraised popular courtesans and detailed their liaisons with the city's male elite.[7] Courtesans also became central figures in Shanghai's rising commercial culture during this period, appearing on calendars and posters advertising soap, toothpaste, and other modern hygiene and beauty products.[8] In these ways, courtesans functioned as harbingers of modern elite culture in China, promoting the modern virtues of cleanliness and commerciality. Ironically, the very culture that they helped to bring about would occasion their demise.

The decline in popularity of courtesans rested on a number of interrelated historical changes that took place in urban China in the early twentieth century. These included the official abolition of the examination system in 1905, the slow but inexorable dismantling of its institutions, and the subsequent decline of the scholar class; the heavy commercialization of prostitution stimulated by a rising male-to-female ratio as the city industrialized; progressive government regulations and social attitudes countering the practice of prostitution and concubinage in the 1920s; the rise of a new commercial and political elite that followed western trends; and the increased social freedom and mobility of urban women.[9] All of these factors contributed to the declining popularity of courtesans among the urban elite, although some were more visible to those affected by the changes. Few who had lived through the late Qing could disregard the variety of social and occupational opportunities opened to women in the emerging society of Republican China, which to some seemed to be the most obvious reason for the shrinking role played by courtesans in the lives of the male elite. As the English-speaking sinologist and sexologist Yao Hsin-nung wrote in 1937: "Modern Chinese women are no longer confined to the inner apartments and fettered by the severe rules of *li-chiao* (Confucian propriety). They go to schools and move in society together with the menfolk. They not only take to art and literature, but are also interested in politics and social work. *In the glorious dawn of their emancipation and ascendancy, the splendor of the sing-song girls has grown dim and probably will never shine again.*"[10]

Meanwhile, spurred by the growth of the magazine, radio, recording, and film industries, a host of new female entertainers arose phoenixlike from the ashes of the dying courtesan culture. These high-profile professions included song-and-dance stars (*gewumingxing*), movie stars (*dianying mingxing*), singing hostesses (*genü*), and dancing hostesses (*wunü*). As the stars of these modern media figures rose, the "flowery world" (*huaguo*) of courtesans slowly and correspondingly disappeared from the tabloid entertainment columns, popular novels, and other narrative and discursive spaces that they had until then dominated. A city as populous and diverse as Shanghai could accommodate many different forms of entertainment, and old brothels and opera houses continued to survive and even prosper throughout the period despite their ebbing fashionability. Nevertheless, in the competitive arena of commercial film and print, where the latest trends and fashions struggled for recognition and advertising space, courtesans fought a hard and losing battle as modern entertainers—particularly Shanghai's cabaret girls—took their places.

A survey of *Jingbao* (The crystal), one of Shanghai's most popular mosquito journals, between the years 1927 and 1940 serves to illustrate this trend.[11] Despite its relatively high circulation, *Jingbao* was a small paper comprising four pages: one devoted to headlines, one to advertisements, one to political and social news, and one to entertainment.[12] Throughout the 1920s, following the mosquito tradition, *Jingbao*'s entertainment page featured daily articles on well-known opera figures and courtesans—the celebrities of the day—often accompanied by their photographs. Through the early thirties the women of the "flowery world" continued to appear regularly in the paper, yet articles about singing hostesses, song-and-dance stars, film stars, and dancing hostesses slowly began to filter into the section as well, sharing space with their courtesan cousins. The names and affiliations of these modern entertainers invariably appeared under their photos. The articles tended to be small and gossipy, dwelling mainly upon the reputations, physical qualities, and relations with the local male elite of these novel media figures.

Following years show a continued rise in the frequency of dancing hostesses and a corresponding decrease in the number of courtesans appearing in the paper. By the mid-thirties, dancing hostesses appeared almost daily, singers and movie stars less frequently, while courtesans were few and far between. By the late thirties, dancing hostesses had become the dominant figures on *Jingbao*'s entertainment page, eclipsing all other professions except male opera stars, who continued to command a large audience despite the increased popularity of dancing and film. In 1939, under a new management,[13] *Jingbao* expanded to six pages—enough space to accommodate a daily half-page section titled "The dancing world" (Wuguo), signaling the institutionalization of dancing discourse. This section appeared directly above a similarly constructed section on Chinese opera, as if in testament to its primary importance in the cultural life of the modern city, surpassing traditional entertainment forms. Articles in "The dancing world" favored gossip about specific dancing hostesses, as well as poems and interviews written about and by dancing hostesses, regular columns such as "Secret news" (Mibao) and "Bedside diaries" (Chuangtou riji), and advice such as "How to speak your heart with dancing hostesses" (Zenyang yu wunü tanquing).[14] At the close of the decade, in the pages of one of Shanghai's most stable and successful "mosquito" papers, the world of the sing-song house was completely overshadowed by the world of the dance hall.

Courtesans attempted to hold their precarious positions in the emerging mass culture by adapting themselves musically, culturally, politically, and commercially to the changes taking place. They expanded their repertoire of opera tunes by learning commercial songs popularized by the budding radio, performance, recording, and film industries. They also served as icons and inspirations for patriotic movements—some were even hired to sing patriotic songs at rallies and patriotic association meetings.[15] Though myopic westerners continued to refer to them as sing-song girls, these women were known in the Chinese popular press as "singing hostesses," a name that both reflects their courtesanly precedents and their narrow professionalization in modern commercial culture.

Who were the singing hostesses, and what separated them from earlier courtesans? Although it was an ambiguous and widely used referent in Republican Chinese print culture, the term "singing hostess" usually referred to women hired to accompany groups of men at parties, dinners, and other festivities, and to regale their party with songs. Following the requests of their patrons, and often with instrumental accompaniment, they usually performed songs chosen from the traditional operatic repertoire. In this sense they were not too different from courtesans of the late Qing and earlier periods. On the other hand, unlike courtesans, whose relationships with their madams, managers, houses, and clients reflected a premodern system of exchange, most singing hostesses belonged to companies or professional associations that used telephones to contact clients, worked on tight profit margins, set up appointments along a clock-based schedule, and netted a substantial portion of their workers' earnings. Not all singing hostesses were hired out to private groups. Many worked in teahouses, restaurants, "storytelling houses" (*shuchang*), amusement centers, and other fixed and floating establishments where they earned tips performing for patrons. Nevertheless, in all cases it was not uncommon for these women to enter into individual relationships with their clients, for which they earned financial support and the possibility of concubinage.

Courtesans in late imperial China had been separated into different classes according to age, talent, beauty, and other standards. Similarly, in the 1930s, at least one journalistic source separated singing hostesses into two basic classes.[16] As with traditional courtesans, the higher ranks of singing hostesses were known as *changsan tangzi*, prostitutes who used singing as a "trademark" (*shangbiao*) to cover for their real work.[17] The lower ranks were organized into associations (*qunfang huichang*) and worked under the tutelage and command of a "group leader" (*banzhu*), who taught them Beijing opera songs and performance techniques, and often subjected them to harsh and brutal treatment in the process.

Despite their efforts to modernize, by the mid-1930s sing-song girls cum singing hostesses in Shanghai were losing ground to other professions. In 1936, when asked about business conditions, one woman complained that the enterprise had suffered greatly in recent times and suggested that the Shanghai population's eternal quest for novelty was in great part to blame. She claimed that while Shanghai had held over forty singing hostess associations in the past, recently the number had dwindled to around ten. Fewer and fewer people were frequenting the storytelling houses and teahouses in which singing hostesses worked. Because of the decrease in business, members of these associations were receiving less pay and thus were forced to find other occupations. Many had found jobs as "girl guides" (*xiangdao yuan*)—the equivalent of the modern escort service—while many others had become dancing hostesses.

From Singing Hostesses to Dancing Hostesses:
An Up-and-Coming Occupation

For decades the practice of ballroom dancing, an important social pastime for the foreign elite of Shanghai's concessions, had been an exotic and misunderstood practice to Chinese city dwellers, who often associated dancing with nudity and sex.[18] A cartoon from the Tianjin newspaper *Beiyang huapao* (The pei-yang pictorial news) is indicative of such a view. Published in 1927, the cartoon shows a set of 3-D movie glasses framing four male-female couples who hold each other tightly while dancing in the nude. Underneath, in English, the caption reads: "Dancing through the eyes of Chinese moralists." Another cartoon, titled "His hand while dancing" (Tiaowu shi ta de shou), shows a man and woman dancing, his hand on her behind.[19] A pornographic work from the late twenties, which the Shanghai Municipal Police confiscated and banned, illustrates in a more radical fashion the Chinese tendency to exoticize and sexualize the institution of the dance hall.[20] In Wu Nonghua's novel *Lingrou damen* (The great door of soul and flesh), a group of Western men and women frequent dark dance halls in shady hotels, where they collectively engage in naked dancing and orgiastic sex, graphically described by the author, in order to "gratify their most basic needs." Part of the reason for such imaginative portrayals of nightlife might have lain in the exclusion of most Chinese from foreign clubs, hotels, and cabarets through the 1920s, a practice that continued in some cases well into the 1930s.[21] In effect, sensationalist Chinese writers such as Wu Nonghua who catered to a public unable to enter these forbidden zones let their imaginations run wild.

Meanwhile, conservative Chinese elites who did have access to Euro-American ballroom culture decried the practice of men and women dancing together, particularly with each other's spouses. In an article exemplary of this viewpoint, which appeared in the Shanghai newspaper *Shenghuo* (Life) in 1927, the author wrote that a friend who had recently returned from a trip to the United States found the practices there of unmarried men and women dancing together, and of married men dancing with each other's wives, particularly offensive. The friend went on to complain about the American social practice of seating husbands and wives at separate tables.[22] Despite invitations to Chinese notables to attend parties held by the foreign elite, such attitudes obstinately persisted. As *Fortune* magazine wrote in an exposé of Shanghai society in 1935, for a long time "Chinese wives did not make their appearance in the night clubs and ballrooms of the foreign rich." In 1923, when Suzanne Tsang, daughter of a high-ranking KMT official, appeared at the Carlton Club with a date, "respectable Chinese families were scandalized." When taipans such as John Keswick of Jardine, Matheson Company began to invite young Chinese men and women to social gatherings, "The Chinese girls . . . came shyly at first, like pretty wax babies, carrying gold and enamel French compacts in their hands, symbols of a new day. Now they circulate around the town quite freely, smoke, drink, drive their own automobiles."[23]

Following the Nationalist Revolution, Shanghai changed radically as the liberal commercial culture of southern China permeated the city, and gangster politics reigned.[24] Chiang Kai-shek (Jiang Jieshi, 1887–1975), the country's *de facto* leader, set a precedent by holding a highly publicized wedding with Wellesley-educated Song Meiling (b. 1902) in the ballroom of the Majestic Hotel.[25] In 1927, the first dance hall to admit Chinese patrons was opened, followed by many others set up by Cantonese entrepreneurs that catered to the Chinese population.[26] As colorfully described in the memoirs of Australian journalist John Pal, the Nanjing era brought the city's touted nightlife to new heights of glory:[27] "Almost from the day the southerners came to town, Shanghai embarked upon an era of whoopee enough to send past emperors spinning in their marble tombs. The pace of the city's world-famed night-life was stepped up out of recognition and the responsibility for this rested almost solely upon Chinese shoulders—youthful ones, for their owners were drawn mainly from the student classes. It wasn't long before they were crowding foreigners off their own dance-floors, and they were big spenders, too."

As Pal notes, Shanghai's vibrant student population, many of whom traveled to Europe to study and witnessed its metropolitan dance culture for themselves, contributed to the popularity of dancing. Students not only populated the cabarets of Shanghai's foreign settlements, but also set up dance classes and social dances in their own colleges and universities. These activities were augmented by dancing schools run by Russian expatriates and attended by the growing middle classes, who, like their counterparts in the United States and Europe, often sent their daughters to school to learn ballet. Dance schools also served as training grounds for Chinese cabaret artists and dancing hostesses. In the words of Pal, "dance academies sprang up all over the place, converting sing-song girls into taxi-dancers and lazy old opium-smokers into spry jazz maniacs rarin' to go."[28] Another factor that contributed to the rising popularity of social dancing among students and other urbanites in the early thirties was the influx of American musical films into Shanghai following the successful commercialization of the "talkie" in 1928.[29] It was no coincidence that when conservative officials during the New Life Movement (*xin shenghuo yundong*) of 1934–37 cracked down on dancing for its "decadent" influence on the student population, they also cracked down on Hollywood films.[30]

Though dance halls were uniformly targeted by ideologues as dens of vice, not all were recognized as such by the reading public. Guidebooks and other accounts tended to categorize cabarets hierarchically on the basis of class and size. According to an article published in the English-language *China Journal*, cabarets in Shanghai could be separated into three classes: "First class, second class, and no class!"[31] Another English guide to Shanghai advised its readers: "Of cabarets there is a range to suit any taste, from those where formal dress predominates, to those not so formal but distinctly bohemian."[32] Chinese accounts categorized dance halls along similar lines. In *Libailiu* (Saturday), one account divided cabarets into large and small establishments, though it claimed that only two, the Paramount (Bailemen) and the Park Hotel (Guoji da fandian), offered pure entertainment, while all others were places for "selling souls" (*mai linghun*), or prostitution.[33] Other high-class cabarets included the Little Club, "the toniest cabaret . . . filled with fine silks and boiled shirts," located on Nanjing Road opposite the racecourse, and ballrooms in high-class international hotels such as the Cathay.[34] These halls catered mainly to the city's foreign and Chinese elite, who often mingled in order to forge economic and political alliances. Patrons included some of the wealthiest and most powerful men in Shanghai, including Green Gang (Qingbang) leader Du Yuesheng (1888–1951), as well as numerous British and American "taipans."[35]

On the middle level were places such as St. George's, Del Monte, Casanova, Vienna Gardens, the Yangtze, and the Canidrome Ballroom—dance clubs and gardens patronized primarily by the middle classes of both the Chinese and foreign communities, who flocked to these halls following an evening's divertissement at the racetrack, restaurant, or theater. American GIs, who in general earned higher pay than other enlisted men, also appeared regularly in these establishments, raising the levels of energy and camaraderie, and occasioning brawls as well.[36] Most other enlisted men frequented the lower strata of Shanghai's cabaret culture. Low-class cabarets included dozens of small bars, cafes, and restaurants that littered the city, each featuring several waitresses and dance hostesses, and often serving as fronts for prostitution.[37] These establishments were attended mainly by lower-income workers and by the multinational hordes of enlisted men stationed in the city since the Nationalist revolution, when they were sent by their respective nations to preserve the lives and holdings of their compatriots in Shanghai.[38] Sailors and soldiers sent to Shanghai in the 1930s flocked to the cabarets of the French Concession's infamous Blood Alley, or Rue Chu Pao San, a tiny street nestled between Sichuan and Jiangxi Roads off of Avenue Edward VII, named for its often bloody brawls.[39] Here could be found Korean, Chinese, Filipino, Indian, Vietnamese, and of course, Russian dancing partners ready to kick up a lindy with the nearest sailor.

Chinese commercial interests, including members of both the Green Gang and Hong Gang (Hongbang), quickly caught on to the potential profits of the emerging practice of social dancing, and collectively invested large amounts of money to set up cabarets.[40] Many of these were small-scale ventures, equipped with a two- or three-hundred-square-foot dance floor, a stage for musicians, and tables and stools surrounding the floor where patrons and dancing girls mingled.[41] If business was low, a cabaret might be sold out to other interests, or revived using novel "gimmicks" (*xuetou*) to lure patrons, including door prizes, free food, and women clad in bathing suits or scanty pajamas.[42] Behind such campaigns lay the entrepreneurial genius of men such as Zhou Shixun, who successfully ran a circuit of dance clubs including the Metropole (Daduhui) and St. Anna's (Sheng Aina), and Ya Tang, manager of the Great Shanghai (Dahu), home to the famous Liang sisters (Liang Saizhen, Liang Saizhu, Liang Saishan, Liang Saihu), stars of stage and screen (see fig. 8).[43] These men competed for the most attractive and popular dancers in the city.

Taken as a whole, cabarets constituted a highly competitive, multimillion dollar industry, which oddly enough seemed to bear an inverse relationship to the economic life of the city.[44] When the city's daytime economy suffered under the impact of recession, inflation, or foreign invasion, the shadow-world of cabarets continued to prosper, much to the chagrin of failing businessmen and patriots alike. Thus, owing to a combination of commercial and cultural forces, the practice of cabaret-going and professional dancing quickly wove itself into Chinese culture, leading to an abundance of Chinese dance halls filled with women who earned their pay by fraternizing and dancing with a mostly male clientele.

By the mid-1930s, several thousand women from various ethnic and professional backgrounds, including a number of college students and many women recruited from the waning profession of the singing hostess, worked as per-

8. The Liang sisters: dancing hostesses cum movie actresses, courtesy of the China Film Archive.

formers or as dancing partners. They worked late hours, often until dawn, in the numerous cafes, night clubs, cabarets, hotel ballrooms, theaters, and department store dance halls that had sprouted up in Shanghai in the early thirties boom years "like bamboo shoots after spring rain" (*ru yuhou chunsun*).[45] Dancing partners, popularly known as "dancing hostesses," were also known as "locomotives" (*longtou*) in local parlance.[46] Patrons, sometimes known as "cabooses" (*tuoche*), purchased tickets at the door, which they used to buy dances.[47] For the price of a ticket and a drink, ostensibly anyone could dance and converse briefly with a dancing hostess, whose age usually fell somewhere between 15 and 25.[48] Often a little negotiating led to more than just a dance, but not all dancing hostesses were prostitutes. While some establishments encouraged such relations between women and patrons, others expressly forbade them, even hiring special buses to take the women home during the wee hours.[49] Yet for most women in the business, because of their meager earnings, relationships with clients outside of the dance hall were a necessity. At the end of the night, a dancing hostess could collect on her tickets, but only after the management skimmed off its own share, often amounting to upwards of fifty percent of her earnings.[50]

For a modest investment of time and money, any young woman with marketable traits and skills could become a dancing hostess. *San wunü* (Three dancing hostesses), a novel by the famous butterfly novelist Bao Tianxiao (1876–1973) published in serial form in the newspaper *Libao* (The guardian) in 1936, offered the contemporary reader a detailed account of the process of becoming a dancing hostess.[51] In chapter 2, "The dancing school" (*tiaowu xuexiao*), a seasoned dancing hostess named Zhou Ruiyun leads her young friend Chen Meizhen, a girl from a poor rural background, through the series of steps needed to enter the world of the dance hall. These include the adoption of a new wardrobe—high-heeled shoes, silk stockings, several *qipao* (Chinese dresses), and an overcoat—a permanent wave, softer hands, and the acquisition of skills such as the use of a lighter. Following these steps, within two weeks Meizhen is transformed from a simple country girl into a city sophisticate, ready to enter a dance academy to learn the latest steps under the guidance of a Russian teacher.

Many of the more popular dance halls had their "number one" hostess, who commanded more money, often fistfuls of dance tickets, for her companionship. Some establishments, in an effort to generate more business, held contests by popular vote to elect the year's "cabaret queen" (*wuguo huanghou*),[52] though it was not uncommon for powerful underworld figures such as Du Yuesheng to fix these contests so that favored women came out on top.[53] Women who earned the coveted title of "cabaret queen" or its sister title, "Miss Shanghai," immediately became citywide celebrities, and some fortunate women went on to successful careers in film. Given its potential, the career of cabaret girl attracted a wide variety of young women for both economic and social reasons. Nevertheless, most popular accounts suggest that the majority of cabaret girls were poor, uneducated women who came in to Shanghai from the countryside to make money and chose to "sell their souls" to the nightlife rather than engage in manual labor, the only other option for a woman without an education.[54]

As dancing gained in popularity among the local business elite, student population, and intelligentsia, the popular press also began to introduce dancing to a larger reading public. In the mid-1930s, the Shanghai women's magazine *Linglong* introduced dancing to its readership through a three-part series of articles. One article described dancing not only as a social activity, but also as a serious subject of study, pointing out the large number of schools and teachers devoted to dancing in Shanghai, as well as abroad.[55] It then ran through a short description of different popular dances, including the quickstep, the slow foxtrot, the waltz, the tango, the New Charleston, and the rumba. The article gave its readers directions on how to dance, and what to watch for when dancing, including one's posture, rhythm, feet, and shoulders. A subsequent article argued that dance was a natural and primitive act that expressed and enlivened the forces within the body. It also asserted that dancing was an effective way to attract a mate, since the act of dancing communicated one's inner emotions. The thrust of such articles was that dancing, while appearing primitive on the surface level, nevertheless accorded with natural and "civilized" impulses.

Dance Hall Protocol: Wang Dingjiu's 'Guide to Shanghai'

Like courtesan culture, dance hall behavior—at least for the upper levels of society—was dictated mainly by a kind of protocol obeyed by all as a matter of mutual consent. Wang Dingjiu's *Shanghai menjing* (Guide to Shanghai, 1932), a popular guidebook, offers many insights into the cultural codes of the dance hall from the perspective of the patron.[56] After introducing the reader to many of Shanghai's high-class dance halls, the guidebook offers a set of rules which when followed should guarantee a satisfied customer. First, one must arrive at the dance hall in a car, since the attendants, the management, and the dancing hostesses look down upon those patrons who are not wealthy enough to own one. One must wear the proper clothing, preferably Western-style suits, although some establishments allow traditional Chinese dress. Upon being seated, it is not proper to move around. One must satisfy the stomach first by ordering a large meal. Only then should one look for a partner among the dancing hostesses present. After dancing with a woman, one should escort her back to her original seat. The guidebook claims that although Chinese society favors men, in dance halls it is the women who have the upper hand.

If a patron took a liking to a certain girl, he might try to win her over with certain "tricks" supplied by the guidebook. Wang Dingjiu counsels the anxious patron to use caution and patience, for the number of patrons far outweighs the number of dancing hostesses. According to the book, it is important to divine the personality of the girl before attempting to win her favor, since different tactics apply to different women. For those women who enjoy the open competition of men, it is necessary to be bold and dashing. Others require more subtle means of persuasion. A bottle of champagne is necessary, but too many are an extravagance. Small gifts such as jewelry, clothing, or even a flowered handkerchief, with a wad of bills inconspicuously folded inside, might be employed to gain the affections of a dancing hostess. If she likes seeing movies, the patron may take her out to see the latest film. If she likes drama, he may take her to see a play. Once a dancer becomes familiar with a patron, she will stay with him at his table, chatting and dancing with him all night. But, the book cautions, do not become too attached to a certain girl, because she will certainly have other clients. Many fights have taken place in dance halls over certain girls, by over-possessive patrons. Moreover, "locomotives" may "derail" (*chugui*) "cabooses" who do not meet their behavioral or financial expectations.

Although she was a commodity, the dancing hostess in the above portrayal was a rational actor within her own economic context, exercising a significant degree of choice over those with whom she fraternized. The bargaining power of dancing hostesses in high-class establishments owed much to the high patron-to-dancer ratio that the high-class dance halls commanded. According to the guidebook, over 300 licensed dancing hostesses worked in these establishments, as opposed to the countless number of men who patronized them.

Here the guidelines for behavior set out by Wang's guidebook again suggest that the role of the dancing hostess was very similar to that of the courtesan, who similarly bargained with clients for money and favors.[57] There were many other similarities between the two cultures. The yearly contest for "cabaret queen" held by some dance halls as a promotional gimmick echoed "flower queen" (*huaguo huanghou*) contests still held in the city in the 1930s. Even the terminology for the dance hall demimonde owed much to courtesan culture. "The world of dance" (*wuguo*) found its counterpart in the "flowery world" (*huaguo*), the widely used term for courtesan culture. Yet despite these superficial similarities, it must be noted that there were pronounced differences between the two cultures. First, as previously noted, dance halls were modern businesses that represented significant investments and generated enormous profits. Second, despite the existence of a protocol that dictated proper behavior, dance halls were nevertheless highly regulated spaces whose histories mark the attempt of the national and colonial governments to penetrate ever further into local society.

Regulating the Girls: Government, Management, and Family

Singing and dancing hostesses were the subjects of many projects of regulation and control, exerted on the three concentric levels of government, management, and family.[58] The primary reason for such controls was the relationship between the professions of singing and dancing and the practice of prostitution. Yet here the forces of government, commerce, and family worked toward contrary purposes, for while prostitution was prohibited by law on the premises at dance halls, teahouses, and other establishments,[59] management in most cases tacitly accepted and often promoted such negotiations among dancers and patrons. Indeed, many managers received a share of the income earned through such transactions. Families often attempted to prevent their female members from entering such professions, but in many cases they too profited from the income that their dancing daughters generated.

Besides prostitution, the main reason for government regulation of the amusement sphere lay in both the Nationalists' and the Shanghai Municipal Council's attempts to curb the spread of Communism by closely monitoring the city's public and semipublic urban spaces.[60] Because many cabarets employed Russian women, these urban spaces were particular candidates for such clandestine political activities. Indeed, several Russian dancing partners were arrested and charged as Red agents for corrupting sailors and extorting them into forming Communist cells during the late twenties and thirties.[61] Again, management came into conflict with government on this issue, resisting penetration into their commercial spheres by refusing to comply with regulations, submitting false information to government bureaus, or bribing police through gangster connections.[62]

Registration was one way for local government to monitor public spaces. The Shanghai Municipal Police kept a close eye on every establishment in the foreign concessions known to employ dancing hostesses, and kept detailed records that included the numbers, names, addresses, and nationalities of the women so employed.[63] Chinese government regulation went far beyond city spaces, encompassing smaller towns in the hinterlands as well. The local government of the town of Bengbu, north of Nanjing in Anhui province, attempted to regulate the activities of its singing hostesses, most of whom were actually prostitutes who "sold" songs as a side job or as a cover.[64] In 1935, the local government took measures to register each singing hostess and collect a tax of 10 yuan from each. The Public Security Bureau (Gong'an ju) restricted singing hostesses to the old town district, which was henceforth referred to as the "singing hostess district" (*genü qucheng*). The town government undertook such measures in order to contain the spread of singing hostesses who had established themselves in large hotels and in private residences, and the subsequent prostitution that their presence encouraged.

As well as registering singing and dancing hostesses, police also conducted frequent raids on dance parlors in order to examine and regulate the behavior of employees and patrons. For example, in 1935 the Qinhuai dance hall was placed under strict police supervision. Singers in the establishment who were caught while engaged in licentious activities with their clients were detained and fined.[65] Government regulations also dealt with the issue of education. In Nanjing during the New Life movement the government prohibited singing hostesses from enrolling in public schools.[66]

While local government attempted to curtail and contain the activities of singing and dancing hostesses and their interaction with local society, management regulations reflected the attempts of owners and investors to ensure the smooth operation of their businesses and to maintain a high level of profitability despite the ups and downs of the economic environment. For example, in 1935, when a wide-scale recession hit the city, dance halls underwent many renovations and their managers instituted a number of new rules.[67] Because dancing hostesses sometimes came to work late, some establishments set limits on the time period during which dancers could exchange the tickets they collected for money. Since patrons often invited them to other clubs, another way of keeping dancers on the job was to hold their coats under lock and key, dispensing them only after certain hours. One more habit that took away dancers' time on the dance floor was the tendency to spend time in the bathrooms chatting together. One way managers prevented such activities was to decrease the size of the bathrooms. Such rules and restrictions hint at the generally antagonistic relationship between dancers and management.[68]

Despite the increasing penetration of both government and modern management into the public and private lives of city people,[69] family members and local communities continued to exert the strongest pressures on their singing and dancing daughters in public lore. In 1937, a story about a father and daughter in Ningbo county became a popular news item.[70] The daughter, Sun Lindi, worked at a perfume factory but wanted to become a dancing hostess. Her father, Sun Xiaohua, opposed the decision. Still, the daughter was adamant. Finally, in desperation her father shackled her to her bed with a steel lock. Eventually the local authorities intervened, arresting the hapless man for violating the physical freedom of his daughter. Another popular story tells of a young female student who, in order to lessen the financial burden of schooling on her parents, sneaked out at night to a dance hall to work as a dancing hostess.[71] One evening while working at the dance hall, she ran into a neighbor. The following day her parents confronted her, asking her where she went during the evenings. Under their interrogation, she reluctantly admitted her secret. The entire family broke down and wept.

While many families discouraged their daughters and sisters from entering the profession, others encouraged them to seek profitable jobs as singing and dancing hostesses. A cartoon in the magazine *Shanghai Shenghuo* (Shanghai life) in 1938 shows a mother shaking money from her dancing daughter, who is depicted as a "money tree" (*yaoqian shu*). Thus, while many stories reveal the strong disapproval of conservative families and communities whose daughters sought the freedom, money, and glamour of life in the dance halls,[72] others represent singing and dancing hostesses as poor, pitiable figures forced by their economic conditions and by their families to work. As we shall soon see, such sentimental portrayals aligned closely with those presented in popular literature and film during the Nanjing decade.

Portraying Modern Girls in the Media

IN THE PRESS: 'LINGLONG'

As is clear by now, singing and dancing hostesses were icons that carried powerful, often contradictory messages about women's roles in society. Their images in the media ranged from innocent, mistreated women to evil seductresses bent on monetary gain. While some journalists and publishers printed sensational stories of licentious, greedy cabaret girls and naive men, others painted a much more sympathetic picture of these women and the hardships they suffered. Earlier we discussed the role that "mosquito" journals such as *Jingbao* generally played in the development of Shanghai cabaret culture. For these newspapers, dancing hostesses were commodities whose skills and personalities were to be advertised and criticized like any other product on the market.

One source that consistently showed more sympathy for the plights of singing and dancing hostesses, as well as their prostitute cousins, was *Linglong*. A popular women's magazine with a large readership in Shanghai and in other major cities and countries where educated Chinese women resided, *Linglong*'s credo was to guide women in their liberation after "five thousand years of feudalism," and to "ease their pains" in an era of famine, imperialism, and war.[73] Like popular women's journals in Europe and America, this weekly magazine offered practical advice on homemaking, health, relationships, occupations, and other issues affecting urban women, along with articles and photographs of society women, film stars, and other female icons.

A 1936 issue of *Linglong* featured a pair of small news items entitled "Wunü lei, genü chou" (Dancing hostess's tears, singing hostess's fears).[74] By their juxtaposition alone, one may discern that these professions were closely related in the public mind. The first item concerned the famous dancing hostess and former movie actress Liang Saizhen, who earned the coveted title of "cabaret queen" in the mid-1930s. According to the item, Miss Liang always pressed her cheek against her partner's face when dancing. The writer ended with the following lament: "Alas, Empress, adept at courting favor in the world of dance, who for 33 cents would be a 'three-minute wife' and press her sweet cheeks [to her partner's face], who says that dancers don't cry?" The second item protested the situation of singing hostesses at the Qinhuai dance hall, which as mentioned above was placed under strict police supervision. A new law, article 239 in the Chinese Criminal Code, was being promoted by the legislature that if enacted would make marriage between singers and their clientele illegal. The writer argued that if such a law were enforced, singing hostesses whose youth was quickly passing would be hard pressed to find lifemates among the men who patronized their establishments.

Both items tied singing and dancing hostesses to licentious practices. Yet in each passage, the author commiserated with the subject. In the first case, the author sympathized with Liang by pointing out the sadness of the situation in which she was forced to sell her body and her intimacy—in this case, symbolized by her "sweet cheeks"—to a stranger for a very low price. In the second case, the author concluded that the stringent laws and police supervision sponsored by the reform movement had taken away singing hostesses' sole chance at finding happiness by removing the possibility of their marriage to patrons. Again, much as in the courtesan tradition, singing was perceived to be an avenue to love and marriage, as well as to monetary success. These news items thus illustrate the tensions between the courtesan legacy, which undergirded both professions, and the commercial and legal boundaries within which they now operated.

A similar approach is found in the previously mentioned article about the man from Ningbo county who shackled his daughter to her bed rather than allow her to become a dancing hostess. The writer went on to contrast the fantasy of life as a dancing hostess—a glamorous life associated with the neon and fashion of the dancing scene—with the harsh realities of the commerce of the flesh. In the words of the writer, such a profession ultimately involved "selling one's soul." The writer also reflected on the piteous condition of women in the contemporary world, arguing that while women now had the opportunity to make a living, they must choose between dull factory work and glamorous but notorious professions such as dancing. "Women in the modern era," concluded the article, "whether dancing hostesses or factory workers, are all sacrificial victims of an evil economic system and captives of evil men."[75]

IN LITERATURE: THE NEW PERCEPTIONISTS AND MU SHIYING

We have already seen how pornographers such as Wu Nonghua and butterfly novelists such as Bao Tianxiao took an interest in the budding dance hall culture of the twenties and thirties.[76] Another genre of writers who approached the dance hall as a focus for urban narrative were the New Perceptionists (*xin ganjue pai*). Influenced by literary trends in Europe and Japan, these writers attempted to portray the cadence, decadence, and chaos of the modern city through a collage of perceptions, sensations, texts, and images. As Heinrich Freuhauf has argued, for many of these writers the dance hall figured into the abstract conceptual space of the modern city and symbolized the liberating energies of Western "civilization."[77]

Beginning in the late 1920s, a number of writers penned stories that included dance halls and dancing hostesses. Lu Mengzhu's short story "Tiaowu tingqian" (Before the dance hall, 1927) features a young man whose primary ambition is to bed a certain girl who works in a dance parlor, but whose efforts are frustrated by other dancing hostesses who continually thwart his intentions by throwing themselves at him. Another example is Zhang Ruogu's *Duhui jiaoxiang qu* (Urban symphonies, 1929), a series of urban vignettes presented together as a montage. In one story, after an evening's adventure in the modern city, several male characters end up in a dance hall in the Japanese district of North Sichuan Road, where one falls head-over-heels for a Japanese dancer. In these stories, the dancing hostess embodies the exotic, seductive, and dangerous nature of the modern urban scene. Never a fleshed-out character, she is instead a prop on which the young urban dandy or flaneur can project his fantasies of easy sex with a "modern girl" (*modeng nülang*).[78]

In the 1930s, a young writer named Mu Shiying (1912–40) took Shanghai's dance hall literature to new heights. Among the short stories he published during this period, several feature cabarets and dancing hostesses. As opposed to previous two-dimensional portrayals, these women function as main characters. Taken together these stories reflect the genius of a talented young writer experimenting with many different styles and genres as he groped for his own personal voice. Given the experimental, subjective, even dreamlike qualities of many of Mu's writings, they also provide an excellent window for exploring the image of the dancing hostess and the role she played in the fecund imagination of a young intellectual.

Stories of Mu Shiying that depict dance hall culture include "Hei mudan" (Black peony, 1934), "Ye" (Night, 1933), "Bengbu xinwenlan bianjishili yizha feigaoshang de gushi" (The story of a discarded draft found in a news editor's room in Bengbu, 1934), "Yezonghui lide wuge ren" (Five people in a nightclub, 1933), and his most famous story, "Shanghai de hubuwu" (Shanghai foxtrot, 1933). Among these works, "Black Peony" is Mu's most approachable story, and the most interesting from our perspective of the courtesan–dancing hostess transformation. It appears in an illustrated version in the popular pictorial *Liangyou* (The young companion) in 1933, as well as in a collection of the same name the year after, attesting to its mass marketability.[79]

The story unfolds in a Shanghai dance hall as the narrator, a young male, admires the exotic glamour of a dancing hostess whose facial features and adornments combine elements of East and West. Yet what most intrigues him is her world-weary aspect, a sentiment that he shares. The two strike up a discussion, where both agree that they live in a "mechanized" (*jiqi hua*) world whose fast-paced tempo, encapsulated in the frenetic energies of the dance hall, has left them jaded. Under the spell of false intimacy created in the timeless environment of the dance hall, the two leave together. The story picks up again one month later, when the narrator is summoned by an old friend, Shengwu, to visit his country estate in order to see his prized "black peony." There he discovers that his friend has adopted a companion, who is none other than the dancing hostess who mysteriously vanished one month earlier. Later, she reveals to the narrator how she arrived there after being chased by a rapist, and how she used her feminine wiles to seduce Shengwu into letting her stay. Ironically, unlike most accounts of dancing hostesses in the press that portrayed the dancing hostess either as victim or as vamp, Mu's Black Peony is both. Tired of being treated like a "Western doll" (*yang wawa*) by her patrons, she has found solitude and comfort as the guest of the wealthy Shengwu, who still regards her as a "peony spirit" (*mudan yao*) even after she has lived in his mansion for a month.

The narrative of "Black Peony" thus travels back in time and space, from the modern setting of the urban dance hall to the traditional environment of the rural estate.[80] Significantly, Shengwu tells his friend that he has renounced the idea of scientific rationality after coming across this beautiful "spirit." In tandem with this wholesale rejection of western thought, the maudlin, ambivalent figure of the modern dancing hostess is transformed into a contented concubine. She is thus saved from the forces of modernization and westernization that have exoticized her, wearied her, and threatened her Chinese identity. As Black Peony—recognizable to Mu's contemporaries as a courtesan's name—

she reclaims her lost identity as a Chinese woman. The story, however, ends with the narrator's rejection of the rural garden paradise in which he, Shengwu, and Black Peony are ensconced: "Again I walk towards life, and as for the white marble room, the flower garden, the pearl-like chain of violets fronting the patio, and the fruity scent of the grape arbor ... I throw them behind." For the narrator, life lies in the city, with its chaotic mix of popular culture and commerce, and its numerous cabarets.

IN FILM: 'STREET ANGEL' AND 'A NEW YEAR'S COIN'

Having surveyed many images of singing and dancing hostesses presented in newspapers, magazines, guidebooks, and novelettes of the twenties and thirties, we are now ready to approach the subject of film and its role in shaping popular perceptions of the city of Shanghai via its cabaret culture. Following the trends of both Hollywood film and Shanghai's own print media, a number of films made by Shanghai studios explored the lives of singing and dancing hostesses. Indeed, such figures proved so popular that leftist playwright Tian Han criticized his contemporaries for not concentrating on more politically cogent topics. Yet as we have seen, singing and dancing hostesses, when seen as victims of modern commercial society, also fit into popular discourses on prostitution. Two leftist films from 1937—Yuan Muzhi's (1909–78) *Malu tianshi* (Street angel) and Xia Yan's *Yasui qian* (A new year's coin)—provide examples of how the fates of these women served as political commentaries on the state of modern urban society.

Street Angel offers us a peek at the life of an ordinary Shanghai singing hostess through the lens of a leftist filmmaker. Starring the popular song-and-dance star turned actress Zhou Xuan (1918–57), the film tells the story of a young woman, Xiao Hong (also Zhou Xuan's original name), who works in a teahouse singing songs for the customers to the accompaniment of her boss's *erhu* (a two-stringed bowed instrument). She and her elder sister live on the third floor, while the owners of the teahouse, an older couple who continually abuse the two sisters, live below. As the story commences, the couple has already forced the elder sister to engage in prostitution, and are planning to do the same with Xiao Hong. Meanwhile, a poor street musician living next door, Xiao Cheng (Zhao Dan, 1915–80), becomes enamored of the girl and courts her from his window across the courtyard. Yet when a wealthy patron takes an interest in Xiao Hong, the couple offers to sell her off. At first, she falls for the patron's charms, and even accepts a gift from him. Later, however, she overhears the transaction being made by the couple and the patron, and decides to run away. The musician and his friends find a hiding place for her. Soon the older sister, who has fallen for the musician's friend, follows. The teahouse owner and the wealthy patron eventually discover their hiding place, and the owner ends up murdering the older sister. The movie ends after the musician and his friends discover the horrible deed, vowing revenge.

This tragedy was meant to illustrate the pathetic conditions of the Shanghai underclass. The singing hostess, the central figure in the story, symbolized the victimization of women in a callous, commercial society. Though elements such as the death of the older sister appear highly melodramatic, *Street Angel* falls within the realist strain that dominated the literary and dramatic arts in China after the May Fourth movement. In other words, this film was clearly intended as a realistic depiction of the life of a singing hostess in Shanghai. Yet by portraying the singing hostess as an innocent victim in a small teahouse, forced by her employers into singing for money and unaware of the impending dangers of her profession, the filmmaker's spotlight fell on only a small part of the rich leisure culture of Shanghai.

Xia Yan's *A New Year's Coin* provides a much richer study of the world of Shanghai leisure from top to bottom, focusing at crucial points on the city's cabarets. *A New Year's Coin* also illustrates the multilayered connections between song and dance, and between the professions of singing and dancing hostess, that colored the history of leisure in Republican Shanghai. The story follows two interwoven themes: the passage from hand to hand of a "lucky" new year's coin, and the story of a "fallen" singing star forced to become a dancing hostess.

The opening shot of the film sets the stage for the story. The credits roll past several dark scenes of Nanjing Road at night, the International Settlement's main drag and the center of Shanghai's nightlife culture.[81] Following this introduction, the scene switches to a small neighborhood where people are celebrating the Chinese New Year of 1934. The camera settles in the home of a moderately wealthy family, who are eating dinner together. The group includes a grandfather, a mother, her six-year-old daughter He Rongrong (Hu Rongrong), her cousin Jiang Xiuxia (Yuan Qiuxia), a popular singing star, and her fiancé Sun Jiaming, the manager of the theater where she performs. The father is conspicuously absent. Rongrong's mother permits her to request a song from Xiuxia. Xiuxia obliges, but only on the condition that Rongrong pay back the compliment. The group then retires to the anteroom, where Xiuxia and Rongrong perform a song-and-dance routine on the stairs, ending in a well-choreographed tap dance. Following their performance, Sun Jiaming compliments Rongrong, calling her a Chinese Shirley Temple (upon whom she is obviously modeled) and asks Rongrong's family to allow her to perform in his theater. The grandfather, skeptical at first, finally relents after Rongrong gently begs him to allow her to perform. The scene ends when the grandfather places a *hongbao* (new year's packet), containing a Mexican silver dollar stamped with the "double-happiness" sign, under Rongrong's pillow. The film then follows a succession of transactions involving the new year's coin as it is passed down the rungs of the social ladder to the lowest levels of Shanghai society.

The story of the coin begins on the level of high society, at a house party held by wealthy socialites dwelling in luxury. One of the housemaids has gone out to buy pastries and has received the coin as change. She returns to the house to find the party in full swing. The male and female members of the party eat, drink, and converse, while a song plays on the latest luxury item, the radio:

> Here is waking dawn, and the clear morning of sleep
> Here are "cloud tresses" (*yunbin*) of a bird, and lips of red
> Here is a laughing red lamp, and jumping music
> Here is yellow gold paper, and a drunken heart....[82]

In the style of traditional love poetry, "Dance Hall Song" (Wu xie zhi ge), which later transforms into a patriotic march and the theme song of the film, portrays a man awakening with his beautiful female lover (the "bird") in the morning after an evening of lovemaking. After the song ends, Yang Lijuan (Li Minghui, b. 1906), a sing-song girl at the party, is asked by the others to perform it once more, but complains of a sore throat. She finally relents after another woman offers to play an accompaniment on piano. Following her performance, Yang is offered a pastry by the maid and returns the favor by letting her keep the new year's coin. Another maid tries to earn a similar favor by offering her cake, but Yang callously refuses to reward her efforts. Subsequently, the two maids fight over the coin.

Song-and-dance hostess Jiang Xiuxia reenters the story several scenes later, when a man who has picked up the coin uses it to pay for a ticket to the theater in which she and the young Rongrong star in a new year's performance, advertised outside with a racy poster showing Jiang clad in a scanty bikini. Dressed as marionettes, the two perform a sword dance on stage, poking each other in a parody of military culture. Later, back in her dressing room, Jiang complains to a female friend, Zhang Man, that her audience is composed of men who only come to see "carnal" (*rougan*) performances. Zhang, a former classmate who is now a music teacher in Pudong, describes the hardships of her own career. Meanwhile, Jiang's fate is sealed when her fiance Sun leaves to meet a woman waiting in a car outside, stopping at the lobby to borrow some money from the cashier, including of course the new year's coin. The following scene shows the illicit couple leaving St. Anna's Dance Hall (Sheng aina wuting), a high-class cabaret on Love Lane—a street so named for its abundance of brothels. As they leave the cabaret, Sun drops the new year's coin to the car boy, who uses it to pay for a doctor to take care of his sick mother.

Parallel to the fate of the new year's coin, the fates of the two main female characters, Jiang Xiuxia and Yang Lijuan, both professional singers, are intertwined in downward spirals, suggesting a perceived hierarchical relationship between the professions of singing and dancing. The sing-song hostess Yang Lijuan appears again when her patron, a banker, flees the city after his bank collapses, leaving her a sum of money for support, with which his assistant absconds. Without the financial support of her patron, Yang is forced to find work at a local cabaret, the Flower Garden Dance Hall (Huayuan wuting), which has written her a letter requesting her services for a "wild dance party" (*kuangwu dahui*) being held on the eve of the Dragon Boat Festival (Duanwu jie). Later, at the dance hall, backed by a Chinese orchestra, she again performs "Dance Hall Song" before a large crowd of patrons and dancing hostesses. Her act is followed by Jiang Xiuxia, who it is assumed has also been forced to find a job as a nightclub singer following her breakup with her fiance. Jiang croons a high-pitched melody into the microphone on stage as dancers waltz by in the foreground. The final act is Rongrong, who innocently performs her Templesque song-and-dance routine while a patron, in what is perhaps the film's most grotesquely comical scene, leeringly eyes her tiny dancing legs.

Later in the film, Jiang has finally reached the nadir of Shanghai's cabaret culture as a dancing hostess in a small and crowded dance parlor that advertises nude performances and fifteen dances per dollar, her fate a cruel combination of the desertion of her fiance and the recession of 1934—in the colorful words of a local mosquito paper, she is "the beautiful detritus from a volcano" (*huoshan qiongxie*). The latest possessor of the coin, a construction headman, enters the dance hall after being attracted by its poster of a nude dancer. When he sees Jiang Xiuxia, the famous singing star, dancing with another patron, he grabs her away and whirls her wildly about in testament to his power as patron. The clock passes from 11:15 to 2 A.M. as the dance hall continues its mad round. When the headman steps on Jiang's foot, she cries out in complaint. He replies by knocking down a table in anger. "I've paid to dance! How dare you use your mouth with me!" The manager intervenes, apologizing to the patron, who then pays for another round of dances using the new year's coin, throwing it disdainfully to the floor. Jiang cries as the two career about the tiny dance floor.

Having had enough of cabaret lowlife culture, Jiang goes to see her friend in Pudong, where she accepts a job as elementary school music teacher, which though not as glamorous or financially rewarding at least offers her back her dignity. Her new job also allows Jiang to play the coveted role of Chinese patriot. In the final scene, it is new year's day of 1935, and Jiang leads the children in a rendition of the melody to "Dance Hall Song," whose lyrics and title have been changed into the patriotic "Song of Saving the Nation" (Jiuwang zhige):

Here is a new life, and fiery passion
Here is a newborn will, and martial spirit

Here is a sword's sting, and the ring of steel
Here are a free people, and the ancient Great Wall....[83]

The beat has also transformed from a sweet lullaby into a strident march, though the melody line remains the same. The children's voices, broadcast on radio, are carried into homes, stores, and parks, reaching people on all levels of society, who listen entranced to the patriotic message. Finally, we once again return to the family that began the movie, also listening to the song on the radio. The absent father has returned, and cradles his daughter in his arms—another potential victim of the dance hall craze, saved by the return of the patriarch to the family fold.

We are now in a position to analyze the contents of this film and the role that Shanghai's entertainment culture, particularly its cabarets, plays in defining the film's major themes. The film follows the downward trajectory of the new year's coin as it falls into different hands via a succession of tainted transactions. People lie, cheat, beg, pilfer, and fight for the "lucky" foreign coin, which contrary to its purpose causes no end of trouble to those who are unfortunate enough to lay hold of it. The female characters in the film follow a similar trajectory, passed from hand to hand and job to job as they descend into poverty—the fate of the unattached woman. Cabarets in the film serve as vortices of "decadence" in this downward process, where both women and men engage in illicit, addictive, and corrupting activities. Cabarets also serve as sites of transaction between the city's upper- and lower-class inhabitants, where the "decadent" rich in a wasteful performance of their opulence disdainfully throw money to the poor. The message of the patriotic "Song for Saving the Nation," carried to Chinese moviegoing audiences on the eve of Japan's invasion of China, is clear: The Chinese people must stop their petty quarreling and interclass disputes and join together as a nation to struggle for the common good. Through the venue of the cabaret, and through the Mexican coin itself, the film also carries another message: Western culture, material values, sexuality, and money serve as corrupting forces in Chinese society. Only when these values are rejected and patriarchal "family values" restored can China once again move toward a bright future.

From Morality to Patriotism: Singing and Dancing Hostesses in Modern Chinese Politics

As we have seen, social dancing was an unprecedented activity in Chinese culture and encountered significant resistance from both conservative and radical elements throughout the Republican era. Never in China's recorded history had social intercourse between men and women *of family* in the public sphere involved such close and constant body contact. Modern dancing so clearly flouted the Confucian precept that "men and women must keep a distance during social intercourse" (*nannü shoushou buqin*) that it inevitably set the stage for conflict. For while Confucian morality was no longer an overriding concern among Chinese elites, the Confucian legacy continued to haunt Chinese perceptions of modernity and morality. In 1926, in the premiere issue of *Liangyou*, a photograph showing an elegant Chinese couple dancing was accompanied by a small explanation that read: "The Western wind floods the East. Chinese youth both male and female embrace each other in pairs, exhibiting the Western style of dancing." The magazine went on to claim: "Dancing was originally among the highest of the arts, existing in China from ancient times. However, never did men and women embrace each other while dancing!" It ended on a note of alarm: "I am not one to entirely oppose men and women embracing while dancing. Yet this trend is slowly spreading in China, and whether it lasts long in Chinese society or not, it is still becoming a problem. Please consider this problem, and find an answer!"[84] This view implicitly likened Western dancing, and the "Western tide" (*xichao*) in general, to a disease that was slowly spreading into the national body, leading to future calamity if not taken care of immediately. Such attitudes persisted despite the increased popularity of dancing in the 1930s. In *Jingbao*, an editorial in 1930 argued that European civilization, though respectable in many other senses, should nevertheless be criticized for having kept up the barbaric institution of dancing.[85] Using the Confucian argument that one should study another's strong points and avoid learning his frailties, the author stressed that dancing should be omitted from the program of Western learning. "The dance hall is a den of decadence for youth," concluded the essay, mentioning several tragic examples, including a large fight that had occurred the previous year at the Sun Sun company dance hall, and the recent suicide of the dancing hostess Huang Baiying.

Many unfavorable representations of dancing youth described their actions as unfilial, thus contravening the primary Confucian virtue required of the son or daughter. A cartoon that appeared in *Liangyou* in 1931 shows an old woman in the countryside being washed away by a flood. Using a washbasin as a boat, she struggles to fight the tide with a broomstick oar. Meanwhile, her son dances away with a lovely partner in a Shanghai dance hall (see fig. 9).[86] An article in *Libailiu* in 1935 described a dancing hostess named Yang Aiyuan, who "leads a life of dissipation and cares nothing for her mother."[87] After a stint at the Black Cat as their number one hostess, Yang left her sickly mother in Shanghai under the care of her little sister and went to Xiamen to find a job as a dancing hostess. *Jingbao* also reported that a certain dancing hostess bought a graveyard for her

9. The son dancing in Shanghai while the mother is drifting in the flooded countryside (*Liangyou*, no. 64 [Dec. 1931]: 42).

mother and grandmother: "Probably the most filial girl among the thousands of dancers in Shanghai."[88]

Others countered this strand of Confucian conservatism by claiming that Chinese culture itself had sullied the once pristine art of Western dancing. Cartoonist and writer Xiao Jianqing, in a Chinese guidebook written for a non-Shanghai audience, argued: "Many people think that dance halls in Shanghai are a decadent industry. Actually, dancing in Western European countries is not an 'evil' (*elie*) phenomenon.[89] However, once it came to the East, it was seen by sex-crazed people and by profit-seeking merchants as a kind of sexual enterprise."[90] Similarly, in the context of the New Life movement, during which dance halls and other foreign institutions such as Hollywood films came under attack by social critics and ideologues, a writer who went by the pen name of "Romantic Scholar" (Langman Shusheng) retorted that dancing itself was a civilized act, but that "immoral" (*beibi*) people "make it indecent" (*shangfenghua*).[91] The answer accordingly was not to ban dance halls, but rather to see that such places maintained a strict standard of decorum. Bowing to the patriotic sentiments of the times, Romantic Scholar ended by stating that "If those with a will act to save entertainment, not to proscribe it, then the nation can also be saved."

Following trends in Chinese political culture, the Confucian conservatism that influenced perceptions of dancing in the twenties sided with and eventually gave way to antidance movements motivated by patriotism. At key moments in the history of the nation, patriots and government officials argued that the proper citizen should invest his or her money and time in saving China from foreign invasion rather than engaging in frivolous entertainment such as dancing. Three news items that made the *New York Times* suffice to illustrate the connections between cabaret and the politics of patriotism:[92] (1) On August 7, 1933, the municipal government of Beiping under the leadership of mayor Yuan Liang banned cabarets, claiming them to be "unpatriotic" while the country was under siege. (2) On November 1, 1934, the presidents of Shanghai's colleges collectively agreed to forbid students to attend cabarets on pain of expulsion. (3) In the wake of the Japanese invasion of China in 1937, following threats from patriots to blow up dance halls in Shanghai that "in the midst of terrible suffering, have been going full blast each night," the government ordered all Chinese dance halls to be converted into hospitals. Whether any of these governmental and collegiate decrees were actually followed is another matter. Despite Beiping's official ban on cabarets, foreign-owned clubs featuring Russian and Chinese dancing hostesses continued to operate under extraterritorial protection. In the mid-1930s, despite the New Life movement's attempts to eradicate dance hall culture, students and other urbanites continued to patronize cabarets and see "bad" Hollywood films. After Japan's takeover of Shanghai in 1937, any cabaret that had been converted into a hospital was just as likely to be converted back.

Nevertheless, threats made on cabarets by zealous patriots were serious and consistent. In 1933, following the second anniversary of the January 28 Incident—the date when Japan attacked northern Shanghai—a patriotic organization sent a number of pamphlets to theaters and ballrooms in the International Settlement, upbraiding them for not closing down to honor the day of infamy, and "requesting" funds for the patriotic cause.[93] In March of 1939, during the citywide celebration of the Chinese new year, the "Blood-Spirit Traitors Extermination Association" sent members out to litter the streets with pamphlets calling cabaretgoers "traitors," and enjoining them to commit their money, time, and lives to the cause of saving the nation rather than dancing while their compatriots died on the front.[94] That same day, bombs consisting of firecrackers tightly packed in cigarette cases were thrown by unknown assailants into Ciro's and other nightclubs, but exploded harmlessly. In 1942, a more powerful bomb went off inside the Grantown ballroom during its busiest hour, killing a teaboy and injuring six others. With the aid of the Japanese constabulary, the Shanghai Municipal Police conducted a detailed investigation of the bombing, and interrogated dozens of the more than four hundred people who had been in attendance during the incident. Again, evidence was found linking the act to patriotic anti-Japanese associations.[95]

Nationalism, as Joseph Levenson discussed in his masterwork, *Confucian China and Its Modern Fate*, was the modern Chinese counterpart to Confucianism, the ideological glue that had held the Chinese empire together for centuries.[96] Patriotism, expressed in radical antidance pamphlets in terms of the physical boundaries of the nation then under seige, was filiality writ large. Like the unfilial young men and women of popular lore who were criticized for dancing while their parents suffered, dance hall patrons during the Japanese occupation were considered by patriotic activists as traitors for having rejected or ignored the commitment to the political, cultural, and territorial integrity of their nation, leaving their compatriots to fight a brutal war while they spent a life of leisure in Japanese-run dance halls. Taken together, both strains of argument viewed nightclubbing as a selfish act that compromised the familial, cultural, and national ties that bound Chinese citizens to each other in times of great crisis.

In 1948, cabarets, no longer under the extraterritorial protection of foreign settlements, once again came under attack by the government for ostensibly patriotic reasons. In the summer of 1947, while the civil war between the Nationalists and Communists was still raging, the KMT issued a declaration forbidding dancing throughout the entire country, on the premise that it was detrimental to wartime morale.[97] At the time, in Shanghai there were still over 800 licensed dancing hostesses working in two dozen establishments, not to mention an equal number of managers and property holders, so that altogether several thousand people suffered as a consequence of the decree to ban dancing. Leading representatives of dancers and management gathered together and held their first meeting on Nanjing East Road, discussing possibilities for action. The association sent a group of representatives to the Bureau of Social Affairs (Shehui ju) in order to persuade the authorities not to carry out the decree, but to no avail.

On January 31, 1948, over 2,000 people met at the New Zealand (Xin xianlin) dance hall for another meeting. During this meeting they received news that the decree was to be carried out, and so again sent representatives to the Bureau of Social Affairs, but were again refused a hearing. Finally, the angry crowd stormed *en masse* to the bureau, where Public Security Bureau police met them at the gates. They fought the police with bamboo staffs and sticks, and whatever other makeshift weapons they could gather, and made their way into the bureau, which they proceeded to ransack. Eventually the police sent reinforcements and arrested over 600 people, whom they then interrogated under the belief that Communists had led the uprising. The female prisoners answered that they had simply been deprived of their livelihood, and that it was the authorities themselves who were at fault in the matter. In the end, the KMT canceled the ban and released the prisoners.

Conclusion

The Chinese elite tradition of courtship and concubinage carried out in the courtesan houses of old was reinvented in the modern urban space of the cabaret, reflecting the emergence of a new moneyed elite that compared and contested their accomplishments within the enlarged arena of the modern cosmopolis. Cabaret hostesses, whose songs and dances were mixtures of native poetry and foreign rhythms (as in "Dance Hall Song"), served as surrogates for the dying institution of the courtesan, yet did so while operating in a modern cultural, economic, and political context. For both men and women in cosmopolitan Shanghai, cabarets, cafes, restaurants, hotels, and racetracks were sites of assimilation into the newly internationalized world order. These women thus played a dual role: they served as substitutes for the dimly remembered pleasures of the courtesan world during its heights, as envisioned by men such as Yao Hsin-nung, and at the same time served to initiate Shanghai natives into the manners and mores of the modern world.

The Good, the Bad, and the Beautiful: Movie Actresses and Public Discourse in Shanghai, 1920s-1930s

MICHAEL G. CHANG

> From a photographic negative . . . one can make any number of prints; to ask for the "authentic" print makes no sense.
> —Walter Benjamin, "The Work of Art in the Age of Mechanical Reproduction" (1936)

Introduction

Movie actresses were some of the most upwardly mobile and visible women in 1920s and 1930s Shanghai. Their rise to fame was part and parcel of a visually oriented mass media revolution, which included the emergence of China's Shanghai-based film industry as well as the pictorial press.[1] Indeed, high visibility and various forms of publicity were the very clouds upon which any actress's career floated.

The use of actresses for female roles had almost disappeared as a popular practice in Chinese drama during the seventeenth century; it only reemerged in the late nineteenth century.[2] The world of silent film, however, stood in marked contrast to that of live theater, and arguments for the presence of women on the silver screen in a 1927 *Funü zazhi* (Women's journal) article were based upon the purely visual nature of early cinematic representation:

> Because movies have no sound and words that might assist in expression, everything depends on movements and gestures. The performance is completely real and is com-

pletely intolerant of disguise. Thus, women must be sought out to play the female roles that must be included in movies.

The central points in art are "beauty" (*mei*) and "authenticity" (*zhen*). When speaking of "authenticity," the use of women to play female roles is, of course, the best. When speaking of "beauty," within one type of art, there is also the need for females.[3]

An even more plausible reason for women taking to the screen was that "in the hearts of the vast audience, they all hope that there is a beautiful woman (*nüxing*) acting in the movie they are watching."[4] Women's direct participation in the movie-making process was related to issues of visual authenticity and a commercial viability based upon sexual desire. An authentic object called "woman"—to be *seen* and then "known" and "had"—was necessary. Whether based on artistic or commercial criteria, film demanded the physical (sexual) presence of women. In fact, the very "essence" and "brightness of movie stars" was defined in terms of a woman's body—specifically her eyes and her neck (see figs. 10, 11).[5] But the notion of a female movie star was, from the outset, fraught with tensions generated by such physicality and visibility. Women who participated in such an unprecedented degree of mass publicity, and in such a bodily manner, epitomized the moral ambiguities of urban life—ambiguities that threatened those would-be gentry members who were nostalgic for a patriarchal order that was clearly in decline in the socially and sexually fluid milieu of early twentieth-century Shanghai. During the late 1920s a negative discourse emerged to delegitimize upwardly mobile actresses, and notoriety became the sibling of celebrity. This early discourse on movie actresses was enfolded in a more general and widespread public discourse on dangerous women.

In the 1920s, movie actresses were categorically characterized as degenerate, corrupted, and deceptive "starlets"—amateurs who, like prostitutes, were morally and sexually suspect. But by the 1930s, full-fledged movie stars (*mingxing*) emerged who were individually praised for courtesanlike talent, virtue, innocence, and sincerity. However, these evaluations were clearly linked, via the standards of "true character" (*bense*, literally "original color") and the "good girl," to movie actresses' standing *as women*.

By the mid-1930s female movie stars in Shanghai were clearly more media darlings than demimondaines. Although the promotional discourse of the 1930s was positive and inclusive, it was as confining or disciplinary as any other discourse. Fiction and gossip, as well as film criticism based upon standards of the "good girl" and "true character" acting, were all critical in defining the bounds of acceptable behavior for movie actresses both on and off screen as well as for urban women in general. Inherent within such discourses were a set of hierarchies and value judgments about how women did and should behave. But instead of drawing attention to itself (its own disciplinary operations and effects,

10. The brightness of movie stars: the eyes (*Beiyang huabao* [Nov. 13, 1926]).

11. The brightness of movie stars: the neck (*Beiyang huabao* [Nov. 6, 1926]).

its own interests and desires), the critical standard of "true character" acting and the "good girl" focused the attention of critics, fans, and actresses themselves on "acting well" with promises of public praise, fame, reward, and assistance.

The entity of *nü mingxing*, then, was a discourse. It "intended to *constitute* the ground whereon to decide *what shall count as a fact* in the matters under consideration [namely, womanhood and female sexuality] and to determine *what mode of comprehension* is best suited to the understanding of the facts thus constituted."[6] Seeing *nü mingxing* as discourse does not reduce or trivialize it to a language game, for the identities of individual actresses ("who" they were) could be separated neither from the category of *nü mingxing* ("what" they were), nor from the discourses that marked them (their bodies) as such. Once one acknowledges this point, one cannot but take the discursive entity of *nü mingxing* seriously as something that produces and regulates subjects linked to concrete fields of institutionalized power.

Even when individual women themselves moved to shape and control the production of those discursive structures in which they lived (through such practices as editing their own screenplays, directing and producing their own movies, writing and publishing their own prose, and/or speaking publicly themselves) they could only grasp at an ideal of "liberation." The costs of constituting oneself as a certain kind of subject (*nü mingxing* and *nüxing*) and then entering the discursive fray were quite real, as the case of Ruan Lingyu's (1910–35) suicide demonstrates.

The rise (and fall) of female movie stars in Shanghai during the 1920s and 1930s must be understood within an even broader context of a shifting social structure—namely, the slow decline of former gentry elites and the rise of a professionalized urban middle class. The gradual displacement between the last half of the nineteenth century and the first decades of the twentieth century of those gentry elites, whose socioeconomic power traditionally derived from landowning and office-holding, by a newly emergent and professionalized urban middle class (bourgeoisie), whose power derived more and more from commercialized activities, was accompanied by the "sexualization" of old-style courtesans who served the entertainment and companionate needs of gentry elites and who were pivotal in reproducing those elites' cultural and social hegemony.[7] The introduction of new technologies such as mechanized printing, photography, and cinematography allowed nouveau riches to assert themselves socially and culturally. The rise of movie actresses in the late 1920s and then of full-fledged female movie stars in the early 1930s coincided with these historical circumstances. As late Qing courtesans, who had once catered to the tastes and values of an urban-based gentry clientele, became more and more "sexualized" in their activities, they eventually melted into the category of common prostitutes. At the same time, female movie stars rose from the notoriety that accompanied being equated with prostitutes to enjoy fame as the "courtesanlike" companions of China's newly arrived urban elites, who came to full-fledged power and prominence during the late 1920s and early 1930s. My argument here is not one of straightforward causality or of class conflict as the engine of history, but rather suggests a number of historical adjacencies and conjunctures.

In this essay, I do not focus on the texts of films that were so powerful because of their realistic qualities. Instead, I will concentrate upon re-presentations of female movie stars themselves and their "private" lives in fan magazines, popular journals, and newspapers. These texts were even more "realistic" than films because they were filled with direct references to "real-life" people and events outside of the movie theater. The phenomenon of the female movie star was a form of discourse consisting not only of written words, but also of a number of new urban practices such as moviegoing, reading fan magazines, writing fan letters, circulating and collecting personally autographed photographs, writing movie criticism, ranking of stars in contests, and so on. The institutionalization of such practices in a number of discourses delineated the possibilities and parameters for two constitutive elements of social being—physical comportment and emotional expression—and thus collectively produced and reproduced a number of interrelated subjectivities (movie star, fan, critic). The subject position of *nü mingxing* was the pivotal element in this constellation. It produced a set of centered subjectivities (via various discourses) in which *nü mingxing* was understood as a naively reflective role through which some interiorized "self" and authentic fact of "woman" ought to be at once identified and then re-presented both on and off screen.

I have found the term "generation" useful as a way to describe a group of individual actresses who rose to stardom in a similar working environment which was dependent upon developments in the film industry alone. It should be read strictly as a reference to changes within China's early film industry itself, not to larger social changes. Thus, a "generation" of actresses may be separated in age by only a few years, rather than 15–30 years as is usually assumed when discussing "generational" changes in a strictly demographic sense. But who were some of China's first "generation" of movie actresses? And how was their rise to stardom enfolded in a public discourse on movie actresses?

The First Generation: Wang Hanlun and Yang Naimei

China's earliest actresses used anonymous performing names like "Miss F F" or "Miss A A" and were mostly part-time amateurs with pretty faces.[8] Two of China's first truly individualized female movie stars, however, were Wang Hanlun (1903–78) and Yang Naimei (1904–60) (see figs. 12, 13).[9]

In 1923 a star was born. Peng Jianping, a typist at Shanghai's "Four Brights" *hong* (Siming yanghang), tried out for the female lead in Mingxing Film Company's first full-length feature *Guer jiuzu ji* (The orphan rescues grandfather) at the behest of her co-worker, Ren Jinping, and got the part.[10] *The Orphan Rescues Grandfather* was completed after three months of filming. The film was a huge financial success that put Mingxing in the black and sent the company well on its way to becoming one of Shanghai's dominant film studios in the 1920s and 1930s. After the release of *The Orphan Rescues Grandfather* in the fall of 1923, Peng Jianqing's family was disgusted that she had sunk to the level of a mere actor (*xizi*). At the age of 20, Peng cut kinship ties, changed her name to Wang Hanlun, joined Mingxing's full-time roster, and immediately began working on a second film, *Yuli hun* (Spirit of the jade pear, 1924). Wang Hanlun went on to star in more than ten films over the next five years and established herself as one of China's first full-fledged movie stars.

Yang Naimei made her first film appearance in *Spirit of the Jade Pear*.[11] In the early spring of 1923 Mingxing director Zhang Shichuan was looking for an actress to play the wealthy socialite protagonist of *Spirit of the Jade Pear*. Screenwriter Zheng Zhengqiu recommended Yang, and director Zhang went along. Yang's performance in *Spirit of the Jade Pear* impressed Zhang Shichuan so much that he asked her to stay on and act in his next film *Youhun* (Seductive marriage, 1924). Yang's father disapproved, since he wanted his daughter to continue her education abroad in England; however, like Wang Hanlun, Yang Naimei went against her family's wishes and became one of China's first movie stars, making more than ten movies in all before leaving the film industry in the late 1920s.

How exactly did Wang Hanlun and Yang Naimei rise to stardom? A former actor from the 1920s, Gong Jia'nong, has made a distinction between "fame" (*chengming*), based solely on name recognition, and "achievements" (*chenggong*), based more on genuine skills or talents. In his memoirs Gong recalls that there was no time to formally study acting technique, nor was it valued, for "it was as if once you entered the film world . . . boring dinner parties and social events geared towards a certain purpose occupied all of our free time."[12] Present-day literary and cultural critics have also written about this distinction between "fame" and "achievements." Indeed, some see the entire notion of "fame" based on concrete achievements as an outdated term that should simply be replaced by a vacuous "celebrity" based on high visibility in the age of mass communications.[13]

During the 1920s, movie stardom was still situated squarely within the world

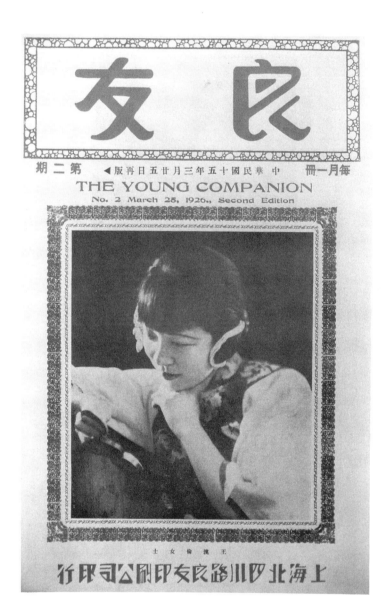

12. Wang Hanlun: an early movie star (*Liangyou*, no. 2 [Mar. 1926]: front cover).

13. Yang Naimei: an early movie star (Gan Yazi et al.).

of live performance and face-to-face interaction. Much of Wang Hanlun and Yang Naimei's stardom was generated by promotional tours. After starring in Tianyi's *Dianying nü mingxing* (Movie actresses) in 1926 with the young Hu Die (1907–89) in a supporting role, Wang Hanlun went on a promotional tour of Southeast Asia. She was booked on an eight-month tour in which she would give live *kunqü* performances at numerous movie theaters where *Movie Actresses* was playing.[14] Yang Naimei also relied on the practice of promotional stage appearances at movie showings in making a name for herself. In winter 1927 Yang promoted the release of *Liangxin de fuhuo* (Rekindling of conscience) by performing a musical scene from the movie live on stage at Shanghai's Central Theater.[15] By the spring of 1928 Yang Naimei had generated a sizeable fan base. When she traveled with the Mingxing film crew to shoot scenes for *Hubian chunmeng* (Spring dream by the lakeside) on location in Hangzhou, hundreds of fans greeted her at the train station. The relationships between movie stars and their fans in the 1920s, however, were limited to these sorts of face-to-face encounters. China's earliest movie fans were not yet cultivated in the flow and exchange of autographs and photos or even fan mail, and the only interaction that Yang Naimei's Hangzhou fans hoped for in 1928 was to catch a harmless glimpse of their idol "in person."[16]

The rise of Wang Hanlun and Yang Naimei was based more upon their outward appearance and "live" or face-to-face interaction than upon pure acting talent as we might define quality acting today (that is, as the art and skill of convincingly portraying a wide range of characters). Both Wang Hanlun and Yang Naimei secured their first roles because they looked the part. This is not to deny that Wang Hanlun and Yang Naimei had any genuine acting skills. My point here is only to illustrate that women were not recognized and rewarded for *acting well*, but rather for *acting good* and acting like "themselves." These standards of judgment were specifically gendered criteria that held only for actresses. The tendency to discourage artifice and deceptiveness in an actress's performances on screen became much more apparent and restrictive in the 1930s.

China's fledgling film "industry" did not, however, exclude women like Wang Hanlun and Yang Naimei from owning the means by which their fame was produced. By the late 1920s both Wang Hanlun and Yang Naimei had made enough connections in the film world and had amassed enough money to finance their own production companies—the Hanlun Film Company and the Naimei Film Company. In 1926 Wang Hanlun purchased the rights to Bao Tianxiao's script *Mangmu de aiqing* (Blind love) and began production. She rented equipment and bought studio time from Mingxing. She starred in the film herself and invited Mingxing's Bu Wancang to direct. Director Bu, however, was unreliable and often failed to show up for filming, and so the project soon devolved into a one-woman show on all fronts—financing, production, and promotion. In the end, Wang bought her own projector and spent forty days editing the movie herself. She then took *Blind Love* on the road and showed it to audiences throughout China. During intermissions, she would take to the stage and get feedback from the audience. The film turned a profit, which Wang Hanlun then used to retire from the film world in 1928.

Yang Naimei's venture into film production was much more financially tenuous than that of Wang Hanlun. In April 1928 Yang was fascinated by the news of a woman from Hong Kong, Yu Meiyan, who had committed suicide in Shanghai at the age of 31, and wanted to shoot a film based on the sensational story.[17] After obtaining the requisite capital from the military governor of Shandong, Zhang Zongchang, Yang set up shop on Jin Shenfu Road in September 1928.[18] She played the lead role in the film version of the Yu Meiyan story, *Qi nüzi* (Extraordinary girl), which was the Naimei Film Company's first and only production; it came and went with little fanfare in 1929.

In the wide-open film industry of the 1920s Wang Hanlun and Yang Naimei were movers and shakers in the spheres of both cultural production and consumption. In 1925 Yang Naimei was living a comfortable life as a trend-setter on the Shanghai fashion scene. The reputations of stores such as Yong'an Company and the Huiluo Company located on the Bund were based upon the patronage of stars such as Wang and Yang.[19] All eyes at the Carleton Dance Hall fell on Yang Naimei, decked out in her sequined dresses; and within a week everyone who was anyone was dressed to match.[20] Yang's residence on Prince Edward Road also served as a social club for her film industry and journalist friends.

Movie actresses were clearly a prominent, if not a predominant, presence and social and cultural force in Shanghai by the 1920s. But their rapid rise coincided with the proliferation of a negative discourse on actresses, for these new arbiters of value and taste transgressed two social boundaries at once: those of class and gender. This 1920s commentary on actresses was hardly monolithic; a hodgepodge of views and voices ranging from those in the film industry to movie fans to social and cultural critics chimed in. However, all but a few of these early perceptions of actresses during the 1920s were shaped by a discourse on urban women in general that appeared outside of the film world.[21]

Sex, the City, and Cinema: The 1920s Discourse on Dangerous Women

There was an implicit danger embedded in the storyline of young men and women taking off for the big city in search of fame and fortune, for cities were populated by free-floating bodies. The consciousness of dangers in the city was often clearly gendered, since sex (both as a biological distinction and as a physical act) was an overriding concern. The mere presence of women provided the underpinnings for many moral misgivings regarding urban life.[22] A woman who had sojourned to the city for the same reasons as men (opportunities for work and advancement) was already suspect and problematic, if not outright dangerous, by virtue of her sex.[23] Such widely shared perceptions were reflected in the characterizations of urban women as pursuers and providers of pleasure and entertainment—as femme fatales, prostitutes, and actresses tied to no kin. The concept of "woman" as a site of moral contention was prevalent in Chinese film and fiction. The portrayal of the city as a corrupting force in women's lives played itself out in many films such as *Yichuan zhenzhu* (A string of pearls, 1925), *Taohua qixue ji* (Peach blossom weeps tears of blood, 1931), *Xiao wanyi* (Little toys, 1933), *Shennü* (Goddess, 1934), *Zimei hua* (Twin sisters, 1934), and *Xin nüxing* (New woman, 1935).[24]

The perils involved in sojourning to and living in Shanghai were the main themes of Mu Shiying, a well-known modernist writer in the 1930s.[25] Mu's "Shanghai de hubuwu" (Shanghai foxtrot), published in 1932, tells the story of a young man who is financially and sexually duped by a slippery seductress while playing the horses at the Shanghai racetrack (*paoma ting*).[26] Mu Shiying was hardly hitting on anything new, for a different story published some seven years earlier—"Dianju yuanzhong" (In the movie theater)—worked off of the same basic formula as "Shanghai Foxtrot."[27] The predictable plot of "In the Movie Theater" provides us with contemporary notions of how a stereotypical Shanghai femme fatale operated.

The male protagonist of this story, Wang Lucheng, goes to see a movie by himself one day. Cai Xiaomei (literally "Smiling Plum" Cai), a brash young woman who has American-style curls and wears seductively revealing clothing, is sitting in the row behind him. Cai asks Wang if he has a light for her cigarette. After some bantering back and forth about movies, Cai invites Wang to sit next to her and help her in reading the script-program for the movie.[28] Throughout their conversation, Wang is both a paragon and a parody of propriety—all formalities and sweaty brow—while Miss Cai is playful and at ease, telling Wang to loosen up a bit. Once the lights go out, Miss Cai gives Mr. Wang an "unspeakable greeting"—a kiss or something less innocent? Then the newly coupled couple moves to the back row of the theater to exchange more intimacies for the rest of the show. After the movie is over, Wang and Cai leave, both smiling (who wouldn't be?), hand-in-hand. Two weeks later, Mr. Wang wears a long and troubled face. Apparently Miss Cai hasn't bothered to stay in touch. In order to cheer him up, Wang's friends take him out to see a movie, *Shanghai yi furen* (A woman in Shanghai, 1925). Throughout the movie Wang overhears a couple behind him whispering sweet nothings to each other and recalls his own fling with Miss Cai two weeks earlier. Predictably, he is shocked when the theater lights come on and he finds the woman sitting behind him with another man is none other than (ho-hum) Cai Xiaomei.

The plot of "In the Movie Theater" draws upon the same premises as Mu Shiying's "Shanghai Foxtrot." The two stories only differ in their settings and in the fact that the femme fatale of "In the Movie Theater" at least leaves the male protagonist with his wallet, though not his pride, intact. The associations between movies, betrayal, deception, and sex in this story serve to fuse the qualities of the femme fatale, the actress, and the prostitute into one. This was the essence of "a woman of Shanghai."

Another short story published in 1926 and entitled "Dianying mingxing" (Movie star) clearly illustrates the prevalent notion in 1920s Shanghai that movie actresses were nothing more than prostitutes in disguise.[29] "Movie Star" parodies the rise of a prostitute named Yan Hong (Crimson) to the ranks of a so-called movie star by setting her success against the backdrop of Shanghai's fledgling film industry when "everyone seemed to be starting their own film company" and when "almost anyone who made a movie was considered a star." Although the story reads more like thinly veiled reportage than imaginative fiction and is much too blunt and didactic in tone to be effective as a parody, it is still indicative of the dubious image that actresses had in the mid-1920s. The narrator of the story attributes the rise of so-called movie stars to the propensity of yellow journalists and the mosquito press to spin "stars" out of thin air as well as to a shortage of actors and actresses resulting from the reluctance of most families to allow their sons and daughters to enter the degenerate world of film. Yan Hong was lured by the prospect of making big money in the film world and began working for the "Boring Film Company." Shortly afterwards she assumes the appearance of a female student by undoing her smooth braids and fluffing her hair into disheveled curls; donning tortoiseshell glasses; wearing short skirts and high heels; and dropping her fluent Suzhou dialect for a more Westernized Mandarin peppered with a few "Miss's" and "Mister's." Indeed, the protagonist's disheveled hair (a sign of disorder) and Suzhou dialect are clear signs that the narrator views her rise to stardom as a holdover from the courtesan era. But the duplicity of Yan Hong's career does not end there, for the entire film world is full of deceit. "Movie Star" ends by describing how the Boring Film Company sets a new trend by hypocritically making films that address social problems, specifically the immorality of the film world itself. There are other pieces of fiction that one might cite as examples of similarly damning portraits of actresses and the film world;[30] however, the negative discourse on actresses spread well beyond the realm of fiction.

In China, actors and actresses had traditionally been associated with less respectable and uneducated members of society—prostitutes, dancing girls, and thieves. These attitudes persisted into the late 1920s as the viability of working as an actress began to attract increasing numbers of young women. A 1927 article in the widely circulated *Funü zazhi* (Women's journal) was derisive of the relationship between women and the fledgling film industry:

> Almost all of the women who step onto the stage are the wives of actors, lowly women, and prostitutes who generally lead the disgusting lives of streetwalkers. We can guess what their values, their principles, and their hopes are.[31]

The same article classifies movie actresses into four different types: (1) those who had no other means of livelihood; (2) those who were lured by the promise of higher salaries and thus abandoned old occupations; (3) unprincipled prostitutes who only sought fame, fortune, and power; and (4) registered prostitutes who were disgusted with selling their sexual services. Wang Hanlun clearly fit into category number two, and she herself recalled, "Because many actors and actresses [in the early 1920s] were only part-time, there were second-rate performers, and also prostitutes."[32] Although the author may not have been too far off, his classification scheme reveals more about the anxieties felt by elites whose own social power was being undermined by the emergence of the cinematic medium. The roots of the problem for these declining elites were the purveyors of film, not the medium of film itself; for the purportedly low social origins of moviemakers and "their" women (actresses) threatened to debase the potentially lofty and respectable cultural form of film:

> What are the characters of these above-mentioned women? No words are necessary! They simply cannot imagine what morality or art are. The male side of the film world and those playboys look down upon them and thus hunt them as so many pieces of meat (*shijian tamen de lieyan zhuyi*).[33]

Here were the beginnings of a discourse on actresses in which the central issue was social mobility of women—an issue of both class and gender. This early discourse on actresses was meant to counterbalance and cordon off the potential for moral degeneracy involved when putting the faces and bodies of women from suspicious social backgrounds up on the silver screen. It was meant to exclude and delegitimize anyone who might become culturally and socially influential via the medium of film. But both delegitimization and exclusion were gendered precisely because they were achieved via the trope of "woman." The negative commentary of the 1920s focused on actresses, and behind the success of movie actresses lay the prospects of success for a whole new group of cultural players—filmmakers. Morally suspect women were classed with those men who engaged in filmmaking and who were thus guilty of degeneracy by association.

Efforts to maintain class distinctions via the morally charged category of "woman" became more pronounced as the likelihood of mistaking movie actresses for women of high society increased. Urban women from various social backgrounds began to strike the same poses, wear the same clothes, and share the same tastes. The power of actresses such as Yang Naimei and Wang Hanlun in setting Shanghai's fashion trends attested to the declining influence of traditional arbiters of value and taste. As women moved into new spheres of activity and became independent wage-earners, attempts to hold more upwardly mobile women in check were expressed through standards of feminine virtue. Outward beauty and material trappings could be had by most anyone in Shanghai in the 1920s, even female cotton-mill workers;[34] but to be truly educated and thus genuinely moral was still very much a privilege of the the upper classes. Morality was the last enclave of upper-class superiority in a topsy-turvy urban landscape. The story "Movie Star" explicitly highlighted the dubiousness of the movie star and former prostitute Yan Hong who assumed the costume and mannerisms of a female student. Appearance was not moral reality.

Class and gender boundaries were also respectively blurred and reinforced in the pages of urban pictorials such as *Liangyou* (The young companion) and *Beiyang huapao* (The pei-yang pictorial news). The front page of any given edition of these Republican-era pictorials might feature a photograph of a movie actress, a female student, or the wife or daughter of some powerful personage, all of whom struck fragile poses of femininity—eyes turned demurely away and hands delicately drawn inwards.[35] One might not be able to distinguish these cover girls in terms of their social positions, but there was no doubt concerning their gender. Although movie actresses and elite women made the same gendered gestures on the covers of magazines, they remained separated by class. Movie actresses never appeared in "women's pages" alongside those genteel ladies of high society: writers, painters, socialites (*dajia guixiu* or *minggui*), the educated and the wealthy.[36] They were always clearly identified and separated out. The category of "movie actress" simultaneously promulgated the quintessence of feminine comportment, yet guaranteed the maintenance of a visual separation needed to reinforce and preserve crucial class distinctions, not only between women of different moral stature, but also between those men with whom they were associated.

The 1920s perceptions of actresses, however, did not reflect some objective reality. Wang Hanlun and Yang Naimei, two of China's first movie actresses, were both from educated and affluent (yet declining) backgrounds. The discourse on actresses in the 1920s, in effect, served to police the nested boundaries of gender and class. The independent power of *women* was not recognized by the 1920s commentary on actresses, and yet women were its primary object of analysis. It was movie actresses, *not* actors, whose moral characters came under direct attack. Women became the lightning rods for class tensions which were often expressed in explicitly gendered terms as male cultural power-holders used negative terms to describe actresses not only to control women themselves, but also to attack male rivals who might rise to cultural power via the medium of film.

Another distinctive feature of the negative discourse on actresses in the 1920s was that it revolved around a categorical indictment of movie actresses. Individuals were never singled out except as fictional characters in short stories that were meant to be interpreted from the "world-in-a-drop-of-water" perspective of imaginative fiction. However, individual actresses soon came to the fore in the discourse on actresses as Shanghai's film industry experienced a number of structural transformations in the late 1920s and early 1930s that resulted in a studio-centered form of organization.

During the early Republican period individual artists and entrepreneurs, both foreign and Chinese, were capitalizing and organizing the Chinese film industry in a major way. The first major institutional breakthrough came in the fall of 1917 when Shanghai's Commercial Press brought together the worlds of publishing and film by opening a film department under the auspices of its already-established photography section.[37] Only five Chinese studios were producing films in the 1910s, but by the early 1920s the film industry took off as the number of studios, theaters, and moviegoers skyrocketed. In 1925 there were some 40 to 60 Shanghai-based production companies, many of which were fly-by-night operations run by amateurs with big ambitions but only enough capital to rent equipment and studio time.[38] Two years later the number of production companies had tripled to a nationwide total of 181, with 151 of these in Shanghai alone.[39] With the rapid development of film technology and the onset of a global economic depression in the late 1920s and early 1930s, many small studios consolidated themselves into larger and more highly capitalized conglomerates; but the vast majority soon discovered that reality truly does bite, floundered by the wayside, and went belly-up.[40] Shanghai was soon dubbed "Hollywood of the East" as China's film industry began to revolve around a handful of studios located there—Mingxing (Star), Lianhua (United), Yihua (China Artist), and Tianyi (Unique). These studios went on to reign oligarchically over China's film industry until the Japanese occupation of the entrepot in 1937.

The rise of the studio system and of individual stars were two sides of the same coin, for a studio's success depended on its ability to create and maintain a stable of stars. This generated a new "promotional discourse" that revolved around particular vocabularies of praise. By the 1930s much of the commentary on actresses originated from within the film industry itself and appeared in fan magazines. Those individual women who worked in the film industry after Wang Hanlun and Yang Naimei followed quite different paths to movie stardom. They had to deal with much more prolific discourses as well as with a body of knowledge about actresses that was generated by a society much more savvy to the workings of the urban mass media, and their careers and public personae were the creations of a highly efficient promotional apparatus.

The Second Generation: Hu Die and Ruan Lingyu

By 1929 both Wang Hanlun and Yang Naimei had faded from the film world.[41] But directors, producers, and film bosses were always on the lookout for fresh faces and new personalities. Following close on the heels of Wang Hanlun and Yang Naimei down the road to stardom were Hu Die (Butterfly Wu, 1908–89) and Ruan Lingyu (Lily Yuen) (see figs. 14, 15). Hu and Ruan both started their careers during the mid-1920s, while Wang Hanlun and Yang Naimei were still in the business, and went on to become two of the most well-known movie stars in China during the 1930s.

14. Hu Die, a.k.a. Butterfly Wu:
the movie queen (ca. 1926, source
unknown).

Like Wang Hanlun and Yang Naimei, Hu Die came from a well-to-do family.[42]
She entered the China Film Academy (Zhonghua dianying xueyuan), China's
first motion picture acting school, in 1924.[43] She made her first movie appearance in *Victory* (Zhan'gong) produced by Zhonghua (China) Film Company in
1925 and signed with Tianyi, appearing in almost twenty films between 1925 and
1927. In 1928 Hu Die joined Mingxing where she worked with well-known directors Zheng Zhengqiu, Zhang Shichuan, and Bu Wancang as well as with Ruan
Lingyu. It was Hu Die's dual performance in *Twin Sisters* in 1934 and her role as
one of the Chinese representatives at both the Moscow International Film Festival and at the Berlin Film Festival in 1935 that put her over the top.

Ruan Lingyu came from a very different social background.[44] She did not attend acting school and auditioned for Mingxing director Bu Wancang in 1926
only at the behest of her brother-in-law, Zhang Huichong. Director Bu recognized Ruan's raw talent and signed her on. She appeared in five films while with
Mingxing, then followed director Bu to Da Zhonghua-Baihe (Great China-Lily)
Film Company in 1929. She made six more movies with Da Zhonghu-Baihe before moving to Lianhua in 1930 where she remained for the rest of her film ca-

15. Ruan Lingyu, a.k.a. Lily Yue
the tragic movie star (*Liangyou*
no. 30 [Sept. 1928]: front cover)

reer. Ruan's career peaked between 1932 and 1935, when she appeared in many leftist-inspired films.[45] Her career ended with her death in 1935.

The careers of Hu Die and Ruan Lingyu can each be divided into two distinct periods that coincide with two very different periods of Chinese film history. During the 1920s Hu and Ruan were merely two actresses among a myriad of others, virtually all of whom were churning out frivolous flicks of love and derring-do to keep the masses entertained. As Hu Die and Ruan Lingyu were each coming into their own in the early 1930s, the film industry was changing in fundamental ways. Film historians in the People's Republic of China (PRC) tend to attribute the rise of Hu Die and especially of Ruan Lingyu to the fact that they came under the influence of directors such as Tian Han, Wu Yonggang, Bu Wancang, and others who were sympathetic to the Chinese Communist Party's left-wing film movement, which had infiltrated big-name studios such as Mingxing and Lianhua in the early 1930s.[46] However, Ruan and Hu's popularity during the 1930s was not simply based upon ideological "progressiveness" and leftist leanings. The institutional structures of Shanghai's studio and promotional systems were also becoming more routinized and refined. New film technologies (namely, the introduction of sound) were changing the process of movie-making, and the proliferation of movie magazines generated new promotional schemes and new forms of fame grounded in a discourse on actresses that departed from their overwhelmingly negative image in the 1920s.[47] New technologies and promotional strategies, not politics, were the decisive factors in Hu and Ruan's success.

With the introduction of "talkie" technology on the cusp of the 1930s, many smaller studios were unable to keep up with the costs of retooling to sound. Undercapitalized companies could not afford to buy new equipment or to build the multiple sound stages needed to efficiently produce sound movies. Likewise, many silent film stars were unable to adapt to the world of the talkies. The biggest obstacle, of course, was that of spoken dialect: many cinematic performers hailed from either Guangdong or the Jiangnan region and did not speak clear or fluid Mandarin, if they spoke it at all. There were also other adjustments that had to be made, such as memorizing one's lines, making sure to project one's voice clearly, and taking directions only in between (as opposed to during) shots. All of these shifts led to a higher standard of professionalization that favored stage-acting skills and Mandarin. Although the impact of sound technology on the film world was jolting, the institutional realities of silent film were not immediately swept away. In fact, silent films lingered on and were widespread well into the 1930s simply because many movie theaters found the conversion to sound projection equipment too costly. Thus, the obsolescence of the silent film industry was not instantaneous. Still, the general trend toward sound movies was clear: it was only a matter of time before silent films would be not only silent, but also invisible.

Hu Die was well poised to make it big in the world of the "talkies" simply because she had spent a number of her childhood years in the Beiping-Tianjin area and could speak standard Mandarin. Prior to the 1930s, Hu Die was a well-known movie actress who appeared in many immensely popular knight-errant films of the day, such as Mingxing's cash-cow series of *Huoshao honglian si* (Burning of the red lotus temple).[48] Given her popularity and her ability to speak Mandarin, Hu Die was Mingxing's natural choice for the lead in their 1931 sound production *Genü hongmudan* (Sing-song girl Red Peony)—China's first sound movie.

The Third Generation: Professional Skills and the Gewutuan

The turn toward song and dance troupes in the early 1930s as pools for new film talent was driven by the technological shift to sound. The world of "talkies" privileged those who spoke Mandarin and possessed the skills of stage performance. The training that young girls received in China's first song and dance troupes fit the bill perfectly.

The man behind the development of these troupes was Li Jinhui (1891–1967).[49] In February 1927 Li started the China School for Song and Dance (Zhonghua gewu zhuanmen xuexiao, also known as Gezhuan). In 1927 Gezhuan's first class was made up of 40 or so students including future movie stars Wang Renmei (1914–87) and Li Lili (b. 1915) (see figs. 16, 17). Although Gezhuan recruited fifteen- and sixteen-year-old adolescents of both sexes, formal training was gendered: most of the girls were groomed for performances, while the boys were mainly trained as musicians. Tuition at the school was free and each day's regimen consisted of six class periods: four classes in song and dance (*gewu ke*) which included voice training, musical instruments, and dance; and two classes in "culture" (*wenhua ke*) which included such subjects as foreign language conversation, basic classes in theater history, musical theory, and so on.[50] When the school was disbanded in late 1927, Li took the remnants of Gezhuan and established the Meimei Girls School (Meimei nüxiao). Li had no idea how long he would be able to finance the Meimei Girls School venture and so began to plan and organize a song and dance troupe to promote China's "national language" in Southeast Asia.[51] Li was forced to disband the troupe in 1929 due to financial difficulties; however, within a few months he had once again reorganized the old members of China Song and Dance into a new troupe called the Bright Moon Song and Dance Troupe (Mingyue gewutuan) which he introduced to northern audiences in Beiping and Tianjin in the spring of 1930.[52] While in the north the Bright Moon Troupe recruited some new members, including future movie stars Hu Jia and Xue Lingxian who, along with Wang Renmei and Li Lili, were dubbed "Bright Moon's Four Heavenly Kings" (*Mingyue si da tianwang*).[53]

In May 1931 the general manager of Lianhua, Luo Mingyou, proposed a merger between the Bright Moon Song and Dance Troupe and his own company. China's first full-length sound film, *Sing-Song Girl Red Peony*, had been released in Shanghai by the Mingxing studio just two to three months earlier, and Luo wanted to increase the viability of his own company in the new era of the talkies. He needed the skills and talents of song and dance girls to do it, for they possessed both the skills and the innocent faces required to play female roles in the 1930s. In June 1931 Li Jinhui and Luo Mingyou struck a deal, and the Bright Moon Song and Dance Troupe changed its name to the Lianhua Song and Dance Group (Lianhua gewuban).[54]

Many actresses who had started their film careers in the 1920s, such as Wang Hanlun, Yang Naimei, and Ruan Lingyu, received no formal training in drama and came to the film industry as amateurs. By the 1930s, however, many of

16. Wang Renmei: the screen wildcat (*Liangyou*, no. 80 [Sept. 1933]: 30).

those women who were to become China's "third generation" movie stars were drawn from the world of "song and dance troupes" (*gewutuan*) and were highly skilled in music and theatrical arts.

The 1930s Discourse on Actresses, I: Acting Talent and the Courtesan Ethic

By the mid-1930s China's second and third "generations" of female movie stars were constituted within the discourse of a well-established urban mass media and a highly efficient promotional system. Their film careers were entirely the products of this system and the speed of their ascendancy attests to the effectiveness of the new promotional machinery.

Hu Die's rise to the top of China's film world provides a convenient window into the construction of *nü mingxing* in the 1930s. Her crowning in February 1933 as China's "Movie Queen" was the result of *Mingxing ribao*'s (Mingxing daily's) efforts to boost its own sales.[55] A new discourse of professionalism presided at ceremonies such as these, where movie actresses were praised for their acting

17. Li Lili: the athletic actress (middle), in a still from *Queen of Sports* (1934), courtesy of the China Film Archive.

skills and talents. Hu's career went ballistic after her coronation, and continued to be fueled by the print media.

Some two years later on February 21, 1935, China's first movie queen, Miss Butterfly Wu (Hu Die), was off to Moscow to participate in the Moscow International Film Festival. She had been specifically invited by representatives in Moscow to be a member of the Chinese delegation, making her a national representative of China. For five months Hu traveled with studio boss Zhou Jianyun and his wife to Moscow, Berlin, Paris, London, Geneva, and Rome. During her tour of Europe, Hu took on the airs of a cultural ambassador, hobnobbing with foreign diplomats, defending China's film and fashion industries as well as China's national pride.[56] Her letters from abroad were published in every venue from newspapers to women's journals and film magazines. Upon returning to Shanghai on June 7, 1935, Hu Die was bigger than ever.[57] She built up her image as a learned and studious woman when she wrote, "I feel very happy because I read two great works: one was 'World Knowledge' (Shijie zhishi) and one was 'A Record of Observations on World Film' (Shijie yingtan canguan ji). I gained knowledge that a lifetime worth of diligent research wouldn't give me."[58] The publication of a memoir of her travels in Europe entitled *Ou you zaji* (Miscellaneous notes from a European journey) in August 1935 reinforced the bookish image Hu wished to cultivate.[59]

The celebration of Hu Die's artistic abilities in the mass media reflected a clear shift from the discourse of the 1920s. A clear line was drawn between the film industry's early days and the present. A 1933 article published in *Dianying yuekan* (Movie monthly) ran:

> When film just came into being, women all shirked away, while men were already a dime a dozen. Because women stayed away, there was a shortage of talent; and there were only a few actresses (*nü yanyuan*) who all became stars (*mingxing*) regardless of their artistic talents.
>
> Those who were reporters or editors all gawked at the female body.... Society was enticed and paid attention to her, to the point of calling her a star. And she? She also used the title "star," made herself up, donned fashionable clothes, swaggered down the street, and put on airs using her so-called stardom to attract the opposite sex....
>
> But this is already a fact of the past, for films have been in society for some time now.
>
> In fact, this group of actresses is already past. It's best not to mention them anymore and to discuss the lucky actresses of the present![60]

The film world of the 1920s was painted as a world of sexpot starlets, while that of the 1930s was a world of genuinely talented *artistes* recognized and rewarded according to their artistic merits. Even actresses such as Ruan Lingyu, who had not yet made the transition to "talkies" and thus seemed more like a holdover from the 1920s era of silent film "starlets," could be praised and remade as a 1930s "artist."[61] After all, during the 1920s "there were many upright and self-respecting actresses who were dragged down and implicated [by the behavior of 1920s starlets]."[62]

The promotional discourse in the 1930s played up the education, training, and artistic skills of the third generation, too. Actresses such as Lu Lixia, Hu Ping (b. 1913), and Li Lili were characterized as having "artistic achievements," as being "studious" and as "highly trained."[63] Thirties fan magazines portrayed actresses as artists in an effort to distance them from common prostitutes and thus make them more respectable. Actresses frequently posed—their diligent faces studying books in hand—for pictures that were published in fan magazines.[64] Li Lili was characterized as having a taste for music as well as books: "Although she's a playful girl, there are times when she feels life's sorrows and is silent. But when our sweet sister is happy, she laughs and jumps, and sings. She plays the piano and rides her bike every day to class at the National Conservatory."[65] And if actresses like Mei Lin were not formally trained painters, the new and democratizing medium of photography enabled them to at least pretend to practice painterly artistry by displaying their photographs in fan magazines under such headings as "Miss Mei Lin's Photographic Artwork."[66]

Such vocabularies of praise resonated and overlapped with an earlier courtesan culture that was most vibrant, visible, and respected during the late Ming, when gifted courtesans, who began as mere prostitutes, emerged as respectable cultural figures.[67] This reassertion of a courtesan ethic as embodied in a new breed of public women was made possible by the slow but sure "sexualization" of Suzhou courtesans (*shuyu*) which "accelerated during WWI and was completed by the early 1920's."[68] Just as artistically talented courtesans were transformed into common prostitutes, actresses shed the trappings of prostitutes and took up the mantle of skilled courtesans. Yet there was an added dimension to the relationship between latter-day courtesans of the silver screen and their "clientele," for *nü mingxing* were the products of urban mass media, while their courtesan predecessors were not.

Aura and Alienation, I: Fame, Photos, and Fans in the Age of Mechanical Reproduction

The fame generated by the 1930s film industry was quite different from those forms of fame enjoyed by Ming and Qing courtesans and even of *nü mingxing* in the 1920s. Courtesans as well as China's earliest female movie stars— such as Yang Naimei and Wang Hanlun—lived in a promotional world of three dimensions and face-to-face interaction. By the 1930s, however, the social category of the actress had been more assimilated into a mass-marketed culture in urban China. The aura of fame founded upon commercialized forms and practices of mass publicity simultaneously produced a veneer of social intimacy as well as an increased social distance. Although female movie stars undoubtedly moved out into the public, an increasingly desirous mass audience was cultivated through continually accelerating and flattened-out forms of interaction with their idols, which eventually revealed the fundamentally commercialized and impersonal nature of this media-based "intimacy." Such revelations resulted in a deep sense of detachment and alienation among *nü mingxing* and their fans alike.

One of the most important rituals involved in the creation and maintenance of this imaginary connection between fans and their screen idols was the exchange of fan mail and personally autographed photos. In 1926, Wang Hanlun had left Tianyi after her private mail had been opened by company employees.[69] By the mid-1930s, however, studios thought nothing of opening the mail of a movie-star wanna-be like Mei Lin, for it was all part of the promotional game:

Although this film [*Wuchou junzi*, or "Unworried gentleman"] hasn't started playing yet and we've only glimpsed a few scenes from the trailers, movie fans have already discovered [Mei Lin's] acting talent. Recently she's received many letters. We have opened a short letter written by a fan and published it for our readers.

Most fan mail consists of requests for a photo of Miss Mei. Dear readers, you can also ask Miss Mei for a personally autographed photo![70]

A fan wrote, "Recently I've heard that you are very warm and gentle and are willing to be close to your audience, not like the disdainful and arrogant airs of most actresses these days. On this point I really respect you."[71] Given the fawning tone of this letter, it's no wonder that letters were published in the pages of movie magazines under such derogatory titles as "The Foolishness of Movie Fans":

[Chen] Yanyan,

I am a movie fan, but I've only been mystified by your films. No matter what movie you're in, I watch them all. There are a few that I've seen 2 or 3 times in a row! Besides the movies you star in, I only watch a few in which Hu Die stars. I don't watch any other movies. Can you understand? I love you. I love your beauty and your youth, your emotions are exquisite and profound. Am I writing you this letter for no actual reason? I hope that you'll send me an autographed picture of yourself. Could you? Yanyan!

A movie fan.

12/1/34

Address: West Ningbo Gate, Jiaoshi Middle School[72]

Actresses with aspirations to stardom were expected to play this picture game, and the editors of movie magazines such as *Qingqing dianying* (who were crucial in maintaining the circuits of desire) fell back on time-tested models. The memories of women such as Hu Die and the now deceased Ruan Lingyu were hollowed out and turned into shells—mere stereotypes. Their physical presence was no longer a priority, for they were now simply categories and molds to be fit. Upcoming starlets such as Mei Lin and Diao Banhua were respectively hailed and then marketed as nothing more than rehashed imitations—a younger generation's Ruan Lingyu and Hu Die.[73] Miscellaneous words of thanks to young actresses who spent much of their precious time conscientiously signing thousands of autographs were published as evidence of sincerity, meant to endear these budding stars to their future fans:

Thanks to Yuan Meiyun, Li Lili, Gao Qianping, Mei Lin, and Diao Banhua for having all donated personally autographed photos of themselves for Yan Ciping's *Nüshen* (Goddess) monthly. They each signed pictures one after another for two days. They all said that their hands were hurting. Nüshen publishing society gave out more than 3,000 photos.[74]

This ritual of writing to ask for autographed photos of the stars and then receiving them became so routine that the aura of the stars began to wear thin, and alienation soon set in. In "A Reader's Outline: Notes of a Movie Fan," a man named Zhu Ping offered some advice on such subjects as how to ask for photos of the stars, how to read magazines, and how to write letters to the stars. But Zhu's final remark points to a certain degree of cynicism: "Don't get in too deep, you'll only be disappointed."[75]

The voice of a young movie fan in an essay entitled "Do I Think That I Know Them?" is also riven with doubt and disillusionment. A twenty-year-old narrator describes how he had collected photographs of female stars, embellished their faces and blackened in their teeth with a marker, and then scribbled various questions and conjectures about their lives along the borders of the photos like so many oracle bones. He concludes:

> Do I think that by doing this, I have come to know them? There are probably a few people who will know them like I have come to know them [by scribbling on their pictures]. . . . Recently I've heard a lot of people say, "I know her." How can she ultimately let me know her? Naturally, this is a problem. Why is it so difficult to interact (*tan shejiao*) with movie stars and why are we limited to only making little conjectures in our heads or on their faces and bodies? By doing this, have I come to know them?[76]

The question was, of course, rhetorical. The very medium of film and fan magazines along with the idea of a mass audience and movie "fans" had radically altered the dynamics of the relationship between entertaining women and their audiences. The commodified relationship of film star to fan belied the promotional trope of a latter-day courtesan. The game was nearly over, for some fans had already clearly approached the discursive limits of *nü mingxing* as centered and knowable subjects.

The 1930s Discourse on Actresses, II: "True Character" and the "Good Girl"

Although second- and third-generation movie stars were lauded because they possessed all of the requisite professional and artistic skills for making movies, the "true character" (*bense*) standard of acting dominated screenwriting and casting practices during the 1930s. Although well-known screenwriters and directors like Sun Yu were well aware of other theories about acting, they had no aspirations to depart from the standards of "true character."[77] Wang Renmei's first starring role in Sun's 1932 film *Ye meigui* (Wild rose) was written specifically for the young seventeen-year-old who aspired to nothing else but acting like herself on screen.[78]

The "true character" standard of acting in the mid-1930s was a holdover of the 1920s notion that it was necessary for women to appear in silent movies because disguise would not work given the realistic quality of photographic and cinematic representation. To attribute the emphasis on "true character" acting in the 1930s to a perception of film as a bald medium of visual realism would be a mistake, however. By the mid-1930s sound technology was in wide use, and directors were already using superimposed images and dream sequences that moved away from a crude realism based on a one-to-one correspondence with reality. In the 1930s, and perhaps in the 1920s too, the "true character" standard of acting functioned more as a *gendered* constraint that held actresses to standards of "authenticity." This "authenticity" was, in turn, grounded in the socially constructed ideal of women as "good girls" who were "natural" (*ziran*), "innocent" (*tianzhen*), and "genuine" (*zhen*). The construction of and adherence to this standard by directors, screenwriters, critics, and audiences as well as actresses themselves reflected an unwillingness to accept and praise women for being anything except centered, knowable, and thus harmless or nonthreatening subjects.

Nowhere was this more evident than in the praise heaped upon Ruan Lingyu. In a 1934 photo spread of stars, a caption reads: "Ruan Lingyu, forever holding a wounded smile. We hope that in the shadow of your wounded smile, even though you powerfully take on genuineness (*zhenzhen*) in your acting, the fruits of that achievement are yours, are yours, do you hear? Lingyu, of all the appearances in the Chinese film world, yours is the most soulful!" (*linghun de*).[79] This caption emphasizes Ruan's acting achievements *and* the "genuineness" of her acting. Ruan is praised for her acting skill, but only when that skill results in her bearing her genuine and authentic soul.

The "true character" standard of praise for actresses was explicitly articulated in the 1930s; and both fans and critics, male and female alike, accepted it. A young fan wrote to the emerging 1930s star Hu Ping:

> I've seen almost all of your movies and the impressions that you give women (*nüren*) are especially deep. Acting that natural, they can hardly find words with which to praise you! I remember there were two girls (*nü haizi*) sitting next to me who didn't stop whispering: "Wow! Those actresses and actors who've received knowledgeable training are really something else. Hu Ping, in my mind, is really beyond many other actresses. Hu Ping really is Hu Ping!"[80]

If Hu Ping really was Hu Ping, women who "acted" in movies were not expected to be anything else but "themselves," too. "True character" discourse held *nü mingxing* to a singularly centered and coherent subjectivity.

Tied to these articulations of "true character" was the cliché of the "good girl"—a moralized media construction of a good woman's "natural" or "genuine" disposition. The captions of a 1935 photo spread featuring a well-known movie star read, "This girl (*guniang*) [has an] innocent, lively, and beautiful face. How passionate (*duo qing ya*)! You know who it is!"[81] We certainly did. It was none other than Miss Butterfly Wu, the lovely Hu Die herself. A caption for two photos of Yuan Meiyun described her as "an upright and innocent girl [*wuxie de guniang*; literally, "a girl without evil"] who doesn't know about the world's love and hate."[82] The 1930s was the era not only of the talented artist but also of the "good girl." The talent, virtue, innocence, and sincerity of movie actresses in the 1930s contrasted greatly with the amateur, degenerate, corrupted, and deceptive qualities of actresses in the 1920s. Although such subjectivities were diametrically opposed, they remained equally flat and clichéd.

The 1930s discourse of praise did not displace the more negative discourse of the 1920s, for the 1920s discourse on dangerous women was still in effect in the 1930s. Women, including movie actresses, who were capable of duplicity could be nothing more than femme fatales of the city. Actresses who might deceptively assume the identity of someone else on screen were a direct threat to a centered subjectivity of womanhood based upon chastity and loyalty. Such was not the case for movie actors. Actors were not strictly held to being "genuine," "natural," and "innocent" on screen. In fact, some actors' on-screen and off-screen personalities were explicitly separated. A photo spread showcasing the "four bastards" (*si ge huaidan*) of the Chinese film world—all of whom were men, of course—drew a clear line between the villains that actor Wang Xianzhai played on screen and his "real" personality. Praise for Wang's acting skills emphasized artifice and his ability to pose as a villain.[83] Although it was acceptable for a man to merely "pose" as a villain on screen, such was not the case for a woman. Indeed, a woman had to transcend simple "poses" of virtuousness in movies and practice it both on *and* off screen. "True character" discourse that praised an actresses' qualities of "naturalness," "genuineness," and "innocence" effected both the fusion *and* the fission of "reality" and "representation," of life and art(ifice).

By the mid-1930s "private lives" of movie actresses became "public" and were packaged and paraded for a mass audience to both see and judge. A four-page photo essay entitled "One Day in the Life of a Movie Actress from Morning Until Night" visualized the life of the actress Gao Qianping, while a smaller four-picture photo essay entitled "The Private Life of Li Lili" showed the young newcomer sleeping, putting on makeup, sitting with her dog, and pumping up her bicycle tires.[84] Actors, on the other hand, never underwent such scrutiny; photo essays on the "private lives" of actors did not exist. Men appeared in photo essays, but only as fictionalized characters, not as "themselves." Indeed, two of the four criteria used to compile a ranked table of actresses published in 1937 fell under the rubrics of "moral conduct" (*pinxing*) and "private life" (*si shenghuo*).[85] The very notion of a "private life" in the pages of a magazine, however, was an oxymoron and belied the idea that actresses were free to behave as they pleased off screen. The lives of *nü mingxing* were, in a sense, perpetually "on screen" and scripted to suit a mass audience. Ruan Lingyu's suicide is a salient example of the disciplining dynamic of "true character" and "good girl" discourse.

Aura and Alienation, II: The Suicide of Ruan Lingyu

Around midnight on March 7, 1935, Ruan Lingyu and her new beau, a wealthy Cantonese tea merchant named Tang Jishan, came home from a dinner party at Lianhua studios.[86] After Tang fell asleep Ruan ate a bowl of rice porridge along with 30 pills of barbitone-sodium and some tea. She then sat down and penned two suicide notes—one for Tang Jishan and one to be published in Shanghai newspapers.[87] Tang woke up shortly thereafter and noticed that something was wrong with Ruan's appearance; he rushed her to several Shanghai hospitals, but numerous attempts at reviving her were unsuccessful. Ruan was pronounced dead at 6:38 P.M. on March 8, 1935, at the age of 25.

Ruan's suicide stunned the entire nation and became both the talk and "the walk" of Shanghai.[88] Magazines ran memorial issues entirely dedicated to Ruan.[89] There was widespread speculation concerning the cause of Ruan's suicide.[90] Because her last words were addressed to her estranged husband, Zhang Damin, and Tang Jishan, Ruan's relationships with these two men were at the center of the controversy surrounding her death. Given that Ruan and Tang had never legally married, the reference to Ruan as "Mrs. Tang Jishan" in her funeral announcement was reported with great irony.[91]

Zhang Damin and Ruan had fallen in love and were living together before Ruan entered the film world in 1925. This was tantamount to marriage, and the fact that Zhang Damin and Ruan Lingyu were never legally married was of little importance, since marriage was vaguely defined in Republican-era China and included a whole range of formal and informal arrangements. The crucial factor was not the legality of such arrangements per se, but rather their morality. The same could be said of divorce at the time.[92]

By late 1932 Ruan Lingyu was estranged from Zhang Damin after he had gambled away large amounts of their money and hit her. At this time, Ruan also had feelings for the manager of the Chahua Tea Company, Tang Jishan, whom she had met at a number of social functions thrown by Lianhua studios.[93] In February 1933 Ruan hired a lawyer, Wu Chengyu, to draw up and publish a statement of her independence from Zhang in various newspapers—a common and accepted means of divorce at the time.[94] In April 1933 Zhang Damin returned from a business trip and found Ruan living with Tang Jishan. All the parties involved sat down and signed a settlement written up by Ruan's lawyer,

Wu Chengyu. The main stipulations of the settlement were that it was not to be made public, that both sides agreed to live independently, and that Ruan would pay Zhang a maximum of 100 yuan per month for a period of two years.[95] Both Ruan and Zhang followed the terms of this settlement until November 1934. Then, Zhang Damin asked Ruan for some money to finance a business venture, for he knew full well that she was only obligated to pay his living allowance for a few more months. When Ruan refused and only agreed to pay him the 500 yuan that she owed him, Zhang hired a lawyer and sued Ruan and Tang for damages. Tang Jishan responded by hiring his own lawyer and sued Zhang for defamation. The case was dropped, but Zhang opened it up again in February 1935, when he sued Ruan and Tang for fabricating documents and forging his seal in order to swindle him out of his property. Two days before the case was to go to court, Ruan killed herself.[96]

While an allegedly spurious set of notes linked Ruan's suicide to a fear of being censured as an immoral woman, a second set of "authentic" notes plainly reveal Ruan's unwillingness to go on suffering the physical abuses and infidelities of both Zhang Damin and Tang Jishan. Still, both sets of suicide notes indicate that Ruan's reasons for committing suicide were ultimately tied to her fear of being stigmatized as an immoral woman. She could not leave her second lover, Tang Jishan, and expect to carry on in her personal and professional affairs as she had previously. Ruan's position as a female movie star only tightened the grip that public opinion had over her and raised the stakes of her reputation. Because the standards of "true character" made no distinction between her talents on screen and her moral character off screen, Ruan's livelihood as an actress and her public image as a harmless and wounded bird were inextricably linked; both were jeopardized by Zhang Damin's legal case against her. The independence and assertiveness that Ruan exhibited in her dealings with Zhang and that she might have exercised by leaving an unfaithful and physically abusive Tang did not coincide with the ideal of her as "forever holding a wounded smile."[97] The discourses of "true character" and the "good girl" virtually guaranteed that she would be judged by the mass media and the general public in terms of her moral character as a woman. These discourses, within which she was constituted, effectively closed down the possibilities of her actions and of a decentered subjectivity. Lu Xun (1881–1936) attacked newspapermen for their irresponsible sensationalism in a May 1935 essay whose title was taken from one of Ruan's own suicide notes—"Gossip Is Fearful."[98] Ruan attempted to assert herself as a morally independent subject against the disciplinary effects of *nü mingxing* discourse, yet her ironic manipulation of the mass media only revealed the constructedness of her own subject position as both "woman" and *nü mingxing*. The fact that Ruan became more human in the eyes of some, but only after taking her own life, was merely another twist of irony. A columnist in *Qingqing dianying* asked: "If Ruan Lingyu hadn't committed suicide, would you still express sympathy with her?"[99]

Ruan Lingyu was not alone in facing the disciplinary effects of being a *nü mingxing*. Hu Die confronted a barrage of criticism and slander when she broke off her engagement with her first lover, Lin Xuehuai. After the Mukden Incident occurred on September 18, 1931, rumors ran rampant that Hu Die had actually danced that fateful night away in Beiping with the traitorous Young Marshal of the northeast, Zhang Xueliang, as Japanese armies invaded and occupied Chinese territory! Such gossip about Hu Die did not subside until she had married again.[100] These rumors may not have been grounded in fact, but they functioned as such because they were legitimated by a discourse of *nü mingxing* founded upon a singular and coherent subjectivity. A movie star was either a "good girl" or a "snake-like woman." Moments of disciplining like these were a clear sign of how threatening such prominent and independent women as Hu Die and Ruan Lingyu could be during politically, socially, and morally uncertain times.

The gossip that plagued Hu Die and that drove Ruan Lingyu to her death revealed a negative side of the 1930s discourse on actresses which was deeply rooted in the 1920s equation of movie actresses with prostitutes. Equating actresses with prostitutes in the 1920s was the flip side of equating them with courtesans in the 1930s. A hierarchy of prostitution in Shanghai during the first half of the twentieth century lent a great deal of elasticity to the term "prostitute" (*jinü*), which was loosely applied to a wide range of women, including elite sing-song girls (*xiansheng*) who performed in "storyteller's residences" (*shuyu*) and regarded themselves as skilled entertainers rather than providers of sexual services, as well as those less fortunate women and girls who worked as streetwalking "pheasants" (*yeji*) or who found employment in "salted pork shops" (*xianrou zhuang*), "flower-smoke rooms" (*huayan jian*), or "nailsheds" (*dingpeng*).[101] Of course, movie critics and detractors of the 1920s were undoubtedly referring to the low end of this hierarchy when they associated actresses with "prostitutes." But the overwhelmingly negative discourse on actresses in the 1920s ran along the same continuum as the more promotional formulas of the 1930s. Placing movie actresses on this prostitute-courtesan continuum gave them ambiguous status, since it might serve promotional as well as sanctioning purposes.

The earlier 1920s version of the prostitute/actress never completely disappeared in the 1930s; it was simply reconstituted as a more individuated and commodified form of scandalous gossip. No matter how much pretension was given to the noble cause of art, making movies was still very much about making money. The commercial viability of Shanghai's film industry was not solely based upon the talent and virtue of Shanghai's brightest female movie stars; pure sex appeal was a factor too. The careers of second-rate starlets such as Tan

Ying (b. 1915) thrived on sex and scandal. Tan Ying, a man-eater of a woman who could always be seen in Shanghai's dance halls, was the centerpiece of the gossip columns that described her in bodily detail as "elegant" and "seductive" (*yao de lai*).[102] She was the film world's femme fatale, and she elicited exclamations like, "Ah! It's Tan Ying! Tan Ying, this snake-like woman! Only a snake-like woman can live up to Shanghai's females" (*she yiyang de nüren, cai goude shang Shanghai de nüxing*).[103] One commentator asked: "If Tan Ying wasn't so licentious (*fangdang*), would Lianhua studios continue their contract with her and ask her to star in a lot of their movies?"[104] Although women such as Tan Ying would never join the ranks of first-rate stars, they had their own niche in the Chinese film world during the 1930s.

Qingqing dianying mapped out these niches in 1937 when it published a ranked table of actresses separated into four classes (*liu*).[105] The practice of marking off different gradations within the category of "prostitute" was clearly at work within the category of "movie actress," and this was the discursive reality in which *nü mingxing* lived.

Conclusion

Public discourse on movie actresses was a function of power, influencing the actions of individual women by opening up fields in which certain kinds of action and production were brought about. The varying discourses of *nü mingxing* opened up specific fields of possibility and constituted entire domains of action, knowledge, and social being via the institutions of mass media and mass culture in which a number of individual women made themselves into *nü mingxing*. Collective understanding of what a movie actress or a female movie star "was" or "should be" shifted from the 1920s as the whole range of moral judgments concerning movie actresses opened up in the 1930s. However, *nü mingxing* (female movie star) discourse, with its standards of "true character" and the "good girl", subtly equated descriptions of "good acting" with prescriptions for "acting *good.*" The discourses on *nü mingxing*, which actually created the very objects and "truths" of their analyses, always did so according to a more familiar trope of "woman," both good and bad.

Cinematic and photographic technology as well as various discourses on *nü mingxing* literally and figuratively "flattened" the social realities and the social relationships through which female entertainers and their fans crafted a sense of themselves. In order to counter the alienating effects involved in marketing the images of individual human beings for mass consumption, it was necessary to recreate and then maintain the aura of genuinely human forms of interaction. The entire enterprise of both making and watching movies floated on the audience's belief in the sincerity, loyalty, and accessibility of those obscure objects of desire—*nü mingxing*.

Attempts to create and then maintain an aura of personalized interaction in the age of mass media, however, did little to hide the commodified and often alienating nature of the social relationships between screen idols and their fans. Movie stars like Hu Die could live by the dual standard of being both a good actress on screen and a "good girl" off screen as dictated by public discourse. Others, like Ruan Lingyu, fit the ideal of a good actress, but could not and would not allow themselves to serve as lightning rods for the moral and cultural crises of the rest of society.

The artifice and posturing inherent in acting *well* (as opposed to acting good) in movies should have allowed for the separation of cinematic art and the daily lives of those women who worked as actresses; but such a separation into private and public personae tore at the ideal of a unified and unifying subject position (called the "good girl") that is easily knowable and nonthreatening to urbanites living in the vibrant but volatile milieu of 1930s Shanghai. A discourse of praise promulgated by the film industry's promotional machinery in the 1930s strove to constitute an aura of the "good girl" within the lives and bodies of young urban women known as *nü mingxing*. But this idealized persona was a fragile veil for the deceptive dynamics of newly institutionalized mass media and the commodified mass culture that pervaded urban life in early twentieth-century China.

Prostitution and Urban Imagination: Negotiating the Public and the Private in Chinese Films of the 1930s

YINGJIN ZHANG

Prostitution and Urban Imagination

As a recurring theme in film and literature, prostitution is endowed with special significance in the urban imagination. Due to the public's conflicting perceptions of it, prostitution has become one of the most compelling metaphors with which to articulate the ambivalence and contradiction inherent in the conceptualization of the modern city: the city seen simultaneously as the symbol of heaven and hell, as the site of civilization and dehumanization, as the agent of progress and destruction. Paralleled to the negative images of the city as "presumption (Babel), corruption (Babylon), perversion (Sodom and Gomorrah), power (Rome), destruction (Troy, Carthage), death, the plague (the City of Dis)"[1] are insidious ideas of prostitution as sexual promiscuity, physical degeneration, moral degradation, and national humiliation. On the other hand, "virtues" such as faithful companionship, fashionable ornamentation, and artistic sensibility have been attributed to prostitutes (*chang*) in Chinese society throughout history, and the city has long been designated as the locus of such traditional cultural achievements.[2]

In *Dangerous Pleasures*, Gail Hershatter succinctly sums up such conflicting perceptions: "In Shanghai over the past century, prostitution was variously understood as a source of urbanized pleasures, a profession full of unscrupulous and greedy schemers, a site of moral danger and physical disease, and a marker of national decay."[3] In other words, prostitution has come to constitute a highly

contested space in the modern era in which diverse urban discourses and ideologies confront one another and compete. In this chapter, I will discuss films
about Shanghai prostitution and use them as markers of urban imagination. I
will further demonstrate that elite modern intellectuals who lay claim to ethical-
moral legitimacy had to confront—and at times to accommodate themselves
to—the epicurean and voyeuristic penchants in mass audiences as well as within their own ranks.

To give the context of urban imagination in Republican China, I will start
with conflicting public perceptions gleaned from original sources as well as recent historical and social-scientific literatures, and then shift the focus from the
question of "facts" to that of representation, by identifying a number of textual
modes used in representing prostitution. My reading of early Chinese films, in
particular Wu Yonggang's *Shennü* (Goddess, 1934) and Shen Xiling's *Chuanjia
nü* (Boatman's daughter, 1935), will further reveal the textual processes whereby
the otherwise "unpresentable" figure of prostitution is presented and distributed as an artistic product for public consumption. In the concluding section, I
will take note of a recent trend toward glamorizing prostitution in Chinese cinema, which has made the idea of prostitution not just "presentable" but instrumental to historical representation itself.

Charles Bernheimer decodes the word "prostitution" in this way: "Etymolog-
ically, prostitution means to set or place (Latin: *statuere*) forth, in public (*pro*).
When Baudelaire wrote that art is prostitution, he may have had this etymology
in mind, for indeed art is the making public of private fantasies, the public exposition of one's imaginary creations."[4] Reading through Baudelaire, Bernheimer detects a potential conflict embedded within the idea of prostitution: to
make "public" something that is usually or at least originally "private"—be it
one's body, desire, fantasy, or artistic creation. Following this exegesis, I would
contend that prostitution involves not only private issues but also public discussion, intervention, and regulation. In some cases, as in China at the turn of the
twentieth century, the house of prostitution might even be imagined as partially
immersed in a "public sphere" of some sort.[5] In this particular type of Chinese
"public sphere" (definitely more erotic—although no less cultural—than the
urban teahouse and wine shop), a young boy might be initiated into the sphere
of male knowledge; a prostitute might be praised by her clientele through print
media; and a literatus might air his political views in addition to displaying his
artistic talents.

Take, for example, Bao Tianxiao (1876–1973), an eminent Shanghai writer of
mandarin duck and butterfly fiction (*yuanyang hudie pai xiaoshuo*) in the Republican period. At the age of 96, Bao still vividly remembered his first experience with the erotic "flower boat" (*huachuan*) in his early childhood, when his

father took him to a festival celebration in the company of gorgeously dressed prostitutes. During the 1910s and 1920s, Bao edited a number of popular magazines that regularly carried the photographs of prostitutes famous nationwide.[6] Take Wang Tao (1828–97), a prominent late Qing Shanghai literatus, as another example. He mingled with prostitutes, politicians, and foreigners, eagerly submitting policy suggestions to the Qing court on the one hand and, on the other, gracefully composing verses to comment on courtesans' character. Wang was so fond of passing clever remarks to Shanghai prostitutes that he once claimed himself to be the "prime minister of prostitution" (*fengyue pingzhang*).[7] Indeed, at the turn of the twentieth century, the house of prostitution was delicately situated at the threshold between the public and the private, and it marked a site where a variety of urban discourses contended and converged. As demonstrated by recent historical studies, hardly any aspect of prostitution in China has escaped public scrutiny in the course of the twentieth century. Issues such as the rules and tricks of the trade, trafficking and regulating, pregnancy and abortion, contraception and sterility, venereal disease and opium addiction have all been detailed and catalogued in public discourses in one form or another.[8] It is precisely such interactions and interplays between the private and the public that make prostitution a fascinating subject for a study of urban imagination.

Public Perceptions and Textual Modes

Gail Hershatter's six "approximations" of Shanghai prostitutes are by far the best summary of various public perceptions of prostitution in early twentieth-century China. The first approximation, "the urbane courtesan," abounds in a popular genre of literati writing, a literature of pleasure, appreciation, or nostalgia, which recounts stories of male youthful indulgences in urban prostitution as the delightful consummation of rare female artistic achievements. The second approximation, "the scheming businesswoman," appears primarily in city guidebooks and tabloids, which warn the male tourists/adventurers of the dangers posed by the untrustworthy prostitutes and their all-too-greedy madams. The third approximation, "the diseased and oppressed streetwalker," touches the darker and more sinful side of urban life, articulated through imageries of filth, violence, disease, and death. From the fourth to the sixth approximations, which pertain to "rational" discourses, prostitution is alternatively regarded as a marker of backwardness (which stands for an "endangered" China waiting to be saved by Christianity or nationalism in turns), as a marker of modernity (which imagines China as taking part in a universal human history), and as object of state regulation (which involves health issues, police strategies, and public campaigns).[9]

It is evident from Hershatter's approximations that the urbane courtesan and the oppressed streetwalker are two extreme figures of urban prostitution, one embodying distinctive cultural achievements, the other social and sexual victimization. This difference, however, does not form a contrast "between good and bad women," but rather is a result of class distinction.[10] What deserves special attention at this point is that, insofar as public discourse is concerned, the courtesan was gradually displaced by the streetwalker in the early decades of the century.[11] I will return to this process of displacement and to a contemporary replacement of the streetwalker by the courtesan later in this chapter.

In spite of the marked difference between the courtesan and the streetwalker, some scholars have recently gathered evidence for a more or less identical, if not uniform, lifestyle and behavioral pattern in all classes of Chinese prostitutes. Virgil Kit-yiu Ho, for one, takes pains to prove that, in spite of common stories of prostitutes' "ruthless exploitation" by their madams, which frequently surfaced in contemporary "moralists' writings," the Cantonese prostitutes of the early Republican period in fact lived a fairly "decent" life, showing off their lavish clothing, enjoying their newly acquired wealth and power, organizing entertainment parties of their own, and conducting their trade either "with some pleasure" or with "thorough" enjoyment.[12] Ho's extensive use of archival materials to illustrate "the generally favorable view, and the widespread patronage, of prostitution in Canton" may look impressive on first reading,[13] but his uncritical, if not indiscriminate, stance toward these materials beg the questions of mediation and representation.

The bulk of public perceptions as recorded by Ho is not so much unmediated *facts* about "the job and life of those in that profession" as their textual *representations* by the historian, the writer, or the government agency, each of them with different and specific purposes in mind.[14] One must not, therefore, equate to "truth" the fictionalized voice of a prostitute in some popular songs. When Ho interprets the song "Repaying the Flower-Debt" (Huan huazhai) in this way—"a prostitute is described as willing to sell her body while still young and attractive, for at this golden age of life she will be admired, appeased, and wooed by a large number of 'followers' who will bring her both companionship and money," he runs the risk of erasing a crucial difference between the voice of the prostitute—speaking as she may be in the first person—and that of the songwriter, who might derive fame, money, and pleasure from a particular type of representation.[15]

Christian Henriot devotes more attention to the problem of representation than Virgil Ho. After drawing our attention to the "undoubtedly strongly idealized" image of prostitution that dominated textual representations in the late Qing and early Republican periods, Henriot writes: "Nevertheless, that the reality was different from the representations the literati gave of it is not so important per se. What matters here is the discourse that was elaborated about this community."[16] Henriot seems to have clarified his position regarding this "positive discourse" when he later contends that "what these [secondary] sources provide are forms of discourse, not evidence of historical practices."[17] As is indicated in Henriot's case, the historian confronts the dilemma of how one goes about knowing and claiming to know the historical reality without any textual mediation. Clearly aware of this dilemma, Gail Hershatter acknowledges the function of textual representations in historical research and recommends that "we need to subject them to multiple readings: as clues (never straightforward) to long-disappeared social conditions, and as signposts for use in mapping the preoccupations of the writers."[18]

Adopting a strategy similar to Hershatter's, but with more emphasis on the preoccupations of the filmmakers and the audience, I will undertake a critical reading of the process of public exposition of prostitution in Chinese films of the 1930s. As I will demonstrate below, what is revealed in the representational process of filmmaking is more often male fantasy or patriarchal self-righteousness than female enjoyment or suffering per se. To facilitate my critical reading, I will distinguish three major textual modes in the public discourse on prostitution in modern China.

The first is the *informative, journalistic mode*, scattered around in city guidebooks, popular magazines, or tabloids, and what cultural elites call "lowbrow" literature, which focus on an array of time-honored procedures (for instance, scripting invitation slips [*jiao tiaozi*] and arranging flower-wine banquets [*hua-jiu*]) as well as practical aspects (such as "professional terms" specific to a city) of urban prostitution. In the early twentieth century, publicity work for prostitution was partially undertaken by literary magazines such as *Banyue* (The half moon journal) and *Xiaoshuo daguan* (The grand magazine). Both magazines included in their front illustration pages a number of photographs of famous or not-so-famous prostitutes from major cities nationwide and used this "erotic" feature as an effective means to attract readers and to boost sales.[19] The increased attention to cataloging relevant information is also striking. A 1906 guidebook contained scattered entries such as poems praising famed courtesans, advice given to prostitutes against footbinding, and fundraising efforts to build a public temple. A 1919 guidebook offered three and a half pages of neatly organized information on Chinese and foreign prostitutes of various classes and prices. And a 1932 guidebook, edited by a man of certain literary reputation, was able to give a 51-page description of nearly all conceivable aspects of prostitution in Shanghai, male prostitutes included, and to present informed choices for its readers.[20] Indeed, by 1932, Shanghai had boasted of at least 38 books on prostitution.[21] Typically, in this first mode of representation, prostitution is presented as a "natural" way of life, an everyday practice in the city, a business beyond good and evil.

The second is the *appreciative, hedonistic mode*, practiced mostly in literati writing, butterfly fiction, or what some scholars choose to describe as "middle-brow" literature, which dwelled extensively on the sexualized female body and the literati's excessive sentiments (*qing*).[22] Female companionship and the cultured tastes of famed and gifted courtesans are described with a connoisseur's apprecia-tion and a stylist's delight, sometimes elaborated in a hedonistic manner, com-plete with textual displays of music, poetry, wine, tears, and sex. For a literatus such as Han Bangqing (Han Ziyun, 1856–94), the house of prostitution was not only a source of literary inspiration but also the actual place of literary produc-tion.[23] It is interesting to read this sarcastic but nonetheless perceptive comment by Lu Xun (1881–1936): at the turn of the century, "talented scholars" went whor-ing in Shanghai and "could surround themselves with ten or twenty girls, . . . till they fancied themselves the young hero" admired by beautiful prostitutes.[24] The appreciative attitude was not altered substantially in the so-called social novels of the 1920s, such as *Renjian diyu* (Human hell, 1923–24) co-authored by Suopo Sheng (pen name of Bi Yihong) and Bao Tianxiao, or *Shanghai chunqiu* (Shang-hai chronicles, 1924–26) by Bao Tianxiao.[25] In these novels, the glamorous life-style of the prostitutes and their wealthy clientele is delineated in minute detail and overshadows occasional social commentary articulated in the intrusive au-thorial voice. In this second mode of representation, prostitution is imagined as a fantastic cultural realm, an exquisite artistic form, and a fountain of nostalgia.

The third is the *castigatory, moralistic mode*, found mostly in political inter-vention, moral discussions, and May Fourth "highbrow" literature, which usu-ally depict the miserable life of streetwalkers and advocate self-righteously for social reform. This literature links prostitution to issues of national concern, such as public health, reproduction, education, and urban security. As my film analysis in the following sections will demonstrate, the ground for representa-tion in the third mode shifts from the cultural to the social and political, while the ethico-moral tone replaces the literary, artistic tone in the second mode, or the factual, descriptive tone in the first. In this last mode, prostitution is trans-figured or refigured as a symbol of infectious social disease, of ruthless class ex-ploitation, and of intolerable national humiliation. Many films in the 1920s and 1930s adopted this critical mode of representation.

Urban Prostitution and Film Narrative
of the 1920s and 1930s

Ever since its early features, Chinese film has devoted unfading attention to the fates of women. For instance, one of China's first short features, *Nanfu nanqi* (The difficult couple, 1913), an early product of Zhang Shichuan and Zheng Zhengqiu's teamwork, was a satire of the ridiculous procedures of the age-long Chinese tradition of arranged marriage, which were carried out regardless of the young couple's mutual feelings. More significantly, the first Chinese long feature, Ren Pengnian's (1894–1968) *Yan Ruisheng* (Yan Ruisheng, 1921), was based on a sensational real-life murder case in which a debt-ridden Shanghai business-man took a well-known prostitute for a pleasure ride in a borrowed automobile, then strangled her to death, ripped off her jewelry, and dumped her body in a wheat field in the suburbs. Featuring a friend of the real-life murderer and a for-mer prostitute for authenticity, the film attracted a large crowd when it pre-miered at the Olympic Theater, one of Shanghai's best cinemas.[26] In the context of Chinese film history, this early box-office hit proved that domestic produc-tions could be profitable. The film also demonstrates the close link between ur-ban prostitution and film narrative in modern China.

In the 1920s, Zheng Zhengqiu contributed many screenplays that drama-tized the fates of Chinese women in their various traditional roles: the chaste widow, the abused child bride, the kindhearted prostitute, the unemployed fac-tory worker, the contract domestic maid, the suffering wife with a child from her previous marriage, and so on and so forth.[27] After Mingxing Company suc-cessfully recruited Xuan Jinglin (1907–92), a prostitute who made her screen debut as an extravagant, unfilial daughter in Zhang Shichuan's *Zuihou zhi liangxin* (The last trace of conscience, 1925), Zheng Zhengqiu wrote *Shanghai yi furen* (A woman in Shanghai, 1925), a script specifically designed for Xuan in the lead role as a kindhearted prostitute. In this film, Xuan's character, Aibao, is sold into prostitution in Shanghai, crowned as the "president of the flowery na-tion" (*huaguo da zongtong*), and purchased by a millionaire as his seventh con-cubine. In spite of the glamor of her courtesan life, Aibao has all along pre-served a heart of gold. In addition to sending ten thousand yuan to her father, she purchases land for her ex-husband, who was crippled in a car accident in Shanghai, and reestablishes him as a small landlord in the countryside. Near the end of the film, when she revisits her former brothel and encounters a young country girl whose family background resembles hers, Aibao decides to use her own money to buy the girl out of prostitution and to pay for her educa-tion expenses. Xuan Jinglin herself gained stardom from *A Woman in Shanghai*, and earned enough money to buy herself out of prostitution.[28]

As evident in *A Woman in Shanghai*, Zheng Zhengqiu's films of the 1920s were moralist in tone and critical in their depiction of social realities. His repre-sentation of suffering women—in particular prostitutes—as victims of social injustice influenced the next generation of Chinese filmmakers. Sun Yu's *Tian-ming* (Daybreak, 1932), for instance, largely followed Zheng's narrative pattern by focusing on an innocent country girl, Lingling (played by Li Lili). Lingling moves to Shanghai in search of a better life but is first raped by her factory boss and then sold into prostitution. In a rather radical move, Sun Yu transforms Lingling from a high-class prostitute into a revolutionary martyr. After helping her former lover, an underground revolutionary, to escape the police, Lingling is caught and sentenced to death. At her execution, she makes the request that the squad open fire the moment she smiles her best. Her death cuts to the inter-title "Long Live the Revolution!" and the images of the revolutionary soldiers marching forward.

Historically speaking, the revolution in question here is the Nationalist-led Northern Expedition in 1927 that placed Chiang Kai-shek in control of China, and the film's explicit political message might not necessarily come as a surprise to the contemporary film audience. However, Sun Yu's efforts to transform the kindhearted prostitute into a revolutionary "new woman" endowed with her own subjectivity remains a rare case in Chinese film history,[29] because prostitutes are more often than not treated as mere objects of sympathy.

Before proceeding to other films, we may pause here for a moment to consider the repeated shots of Lingling's smiles in *Daybreak*, which foreground her as the *ideal* image of a kindhearted and self-sacrificing prostitute in Shanghai. When Lingling is first introduced by her cousin to attractions in the city (such as the Bund and Nanjing Road), she is under the impression that "Shanghai is such a fun place that everyone smiles." When she is sold into prostitution, she has to put on a forced smile that is the trademark of the profession. When she is elevated into high-class status, she wears her contemptuous smiles all the time while dealing with her morally corrupt clients. But it is her sincere smiles that comfort her sick factory friends and their children the most, for she regularly brings money and food to those in need.[30] As we will see in the next section, Ruan Lingyu acts out with brilliance these various kinds of trademark smiles in *Goddess*.[31]

Female Virtues and Patriarchal Order in 'Goddess'

In 1934, Wu Yonggang chose to tackle the issue of prostitution in his first feature, *Goddess*, a silent film that earned him immediate critical acclaim and was later judged to be a masterpiece in early Chinese cinema.[32] Wu studied fine art at the Commercial Press and worked as art designer for Da Zhonghua-Baihe (Great China-Lily) Film Company before moving to Tianyi Company in 1928.[33] One of his off-duty experiences during the period was his daily encounter with streetwalkers who forced smiles on dark street corners. As he watched them from the trolley, Wu was so disturbed by the fate of these women that he envisioned an oil painting: under a dim street light stands a sorrowful woman with thick powder and lipstick. "The painting was never completed," Wu reminisces, "but the image of this miserable woman had been deeply imprinted in my memory."[34]

Instead of a painting, Wu submitted a screenplay to Lianhua Company, and the result was the silent film *Goddess*. Following the narrative pattern established by Zheng Zhengqiu in *A Woman in Shanghai* and refashioned by Sun Yu in *Daybreak*, Wu presented a memorable screen image of a kind and self-sacrificing prostitute. Using a more sophisticated film language than its predecessors, *Goddess* portrays a Shanghai streetwalker, despised by the local community, who has a heart of gold. By concentrating largely on moral issues (such as the child's education, the mother's virtue, and the principal's integrity) and by presenting urban prostitution as "a problem of our entire society, a disease of our social and economic system,"[35] the film succeeds in making publicly visible an otherwise invisible mother figure, who struggles in the lowest social stratum to fulfill her expected role in cultural reproduction. As the camera lingers lovingly and "excessively" on the female star Ruan Lingyu, the viewer is compelled to "experience an innocent pleasure" and to feel the virtue of the suffering mother, "an ideal mother" in the filmic imagination.[36]

The newly established visibility of the "virtuous prostitute," however, is framed in a *patriarchal discourse* about the self-sacrificing mother: "*Goddess* affirms a woman's self-denial," a woman whose "mission in life is to provide her son with an education."[37] In gender terms, it is evident that the objective being pursued in the film is not the articulation of a female voice, nor the attainment of "woman's self,"[38] but rather the realization of a particular type of male fantasy. This male fantasy is played out by the old school principal, a morally upright paternal figure who intervenes on behalf of the mother and eventually takes over her role. In a touching scene near the end of the film, the principal visits the mother in jail (after she killed the gambler who had stolen all her savings for her son's education) and promises to raise her son as his own (instead of letting the child stay in an orphanage). By assuming his new role of surrogate father, the principal secures patrilineal continuity on a symbolic level, relegating the despised mother once and for all to the realm of oblivion, and thereby marking the film as conservative (see fig. 18).[39]

A film full of the pathos of unrewarded virtue, *Goddess* participates in a male discourse on prostitution typical in Republican China, which dictates that sexual dangers be contained, public disorder be reduced, and male offspring be legitimately adopted. In conformity with this discourse, *Goddess* sees to it that the woman of ill repute is safely locked behind bars, though she is still seen pacing uneasily like a "caged animal," and that she willingly erases herself—and her motherhood—from the male narrative. Hence her tearful plea to the principal:

18. A virtuous prostitute in *Goddess* (1934), courtesy of the China Film Archive.

"When [my son] grows up, please tell him that his mother died long ago, so that he will never know he had a mother like me." In a sharp contrast to an earlier chaotic scene where the police are busy chasing the unlicensed streetwalkers at night, the final prison scene, with the camera focusing on the securely locked iron gates, reassures the audience that male control of the city has been firmly restored. With this twist in male fantasy, *Goddess* turns out to be one more example of the "masculine quest to stabilize the mobility of a sexually imaged reality,"[40] which is the modern city of Shanghai. In a montage, Shanghai is fantasized as an alluring prostitute smiling directly at the audience against a background of skyscrapers and flashing neon lights.

In spite of its focus on prostitution, *Goddess* is marked by its lack of an explicit display of female sexuality. A few sequences show the prostitute soliciting her clients on the street at night. One scene is especially striking in terms of its artistic quality and its possible influence by a German film: we first see a medium shot of the woman's feet, which uneasily tap on the pavement until they are joined by a man's feet, and then follow a tracking shot of the man's and the woman's feet walking together along the street and disappearing in a doorway.[41] As a rule, these solicitation sequences in *Goddess* quickly cut to the morning scenes where the mother takes good care of her lonely child in a shabby room. The only evidence betraying the mother's unpresentable trade (and her concealed sexuality) in the room are two pretty dresses she hangs on the wall, but the association of these dresses is beyond the comprehension of her innocent child.

One exception to the concealment of sexuality in the film is found in what William Rothman sees as "an erotic bond" between the prostitute and the principal. In his two brief encounters with the prostitute, the principal manifests an almost irresistible desire to *touch* her physically: he fails the first time in her room (instead he pats the boy on the head—a gesture of misplaced or displaced desire) but succeeds the second time in the prison (when the mother is beside herself with grief over her dilemma).[42] In these two "touching" scenes, I would suggest, the principal's desire to touch the woman is more than a physical desire, for it also powerfully articulates the desire of the male intellectual to penetrate the unknown world of urban prostitution (unmistakably gendered as female) and to narrate it in a rational (that is, male) discourse. The otherwise concealed *narrative desire* is fully articulated when the principal, after his first meeting with the mother, makes an eloquent speech at the school's faculty meeting in an attempt to retain the boy as a legitimate student. Unfortunately, the principal's attempt fails, and he chooses to resign, thus distinguishing himself as a benevolent figure standing alone in an unsympathetic society.

In his reading of *Goddess*, Rothman is puzzled by the film's evasion of female sexuality: "Then why does he [the principal] not marry her? How can it be that this possibility is not even considered, as it could not fail to be if this were an American film?"[43] My response to Rothman's question is that, in *Goddess*, the Chinese concern with patrilineal continuity precludes any effort to explore the issue of happiness in an individual's case. Individual pursuit of happiness was still perceived as a Western concept in 1930s China, although such a concept had shaped the happy endings in Western prostitution films such as Frank Borzage's *Seventh Heaven* (1927) and Josef von Sternberg's *Shanghai Express* (1932).[44]

The evasion or concealment of female sexuality in *Goddess* does bring out further questions. If one agrees that the image of a "loving prostitute exemplifies the renunciation of a predatory female sexuality in submission to paternal Law,"[45] then *Goddess* may have reaffirmed this paternal law, even if unconsciously, by resolutely denying a narrative space to female sexuality. To guarantee the working of this paternal law, the idealized mother in *Goddess* is "saved" from contracting contagious disease, which was a common danger to Chinese streetwalkers at the time and which made them a species of urban predator in the eyes of the public.[46] The predatory female sexuality of the streetwalker was discussed in print media with great concern in the 1930s. Among other things, it was deemed particularly detrimental to the health of the nation, because the venereal disease husbands contracted from prostitutes would unavoidably be passed on to wives, who would then pass it on to the next generation through pregnancy.[47] In the fictional world of *Goddess*, however, the audience is ensured that the potentially predatory prostitute is now safe behind bars, and that her existence will be erased from the public memory, perhaps even from that of her son. Read against the serious public concerns with the moral and medical implications of urban prostitution in the 1930s, the ending of *Goddess* is doubly significant: at the symbolic level, it restores paternal law and reaffirms the sense of urban security; at the narrative level, it gives a seamless closure to a tragic tale of the kind and self-sacrificing prostitute.

Female Body and Male Fantasy in 'Boatman's Daughter'

The final shot in *Goddess* consists of a split screen: in the lower left corner, the prostitute looks up at her son, who appears in the upper right corner, whispers to her, smiles, and then fades out; she turns around with a deep sigh and a faint smile, and her image fades out, too. As mentioned earlier in the case of *Daybreak*, the screen image of the prostitute's smiles seems to have attracted particular attention from Chinese filmmakers. In his 1936 critical profile of Shen Xiling, Ling He points to the "troubled smile" Shen's films usually bring out in the viewer—a kind of bitter smile that appears the moment one is about to burst into tears. According to Ling He, the troubled smile has become a stylistic feature of Shen's films, such as *Nüxing de nahan* (The protest of women, 1933), *Shanghai ershisi xiaoshi* (Twenty-four hours in Shanghai, 1934), *Xiangchou* (Homesick, 1934), and *Boatman's Daughter*.[48] Like Zheng Zhengqiu, Sun Yu, and Wu Yonggang, Shen wanted to expose social injustice and to show his sympathy for suffering women. In his *Boatman's Daughter*, a sound film about an innocent and lovable girl who is forced into prostitution, Shen includes a brothel scene in which a prostitute, after drinking a cup of wine, sings of her tragic fate: "Today, only today / Can I tolerate such suffering. / Tomorrow, yet tomorrow, / My voice lost, / My skin decayed, / I'll be abandoned in a deserted lot, / like useless coal cinders. . . ."[49]

The performance of this sad song occurs near the end of *Boatman's Daughter* and is intercut with a chaotic scene in which a factory worker, Gao Tie, breaks into the brothel to rescue his former sweetheart, A Ling, but is overpowered by the police. By highlighting such a dramatic—albeit futile—attempt at justice, Shen continued Chinese filmmakers' narrative effort to construct the meaning of urban prostitution. Unlike the dominance of dull urban scenes in *Goddess*, however, Shen's film provides many scenes where the audience can smile happily, at least for the time being. In the opening scene of *Boatman's Daughter*, the natural beauty of Hangzhou's scenic West Lake is displayed to the viewer as if in a traditional scroll painting: tourists boating in the lake, the ripples shimmering in the sunshine, and the distant hills half-hidden by the morning mist. For a contemporary critic like Ling He, Shen's opening scene is as fine as the waterfall scene in Frank Borzage's *Little Man, What Now?* (1934). Indeed, the opening scene of West Lake reveals Shen's penchant for "sentimentality" (*shengdi mente*), "emotionalism" (*chunqing zhuyi*), and a kind of "realist romance."[50]

Another good example of Shen's sentimentality is his narration of the romance between A Ling and Gao Tie according to the convention of the Chinese fairy tale. In this traditional genre, a flower spirit or a fairy maiden would do all the housework for the unmarried male protagonist (usually a poor scholar or a hardworking cowherd) while he is not home, and the two usually fall in love when they finally meet. In *Boatman's Daughter*, Gao has been helping A Ling and her old father row a boat full of people across the lake in the daytime. One evening, A Ling notices Gao is clumsy with needlework. She sneaks into his room, steals his worn clothes, and secretly returns them after she has mended them. Naturally, Gao is all too happy when he catches his "fairy/spirit" in his room and finds out that she is none other than his beloved A Ling. The two are later seen in a romantic tryst on the lake, rowing a small boat under the full moon. Shen's romantic fairy tale, besides being simply pleasing to his audience, also reveals the persistence of fantasy in Chinese narrative across time.

A different—and certainly more modern—type of male fantasy is elaborated in *Boatman's Daughter*. As is clear from the start of the film, A Ling's youthful body is delivered to the gaze of not only male characters in the film but also of the contemporary film audience. Voyeurism is fully at work in the film, especially in the modeling scene in which A Ling is hired to model for three urban playboy-artists. In a spacious modern setting, she appears completely changed, dressed fashionably and made up. Under an intense voyeuristic gaze, she first lies down on a couch, then sits up biting a flower between her lips, and finally stands still with her hands stretching upward in a gesture that reminds one artist of certain French paintings. The playboys take turns photographing and painting, and they enhance their "aesthetic" pleasure by playing Western music on the gramophone. Obviously, the playboys' epicurean taste is relished by the audience in this scene, in which the sexualized female body is objectified as an concrete embodiment of male artistic talents.

In moral terms, the discrepancy between this modeling scene and the fairy-tale romance mentioned above may be quite striking, but Shen Xiling's formal training in Western art accounts for their connection. A native of Hangzhou, Shen studied engineering at a local school before pursuing industrial design, oil painting, literature, and experimental theater in Japan. He returned to China in 1929 and participated in the drama movement. In 1931 he became an art director for Tianyi but soon moved on to Mingxing where he started directing. Shen's familiarity with Western art is manifest in his mise-en-scène for the modeling scene. In an ambience that smacks of aestheticism and decadence (both with strong French "high-culture" flavors), the modeling scene constitutes the first stage in which the "corrupt" moneyed society forces poor girls into prostitution: A Ling's debt-ridden father is sick, and modeling is the only way she can make quick money to pay for his medical treatment. By dwelling on A Ling's agony in a close-up shot (she is so worried about her father that tears start trickling down her cheeks), *Boatman's Daughter* condemns the Westernized artists from a Chinese ethico-moral point of view: the decadent lifestyle is thus contrasted with the traditional virtue of filial piety.

One may suspect, however, at the level of textual representation, "moral condemnation serves the purpose of libertine titillation,"[51] for this scene offers plenty of space for male fantasy to run wild. When one of the playboys suggests that A Ling pose nude for them, as in French painting, it is evident that the same type of male fantasy experienced by the characters is being tactfully projected or relayed to the contemporary film audience as well. Indeed, what the character suggests in the film (and, by extension, what the audience would presumably have in mind) might be something like the scene of nude modeling in Chen Tiansuo's *Zaisheng* (Resurrection, 1933), where an artist is painting a female model in a spacious room with elaborate, Western-style decorations, and his underage son is sitting beside him and painting the houses of his imagination (see fig. 19).[52]

At this juncture, let us look at another—perhaps subconscious—level of signification in the modeling scene. In the process of objectifying the female body as an artistic product, the playboys are engaged in a different type of display as well: that is, to display themselves as model artists—who fully appreciate feminine beauty—to the film audience. To a certain extent, the scene stages a narcissistic quest for the concealed male body, which seems to be revealed only through the fetishized object of male desire—the sensuous, erotic body of a female model. It is in this sense that Baudelaire's idea of art as prostitution becomes relevant here, for modeling provides the male artists with a perfect occasion to make public their otherwise private (concealed or repressed) fantasy.

The connection between modeling and prostitution is established in the film narrative as a turning point of A Ling's life, but her posture, lying on the sofa, carries rich connotations in the culture of prostitution in both China and the West. In the June 1916 issue of *The Grand Magazine*, for instance, a Shanghai prostitute is displayed in a photograph in the same posture, and the posture is designated as "spring sleep" (*chunshui*) in the caption.[53] As the magazine editor Bao Tianxiao recalls, the prostitutes were the first group of modern Chinese women who were willing to make their photographs available to the reading public, and some Shanghai publishers, like Di Pingzi (pen name of Di Baoxian, style Chuqing, 1872–1940), were quick to take advantage of the prostitutes' will-

19. A still of the nude modeling in *Resurrection* (1933) (*Liangyou*, no. 78 [July 1933]: 31).

ingness to display themselves by setting up photography studios of their own and offering free services to the city's *demimondaines*.[54] In this sense, the posture of "spring sleep" as a public image in modern China was an outcome of the introduction of Western portrait photography and printing technology.

But the "spring sleep" posture can be traced to earlier precedents in the tradition of Western painting. Edouard Manet's controversial *Olympia* (1865) deliberately transformed the previously "innocent" posture in classical painting—as in Titian's *Venus of Urbino* (ca. 1538)—to highlight the morally troubling connection between art and prostitution.[55] Interestingly, such a highly provocative Western posture traveled to modern China via photography, painting, and print media. A Chinese photograph of a famous late Qing courtesan, for instance, features her in a posture similar to the one in *Olympia*: both figures stare directly at the viewer, though the Chinese prostitute is fully clothed in a traditional costume while lying on a Western-style sofa (see fig. 20).[56] A similar posture is found in *Beiyang huapao* (The pei-yang pictorial news), which regularly carried full-bodied nudes in Western painting in its attempt to promote art and common knowledge in the 1920s and 1930s. On December 10, 1927, the pictorial published a sketch carrying its own English caption—"A study of pose for model . . . By a famous artist in Paris"—in which the female model displays herself in a posture almost identical with that of the late Qing courtesan mentioned above, except that the foreign model poses completely nude. A question printed in the Chinese caption—"Is this pose OK?"—returns us, intertextually, to the modeling scene in *Boatman's Daughter*, where the playboy artists take pains to get A Ling's poses right: right, that is, according to the tradition of French painting (see fig. 21).[57]

It should be evident by now that the modeling scene in *Boatman's Daughter* illustrates the way a particular type of male fantasy comes to be a driving force behind urban imagination. What is worthy of special attention here is that, in the Republican period, it is often the prostitute who is chosen to constitute the central object of male desire. Two other film examples here will suffice to foreground the erotic nature of urban imagination. In Cai Chusheng's *Xin nüxing* (New woman, 1934), a woman writer (played by Ruan Lingyu) is fantasized by a playboy banker as cheerfully volunteering sexual services to him and his friend in a private mansion. When they walk into the living room, the writer welcomes them with her charming smile and, without further ado, sits right on his friend's lap. In an early scene of *Goddess*, the streetwalker is made to act as if she willingly accepted her fate as a sex partner in a gambler's room, which she enters by accident while escaping the police. Realizing her difficult situation, she gracefully walks past the gambler, sits on his desk, waits for him to deliver a cigarette and light it, and then puffs rings of smoke in his face.[58] In both cases, the em-

20. A late-Qing courtesan lying on a sofa (Tang Zhenchang, p. 232).

21. A study of a pose for a model (*Beiyang huabao* [Dec. 10, 1927]).

phasis on the prostitute's sexuality works to arouse not only male sexual desire (at the level of film narrative) but also male narrative desire (at the level of film-making)—a desire to probe into and write about the enigmatic city woman.

If, in *Goddess*, the male narrative desire is sustained by a single character (the school principal), in *Boatman's Daughter*, it is articulated in a more complicated way, relying on three levels that frame the narrative. The first level is the newspaper accounts of how innocent girls from good families were forced into prostitution; the second level the two old gentlemen who read the newspaper under the trees by West Lake and deplore the deterioration of public morality; and the third the political activists who speak eloquently at a meeting on the "abolition of prostitution" (*feichang*). Historically, the Nationalist government launched "intermittent campaigns to ban unlicensed prostitution" in the Republican era,[59] but the framing device in *Boatman's Daughter* has specific aims to achieve. By comparing the three levels of framing in the film with the three major modes of public discourse on prostitution discussed earlier, we come to realize what kind of value judgments the film has implicitly made: (1) the informative mode (exemplified by news reports) becomes utterly meaningless, since no one cares to listen to warnings about evil practices; (2) the hedonist mode is still being practiced (as in the scene of a flower-wine banquet near the end of the film), but the modern clients are morally corrupt and culturally impoverished, no longer capable of comparison with the talented scholars in the previous generations; and (3) the castigatory mode is represented as a mere show of rhetoric, a publicly staged fanfare without any practical effect. An ironic contrast is formed in the film between the framing sequences (beginning and ending), where neatly dressed male figures speak to an audience applauding in excitement, and the bulk of the narrative, where the reality of urban prostitution is basically unchanged as a new supply of young girls keeps arriving from impoverished rural areas and bankrupt factories.

Apart from revealing the epicurean taste in the popular discourse on prostitution, both *Goddess* and *Boatman's Daughter* did not break away from the entrenched ethical-moral representation first established by Zheng Zhengqiu in the 1920s. What remained as a consistent narrative pattern in both films is that the ill-reputed must always be represented as ill-fated: the kindhearted mother loses her son and her freedom in *Goddess*, and the innocent A Ling loses her body and her love in *Boatman's Daughter*. The same narrative pattern is also found in other films of the 1930s, though often with more tragic ends. In *Daybreak*, the self-sacrificing prostitute is executed; in *New Woman*, the woman writer, who is almost forced to sell her body once in order to afford her daughter's hospitalization, finally commits suicide in total despair; in Yuan Muzhi's *Malu tianshi* (Street angel, 1937), an ill-fated streetwalker, who always moves in darkness and seldom speaks in the film, is stabbed to death in the end.[60] Traceable to *Yan Ruisheng* in the early 1920s, this discursive strategy of representing the ill-reputed as the ill-fated fortuitously predestined the star Ruan Lingyu, who played the female protagonist in both *Goddess* and *New Woman*, and who functioned as a public embodiment of male fantasy in early 1930s Shanghai, a city that indulged in the endless tabloid reports of her lurid private life (an actress torn between two unfaithful husbands). Ruan's tragic suicide in 1935 inscribed a conspicuous mark on the urban imagination in Republican China. What is more significant is that, half a century later, her story returned to the screen to haunt urban audiences in both mainland China and Hong Kong.[61]

From the Perspective of the 1990s

The idealization of ethico-moral virtues in *Goddess* and the glorification of potent proletarian power in *Boatman's Daughter* (embodied in the male factory worker who breaks into a brothel to try to rescue his beloved A Ling) may appear a far cry from the perspective of the 1990s. After decades of clandestine existence in the 1950s through the 1970s, prostitution in China has become widespread again since the mid-1980s and public tolerance seems to have increased accordingly.[62] It is, therefore, not merely a historical irony that prostitution has returned in its more glamorous form in the recent cinematic rewriting of modern Chinese history. *Yanzhi kou* (Rouge, 1987) by Stanley Kwan (Guan Jinpeng, b. 1957) attempts to reconstruct a local history of Hong Kong by comparing drastically different forms of sexuality in the 1930s and the 1980s, and *Bawang bieji* (Farewell my concubine, 1993) by Chen Kaige (b. 1952) reflects on the political history of mainland China by following the fate of Peking opera as a repeatedly violated cultural form.[63] Rather than the previously fragile, gentle, and self-sacrificial figures, recent Chinese films prefer to feature strong-willed and aggressive woman characters, who want to control not only their own fate but in varying degrees that of their husbands and lovers as well. In *Rouge*, for instance, Fleur decides that she and her lover are to commit love suicide by swallowing an overdose of opium (and on top of that she secretly adds poison to the wine they later drink together). In *Farewell My Concubine*, Juxian throws a bundle of jewelry to her madam and buys herself out of prostitution in order to marry the actor she loves (and she does it without obtaining his consent in advance). In both films, the prostitutes are morally stronger than their male counterparts and are more dedicated to their chosen goals. They are no longer merely objects of sympathy for the audience or the filmmaker.

With a notable exception of *Kongbu fenzi* (Terrorizer, 1986) by Edward Yang (Yang Dechang, b. 1947), which traces a dangerous, mysterious Eurasian girl in the underworld of Taipei, recent Chinese films—by male and female directors alike—prefer the glamorous courtesan to the miserable streetwalker.[64] In aesthetic rather than moral terms, the glory and glamor of prostitution are represented in greater detail to invoke *nostalgia* in the viewer.[65] As far as textual representation is concerned, it seems as if the discourse on prostitution in modern China had traveled full circle: starting with an idealization of the highly cultured courtesan at the turn of the century, through an exposure of the ruthlessly exploited streetwalker in the 1930s, to a reglamorization of the courtesan culture from the 1980s on. Perhaps what Sue Gronewold observes of prostitution in modern China in general applies to contemporary Chinese cinema as well: "Condemned in law and reviled in rhetoric, prostitution was condoned in practice and merely regulated in reality."[66] In recent cinematic representations, condemnation of prostitution on moral grounds does not merit much attention, not even at a rhetorical level. Instead, on the pretext of retelling Chinese history, condoning prostitution projects a fantastic dream world, where the lifestyle of the bygone *demimondaines* is preserved as a Chinese cultural tradition and stored forever in public memory.[67]

In a striking way, recent Chinese films have much in common with the Hollywood representation of East Asia in the 1930s and 1940s. Beneath the historical script in *Rouge*, for example, is a rendition of prostitution as an essential experience of urban phantasmagoria. The same can be found in Josef von Sternberg's film *The Shanghai Gesture* (1941), in which a Eurasian girl flaunts her sexuality amid the smoke of opium, the smell of wine, and the sound of gold, albeit to a rather tragic end. Sternberg's earlier film, *Shanghai Express* (1932), again prominently features prostitution in the narrative, but with a happy ending. In juxtaposing von Sternberg's films to contemporary Western literary representation, I discovered that the dream quality of urban life had already been noted by Hendrik De Leeuw, who prefaced his 1933 investigative report of prostitution in Asia with "Dream of Lost Women," composed in a highly poetic style:

> The dream is confused and broken. The unearthly melody becomes a strange loud discordance, the cries and wailing of women rise over the sound of flutes, and, suddenly, the cities fade, the cities of Tokyo and Yokohama, of Shanghai and Hongkong, of Port Said and Singapore and Macao. The texture of the dream roughens; the shifting designs are new and fearful, until, at last, the faces gleam clearly in the mist, the features of thousands and thousands of girls and women, streaming in nakedness over the face of the earth, tossing their arms in despair, laughing in wild abandon, walking languidly in the grip of opium. White and brown and yellow and black, they engulf the landscape, drifting in a pandemonium of joy and grief and anger into that yawning cavern, over whose black, insatiable mouth, in all the languages and characters of Asia, is written the one word: Lust.[68]

De Leeuw's case is symptomatic of public discourse on prostitution in general. The bulk of his book is written in the informative mode, detailed with plenty of interviews and firsthand observations; yet, in spite of his moralist purpose (hence his title *Cities of Sin*, which conveys a castigating tone), he ended his poetic "Dream of Lost Women" with a cluster of blurred images of cities and women in Asia. To a considerable extent, his final private vision of a stream of naked, languishing, and hysterical women careening toward the cavern of lust is projected to the public in a fairly hedonistic manner, visually resembling the typical Hollywood representation of prostitution (as in von Sternberg's films mentioned above). A conflict between the moralist intent (the public) and the hedonistic force of visual images (the private) is embedded in the discourse on prostitution, just as the idea of prostitution itself contains a conflict between the public and the private.

From the perspective of the 1990s, what can we make of De Leeuw's connection of urban imagination and Asian prostitution? To be sure, "dreams of lost women" continue to be produced by film technology, but the ideas of sin and guilt De Leeuw attributed to prostitution rarely surface in contemporary Chinese films. Morality is hardly an issue now, and visual images seem to be the only thing that prevails in the space of urban imagination: images of flower-wine banquets, of gorgeous fashions, of shining jewelry, and, most important, of the alluring smile of the enigmatic city woman. In retrospect, the lack of moral concern in the 1990s foregrounds the 1930s Chinese films: films like *Goddess* and *Boatman's Daughter* appear almost unique—although somewhat naive—in their puritanical ideological stand. What emerges as particularly ironic in my juxtaposition of cinematic configurations of prostitution between the 1930s and the 1980s and 1990s is the triumph of visual images over any moralist intent. Insofar as visual imagination is concerned, I would conclude by suggesting that contemporary Chinese filmmakers have rediscovered the fin-de-siècle ambience of *hedonism* in the late Qing and early Republican periods, reworked a few ideologically ambiguous but visually provocative scenes of male fantasy in the 1930s Chinese films (such as scenes of modeling and street solicitation), and redelivered them as a full-scale spectacle of repressed—indeed, reinvented—Chinese sexuality, perfected in the latest Hollywood fashion of glamorization but packaged as essential to an inscrutable oriental culture.[69]

PART **THREE**   CONSTRUCTING IDENTITY: NATIONALISM,

METROPOLITANISM, PAN-ASIANISM

Constructing a New National Culture: Film Censorship and the Issues of Cantonese Dialect, Superstition, and Sex in the Nanjing Decade

ZHIWEI XIAO

Although much has been said about the Nationalist efforts to consolidate their political power, promote the nation's economy, reform the education system, and increase their social control during the Nanjing decade (1927–37),[1] little attention has been given to their cultural policy during this period. In this chapter, I will discuss how the Nanjing government attempted to reconstruct a "new" ideology and cultural values by examining its censorship of motion pictures. While Cantonese dialect, superstition, and sex may seem to have nothing to do with each other at first glance, they were some of the most critical issues on the Nationalist film censors' agenda. One of the consistent policies of the Nanjing government with regard to film censorship was to ban all dialect films because they were deemed to be threatening to the country's political unity. Meanwhile, in a zealous drive toward modernity, the Nanjing censors prohibited anything they viewed as unscientific in the films. Hence, all films dealing with superstitious or even religious subjects were banned. Finally, like censors elsewhere in the world, the Chinese censors frowned upon racy pictures because they saw those films as incongruous with China's immediate national goals. By looking at cases in which the National Film Censorship Committee (hereafter NFCC) and the Central Film Censorship Committee (hereafter CFCC) handled dialect (mostly Cantonese), superstitious, and "racy" films, I hope to shed light on some aspects of the Nationalist cultural policy during the Nanjing decade.[2]

The Issue of Cantonese Dialect Films

The first Chinese sound film was not made until 1930.[3] During the silent era, the question of what dialect should be used in the movies was never raised. During the 1920s, the controversy centered mainly on whether classical or modern vernacular styles of writing were appropriate for subtitles.[4] After the NFCC was founded in 1931, it insisted that all Chinese films use easy-to-understand vernacular captions. After Chinese studios began producing sound films, the NFCC further decided that Mandarin Chinese, or *guoyu* (the national language), be used as the spoken language in films and prohibited the use of dialects. To further the cause of *guoyu*, the NFCC requested that film studios in China print the standard syllable chart at the beginning of each film, and that the characters in subtitles be marked with standard pronunciation.[5]

Guoyu, as one of the many dialects spoken in China, was proclaimed the official language of the nation in the 1910s and gained popularity and political significance as modern mass media became an important vehicle of communication.[6] When Sun Yat-sen (Sun Zhongshan, 1866–1925) addressed audiences in public with his labored *guoyu*, he set an example: despite his fluency in Cantonese, he would strive to speak a language that represented national consciousness.

In Canton, local people spoke Cantonese and never fully accepted *guoyu* as a spoken language. After Chiang Kai-shek (Jiang Jieshi, 1887–1975) took power in 1928, Hu Hanmin (1879–1936), another leader who held much prestige within the Nationalist Party, refused to acknowledge Jiang's political legitimacy. With the help of Chen Jitang (1890–1954), a Cantonese militarist, Hu formed a separate government in Canton, opposing Nanjing's authority. Although in January 1932 the political leaders in Guangdong and Guangxi publicly acknowledged Nanjing's authority, in reality, both of these provinces insisted on autonomous rule. In this political context, local dialect became an issue for both the central and local governments. In the eyes of the central government, local dialect was a factor supporting regional separatism, whereas the regional governments saw in local dialect a legitimate claim of "regional uniqueness."

As far as the film industry was concerned, Canton was second only to Shanghai in importance. Together with the southeast Asia Chinese communities, Canton was also a major film market for the Shanghai studios.[7] Because of its importance as a market for domestically made films, many Shanghai studios had branch studios in the Cantonese-speaking cities of Hong Kong and Canton. For instance, the Lianhua and Tianyi studios both had operations in Hong Kong. Although Mingxing Studio did not have a branch in the south, it did commission work for studios in Canton. After the advent of sound technology in the late 1920s, these branch studios in the south all began to make films in Cantonese to cater to local audiences as well as overseas Chinese communities. These activities directly violated the NFCC's *guoyu* policy. Throughout the Nanjing decade, the issue of Cantonese-language movies was a battleground between Nanjing and Canton. The Canton regime challenged not only Nanjing's political policy but also its cultural policy by allowing studios to make dialect films, because the Film Censorship Statute promulgated by Nanjing stipulated that the NFCC was the only authority in the country to control films. The Canton government set up a local censorship committee with its own rules about what kinds of films were permissible in theaters throughout the region. The NFCC's decisions were meaningless in Canton.

With the political protection of the Canton government, film studios in Canton ignored Nanjing's ban on making dialect movies. As a result, only the Shanghai studios were prevented from making dialect films because they were under tighter control from the NFCC/CFCC. Unhappy about losing the Canton and overseas market to their competitors in the south, Shanghai filmmakers bitterly complained about the unfairness and inconsistency of the NFCC's policy.

In fact, the NFCC/CFCC's policy regarding dialect movies was consistent. In 1931, the NFCC issued its first circular to studios throughout the country, warning them that no films made in local dialects would be tolerated.[8] In 1934, after the NFCC was reorganized, the newly appointed director of the CFCC, Luo Gang (1901–77), restated the policy.[9] The problem was that the peculiar political relationship between Canton and Nanjing posed obstacles to any effective implementation of the policy. Canton's political autonomy made it impossible for the NFCC/CFCC's power to extend to that region. It was not until the summer of 1936, when the Canton regime collapsed after an aborted revolt against Nanjing, that the CFCC began to extend its authority there.

Cantonese studios found both political and economic reasons to resist Nanjing's ban on dialect movies, on which they were fiscally dependent. Such films usually catered to the tastes of Cantonese and the overseas Chinese communities and were never intended for distribution in northern China. If the ban on dialect films was effectively enforced, most of southern studios would have been driven out of business.

But the Canton government's protection of the local film industry from Nanjing's "harassment" was motivated more by political considerations than any other. Apparently, Hu Hanmin's political prestige alone was not enough to protect the Canton regime from the unifying rigors of the central government. The political leaders in Canton thus sought other sources of strength to resist Nanjing. They saw Cantonese local culture, especially local dialect, as an effective bolster to maintaining regional autonomy. From their point of view, to allow the assertion of Nanjing's ban on Cantonese films in Canton would amount to ac-

knowledging Nanjing's legitimacy and would open more channels to further influences from the central government.

While resisting the imposition of "national culture" from the central government, the Canton regime made nationalistic gestures in its own way. It required
all movie theaters in Canton to schedule no less than 60 percent of their showing time for domestically made films.[10] This policy was even more "nationalistic" than Nanjing's policy because it guaranteed Chinese filmmakers the advantage in competition with foreign film studios. The filmmakers in Shanghai were
envious of their counterparts in Canton. However, the film distributors in Canton resented the Canton government's policy, feeling that it favored the production side of the industry while putting distributors at a great disadvantage. Theater owners in particular protested that the policy only encouraged studios to
produce films of poor quality while they would ultimately suffer the financial
consequences.[11] Understandably, when the Canton regime collapsed, theater
owners in Canton immediately stopped following this 60 percent rule.[12]

In May 1935, when Hu Hanmin died, the Canton regime lost the shield of Hu's
prestige and personal influence. In anticipation of Nanjing's actions against Canton, the military governor of Canton, Chen Jitang, staged an open revolt against
Nanjing in the summer of 1936. The revolt was soon aborted due to the massive
defection of Chen's forces to the central government, and Chen fled to Hong
Kong. Canton was thus brought under Nanjing's control.

Shanghai filmmakers enthusiastically welcomed these developments in Canton. As one editorial article put it, with the southwest region under the central
government's control, "a unified film censorship is finally possible."[13] Indeed,
following the collapse of the Canton government, the CFCC reemphasized its
policy with regard to dialect films. At a news briefing, Luo Gang, the director of
the CFCC, told reporters that several CFCC officials were preparing to go to that
region to "investigate the situation," so that the CFCC could establish its authority there. On a number of other occasions, the CFCC repeated its position on
banning Cantonese films. In the words of one movie magazine, Nanjing "was
determined to settle the issue once and for all."[14]

Knowing that they no longer had the political protection of the local government, Canton's filmmakers did not wait passively for the CFCC to decide
their future. They held a meeting in the Jinlong Restaurant in Hong Kong in
December 1936 and invited more than three hundred people from the business
sector, news media, and educational institutions. The spokesman for the Cantonese filmmakers, Li Hua, solicited sympathy from the participants and argued that schools, not filmmakers, should be responsible for promulgating
guoyu. He further protested that it would be unfair if Cantonese was permitted
as the language of instruction in school but banned in movies. As an important
and influential figure in cultural circles, Hong Shen, the playwright who earlier

led the protest against Harold Lloyd's offensive film, *Welcome Danger* (1929), was also invited to the meeting. When asked to express his view, he said that the filmmakers in Canton should be given more time to make the transition, which implied that he was not opposed to the principle of the CFCC's policy, but was willing to be flexible regarding its implementation.

Nevertheless, the conference resolved to send a telegram to Nanjing, asking the latter to revoke its policy. It stated that *guoyu* was not yet popularized in Canton. For the purpose of enlightening the masses, Cantonese remained the most effective means, an assertion supported by the fact that the central government regularly broadcast its orders and policies in both English and Cantonese. To further convince Nanjing that Cantonese movies would strengthen and not dissipate central government control, the statement promised that Cantonese movies would advocate nationalism, encourage economic construction, promulgate scientific knowledge, strengthen national ethics, and stimulate the peoples' noble emotions. It further guaranteed that Canton studios would make two short films in *guoyu* for every feature film in Cantonese in order to promote *guoyu* in Canton. In addition to sending this telegram to Nanjing, the Association of Filmmakers in the Southwest (mainly comprised of Cantonese) also sent a delegation to Nanjing in a lobbying effort. Their endeavor was apparently successful because Nanjing agreed to postpone the enforcement of the ban until July 1, 1937.

A CFCC official, Dai Ce, arrived in Canton in May 1937 in anticipation of the deadline. He brought with him a letter from the CFCC's director, Luo Gang, to Li Hua, Zhao Shushen, and Zhu Qingxian, the representatives of the Association. Dai's presence in Canton and the contents of Luo's letter were both meant to convince the Cantonese filmmakers that the CFCC's stand on prohibiting the making of Cantonese films was adamant and unflinching. While there, Dai turned down a request from the Cantonese filmmakers to set up a CFCC branch in Canton on the grounds that such a precedent would lead to similar requests from other provinces.

Although the CFCC seemed to be determined to carry out its ban on Cantonese movies, the actual implementation was not easy. As one commentator sarcastically commented, "the CFCC has set deadlines many times and every time the deadline is pushed back."[15] Many wondered whether the July 1 deadline would also quietly lapse. Such doubts were not unfounded. On June 17, the Ministry of Propaganda invited representatives from the party, government, film industry, and news media to an open discussion on the issue of Cantonese films. A delegation from Canton was present at the meeting. There was a heated debate. The representatives from Canton argued that Cantonese was the only language that people in Canton could understand. If Nanjing wanted to use films to instill nationalism into the populace there and in overseas Chinese communities, films had to be made in Cantonese. Besides, Sun Yat-sen himself was from Canton; maybe his home dialect should receive more acceptance nationwide.

The filmmakers in Shanghai, on the other hand, continued to pressure the Nanjing government on the issue. They argued, if Cantonese films were allowed to exist, other dialect movies should also be allowed, and the filmmakers in Shanghai should be permitted to make Cantonese films themselves and sell copies in southeast Asian markets. Nanjing faced a dilemma. In the words of one official from the Ministry of Propaganda, "we had no intention of lifting the ban on dialect movies, but neither could we enforce the ban effectively [because of the resistance from filmmakers in Canton]."[16] Almost to footnote this quandary, a telegram from the Canton government arrived on June 18 while the conference was still in session. The telegram stated that the drive to ban Cantonese films was a scheme designed by the Shanghai studios aimed at wiping out business competition in the south. It cautioned the central government to consider the issue carefully. The telegram was signed by Wu Tiecheng (1888–1953), the governor of Guangdong, and Zeng Yangfu (1898–1969), the mayor of Canton City, both highly influential figures in the Nationalist government. Apparently, they placed their local interests above those of the nation.

During the conference, the director of the CFCC, Luo Gang, was the only government official who opposed any further delay in the implementation of the ban. The Minister of Propaganda, Shao Lizi (1882–1967), was reluctant to take decisive action because if he insisted on the ban he would make enemies of Wu Tiecheng and Zeng Yangfu and aggravate the antagonism between Nanjing and Canton; if he revoked the ban the ramifications were equally serious. In the end, Shao managed to avoid directly addressing the issue. Instead, he proposed that studios in Canton be subject to the CFCC's licensing authority. Any studio that intended to make films must meet certain standards, which included a working studio, a basic cast, and a certain number of screenwriters and directors. Failure to meet these standards would result in denial or revocation of the license to operate. This was a rather cunning scheme because there were only four studios in Canton that could meet these standards. If this proposal was carried out, it was hoped, the number of Cantonese film productions would be dramatically cut back. Ironically, this new regulation also had an unintended consequence for studios in Shanghai. Of the twelve members of the Guild of Shanghai's filmmakers, one-fourth of them did not have working studios and were thus subject to elimination.

Shao's proposal was accepted by the Conference. The Ministry of Propaganda further decided to give the Cantonese filmmakers another three years to prepare for the transition to make *guoyu* films. Each year the Cantonese filmmakers were required to produce a quota of films in *guoyu* which would increase each year.[17] Also reemphasized in the Ministry's decision was that the Cantonese filmmakers send their works to Nanjing for review, and that they respect the CFCC's authority. With this, the question regarding Cantonese films seemed to be solved. Weeks later, a large number of Cantonese films arrived in Nanjing for the CFCC to review, an indication that Canton was finally beginning to submit to the CFCC's authority.[18]

However, the battle was far from over. A showdown between Nanjing and Canton came a few weeks after the settlement, when a number of Cantonese business organizations and leaders of overseas Chinese communities sent a petition to Nanjing. The move was a direct result of Cantonese filmmakers' lobbying efforts. Their petition included two requests. One, they wanted a six-year extension, not just three years; two, they wanted the CFCC to set up a branch in Canton. Nanjing was uncompromising this time and turned down the request. The Cantonese filmmakers responded by withholding their films from review. Meanwhile, the municipal government of Canton issued an edict, authorizing the old Board of Censors for Films and Theaters, which had been organized under the former regime, to resume its duties.[19]

As Nanjing and Canton reached this stalemate, the Japanese launched a full-scale attack on China. By August 1937, Shanghai was under the threat of attack by Japanese troops. With the memory of the destruction caused by the Japanese attack on Shanghai in 1932 still fresh, many studios in Shanghai began to move to Hong Kong. For a while, film production in Shanghai virtually came to a halt. This new situation required Nanjing to adjust its film policy in the south. Finally, in late 1937, the CFCC set up offices in both Guangzhou and Hong Kong. By late February, Japanese warplanes began bombing Canton. Hong Kong became the only place where film production remained active. By necessity, the CFCC's Canton office joined the Hong Kong branch, with Xu Hao as regional director. With very little help from the central government, which was preoccupied with the war with Japan at the time, the CFCC's Hong Kong branch had to rely on the financial support provided by the Association of Hong Kong Filmmakers for its operation. Since the number of films made in Hong Kong and Canton was limited, the reviewing of those films was soon finished. The Association of Hong Kong Filmmakers was no charity organization. The only reason it financed the CFCC's operation in Hong Kong was that it was convenient for the filmmakers in Hong Kong to have their films reviewed locally. Now that there were no more films to review, it told the CFCC officials to go back to Canton and come to Hong Kong only when new productions were completed.[20]

However feeble the CFCC's control in this region, it remained a symbol of the central government's authority. The Ministry of Propaganda further decided to authorize the Guangzhou office, which had only three officials, to be in charge of all matters related to film censorship, which elevated its status to one of national importance. In reality, the Guangzhou office did not have nearly as much power over studios in Guangzhou and Hong Kong as the former CFCC had over studios in Shanghai. The filmmakers in Hong Kong and Guangzhou openly defied the authority of this office, continuing to produce films the contents of which were unacceptable by CFCC standards, and refusing to send them for review by late 1938.[21] Under such circumstances, it made little sense to retain the CFCC's office in that region. With the Japanese troops approaching Canton, the Nationalist government decided to recall the office.

The Antisuperstition Campaign

One of the most significant developments in China after the 1911 Revolution was the rapid and widespread absorption of modern ideas, particularly the popularization of scientism. The coining of catch phrases like "De xiansheng" and "Sai xiansheng" (Mr. Democracy and Mr. Science) during the May Fourth era illustrates the enthusiasm for science that continued to shape the development of thought and culture in the 1920s and 1930s.[22]

This faith in science was inseparable from China's drive to modernize. The Nationalist state, striving for modernity, saw the realm of popular religion and culture as a "principal obstacle to the establishment of a disenchanted world of reason and plenty."[23] According to Prasenjit Duara's study of the antisuperstition campaigns during the Republican era, the second phase of this campaign began with the ascendancy of the Nanjing government. In 1928 and 1929, the party launched a vigorous "antisuperstition" drive. In rural areas, Nationalist cadres restrained religious activities, attacked clergy, and turned temples into modern schools. In urban areas, they focused on suppressing any expressions in the mass media that could be linked to religion. The ban on films presenting religious subjects was an important part of that campaign.

The category "superstitious films" (shenguai dianying) covered a wide range of subject matter. It included films dealing with religious subjects, such as The Ten Commandments (1923) and Ben-Hur (1926), both of which were banned in the 1930s.[24] Here, the emphasis was on shen (gods and deities). Very few Chinese films fell into this category because Chinese films rarely dealt with religious subject matter. "Superstitious films" also included films whose plot, characters, or narrative were clearly unscientific. For instance, Alice in Wonderland (1933) and Frankenstein (1931) were banned for their "strangeness." Here, the emphasis was on guai (bizarre, exotic, and strange). Numerous Chinese movies made in the 1920s fell prey to this criticism, often portraying martial arts masters with magical skills, throwing fireballs, flying in the sky, summoning ghosts, and so on. The Chinese term referring to this genre of films was wuxia shenguai pian (films about knights-errant, immortals, and ghosts), suggesting the close connection between the display of martial-arts skills and superstitious elements. The Chinese fascination with such stories is deeply rooted in folklore and popular beliefs, topics too diverse to discuss effectively here. Suffice it to say, as mentioned previously, that such films were myriad and extremely popular.[25]

Since audiences for such films were predominantly from the lower strata of society and were usually uneducated or illiterate, the Nationalist censors felt a paternalistic obligation to "guide" them. A few incidents further convinced the ruling elite of the necessity to ban such films. For instance, it was reported that during the showing of *Nezha chushi* (The coming of Nezha, 1927), a story about Chinese folk deities adapted from the classic novel *Fengshen yanyi* (The investiture of the gods), some audience members held a worshipping ritual in the theater. They mistook the image of Nezha, who is only a fictional character in the movie, for the deity's real manifestation and went on the stage to burn incense for him.[26]

From the state's point of view, these films served to encourage and perpetuate superstitious beliefs among the populace. As early as 1928 the Ministry of the Interior announced a policy that banned films on religious subjects.[27] The Film Censorship Statute published in 1930 explicitly stated in clause four of article two that no films advocating superstition were permitted.[28] Only weeks after its establishment, the NFCC issued a circular to all studios and movie theaters in the country, asking them to produce and exhibit films pertaining to "science, patriotism, and exploration."[29]

The Chinese authorities and cultural elite agreed that movies were more than mere entertainment.[30] One observer noted, "if we look at magic/ghost movies simply as entertainment, they are harmless. However, film is a serious form of artistic expression; therefore this type of film cannot be tolerated."[31] The major film studios and cultural elites welcomed the antisuperstition policy and actively participated in the campaign to eradicate superstitious films.[32] An article in the *Minguo ribao* (The republican daily), the Nationalist Party's official newspaper, stated that magic/ghost movies were obstacles impeding the government's campaign to eradicate temples in the countryside.[33] Another commentator praised the government's action to ban magic/ghost movies as timely and justified.[34] Mao Dun's (1896–1981) criticism of the genre is typical. In a famous essay he denounced them for perpetuating feudal ideology and inducing audiences to escape into a fantasy world rather than face their problems in reality.[35]

The major studios supported the policy because they saw it as an opportunity to eliminate their business rivals.[36] For years, the smaller studios had produced a disproportionate number of martial arts and magic/ghost movies.[37] In doing so, they competed with the big studios for audience. The major companies had long hoped to squelch their competitors and saw in the state's antisuperstition policy a means to suppress the smaller studio's activities. The state, however, wanted to act evenhandedly. On the one hand, the government wanted to ban superstitious films; on the other, it did not want to hurt business interests, because economic growth was also part of the state's modernizing project. One of the NFCC's tasks was to ensure the healthy development of the Chinese film industry. The ban on magic/ghost films put many small studios on the verge of bankruptcy. So the NFCC adopted a "go easy" policy toward the small studios. Some people even proposed setting up a fund to help them to make the transition to producing more ideologically acceptable films.[38]

The smaller studios quickly exploited the situation. Led by Huawei Company, a major distribution agency, they appealed to the authorities for leniency. The petition promised that they would not make such films in the future, but requested that the ones they had already produced be allowed to be shown in theaters.[39] The NFCC granted the petition and agreed to do two things: first, they would reexamine those films that had already been banned and select some for release; second, for the "unsalvageable" films, the activation of the ban would be postponed until the studios made sufficient profits from them. In the words of the NFCC officials, "We will do anything to ensure that the studios not suffer financial losses."[40]

Some in the film industry criticized the NFCC's softness regarding magic/ghost movies. They complained that the NFCC was too lenient with the small studios, had spared too many problematic films under the pretext of being considerate of the difficulties faced by businesspeople. Others pointed out that in the long run, the NFCC's "business consideration" was not going to save China's film industry because by tolerating those films, the NFCC not only "obstructed the important antisuperstition campaign, but also allowed the small studios to continue to tarnish the image of China's film industry as a whole and ruin the audience's appetite for domestically made films."[41]

In fairness, the NFCC only meant to be lenient toward films that had already been made and never intended to abandon its policy banning new productions. From 1931 to 1938 the NFCC carried out a number of operations to halt production of magic/ghost films.[42] Because of the NFCC's vigorous efforts, the genre disappeared from major circulation and studios that continued producing them were mostly driven underground.[43]

However, as leftist films began to emerge as a formidable force by the early 1930s, the Nationalist government shifted the focus of its film policy. The suppression of politically dissident voices now gained priority over the restriction of magic/ghost movies. Yet to pursue a policy that simultaneously banned politically dissident films and superstitious films would really hurt the film industry; some officials even proposed that the ban on magic/ghost movies be lifted. Although the government never reneged on its policy to ban superstitious films, enforcement was greatly relaxed. By the mid 1930s, many magic/ghost movies that had previously been banned were rereleased with few deletions and some movie theaters openly showed them under the thinly disguised pretext of "ridiculing the superstitious beliefs in these films."[44]

Modernity and the New Sexual Morality

In China modernity has never been separable from foreignness. As one Chinese writer of the 1930s put it: "Anything foreign is modern, whether it be a social usage or a style of dress."[45] Films played an important role in popularizing Western values and goods. The Nationalist state wanted modernity in China, but rejected its inherent foreignness. This stand was best illustrated in Nanjing's policy toward so-called sexy pictures, with which modernity and foreignness were most intimately linked. It was not incidental that the presentation of women's bodies in these pictures became a focal point in both the boardroom of the film censors and public discussions.

The changes in sexual mores during the Republican period were astonishing. In cities like Shanghai, kissing in public became more and more common, a practice that had not been a public aspect of traditional Chinese lovemaking; young men and women began living together without getting married; revealing and provocative styles of clothing were preferred by both men and women; nude pictures of women appeared on the covers of magazines.[46] The rise of movies provided a further venue for sexual displays. As one commentator put it: "Most of the people who go to movies are not going for the movie per se, but to enjoy the images of female stars."[47] As the number of movie theaters increased rapidly, the consumption of pornographic films was no longer confined to private residences.[48]

Once the Nanjing government was established, the state began to take steps to curb this "liberal" trend and channel it to the service of the state's modernization project. By suppressing certain types of films and promoting others, the state endorsed a new sexual morality. From June 1931 to June 1932 alone, a total of 71 films, both domestic and foreign productions, were banned by the NFCC. While the majority of foreign films were banned for their offensiveness to Chinese sensitivities, most of the Chinese films were banned for moral reasons.[49] Sexual subjects in particular were most sensitive and controversial.

When banning a film or requiring a deletion, the NFCC often used the phrase *you shang fenghua* (injurious to social mores) to justify its action. In 1932, the NFCC issued a guideline to interpret what "injurious to social mores" meant. The following were considered unacceptable: depicting obscenity and unchaste behavior; depicting the use of intrigue or violence on the opposite sex for the purpose of sexual satisfaction; directly depicting or suggesting incest; showing women undressing in an inappropriate manner; and showing women giving birth or having an abortion.[50] Even in these clarifications ambiguities abound. What is considered "obscenity and unchaste behavior"? What manner of undressing is deemed "inappropriate"? To understand the Nationalist government's film policy, we must not focus on the rules only, but also look at how the rules were interpreted through their implementation.

Of course, pornographic films were always out of the question and subject to the most strict censorship. Even though they were not totally eliminated and smaller studios continued to make them, for the most part they became an underground phenomenon. According to contemporary descriptions of these films, they were quite similar to the kinds of pornography that exist today, often graphically presenting intercourse and sexual organs. Such hardcore pornography was easy to recognize and deal with, but the so-called sexy pictures were much more ambiguous. The NFCC's approval of *Ecstasy* (1933), a notoriously erotic film from Czechoslovakia, and the ban on *Top Hat* (1935), a Paramount light romantic comedy with Ginger Rogers and Fred Astaire, illustrate the confusion and arbitrariness on the part of the censors. Nevertheless, there was a pattern in the NFCC's rulings. For instance, scenes of nudity were always prohibited.[51] Although the language used by the movie advertisers was always sensational and tantalizing, the actual films rarely showed what the ads had led people to expect. In fact, audiences were often disappointed, and complained about the exaggerated terms the ads used.[52] As one critic wrote, "The movie ads purposely teased the audience and made people believe they were going to see something really racy. In fact, more often than not the actual films failed to deliver what the advertiser promised."[53] Another letter writer protested to a movie magazine and condemned the "degeneracy of movie ads."[54] The abuse of advertising language made the NFCC decide to censor movie ads in January 1934 and ban any advertisement that used excessively racy language.

Suggestive advertisements aside, in reality no Chinese film showing full nudity was ever approved by the NFCC for public screening. This was a telling contrast to the 1920s, when scenes of female nudity in movies such as *Pansi dong* (The spider queen, 1927) were permitted by the authorities (see fig. 22).[55] According to one estimate, prior to 1931 there had been ten Chinese-made films with scenes of female nudity.[56] The number of foreign films with nude scenes probably exceeded that of Chinese films because in general "foreign films were more daring in their presentation of sexuality."[57] After the NFCC was founded in 1931, by all accounts, nude scenes disappeared from the screen. Occasionally, when the plot justified it, the NFCC allowed a few partially nude scenes. For instance, it was reported that during the shooting of *Gucheng lienü* (The heroine of the besieged city, 1936), there was a rape scene in which the villain was supposed to rip the clothes off Chen Yanyan (b. 1916), the female lead. The actor who played the villain was a little too rough, and as a result, one of Chen's breasts was exposed. Chen's husband, Huang Shaofen (b. 1911), was very upset and made the director promise to cut the scene. Yet when the film was released Huang found the scene still intact.[58] Such a case was more an exception than a rule. In general, the NFCC was very strict with nude scenes. When Yuan Meiyun, who later became a star, was recruited by Yihua studio, her parents insisted that the studio write in the contract that no nude scenes would be required of her. The studio representative replied that it was really not necessary because the NFCC would not allow such scenes to be filmed anyway.[59]

The NFCC's concept of "racy" applied not only to nude scenes. In 1934, a film titled *Renjian xianzi* (The worldly immortals) was condemned as "lewd" because during the dance sequences the female dancers in the film "exposed their bras and panties."[60] The NFCC ordered the studio to cut those scenes before the film's release. Another film was banned because the producer refused to cut a scene that showed a woman giving birth.[61] The Nationalist film censors' standard of decency was indeed restrictive. In one case, Yucheng Studio submitted a film script to the CFCC, which killed the script because the woman character married seven times in one month. One censor wrote on the margin of the script: "This is not a light romance comedy, but virtual pornography"; and the CFCC sent back the script to Yucheng with a note: "Please don't send us this kind of script in the future."[62]

Under the CFCC's rules, scenes of kissing were also taboo and were usually ordered cut.[63] This policy applied to foreign films as well. The Chinese censors' aversion to kissing, in part, had to do with the foreignness of the practice. As one commentator wrote, "kissing is a more primitive way of expressing intimacy. As human beings further evolved from their animal stage, they embraced more civilized and healthy forms of intimate contact. For instance, the Chinese usually expressed their intimate feelings through eye contact."[64] It seemed to be true that Chinese actresses of the 1920s and 1930s did not feel comfortable participating in kissing scenes. As one commentator sarcastically pointed out, "they are more willing to do a nude scene than a kissing scene because the latter involves real contact."[65] Another movie critic complained that Chinese actors and actresses seemed to be so awkward doing kissing scenes in front of the camera that they ought to learn the art from their Western counterparts.[66] Even during the 1930s it was still a "big deal" for movie people to perform kissing scenes. For instance, a jealous man resented his sweetheart's kissing scenes in a movie and protested to the director.[67] The predominant views expressed in public debate usually denounced kissing as an un-Chinese practice. Sometimes, the attack on kissing was conducted more subtly. By translating and referring to

22. Eroticism and nudity under attack in *The Spider Queen* (1927), courtesy of the China Film Archive.

the writings of certain Western medical experts, Chinese critics tried to carry out their crusade against this "non-Chinese" sexual practice behind the facade of "modernity" and "science."[68]

Prohibition was only part of the story. The NFCC/CFCC was also actively involved in constructing or redefining sexual mores through censorship. In 1936, a Czechoslovakian film titled *Ecstasy* scored a tremendous amount of publicity even before it was brought to Shanghai, simply because its female star, Heidi Keisler, appeared nude in a number of scenes.[69] The film was banned in the United States because of its provocative nature. Interestingly, the CFCC decided to allow the film to be shown in China. When first released, the Chinese translation of the title was *Yuyan*, meaning "flame of desire," which quite appropriately rendered the theme of the movie, which was about a woman's sexual awakening and eventual reconciliation with her alienated husband. The censors, however, did not like the title and changed it to *Ai de xietiao*, meaning "harmony of love." Then they cut all the nude scenes.[70] In doing so, the censors reconstructed the meaning of the movie. Audiences, titillated by the publicity about this film and unaware of the cuts, rushed to the Central Theater in Shanghai where the film was shown, only to experience a bitter disappointment. The angry audience broke into a riot and asked for refunds. In the end, the theater promised to donate half the ticket sales from the show to the soldiers fighting in the north.

The NFCC/CFCC also influenced the imaging of modernity by promoting an athletic ideal. It encouraged the creation of screen images of young men and women who looked healthy and physically fit, and banned those which fell short of this ideal. In 1935, a film titled *Mofan qingnian* (A model youth) failed to get the censors' approval, despite the fact that the script was written by Chen Guofu (1892–1951), the governor of Jiangsu Province and brother of Chen Lifu (b. 1890), the man in charge of the propaganda apparatus of the Nationalist Party. The main reason for the ban was that the male protagonist in this film was, in the words of the censors, *youtou fenmian* (an oily hair and powdery face), a reference to an effeminate male type who is meticulously groomed, covered with makeup, and dandyish. The censors did not think such an image should serve as a model for Chinese youth.[71]

Indeed, the effeminate male movie stars from the 1920s were replaced by a much more muscular group of actors in the 1930s. During the 1930s, the most popular male stars were Jin Yan (1910–83) and Gao Zhanfei (1904–69), both with much more manly physiques than the actors of the 1920s. A survey also suggested that a trait shared by popular male stars was their athletic look.[72] Some even suggested that what women enjoyed most in movie theaters was "seeing their male stars weight-lifting."[73] Gone were the days of the traditional *xiaosheng* type (cultured, feminine-looking male actors);[74] with the NFCC/CFCC's promotion, the athletic-looking man dominated the screen.

It should be pointed out that physical well-being and athletic looks were also expected of women. As one observer put it, "physical fitness and flirtatiousness" (jianmei he mei) were the two features of modern beauties.[75] Another commentator reminded his readers that the criterion of female beauty no longer involved only a woman's face but her whole body.[76] Female movie stars like Wang Renmei and Li Lili were frequently cited as examples of "modern beauties." There was openly expressed scorn for actresses who were not athletic looking. For instance, an advice columnist suggested that Hu Die, the most popular female star of the time, play tennis to become more physically fit.[77] Swimming became a required skill for female movie stars in the 1930s because it provided them the opportunity to show off their beautiful bodies, if not in movies, at least in publicity photos. All this contrasted quite strikingly with the attitude toward female beauty during the 1920s, when vulnerability was perceived as an essential feature of femininity.[78]

The state's promotion of physical fitness was directed toward building a

strong nation. Yet in popular culture, the emphasis on the body was often translated into displays of sexuality, which the state wished to suppress. A movie magazine essay instructing women how to look attractive emphasized two points:
physical fitness and sexiness.[79] Both criteria were consistent with contemporary standards of modern beauty.[80] Physical fitness was seen as part of women's
sex appeal; the censor's desire to distinguish nationalist athleticism from inappropriate displays of sexuality would be invariably frustrated where women
were concerned.

With more and more women wearing low-cut fashions, having their hair
done in the latest Western styles, and even baring their legs in public places,[81]
the authorities began extending their reach beyond the movie screen, from controlling images of women to controlling women's bodies. In many places, local
governments regulated women's fashion and bodily adornments. In Shandong,
permed hair and high heels were prohibited. The governor, Han Fuqu (1890–
1938), had arrested women who defied the rule.[82] In Shanxi, the local authorities ordered that all prostitutes wear permed hair and high-heeled shoes as their
professional markers so that other women would not dare to adopt these
styles.[83] In Beijing, the city government prohibited women from baring their
legs in public places.[84]

There was nothing new in the government's efforts to control people's bodies. After the 1911 Revolution, the Republican government prohibited men to
wear queues and women to have their feet bound. In 1927 there were calls from
both government officials and social elites to ban the practice of breast-binding
among women.[85] In December 1929, the Ministry of Interior of the Nanjing
government issued a decree officially prohibiting the practice. The argument
was that breast-binding inhibited women's ability to produce healthy babies,
and that this would lead to the weakening of the nation. If unchecked, the decree warned, "the Chinese race will wither and the country will be finished."[86]

The focus on women in particular was worth noticing. Men had long felt re-
sentment toward the "emancipation of women." Many conservatives denounced
the "modern woman" and insisted that the proper place for women was home.[87]
Some warned women of the dangers of deviating from their traditional roles.[88]
Others gave "friendly advice" to women. Often, the advice was from a Westerner,
which allowed the conservative thrust to be hidden behind a seemingly modern
facade.[89] When an American film titled *The Unchastened Women* was brought to
China, it was immediately used as a "women's guide." One critic wrote: "This
film shows the proper manner in which women should serve their husbands.
Although the woman protagonist suffers some injustice from her husband, she
endures it and the end result is complete happiness. Chinese women must go to
see this film."[90]

Concluding Remarks

The overall achievements for the NFCC/CFCC in controlling the film industry and using film as an instrument for nation-building are mixed. One cannot find any case in which the NFCC/CFCC demonstrated a clear and clean success. The ban on dialect movies was strongly resisted in Canton; the campaign to eradicate superstitious movies was derailed by the antileftist reorientation in the mid-1930s; the attempt to cleanse "erotic" images from the screen seemed to be most successful, but even in this case the victory was less than total. However, if we look at the general trend, it is clear that in all three areas the NFCC/CFCC successfully set the direction for China's film industry. Although Cantonese dialect films continued to exist, their number and scale of distribution were increasingly limited. Especially after the fall of the Canton regime, makers of Cantonese film were more and more on the defensive. The antisuperstitious film campaign might not have eliminated all magic/ghost/martial arts movies, but it did succeed in marginalizing the genre and driving it out of mainstream theaters. The prohibition of "erotic" images and promotion of physical fitness through film also achieved mixed results. Though displays of sexuality were not eliminated, the state succeeded in establishing a new physical ideal.

Furthermore, for every prohibition, there was a positive thrust. While banning dialect movies, the NFCC/CFCC campaigned to promote *guoyu*; while suppressing superstitious film, the NFCC/CFCC encouraged educational and informative films; and behind the purging of erotic images on the screen lay the promotion of physical fitness. In all these cases, the state was generally successful in using film to construct a new national culture and a set of values that best suited the drive to modernity.

Chinese cultural elites, including the leftists, fully supported the state's endeavors in all three areas. To some extent, the success of the NFCC/CFCC's operations in these areas could be attributed to the cooperation of cultural elites within the film industry. Even the leftists shared the censors' view on the benefits of prohibiting these kinds of films.[91] This suggests an intriguing relationship between Chinese intellectuals and the state. Both shared a common vision of a strong and modern China and considered all else as secondary. As the censorship of Cantonese, superstitious, and "racy" films shows, the need to build a strong and modern nation was the central motivating factor behind the state's film policies. Films were measured by how well they would serve the enterprise of modernization.

Chapter Nine

Metropolitan Sounds: Music in Chinese Films of the 1930s

SUE TUOHY

The films produced during the mid-1930s in Shanghai, particularly those films intent on mobilizing social-political action, provide a richly textured case study of the role of the arts in cultural commentary and change. Bypassing an aesthetic critique of the film music, this chapter focuses on the ways in which the films used music to engage audiences in the problems and choices faced by Shanghai and the nation as a whole. During this time of widespread concern for the nation's survival as well as of experimentation in film and music, Shanghai was a metropolitan center for both concerns. I argue that the films went beyond a simple reflection of society to produce an on-screen enacted discourse that encouraged audiences to move from being passive spectators to being emotionally and physically engaged actors. Those influential musicians who chose and composed film music participated in the debates about China's future and about the role of the arts in the process of social transformation, debates that made their way into the music. The films thus provided a context in which musical meanings were recast through dramatic and emotional associations. Spilling out of the bounds of the screen to become part of contemporary social-political movements, the music linked the actions taking place on the screen to those on the streets. The choices of music in the films were as diverse as—and, in fact, reflected the ambivalence about—the alternatives put forth for Chinese society.

In spite of the importance of the music heard throughout these films, however, the classic Chinese film histories and more recent film scholarship seldom mention the music or the composers who participated in their production. As Claudia Gorbman writes, "The classical narrative sound film has been constituted in such a way that the spectator does not normally consciously hear the film score."[1] From the lack of attention they have paid to music, film scholars might be included among those spectators who have not consciously heard the film scores. Of those who have written in passing about early Chinese film music, most have remarked upon the "incongruity" of foreign music accompanying Chinese images:

> Only the hodgepodge of random music recordings added to make an accompaniment weakens the effect of the film today.... It is fairer to see *Spring Silkworms* [Chuncan, 1933] without its meaningless soundtrack: dinner music, Parisian and Viennese operettas, jazz, "Old Black Joe," Aloha, church hymns make no attempt to reflect or to comment on the film's action or meaning.[2]

Paul Clark similarly comments on the *Spring Silkworms* score: "Most versions of the sound track are made up of popular Western classical music. The joys and trials of the Zhejiang peasant heroes are accompanied by Polish mazurkas and marches. The incongruity is a reminder of the foreign associations of the film medium."[3] And Ma Ning uses words such as "mismatches," "incongruity," and "contradictory" to assess the music in *Malu tianshi* (Street angel, 1937).[4]

When listened to with ears of the 1990s, the film music indeed may sound incongruous. But if we attempt to listen to and make sense of the film music with ears of the 1930s, as members of Shanghai audiences and intellectual communities, we can hear the music as consistent with contemporary Chinese metropolitan life. This recontextualization—attending to musical meanings within the context of production rather than with associations the sounds may hold today—recognizes the role of music in the period's artistic and intellectual discourse. For instance, many of the films of the 1930s put the category of "foreign" in opposition to that of "Chinese," as the characters in *Chuanjia nü* (Boatman's daughter, 1935) lamented factory closings brought on by the influx of foreign goods, and "western-style" businessmen were portrayed negatively. We must be careful not to read these categories and associations into the music, however. Kreisler's virtuosic "Gypsy Song" was played as background music in that film with no attempt to comment upon that music as negative, contradictory, or, for that matter, even foreign.[5] Instead, the music accompanied the depiction of characters' deep emotions of love and sorrow. The films may have criticized certain types of music associated with the West, such as music of the dance hall, but neither the films nor their contemporary critiques presented foreign music as a whole as a negatively charged symbol. Some of the most patriotic national sounds of the time were set to harmonies, rhythms, and forms considered characteristic of Western music.

The film music brought to the fore some of the central issues debated by Chinese intellectuals, such as the correct path for China's future and the relations between the Chinese past and colonial present. The film music echoed and worked out these issues aurally as the music used inside and outside of the films formed a type of critical, cultural commentary that fed back into the written and spoken discourse. In later decades in China, film music and commentaries followed a different track, one that was concerned, perhaps, with defining more explicitly "national" sounds. But the music in the films produced in 1930s Shanghai grew out of and illustrates that particular social-historical setting. If the musical choices sound random or contradictory today, that may reflect the unsettled nature of the goals within the musical community of wartime China. This community's ambivalence about the role of music in society can be seen in the arguments over opposing ideas heard in the musical discourse of the films. Uncertain about which musical course to follow, the musicians experimented with combinations of Chinese folk and regional music, with national and international forms. In the process, they continued to revise both the contents and social construction of these unstable musical categories through films that dramatized concrete contexts for and new interpretations of the musical sounds. The musical experimentation, bricolage approach to scoring, and the wide range of musical styles combined to produce characteristic metropolitan sounds.

Analyzing the Film Music

The twofold problem of translating into words the sounds and images of cinematic discourse makes a discussion of Chinese film music a complex task, one made more difficult because writings often did not address the contemporary significance of the musical choices. For instance, most of the scripts do not specify the music to be used. Adding to the difficulty is the ambivalence scholars and artists had toward film music. The hybrid genre of film music did not fit neatly into preexisting categories in the art world. The central musical establishment did not consider film music to be a serious musical form. And many directors and scenarists, perhaps because they were not trained in music, left musical decisions to the handful of musicians and composers working in film studios. There was some indifference toward that group as well. In an article on the responsibilities involved in film production, the director Shen Xiling referred to screenwriters, directors, actors, and sound technicians but neglected to mention composers.[6] A few composers of popular songs were named, but the written literature seldom discussed composers and arrangers of background music, although the film credits usually listed their names. While they were central to the films, the music and musicians were peripheral in the writing about film.

In that case, why is music important to an understanding of the films? First of all, the frequency with which scenarists and filmmakers chose music as the topic or organizing principle of their films is striking. Films such as *Genü hongmudan* (Sing-song girl Red Peony, 1931), *Dushi fengguang* (City scenes, 1935), *Street Angel*, *Muxing zhiguang* (Light of motherhood, 1933), *Yasui qian* (A new year's coin, 1937), and *Yuguang qu* (Song of the fishermen, 1934) featured musicians as central characters or music as a central framing device; the titles of films such as *Kaige* (Song of triumph, 1935), *Lianhua jiaoxiangqu* (Lianhua symphony, 1937), and *Qingnian jinxingqu* (March of the youth, 1937) are musical genres. Even before the advent of sound films, live or recorded music constituted a primary feature of the films. As early as the 1920s, music became attached to emotion as "mood music" compilations, arranged numerically according to emotion, were distributed to accompany film showings.[7] Shanghai audiences learned to read and feel the music—consciously or not. Sitting together in theaters, they not only listened to the musical performances but also heard the film characters as they discussed and often transformed their musical society within the film.

In this chapter I will follow Gorbman's advice as she encourages us "to start *listening* to the cinema's uses of music in order to read films in a literate way."[8] This analysis of film music sounds, techniques, contexts, and composers focuses on films produced in Shanghai, particularly films from 1933, when sound films began to dominate, to 1937, when many of the musicians and filmmakers left Shanghai. The films selected are called leftist today, and film scholars from the People's Republic of China (PRC) in the following decades have emphasized the role of the Communist Party in their production. Yet the discourse of the time shows the ideologies and the musical choices made were far from homogeneous. Some of these choices may sound confusing today, perhaps because later processes of canon formation have imposed tidy categories on the terms and goals of film production that were not present then. The analysis reveals a complex process of intellectual debate within the technical and political constraints of producing sound films.

My approach to the music in films and the musicians responsible for it attends to the meanings created through a complex web of relationships between genres and contexts of performance. To understand the meanings within specific instances of musical discourse, theories concerning intertextuality and contextualization are particularly useful.[9] The genres of music heard in Shanghai dance halls or concerts, from Strauss waltzes to revolutionary songs, were recontextualized in the genre of Chinese films. And songs from the films were recontextualized in massive National Salvation assemblies and political marches. As we see music moving between films and beyond into recordings and live performances, the interplay between genres of social-political and artistic discourse stands out as a process in the transformation of meaning. As Charles Briggs and Richard Bauman point out,

> Genre is quintessentially intertextual. When discourse is linked to a particular genre, the process by which it is produced and received is mediated through its relationship with prior discourse. . . . Invoking a genre thus creates indexical connections that extend far beyond the present setting of production or reception.[10]

Film musicians drew upon music of the time, detaching it from previous contexts and reconstituting it in the new context of the film. The music accumulated meaning through intertextual associations that were then transformed as these musical crossovers were combined in the critical commentary within the films and within the film community.

Although music may be considered a nonrepresentational art form, I argue that these processes of intertextuality and recontextualization also helped audiences to "read" film music, often through the aid of recognizable tropes. Chinese film music composers used strategies similar to those of their counterparts in the United States, including "the methodical exploitation of certain musical and extramusical tropes which, for whatever reason, evoke automatic responses in the listener."[11] The process is complex, however, for these "automatic responses" were learned and modified through their experience. The film music created a framed context in which to transform images from other social contexts and to put forth new meanings.[12] Important in this process are the techniques and formal aspects of film and music, as will be discussed in the section on film music techniques.

As will be seen, many of the Chinese filmmakers and musicians wanted more than the transformation of meaning; they wanted their audiences to feel and to act. The musical images were intended to represent and to transform the social-political scene. The dual nature of the intertextuality of genres and transformation of meaning thus extended to social practice. My analysis considers film music as a musical portrayal of metropolitan intellectual thought, a portrayal that may have been experimental and ambiguous but which was broadly disseminated. Listening to the music, we hear and see the multiple visions of society and its future.

New Technologies, Institutions, and Contexts

One hundred years ago, Paris audiences heard the first musical accompaniment to a film and the first foreign films were shown in China. By 1905 China was producing short films which, although silent, were nonetheless about musical topics, particularly national genres such as Peking opera, which featured famous performers such as the opera star Mei Lanfang. The films frequently were placed on a menu of live performances in theaters. Musicians sometimes performed music chosen from scores for film accompaniment produced in the

United States, to suit specific moods and scenes.[13] Larger theaters hired orchestras to perform during the films and, later, played recordings issued to accompany them. This background music, coming from "outside" of the film and separated from the film reel itself, formed the earliest model for film music and influenced its later development in terms of expectations, techniques, and structure.[14]

By 1929–30, Chinese theaters were beginning to change equipment to accommodate sound films. What were the models for these first sound films? Again, musical subjects took a central position. One of the first sound films produced in the United States, *The Jazz Singer* (1927), was shown in China in 1929. And one of first Chinese sound films, *Sing-Song Girl Red Peony*, about a cabaret singer and actress, was a sonic version of the earlier silents and was accompanied by a record produced by the Baidai Changpian Gongsi (Pathe record company). The majority of the sound films shown in Shanghai during the late 1920s and early 1930s were produced in the United States. As Yuan Kao wrote in 1935, "The story of motion pictures in China is the story of American films in the country for these have . . . wellnigh monopolized the business."[15] Film technicians from the United States worked on Chinese films, and Chinese producers and technicians went to the United States to study the new technology. Chinese musical genres could be heard in films, but the Hollywood film music tradition, itself only a few years old, seems to have dominated the early cinematic use of music. The same musical genres from opera, vaudeville, and melodrama could be heard in Chinese films. Ma Ning also has discussed the influence of the Hollywood melodramatic tradition in Chinese leftist films in the "construction of a social allegory that frames the melodramatic narrative of the text."[16] That "narrative," on the other hand, is accomplished through both the visual drama and the "melos," song or tune, of melodrama in the films.

Neither China nor the United States had a cinematic tradition from which to draw. In 1934, Si Bai lamented that sound film had not yet developed as an independent art form but depended on other arts.[17] It also depended on the new technologies. Cinema brought with it new machines and new problems. Two types of sound recording were used at first—sound on disk and sound on film; the former, although less expensive, had the disadvantage of the visual image and sound becoming separated easily. Stories abounded of the ordeals of coordinating eighteen reels of film and eighteen sound disks for one film showing. Problems of synchronization characterized both forms, however. Live orchestras—along with their performance errors—were heard often; the technology for post-recording did not exist; and the separation of film and sound created nightmarish problems in the editing process. The technology of sound itself was of interest and subject to display. In 1926 at the Shanghai Baixing Daxiyuan (One hundred stars theater) audiences viewed the machines, and a projectionist explained the principles of sound projection.[18] By the mid-1930s, the provenance of the film equipment itself became an issue of debate, with many advocating the use of Chinese-made equipment.

Many other musically related institutions of the 1920s and 1930s were also foreign-owned or -influenced. For instance, the leading music education institution, the Shanghai Conservatory, established in 1927, was based on a German model. Its faculty, primarily made up of foreign-trained or foreign musicians, "came to dominate the musical life of the intelligentsia of the treaty ports and to be regarded as authorities for acceptable musical standards and behavior."[19] The conservatory was a center for "new music," music connected to ideologies called progressive and modern that advocated the creation of new musical forms based on European models. Out of the conservatory came symphonies, primarily based in tonal harmonies rather than in musical styles historically used in China. Simultaneously some film music composers were influenced by the folk song movement that grew out of the May Fourth period and that encouraged the collection of Chinese folk music and, later, the songs of the workers in the city. Leo Ou-fan Lee has pointed out the close connection between Chinese drama, cinema, and the new literature movement;[20] the film composers of the time discussed this connection as they sought to compose new music for plays and films that would be the equivalent of the vernacular of the New Literature Movement. Composers went to factories, dance halls, and wharfs to collect workers' musical sounds as raw materials for their film music; they also taught classes and organized singing groups in factories. The musical situation was far from simple: traditional Chinese music and foreign music were simultaneously rejected and admired; musicians sought a vernacular national music rooted in the Chinese people and a modern music for China's future. What this "Chinese new music" was to be, however, had not yet been settled. Nie Er (1912–35), a founding member of the Zhongguo Xinxing Yinyue Yanjiuhui (Chinese new music research society), wrote in his diary at the time: "What is Chinese new music? That is the first question those involved in the movement now must resolve."[21]

Shanghai was an overtly metropolitan and commercial society; and film production required tremendous capital and affiliated institutions. The host of European and American record companies located in Shanghai produced the records that accompanied the films and that played in homes on radios.[22] As these institutions disseminated popular cultural forms through the electronic media, the same music was performed live in dance halls, in coffee houses, and in more overtly political gatherings such as the massive National Salvation assemblies held in Shanghai in 1935–36.[23] While it may be tempting to posit meanings on the basis of a formalist analysis of musical characteristics and structures, the ease by which these surface features crossed between contexts—

from concert halls to activist rallies—and through media illustrates the importance of listening to the sounds in relation to their social settings.

This was a time when ideas and movements were not yet standardized, although later authors have constructed more coherent categories such as "left-wing or leftist films," "Communist films," "patriotic films" and the "underground film movement."[24] The 1930s saw these categories in the process of formation; similar ideas and techniques could be found in films later categorized as different types. Even the films produced at particular studios resisted easy categorization as personnel moved from studio to studio, as film companies struggled to make commercial successes, and as filmmakers constructed their films to pass the government and Japanese censorship. Leyda provides the example of the Lianhua film studio during 1934–35:

> The interesting result of this contradiction was that for two years Shanghai's most "reactionary" films and most "progressive" films were coming from the same studio. Such a situation, in which Japan was both mollified and resisted by the same Chinese organization, is typical for these years.[25]

In this complex context, with its shifting genres, filmmakers incorporated new technologies in a newly formed medium.

Film producers and audiences together were implicated in the process of constructing and deconstructing techniques through which to communicate meaning grounded in contemporary contexts. Composers and producers attempted to bring ideas, music, and technologies together in a new form. For instance, the director Cheng Bugao wrote that, with 1932 films such as *Kuangliu* (Wild torrents, 1933) and *Spring Silkworms*, the filmmakers brought together the cinematic and New Literature worlds.[26] The film audiences as well must have been learning to read and hear an entirely new medium. Both consumers and producers were moving through an experimental learning process, a multichanneled process that included music.

Music and Musicians

Two types of musical formats had to have been learned by film audiences of the period: (1) background music, music coming from off the screen and not audible to the characters; and (2) source music, music coming from within the film and which was produced by or audible to the characters (the source of the sounds was often visible to the audience).[27] Taken as a whole, the types of background and source music used in the mid-1930s films could be heard in various settings in Shanghai at the time (including in the Hollywood films shown there), illustrating its metropolitan character. The number of film music composers and arrangers was small, however, and they were drawn from a close community. Most of the musicians composed for other genres and contexts, from the theater to the international concert stage. Among those people responsible for the background music or for heading the music sections of the film companies such as Mingxing, Lianhua, and Diantong were musicians who had gained part of their musical training abroad: He Luting, Huang Zi, Lü Ji, Ren Guang, and Xian Xinghai.

In the beginning, filmmakers seldom commissioned musical scores for their films; instead, musicians selected and arranged pieces drawn from the repertoire surrounding them. Background music consisted mostly of well-known pieces from the European classical and romantic symphonic traditions, opera overtures, late nineteenth-century light opera, waltzes, and marches, as well as symphonic pieces from the contemporary Chinese art music tradition. A few of these latter pieces, such as Huang Zi's (1904–38) "Dushi fengguang huanxiangqu" (City scenes fantasia, conducted by Lü Ji, for the film *City Scenes*), were composed for specific films. Most of the background music was instrumental. While the terms used to describe this music today—"Western art music" or "classical" music—are problematic, here they refer generally to the structures, provenance, and instrumentation of the music: music based in tonal harmony; sites of production historically located in Europe, America, and Russia; and instruments generally associated with the West rather than with China prior to the twentieth century. Considered both cosmopolitan and modern, this was the music of the urban middle class and the expatriate communities in China.[28] These categories were neither immutable nor exclusive, however, as their use in different Chinese contexts served to reconstruct prior associations of time and place, just as did the recontextualization of "classical" music within American popular music genres occurring at the same time.

Source music in the films, on the other hand, drew from more popular American and Chinese traditions, including American big band and dance music of the 1920s, Chinese traditional narrative and opera forms, and popular vocal music. Original source music, most likely developed along with attempts at "film realism" in that sights and sounds of the environment are recorded, can be heard in street scenes. Audiences heard the sounds that a film character walking down the street might have heard: simultaneous snatches of three Latin American dance band songs emanating from dance halls in *A New Year's Coin*; in *Boatman's Daughter*, the rhythmic chants of the boatman and his daughter calling passengers; in *Taolijie* (The plunder of peach and plum, 1934), the musical bells of the passenger ship docking; rhythmic sounds of factory machines; the narrative music (particularly northern forms) of a singer walking down the street; and so on. In some cases, this type of music (in the sense of "organized sound") was enhanced by background music, as when characters buying tickets for the train in *City Scenes* rhythmically chant "Shanghai, Shanghai, Shanghai" to the accompaniment of off-screen musical instruments.

A primary genre of original source music, unique to the Chinese films, was that of Chinese songs composed specifically for the films. Off-screen instruments such as the piano often accompanied the songs. It is the music of this latter group—individual songs composed either as theme songs or interludes for specific films—that was most often mentioned in the Chinese literature of the time and subsequently.[29] Film credits listed the titles and composers of such famous songs as Nie Er's "Biye ge" (Graduation song), for *The Plunder of Peach and Plum*; "Dalu ge" (Song of the big road) and "Kailu xianfeng" (The pioneers) for *Dalu* (Big road, 1935); "Tieti xiade genü" (Oppressed singing girl) and "Yiyongjun jinxingqu" (March of the volunteers) for *Fengyun ernü* (Children of troubled times, 1935); and "Xinnüxing" (New women, for the eponymous film, 1934); Ren Guang's "Cailing ge" (Water chestnuts) for *Song of Triumph* and "Yuguang qu" (Song of the fishermen, for the eponymous film); Xian Xinghai's "Yeban gesheng" (Singing at midnight) and "Qingnian jinxingqu" (March of the youth); Zhao Yuanren's (Yuen Ren Chao, 1892–1982) "Xiyangjing ge" (Song of the peep-show man) for *City Scenes*; and Lü Ji's "Ziyou shen" (Goddess of freedom, for the eponymous film). Tian Han, Xu Xingzhi (1904–91), An E (1905–76), Shi Yi, and Sun Shiyi (1904–66) often wrote the lyrics for songs in this genre. The purported sources of these songs varied. For instance, Sun Yu, director of *Big Road*, asked Nie Er for a song similar to the Russian "Volga Boatmen Song." According to Nie Er's analysis, Ren Guang based his "Song of the Fishermen" (the lyrics describe the hard life of the fishermen) on a folksong popular throughout the Jiangnan region after he "entered into the society of the fishermen" to gain experience.[30]

These composed songs were influenced by the style of *xuetang yuege* (public school music), with lyrics on such topics as social inequities, foreign oppression, women's equality, and national unity and salvation in the face of imperialism.[31] They were short, self-contained pieces and were usually strophic, with two to four verses, sung in national dialect and repeated to the same melody and a refrain. These formal properties of the genre, which were followed consistently, contributed to individual pieces "fashioned for ease of detachment from the situational context."[32] Once they left the movies, these songs were recontextualized in a variety of settings. Many of them took on the status of masses' songs, becoming part of the repertoire for the National Salvation singing assemblies and the larger movement in the mid-1930s. For instance, the list of fourteen "heroic" songs from a 1936 report on the assemblies includes songs such as "Song of the Big Road," "The Pioneers," "New Women," "March of the Volunteers," "Goddess of Freedom," and "Graduation Song."[33] Records of songs released prior to the films served to promote the films, and films then promoted the songs. In some cases, such as Nie Er's "Kaikuang ge" (Miners' song) from *Light of Motherhood*, the song remained popular although the censors banned the film.

The songs crossed over into many forms of mass media and of live performances, particularly to promote social-political movements and ideas. They were released as recordings and in sheet music, were published in newspapers, and sung in rallies in Shanghai—the ultimate in "cover songs." Take, for instance, the theme song from *Children of Troubled Times*, "March of the Volunteers," also released on the Pathe label. Cheng Bugao wrote that, as soon as the film was shown, the song "spread like wildfire" and was sung continuously throughout Shanghai because of its "impassioned, national feeling" that realistically portrayed the "sound of the hearts of the Chinese people against imperialism and Japan."[34] According to Tian Han, film studio personnel often began meetings with the song. Liu Liangmo conducted "March of the Volunteers" in the mass meeting in the Shanghai stadium in 1935. The power and popularity of this song is made all the more interesting by the situation of its composition. Nie Er, who had been asked to compose the music, was in Japan to avoid political persecution and mailed the score back to China when he was finished. Tian Han hurriedly wrote the words to the song on pieces of cigarette rolling paper.[35]

Musical intertextuality characterized the films of the mid-1930s as well. Different films employed the same compositions, also illustrating the consistencies in the use of music. For instance, Franz Lehar's "Merry Widow Waltz" was heard in *Boatman's Daughter* and *Fengren kuangxiangqu* (Madman's rhapsody, episode no. 7 in the *Lianhua Symphony*); Schubert's "Ave Maria" in *The Plunder of Peach and Plum, Boatman's Daughter*, and *Song of the Fishermen*; Nie Er's "Song of the Big Road" in *Big Road* and *Lianhua Symphony*; Stravinsky's *The Firebird* in war-related scenes in two of the short films from *Lianhua Symphony*; the same American big band pieces in *The Plunder of Peach and Plum* and *A New Year's Coin*; and even the "Wedding March" (from *Lohengrin*) in *Sanren xing* (Three men, episode no. 4 in *Lianhua Symphony*) and *City Scenes*. The detachable and transportable nature of musical genres enabled them to cross within, between, and outside of the films.

The crossover of the musicians responsible for the music assisted the interchange between genres. They composed music for spoken dramas, worked in record companies and film studios, wrote articles in newspapers and magazines, and participated in social movements. They constantly shifted their positions as societies were reformulated during the mid-1930s. Members of the music group of the Left-Wing Dramatists Association (1933–34) included An E, Lü Ji, Nie Er, Ren Guang, and Zhang Shu; Tian Han organized the Nanguo she (Southern society), bringing in Ren Guang and Xian Xinghai; similarly the Sulian zhiyou she

(Soviet Union friendship society) included Ren Guang, Nie Er, Tian Han, Zhang Shu, Lü Ji, and An E; in 1933 Ren Guang and Nie Er were the principal organizers of the Chinese New Music Research Society. Ren Guang (beginning in 1932), Nie Er (1933–34), and Xian Xinghai all worked in the Pathe record company.[36] The people involved in film music formed a local community in Shanghai, one built on personal connections and continued reformulations of groups dedicated to related film, music, and social-political purposes. Through reminiscences such as Cheng Bugao's, we gain a sense that they were a group of friends. The director recounts a story of reunited Nie Er and Tian Han singing songs in a hospital in the early 1930s, after having been separated during the Japanese invasion. Cheng writes that in 1934, he, Tian Han, Ren Guang, and An E were together nearly every day watching films and talking. And Tian Han remembers that they frequently met at Ren Guang's house where they argued vehemently, played music together, and worked cooperatively on songs.[37]

The politics of fame were at work in terms of composers and musical pieces. One has to assume that people such as Nie Er did not get a job composing music for films because he was a famous composer. At the time he was only a teenager. Instead, Nie Er seems to have broken into the film music business through personal relations within this community, particularly with Tian Han. Nie Er first began working as a clerk in the film company office and had acted in several films such as *Light of Motherhood* and *Song of the Fishermen*. By 1935, Nie Er was the head of the music section of Lianhua Film Company; he did the background music for *New Woman* and conducted the Lianhua symphony and chorus. Today, after decades of writing, it is difficult to determine if Nie Er was a great composer, a great revolutionary, or both. Judging from the number of articles written and memorials conducted upon his death in 1935, he was popular in what were called progressive circles at the time. In later commentaries, Nie Er takes on mythic qualities as stories and anecdotes are repeated and, perhaps, embellished. In 1960, a movie about his life, which dramatized a portion of these stories, was produced in the PRC.[38] By the 1970s, he became perhaps the most celebrated of the film composers within the Chinese scholarship.

If Nie Er became a symbol of the revolutionary and progressive film musician, Li Jinhui became his opposite, at least during the mid-1930s when film composers carried out in magazines their debates on healthy and unhealthy tendencies in music (these debates moved into the films, as will be seen below). Before then, Li was involved musically in the May Fourth, Beijing University folksong, and national speech movements, and he composed well-received children's songs. In the 1930s, however, Li organized the Mingyue Gejushe (Bright moon opera troupe) which performed songs such as "Taohuajiang" (Peach blossom river). After leaving Li's opera troupe and joining the Left-Wing Dramatists

Association, Nie Er became one of Li's fiercest critics. In articles such as "A Brief Commentary on Chinese Song and Dance" (Zhongguo gewu duanlun, under the name Hei Tianshi, published in 1932 in *Dianying yishu*), Nie Er criticized Li for composing "music for music's sake." He called Li's songs "soft tofu," gaudy and amorous, composed to appeal to the senses. During this time of national crisis, Nie Er said the songs poisoned the youth rather than providing the "musical knives" needed for the national struggle.[39]

Why Nie Er singled out Li Jinhui as a venomous symbol is not clear, although his participation as a musician in Li's troupe meant that they had some sort of personal acquaintance. But Li was not the only composer producing such songs. The distinction between songs written for art, entertainment, and commercial success and those written for patriotic reasons—especially in light of the commercial success of Nie Er's own songs—is no longer clear today, if it ever was. In succeeding decades, the Chinese literature gradually sifted through and categorized the composers much as it did the films, but as Richard Kraus writes, He Luting "combined activism for revolutionary change, cultural iconoclasm, and enthusiasm for European classical music in much the same way as Xian Xinghai, with a similarly odd mix of Communism, movie music, and service in Yan'an."[40]

This characterization of He Luting can be extended to the majority of musicians of the time. Intellectuals and leaders, many of the musicians discussed in the chapter were concerned with formulating and forming a new national culture. Their discussions reflected disagreements and ambivalence about the proper path for Chinese music: Westernization, reformulation of Chinese music, the Chinese folksong movement, public school music, composed songs, and the musical synthesis of Chinese and foreign styles were all among the possible paths discussed, as were "national" styles based on reformulated local and regional music which went beyond its locale.[41]

Film Music Techniques

In these films, however, it is not merely *what* music is used but *how* it is used which is important to our listening. Many explanations have been given for the inclusion of music in early film: it covered projector noises; provided continuity; gave an aural illustration of the picture; and assisted in the framing, narration, and segmentation of the film. One of the more important technical uses of music falls into the category of framing; music supported the structure of the film through aural forms of organization and patterning. Although Gorbman writes that, as a nonrepresentational discourse, music "lessens awareness of the frame; it relaxes the censor, drawing the spectator further into the fantasy-illusion suggested by filmic narration," in these Chinese films music was used precisely as a frame for the content and structure of films, and it sometimes did not get by the censors.[42]

As mentioned above, music and musicians were often the topic and a type of frame for the films. As an example, we can look and listen to *City Scenes*, in which the excitement, luxury, despair, and dangers of Shanghai metropolitan life are displayed to a rural family.[43] The overture, a carnivalesque symphonic band piece, "City Scenes Fantasia," accompanies a kaleidoscope scene. Following the credits, the entire film is framed through the more traditional peep show in which still scenes of city life shown in the peep-show box become animated through musical performance. The theme song, "Song of the Peep-Show Man," is sung by the peep-show musician, played by the director Yuan Muzhi (1909–78). Actually, we see Yuan singing the lyrics but hear him merely humming several of the verses, those that were banned by the censors.[44] The singer, accompanying himself with percussion instruments, sings a song to draw the crowd to look inside the peep-show box: "Come on, take a look! Come on, look inside! See all the street lights shining bright." While the music heard is supposed to be source music, the peep-show musician sings the verses to a background orchestra. As the rural family looks into the holes in the box, the still shot of the city transforms into a moving city-scene montage with background music, which ends and returns to the next still frame of the family, now in the city. From then on, the film progresses with the hypothetical drama of the rural family once they have moved into the city. Although the opening of the film cues the audience to think in terms of this rural family watching the city scenes through the window of the peep-show box and listening to the musical narrative, there are only two later reminders of the musical frame of the film—still scenes in the style of the musical peep-show.

Lianhua Symphony, also framed by music, uses music to index another Lianhua film, *Big Road*. Composed of eight short films, *Lianhua Symphony* begins with close-up shots of the chorus—made up of Lianhua Film Company personnel—singing Nie Er's "Song of the Big Road." The camera moves back to reveal the conductor, microphone, and camera and the scene ends with the chorus laughing. The entire film closes with a similar scene; the same chorus, now singing Nie Er's "The Pioneers," concludes by laughing and the camera again reveals the movie-making apparatus. In this case, the music structures the film in such a way that the entire context—of the Lianhua Film Company making films and music—is revealed, thus breaking the cinematic frame through musical performance.

Examples of music used to segment the internal structure of films by paralleling scene changes can be found in nearly all of the sound films. For instance, all eight short films within *Lianhua Symphony* begin with black screens and music, marking off the film's internal subdivisions at the largest level. Within films, discrete musical pieces often begin and end discrete visual scenes, and the structures of the musical and visual images work together. Many scenes in *Boatman's Daughter* illustrate a concerted attempt to match musical, filmic, and dramatic structures as musical cadences coordinate with the ends of particular scenes or musical climaxes coordinate with dramatic ones.

In other cases, the continuity of music across scenes marks the continuity of the structure or content of scenes. In the opening to *Song of the Fishermen*, the music that plays to changing visual images enables the audience to understand that these discrete visuals are of a boy growing up. At a larger level, the replaying of the "Song of the Fishermen" at key points reminds the viewer of the characters' emotional attachments as the past is represented in the present through music. As the composer Virgil Thomson has commented, music can be used to sustain continuity in film, which is a "discontinuous medium."[45]

Music marks the assumed simultaneity of events that, because of the visual and narrative structure of the film presentation, must necessarily be presented in linear sequence. In *The Plunder of Peach and Plum*, music connects what should be simultaneous scenes, as when the two central characters, Tao Jianping and Li Lilin, have found jobs. Waltz music continues as scenes switch from her office to his. Later, after Tao has lost his job, the same musical technique occurs, this time indicating diachronic and synchronic continuity. But now, as the waltz plays, scenes switch between Li Lilin working in her office and Tao Jianping, unshaven, at home. The music points out the continuity of ideas and scenes over time, and serves as a reminder of Tao's earlier success.

Examples of the technical use of music to provide continuity occur in *Chungui duanmeng* (Young women's short dream, episode no. 2 in *Lianhua Symphony*), a rather obvious criticism of Japanese imperialism. First the viewer sees two women sleeping, to a slow melody from Stravinky's *Firebird* (background music); a trumpet interrupts the scene, although not their sleep, and the visual switches to an army camp where the viewer sees that the background trumpet playing "Taps" is actually source music for this new scene. Later, Stravinsky's *Firebird* continues from the scene of the madman / sex villain / imperialist, connecting it with the scene of the two women sleeping as well as with the dream scenes of both women. Now and again, the music is interrupted by the trumpet. Although an early film audience might find it difficult to follow these visual shifts between two "real-life" scenes, the inserted scene of the imperialist madman twirling the globe in a fire (accompanied by *The Sorcerer's Apprentice*), and dream scenes of two different women, the use of music helps make a visual reading understandable. *The Firebird* continues through the women's dream scenes as they fight with the man and into the army battle scene, creating a musical equation of the two fight scenes. As *The Firebird* ends, the trumpet is heard again. Thus music connects the different real-life scenes and the dream scenes, as well as the ideological concepts (the oppression of women and the oppression of the nation) that are being discussed outside the film in Shanghai. Similar musical techniques occur in *Madman's Rhapsody* as the music marks flashbacks, another means of framing scenes and indicating temporal shifts. *The Firebird* connects the opening scene set in the insane asylum with the war scenes occurring within one inmate's flashback as a musical indication of the causal relationship between the man's insanity and the war. The waltz can be heard as the madman flashes back to his life with his family before the war killed them and made him insane.

Musical flashback similarly structures *The Plunder of Peach and Plum* as the story is told as a narration of the past and of the school principal trying to make sense of what happened to his student's life after graduation. When the principal goes to visit his former student Tao Jianping, who is now in prison, the blank screen and Nie Er's "Graduation Song" mark the beginning of Tao Jianping's flashback to his school graduation ceremony. His graduation class sings:

> Today we're blossoming peaches and plums,
> Tomorrow the mainstay of society;
> Today we're singing together,
> Tomorrow we'll surge in the tidal wave of the nation's survival!
> Tidal wave! Tidal wave! Rise unceasingly!
> Classmates! classmates! Take up strength to shoulder the nation's
>   burden!

During the song the camera moves from the back of the room, to come to rest on the principal by the end of the song. This famous song does not reappear until the end of the film, after the end of the long flashback and after Tao's execution. As the principal looks at Tao's graduation picture, it now plays as remembered background music (or as source music emanating from the principal's mind). Marking the decline of Tao's life within the corrupt social-political-moral context of metropolitan life in the 1930s, the song ends the film with "shoulder the nation's burden."

The musical meanings of the films build in considerable ambiguity through the simultaneous presence of or shifts between background and source music. He Luting's well-known "Yaochuan ge" (Boat-rowing song) is sung several times in *Boatman's Daughter* as source music as the characters row across the lake; but background piano accompaniment is heard by the audience. At times the ambiguity occurs because music is heard prior to seeing the scene in which the visual indicates that it is source music. In *City Scenes* music plays as characters sit in a theater, but when the camera moves to the screen that they are watching, it becomes clear that it is source music coming from an animated film by the Wan Brothers (another type of genre intertextuality found in the films).

Another important use of mixed source and background music occurs in *The Plunder of Peach and Plum*. During a restaurant scene—in which Li Lilin's boss attempts to seduce her in a hotel-club as her husband searches for her—music creates a sense of spatial depth. As the taxi arrives at the door of the club, American big band music in the club plays faintly. As Li Lilin and her boss walk in, the band music grows louder, indicating it as source music (the band playing in the bar). As they move to and up the elevator, the music grows fainter. Later as Tao Jianping, in an agitated state, enters the restaurant and searches for his wife, the source big band music mixes and alternates with Mendelssohn's *Midsummer Night's Dream* as a representation of his agitation. Finally, when Jianping and Lilin meet at the club door, the band music grows fainter as they walk back home. Complex film music techniques such as these were incorporated meaningfully into films in a matter of a few short years after the technology for sound became available. In many cases, these musical techniques served to dramatically express social-political situations and goals of the time.

Musical Representation

Other techniques of musical representation heard throughout the films are made through associations with visual and dramatic meanings developed within one film as well as associations with previous contexts of performance.[46] *City Scenes* contains many obvious attempts at direct musical representation. The visual montage of city scenes is accompanied from beginning to end by a musical montage—fast, lively music with night scenes of the city and neon lights flashing in rhythm to the music; slower, more serene music with views of the park; the bells heard as the viewer sees church steeples turn into clock bells as visuals shift to the city's clock towers. *City Scenes* uses music as a representational ornamentation of action through sound effects or "mickey-mousing." The filmmakers seem to have delighted in this musical-visual synchronization, the most obvious being the synchronization of movement up and down the musical (diatonic) scale as people walk up and down stairs.[47]

Broader representations occur as associations with foreign films are strengthened by borrowing musical elements and sound effects. For instance, the association between Hollywood's Shirley Temple movies and *A New Year's Coin* is particularly clear with the explicit discussion of the six-year-old tap-dancing and singing girl (with curls) as "China's Shirley Temple." Later in the film, an instrumental version of "Hark! The Herald Angels Sing" is heard as a character walks into a toy store to buy a Christmas present. And, although there is no documentation of the process of choosing the music for *Young Women's Short Dream*, Dukas's *Sorcerer's Apprentice* most likely was used for its programmatic title in the scene of the imperialist madman twirling the globe in a fire.[48]

But we cannot assume that music is representational in the sense of particular pieces chosen for their programmatic nature. Even in cases where such a programmatic intent existed, it would be difficult to gauge the extent to which the Chinese audiences might hear that program. While some analyses of Western film music have posited the ideas of music's use as cultural code, how would these codes be read in the context of Chinese cinema of the 1930s? What associations did viewers have with sounds such as "Ave Maria"? It is a truism that meaning is inherent in the musical sounds per se. The films provided the context for transforming the emotional representations of music. Music is repeated with certain types of visual images, as in *Song of the Fishermen*, where both "Song of the Fishermen," a composed Chinese song, and Schubert's "Ave Maria" consistently mark major emotional scenes. "Ave Maria" is used in unhappy emotional climaxes (it plays in the death scenes of the father, the blind mother, and the brother). "Ave Maria" accompanies scenes of death and parting in *The Boatman's Daughter* (where it is heard as the daughter discovers her father is ill and she is to be sold to a brothel) and in *The Plunder of Peach and Plum* (after Li Lilin dies and Tao Jianping decides to give up their baby).[49] Musical meanings, learned through sonic associations with visual images or through previous contexts of performance and discussion, were used to represent and stimulate emotions.

A New Year's Coin, with music arranged by He Luting, uses many of the techniques discussed above. Following a coin as it passes from one person to the next, the viewer sees film characters in a variety of urban musical performances and hears their critical commentary on music of the time. This featured discourse about music and society shapes the on-screen portrayal of the music. The film concentrates on musicians and urban musical performance; the viewer sees variety shows and street musicians, listens to American big band music in dance halls, and hears one of the singers and dance-hall women tell the female music teacher that people look down upon her. The teacher responds, saying that "in this society it is difficult for women who work." Later, after an incident at one of the dance halls, the performer leaves her job in the world of urban entertainment and joins the schoolteacher. Again musical sounds are accompanied by narrative and dramatic interpretations of their meanings.

Musical performance presses forward *A New Year's Coin*'s message of transformation in the setting of 1934–35 China. In the beginning of the film, the family eats their new year's eve dinner with a man and woman who are members of a song-and-dance troupe preparing for special new year's performances. The grandfather asks them if they will sing "Maomaoyu" (Misty rain), and they respond by saying, "We don't sing that anymore; we are singing a new 'Misty Rain'." This short dialogue indexes a much larger debate over the role of music in society and in film. Within progressive and leftist circles, the song, composed by Li Jinhui, had become one of the musical symbols of decadence in urban society. The first instance of a song heard throughout the film plays at a party. It comes from a radio: the announcer of the Mingxing broadcast station announces it as "Wuxie shaoge" (Song of the dance hall).[50] The partygoers discuss its popularity—"now all the people on the streets can sing that song but not as well as Miss Yang"—and they convince Miss Yang, who is at the party, to sing the song (see fig. 23). In both the radio and live performances, the solo, melismatic voice is accompanied by a piano. The song is heard several times in the film, such as in Miss Yang's performance with a live band at a club, and it indexes the dance halls seen in the film. Toward the end of the film, the song is sung yet again, now with new lyrics and renamed (as the Chinese subtitles point out) "Jiuwang zhige" (Save the nation song). In its new form, it is sung by a chorus of schoolchildren and their teacher, accompanied by a band and in a straightforward, triumphant, strong style with a steady rhythm much different from the performance style of Miss Yang.[51] This performance continues as the visuals switch from scene to scene of smiling people in their homes listening to the new song on their radios and televisions. The "Chinese Shirley Temple" is now in her father's lap as he asks, "Do you think this year will be better than last year?" This section continues with other live performances, all choral and sometimes with four-part harmony, in different locations. This transformation of the lyrics and the performance style of the one song—from a solo performance of the decadent urban dance halls and to a choral song of concerted, unified struggle against Japan for the future of the nation—creates a musical metaphor of the transformation of the characters' lives, the consciousness of the people, and the country.

The music and musical discourse in the film index a range of contexts and actions outside of the theater. *A New Year's Coin* serves to point out the intertextuality and intercontextuality of music found in nearly all of the films. The theme of transformation, represented metaphorically through the film music, was echoed in the literature of the time. This change in the musical sounds heard in *A New Year's Coin* was linked to representation of social change. According to a June 25, 1936 report in the *Jiuguo shibao* (Save the nation newspaper):

Three or four years ago, Shanghai was still a world of songs such as "Peach Blossom River," "Kelian de qiuxiang" (Pitiful Qiuxiang), "Misty Rain"—solo songs sung by

23. A singing hostess at a family party in *A New Year's Coin* (1937), courtesy of the China Film Archive.

single people. Although they were very sweet and beautiful, the tunes were actually weak and dispirited. As the days of national calamity deepen, heroic roaring masses songs are appearing, such as those of the famous musician Nie Er, "Song of the Big Road" and "The Pioneers."[52]

The use of music outside the films to serve as a metaphor for and instigator of transformation points to a significant feature of film music and its intertextuality. While many may tend to look at music as "representative" of change, these musicians used music to promote change.

Conclusions

Those in progressive film circles seemed to have shared a concern with the modern—a New Literature movement in music. Kraus writes, "Musical pioneers such as Xiao Youmei and Zhao Yuanren suggested the possibility of participating in the creation of a new Chinese music that would replace feudalism with modernity, just as the stars of the May Fourth Movement were doing in fiction and poetry." And, as Paul Pickowicz points out, the May Fourth movement "came late" to cinema; he reminds us that, unlike literature, "there was no Chinese tradition of filmmaking to reject."[53] Nor do the films and discourse indicate a rejection, as a broad genre, of music associated with the West. The foreign musical models extended far beyond the silver screen to include the establishment of conservatories and orchestras, the presence of foreign teachers and composers, and the return of musicians who had studied abroad. Ren Guang, who composed theme songs and background music, returned from study in France in 1929, Huang Zi studied at Oberlin College, Xian Xinghai in Paris, and Zhao Yuanren in the United States. In this context, it seems anything but incongruous that European symphonic literature, big band songs, and Strauss waltzes were chosen for the films. The formally diffuse ideologies and practices operated, it seems, according to many of the same intertextual processes characteristic of the music.

In his analysis of the urban as exotic in Chinese literature, Heinrich Fruehauf writes that "In the context of nationalist exoticism, the Shanghai phenomenon thus did not primarily connote a cause for shame but became the prototypical setting where the formation of a Chinese-style *civitas* was to take place."[54] The film music world of Shanghai was a metropolitan one, and many of the films single out the urban and metropolitan—*Shanghai ershisi xiaoshi* (Twenty-four hours in Shanghai, 1934), *A New Year's Coin*, *City Scenes*, *Street Angel*, and so on. The metropolis was the site of the film audience, entertainment, technology, and intellectuals.

The period does not present a unified theme or monophonic musical language. This time of transition, as studios moved away from silent films, gave musicians the opportunity to compose original film music and to explore new musical genres and technologies. They experimented with Hollywood models and with new social-political forms. Within a few years, they had developed a wealth of sophisticated techniques in the use of music as film structure and as a means furthering the films' content. Musicians saw film as a medium to promote their ideals for the future of Chinese music and of China, whether they be modernization or nationalization, patriotic or popular. The films and other activities served to situate the music in concrete contexts and a web of intertextual references. The musical sounds and the musicians' critical commentary reflect their different ideals as well as the ambivalent stance taken at the time toward foreign and Chinese musics and cultures. Listened to as a whole, the music of the films does not put forth a master soundtrack. Its composition was characterized by creative hybridity, experimentation, and openness to a range of musical forms. Simultaneously, it was limited by ideological debates, individual power, and government censorship. Some of the films and songs may have been canonized later as leftist, but the musicians, the ideas portrayed, and the sounds themselves reflect the varied and often conflicting thought characteristic of urban China in the 1930s.

"Her Traces Are Found Everywhere": Shanghai, Li Xianglan, and the "Greater East Asia Film Sphere"

SHELLEY STEPHENSON

A May 1943 article in *Xin yingtan* (New film forum), organ of the Japanese-controlled film studio Zhonglian (Zhonghua lianhe zhipian gufen gongsi, or China United Film Company), begins this way:

> Everyone harbors some suspicions toward Li Xianglan, invited specially from Manchuria to collaborate on the film *Wanshi liufang*. Zhonglian has plenty of actors; why be so perverse as to invite a Li Xianglan to come? Since the Manchurian film industry has long fallen behind that of China [*woguo*], it's really difficult to make people completely trust Li Xianglan. Even though we've gone through all manner of propaganda, still propaganda is, after all, only propaganda. Everyone wants to see facts.
>
> OK, now the facts have been placed clearly before us. . . .[1]

While the paragraph serves only as a foil to the remainder of the article, which is a litany of superlatives describing the singer/actress's performance in the block-buster film *Wanshi liufang* (Eternity, 1943), it is unique in its clear expression of distrust toward Li for her attempted invasion of the Shanghai cinema market. While resistance to the star is expressed in nationalistic terms, it is motivated not by politics but by aesthetics: her legitimacy is eventually affirmed by her acting technique, which "doesn't fall one bit behind" that of her Chinese co-stars. Li's superior performance, on terms established by the Shanghai market, are read as clear "facts" presented for our verification.

In truth, however, there is little that was, or is, clear about the star Li Xianglan (see fig. 24). Mysteries surrounded the Manchurian-born Japanese actress with the Chinese stage name, as different sorts of mysteries do now. The received image of Li Xianglan, furthered in no small part by Yamaguchi Yoshiko's (b. 1920) autobiography,[2] presents a movie star famous for masquerading on- and off-screen as a Chinese woman, and with her true nationality known to only a few top executives of her home studio Man'ei (Manchu eiga kyokai, or Manchurian Film Association). As such, she stands as a physical embodiment of the principle behind Japan's "mainland policy."[3] This policy, adopted following the box-office failure of the occupiers' initial efforts, was designed to mask Japan's role in filmmaking so as to assure commercial success with nationalistic Chinese audiences. In this capacity, Li Xianglan may be read as a classic case of a colonizer passing for colonized.[4] However, the ways in which Li Xianglan was portrayed by the contemporary press, and to some extent the ways in which she was taken up by contemporary fans, suggest that the star cannot be reduced to something so simple as a ruse.

In this chapter I explore the construction and reception of the star Li Xianglan in Shanghai, through an examination of that city's wartime film publications, most particularly those sympathetic to or controlled by the Japanese, as well as through interviews with occupation-era filmgoers. Li appears to have been a far more popular star in her home territory of Manchukuo than she was in Shanghai, and Manchukuo also claims a longer and perhaps more famous history of occupation filmmaking.[5] But that history remains in essence one of Japanese filmmaking transported to the Chinese mainland, and a study of the national dimension in spectatorship in that location would be complicated by the fact that Manchukuo was, from its inception, cast theoretically as an independent state—that is, as separate from both China and Japan. Shanghai, on the other hand, offers a site from which to examine the ways in which the star cult played out in an urban audience already regarded as the undisputed center of a distinctly Chinese film culture, albeit one that had been subject to continuous and various influences (from that of Hollywood to the Chinese Communist Party). That Shanghai was popularly seen (by Shanghainese, at the very least) as the heart of the Chinese film industry is evidenced clearly in the above article, which initially begrudges a position to Li in the already teeming Shanghai star system.

One important quality this article shares with other journalistic writings of the time is its frank attitude toward the role of propaganda in the operations of the Chinese film industry. While in this case the reporter expresses more skepticism regarding the practical effects of propaganda than did most writers, there is no censuring of its involvement. Indeed, if the propaganda in this case had been successful in convincing Shanghai fans to accept the Manchurian star, there would presumably have been no reason to mention it, except perhaps by way of praise.

Regardless of political orientation, 1930s and 1940s Shanghai film publications express an awareness of, and often a reverence toward, the filmic medium's

24. Li Xianglan: the mysterious actress,
courtesy of the China Film Archive.

presumed unmediated access to the human heart. In some cases reverence may hide undertones of fear, but most of the journalistic writings on film express rather a utilitarian attitude to the medium, a wish to harness the immense power of film to the advantage of whatever political agenda is supported by that particular publication. In occupied Shanghai, pro- and anti-Japanese publications employ identical language to discuss the "responsibility" of film to realize its full potential as "military instrument" or as "educational tool." Readers are assigned an important role in this enterprise, the fan magazines in particular offering a large variety of articles instructing the spectator on such matters as how to watch a film, how to appreciate a screenplay, and how to critique an actor's performance. At times the lessons are even delivered in the words of the audience, such as when readers write to the fan magazine editors scolding studio heads for offering a steady supply of empty entertainment in the form of romantic and horror features, rather than the sort of educational features for which the Shanghai audience so clearly goes hungry.

Then-prevalent attitudes in the occupied Shanghai press to the potential uses of film are evoked perhaps most succinctly in the Japanese voice, through the phrase "Greater East Asia Film Sphere" (*Da dongya dianying quan*). A perfect synthesis of cinema and political agenda, the phrase is a compact embodiment of the Japanese expectation that film could be used to change minds, and that it could therefore play a key role in the construction of a new world order. While in my examination of occupation-era Shanghai film magazines I have found the phrase invoked only twice, both times in the magazine *New Film Forum*, according to occupation cinema scholar Shimizu Akira the slogan was used fairly regularly in the domestic Japanese press.[6]

It is, of course, a variation on the more encompassing and more heavily invoked phrase, "Greater East Asia Co-Prosperity Sphere" (*Da dongya gongrong quan*), an expression signifying interracial solidarity among the nations and peoples of Asia. The phrase, introduced by Japan in 1940, proposed a future Asian community founded on the notions of cooperation and interdependence and, especially after the outbreak of the Pacific War in 1941, resistance to the powers of the West. Japan was, on the basis of its presumed superiority to other Asian nations, to have a leading role in both the formation and the eventual governing of such a community, and it is in this capacity that Sphere ideology provided the motivation and eventual goal behind Japan's militarism toward its Asian neighbors.

In the intervening fifty years and with the contributions of critical analyses such as John Dower's, the Co-Prosperity Sphere has long left behind the romanticized idealism of its original conception, that of a liberated and harmonious united Asia. Rather, it has taken on the flavor of a thinly concealed ideology of racism, a failed attempt on the part of Japan "to establish permanent domination over all other races and peoples in Asia—in accordance with their needs and as befitted their destiny as a superior race."[7] This much seems evident in light of post-1945 developments; we do not, however, know much about the ways in which people at the time may have been trying to talk about the concept, or the ways in which it was received. Insofar as possible, then, I attempt to forego the presupposition, afforded to us by time and analysis, that Co-Prosperity Sphere ideology was at the time recognized as a sham or as doomed to failure. Taking the ideology on its own terms, in this case through an examination of the ways in which it appeared in the realm of cinema stardom in occupied Shanghai, enables a more reflective examination of the ways in which the concept was evoked and read in its heyday.

If Japan's destiny was to be the leader of a unified Asia, then it had the obligation both to learn about its inferior neighbors, as well as to teach them about itself. In both of these tasks, film was to play an integral part. Japan had been involved in film production in both Korea and Manchuria from the early 1920s, but backed by Sphere ideology in the first half of the 1940s this involvement became increasingly formalized, not only in these two locations but in China and throughout Southeast Asia as well. Film units were set up in some areas, local technicians being trained in film art under the guidance of Japanese managers. In other locales, such as Shanghai, preexisting film studios were taken over. Upon occupying a new territory Japan would ban all American and British films and screen its own products to a captive audience. Meanwhile, documentaries and fiction films alike introduced to the domestic Japanese audience the customs of Japan's newest colonies. The Japanese government intended to play, through its film activities abroad, the role of "older brother to one slightly younger," the eventual goal being assimilation through mutual knowledge.[8]

The Greater East Asia Co-Prosperity Sphere, operative as a political concept between the years 1940 to 1945, coincides almost exactly with the screen career of Yamaguchi Yoshiko under the name of Li Xianglan. Hence it is not surprising that she should come to be associated in the journalistic imagination with the filmic manifestation of Sphere ideology as expressed in the phrase Greater East Asia Film Sphere (both *New Film Forum* references to the phrase, in fact, are linked with her name). And just as the film medium is, in this phrase, assumed to have propagandistic uses, so too are film stars. In fact, since stardom can be defined as the state in which a film personality's off-screen activities equal or surpass in importance those on screen, one might well argue that it was in the film stars' various promotional appearances at the request of the studio that their star status was most manifest.

Certainly, Li Xianglan was not alone in being used to the advantage of the Japanese cause.[9] She does, however, provide a particularly rich example of the ways in which stardom could be manipulated to reflect a political agenda. While the Chinese star system mirrors Hollywood in its use of film personalities as sellers of a product (in 1930s and 1940s Shanghai, star images were used to sell everything from face lotion to cigarettes, from raincoats to herbal medicines), the product here is the idea: a unified Asia through the medium of film. As a star, Li Xianglan was, if not uniquely qualified, then at least uniquely constructed to represent the importance of film within the Greater East Asia Co-Prosperity Sphere ideology.

"Gazing with Eager Anticipation": Li Xianglan and Absence

The February 1942 issue of *New Film Forum* carries a story entitled "Filming Diary." While ostensibly a record of two days on the *Eternity* set, the journalist seems most struck with the fact that Li Xianglan, one of the stars of the production, is absent from the set. (In demand for other productions, she had arranged to finish her scenes for this one in just three weeks.) Before reporting on the other stars and their roles in the production, the reporter deals first with the curiosity of her absence: "Li Xianglan, travel-worn and weary, who had left Manchuria for Japan, then Taiwan, then Shanghai, has [now] returned to Manchuria. But even though she is gone, the filming of *Eternity* has still not finished. . . ."[10] This sort of writing about Li Xianglan, in which her most striking feature is the fact that she is not here (where, it is implied, she should be), is typical of the ways in which she is represented in occupation-era Shanghai publications. From the looks of these publications, the most significant aspect of Li's presence in the Shanghai star system is, quite simply, her absence.

Before discussing the Shanghai press, though, it is essential first to examine the extent of Li's presence on Shanghai's screens.[11] Li Xianglan's earliest films were screened upon release in cinemas located within Shanghai's Japanese concession. The three most well-known of these early films—*Bailan zhi ge* (Song of the white orchid, 1939), *Zhina zhi ye* (Night in China, 1940), and *Shamo zhi shi* (Vow in the desert, 1940)—are known collectively as the "Continental Series."[12] Each film depicts a love story between a Japanese man and Chinese woman on the Chinese mainland: Beijing in the first film, Shanghai in the second, and Manchuria in the third. Each coupling, surmounting as it does all manner of obstacles including some strong anti-Japanese elements, symbolizes Chinese collaboration with Japanese interests as well as peaceful cooperation guided by a paternalistic Japan.[13] The films, blatantly propagandistic (*Vow in the Desert* has the hero's brother, on his deathbed, converting Communists to Pan-Asianism) and showing little understanding of the Chinese, were later to prove embarrassing to the young star.

The films were not, however, seen widely upon their initial release, probably because of their undisguised Japaneseness and their restriction to screenings in the Japanese concession. According to my informants, it was not until after the May 1943 release of her hit film *Eternity* that Li Xianglan became widely known in Shanghai. A period piece describing the 1839 anti-opium campaign of Lin Zexu, this film proved popular with its theme that could be read, depending upon one's attitude toward the war and Japanese occupation, as either anti–Western imperialism or more generally antiforeign. The casting, with Li Xianglan at the heart of an all-star, all-Chinese ensemble, represented for the Japanese a successful insertion of Japanese film interests into the established Shanghai star system.[14] Following the success of this film, Li's earlier films were rescreened, this time in Shanghai's Chinese cinemas as well as the Japanese ones. Thus while Li can legitimately claim popularity in the city after May 1943, prior to that time she appears to have been, among Shanghai's Chinese filmgoers, a virtual unknown.

Li's presence on Shanghai's screens being largely dependent upon political factors—that is, the national affiliation of the cinema in question—it is not surprising that her presence in the Shanghai press should be dependent upon the same. In fact, news items concerning Li Xianglan appear to be entirely contingent upon a publication's political affiliation: absent in publications either independent of or hostile to the Japanese, she is if anything overexposed in Shanghai's pro-Japanese publications such as *New Film Forum* and *Shanghai yingtan* (Shanghai film forum).

But her presence in even the latter publications lies mostly in the form of absence, though in this case it is an absence of the geographical sort. In these magazines any references to Li almost invariably include, and often capitalize on, her geographic location: generally, much to the chagrin of the writers, not in Shanghai. She is, according to these articles, always on the verge of appearing in Shanghai, or always just departed. *New Film Forum* and *Shanghai Film Forum* both carry long series of teasing headlines promising Li's imminent arrival in Shanghai, a typical item being the latter's October 1943 header, "Li Xianglan's arrival in Shanghai will soon be reality."[15] In time, the unfulfilled promises seem to prove wearying: in the following issue, under the headline "There is hope that Li Xianglan will come to Shanghai!," is somewhat impatiently reported the following:

> "Li Xianglan has already arrived in Shanghai"! "Li Xianglan will soon arrive in Shanghai"! I don't know how many times, among movie fans or in the words of the movie magazines, we have heard this or read this.
>
> But Li Xianglan's arrival in Shanghai, from start to finish, is like a riddle. "You only hear the sound of the elevator, you don't see anyone come down." Up until today, we still haven't seen any trace of her.[16]

The piece goes on to speculate that, although plans for a Shanghai film production have "fizzled out," there are still reports that she will return:

> Probably, on the day that her [current] work in Japan finishes, that will be the start of her time in Shanghai.
>
> There's also a report that Li Xianglan will probably come to Shanghai at the end of this month.
>
> Meanwhile, there's another report that Li Xianglan will come to Shanghai together with Bai Guang.
>
> [But] wait, I think Li Xianglan will definitely arrive someday. It's just a question of time.

The name Li Xianglan in these journals functions as sign: literally absent from the anti-Japanese publications, it remains heavily present in the Japanese ones. But even in the latter Li functions only as sign: she is present in name but absent in body. It may be that the more accurate account of Li's importance is, then, contained within the anti-Japanese press, where she exists not at all: there her absent sign is, at least, consistent with her absent materiality. Her constant presence in magazines such as *New Film Forum* can be read as an ongoing attempt on the part of pro-Japanese journalists to wedge reference in (thereby creating fan enthusiasm and selling political ideals) where there exists no referent.

What is remarkable about many of these reports is the degree of exaggerated longing attached to the figure of Li Xianglan. One reporter notes upon her departure that although Li was in Shanghai a mere four weeks, "she gave us in the film world a rainbow-colored resplendence. Now the only thing we desire is that Miss Li will someday return to Shanghai! We wish Miss Li in this parting a pleasant journey, amen!"[17] Overstated expressions of desire are also typical of the writing used to describe Li's feelings toward the city of Shanghai. The December 1942 issue of *New Film Forum* reports in a photo caption, for example, that "On November 21, Miss Li Xianglan already rushed back up north. On the point of departure, she embraced limitless emotions; whether it be one blade of grass or one tree, she felt toward them all a strong unwillingness to part."[18]

As Christine Gledhill suggests in her essay "Signs of Melodrama," there exists a close relationship between excessive displays of emotion and the star phenomenon itself: "If the excessive moment in melodrama infuses ordinary characters and relationships with excitement and significance, stars represent ordinary people whose ordinary joys and sorrows become extraordinary in the intensity stardom imparts to them."[19] While Gledhill is here referring primarily to the role of melodramatic excess on screen, her comments can equally illuminate the sentiments behind off-screen representations of the star as found in these writings. Readers of the fan magazines may not know who Li Xianglan is, but the writers can only hope that their constant reassurances of Li's attachment to Shanghai, and of Shanghai's attachment to her, will actually function to encourage such attachment (on the part of the fans, at any rate). Her absence creates a sort of romantic longing, Li's star status growing with each repetition of overstated emotion. The fans who "gaze with eager anticipation" forward to Li's arrival in the city have but to await, fondly and at times perhaps impatiently, the arrival of their object of desire.[20]

"Hurrying Here and Hurrying There": *Li Xianglan and Motion*

Closely tied up with the image of Li Xianglan as a figure absent from the star system in occupied Shanghai is her image as a traveler. What keeps her constantly away from Shanghai is her busy shooting schedule in Manchuria and Japan as well as, increasingly throughout the early 1940s, other locations in China and East and Southeast Asia. Thus, the Shanghai publications keep themselves busy reporting not only her absence but also the reasons behind it: what is it, they ask, that is keeping her away from us?

In the contemporary press, Li's name is linked constantly with verbs of motion. She "comes trippingly" to Shanghai, and then "flies" back to Japan.[21] She "busily rushes to perform, with appointments everywhere."[22] Almost without fail, each time that Li's name is introduced into an article concerning the production of *Eternity*, it is modified with phrases emphasizing the speed with which she moves or the distances she has traveled: "Li Xianglan, hurrying here and hurrying there" or "Li Xianglan, who has once again been invited here from the 1,000-mile–distant Manchuria."[23] In a *Zhonglian yingxun* (Zhonglian movie report) piece, the distance Li has traveled is invoked as a demand for legitimacy: "Li Xianglan is a very popular Man'ei star, who hurried here specially from beyond the Shan Hai Pass, [thus] you could really say that she should 'be treated with seriousness.'"[24]

To illustrate the demanding nature of Li's travel schedule, an interviewer for the pro-Japanese journal *Nüsheng* (Female voice) notes that, although released the year before, Li has yet to see her own film *Eternity*:

> She has so many responsibilities, that she is not able to stay long in one place. Because of her filming schedule, when her part was done, [without] waiting until the whole thing was finished, she had already flown off from Shanghai to Beijing. When the film came to Beijing, she had once again gone to Manchuria, and then by the time she arrived in Japan, the papers had announced that *Eternity* had already rotated [out of town], and was no longer there.[25]

This fragmentary, illusory presence again delineates the division between the star as sign and as object. Li Xianglan the object exists in one space and, ironically, in this capacity she exists only as object, lacking a sign. (That is, since the fan magazine writers never seem to know where she is at any particular time, her actual physical presence is never accompanied by the reference which so proliferates wherever she is not.) The current film project is located at another site but, as Li has completed her part and moved on, the set is lacking her object, left only with her traces (her signs) in the form both of journalistic reports and cinematic images. The completed film, existing not only at a different location from the other two but also constantly moving from theater to theater, city to city, contains as much of Li Xianglan's embodiment as most Shanghainese fans are ever able to see. But because of the "photo-effect," Li can in fact never be as present in the cinema in the same way that a stage actor can be present for the theater audience. Rather, her presence exists only as shadow on film, a marker of what once stood before the camera and is now absent. "This poignant 'presence in absence,'" comments Christine Gledhill following Christian Metz, "lies at the heart of the desires stimulated by stardom."[26]

Mirroring the constantly rotating film, Li Xianglan's own physicality, when it can be located, is fleeting. One item in the July 1945 issue of *Shanghai Film Forum* is particularly evocative in its representation of the perpetually mobile Li Xianglan. Under the headline "Li Xianglan restless in her lodgings," the piece reports that although her whereabouts during her current trip to Shanghai were to have been kept secret, Li is in fact known to be staying at the Grand Hotel. Because of that hotel's new policy prohibiting stays of more than three days in the same room, however, the star has had to keep moving:

> To save trouble, at first she stayed in room 631, afterwards moving from the sixth to the fifth floor several times, and most recently staying in room 707. Most likely, in a few days she will move once again. The traces of Li Xianglan are found everywhere, [but] who could have imagined that they would [also] be found in every room in the Grand Hotel![27]

Even when Li Xianglan is sitting still to give an interview, it is her energy and her movement which seem to capture the attention of the interviewer. *Shanghai Film Forum*'s September and October 1944 issues, for example, contain a two-part interview that begins with the star's greeting the interviewer, Lu Ping, at the door. Li quickly apologizes for not yet being dressed, and the interviewer comments, again emphasizing the fleetingness of Li Xianglan the object: "So fast that I almost didn't see the dazzle of those pretty red pajamas, like lightning she entered the side room." Later, "having changed clothes she came out, but she didn't immediately settle down. She inquired laughingly of her guest's opinion, then called to the servant for food and cold drinks, [and then] having just begun her little 'Excuse me' 'Excuse me's, she sat down." Throughout the interview, the star is constantly moving: looking up at the ceiling while answering a question, squeezing her handkerchief, fluttering her eyelashes, fixing her hair, jumping up to answer phone calls and get more drinks.[28] The inclusion of such details is not, of course, unusual in the style of many fan magazine interviews, which rely on details in an attempt to satiate the curiosity of readers invested in knowing all about their favorite stars. I have found, however, such minutiae of motion to be more typical of press coverage of Li Xianglan than of her female contemporaries, however "lively" (*huopo*) they are all described as being.

The larger purpose of Li Xianglan's mobility is not, however, to charm interviewers and fans; in this sense she is portrayed by the press as somewhat more seriously engaged than other figures in the Shanghai star system. Rather, Li's activity is suggested as ultimately benefitting the cause of a unified Asian film industry and, indeed, the ideology of the Greater East Asia Co-Prosperity Sphere in general. This is a role with which she becomes more and more closely identified throughout 1943 and 1944, and it is represented nowhere so clearly as in a cartoon accompanying a two-page spread of *Eternity* in the February 1943 issue of *New Film Forum.* The cartoon depicts an enormous-eyed Li Xianglan, dressed in a traditional Chinese *qipao* and toting a suitcase covered in travel stickers, walking over the Asian continent on a globe. Under her feet, superimposed over the Asian continent, are the characters for East Asia Co-Prosperity Sphere, while the cartoon is captioned "Li Xianglan, hurrying to and fro."[29]

The cartoon refers most concretely to Li Xianglan's public role as a movie star, hurrying from one shoot to another throughout Asia and thus promoting the ideology of a unified Asia, if only through the existence of its film industry. But what makes Li Xianglan an especially interesting figure, and what makes possible a more profound reading of the cartoon, is her perhaps more private role as traveler through identities. Born in Manchuria of Japanese parents but schooled in China and masquerading as Chinese in her trademark *qipao*, Li travels not only with her suitcase, geographically, but through her various identities as well.

These identities are linked to (though not limited to) the various names by which she has been known: Born with the name Yamaguchi Yoshiko in 1920, she was enrolled under the name Pan Shuhua at her Beijing school from 1934 to 1936, where she lived, by her accounts, a completely Chinese lifestyle with family friends, the Pans. Li Xianglan is the name previously given her by her adoptive father (*gan baba*), Li Jichun, in 1933. Yamaguchi stresses in her autobiography that the name functioned purely as a symbolic marking of the closeness between the two, and that for the sake of convenience, she took the same name when she began to sing professionally on the radio in the year following, as well as when she debuted at Man'ei in 1938.[30]

Li Xianglan's persona could not, of course, be tied down to just one of these identities, a point quite evident, though perhaps unintentionally so, in the contemporary press. Rather, she represented a blurring of them all, a traveling through the various identities even as she traveled through Asia in her mission for the Japanese. She provides, in consequence, a model of what a true child of the assimilated Greater East Asia Co-Prosperity Sphere might be.

"Native Place: ?": Li Xianglan and Pan-Asianism

She appears more emblematic of the Sphere in retrospect, however, than anyone at the time seems to have realized. There is a good deal of controversy concerning public awareness of her background during the war, a controversy I have discovered through interviews with occupation-era filmgoers as well as through conflicting representations in the contemporary press.

The responses given by two of my informants typify the controversy: one woman, an avid moviegoer in the 1940s who worked as a radio announcer, recollects that it was only after liberation in 1949 that anyone discovered Li Xianglan was anything other than Chinese. That news, circulated sometime after 1949, made quite an impact on this woman and her friends. Though professedly not a big fan of Li Xianglan, this woman does recall feeling duped upon discovery that the star was, in fact, the Japanese Yamaguchi Yoshiko. Another of my informants, however, a woman pursuing a graduate degree in sociology during the war years, contends that though Li Xianglan was presented to the Shanghai audience as a Chinese movie star, she and her friends were long cognizant of the fact that she was really Japanese. This woman remembers no moment of revelation. She also rejects suggestions that the knowledge of Li's nationality is something she came to afterwards that, through the intervening fifty years, may have gradually served to revise her wartime memories.

These two informants, though they disagree on what they knew of the star at the time, are in accord on one point: that is, that the actress was represented to the Shanghai cinema audience as ethnically Chinese. This notion is confirmed repeatedly in Yamaguchi's autobiography, *Li Xianglan: My Half Life.* Here she indicates that, though the fact of Li Xianglan's being born of Japanese parents was known to some in Japan and suspected by many in China, it was a detail which Man'ei studio executives preferred to keep secret if at all possible. Accordingly, when reporters asked Li about her background, she resorted to evasive answers. During her first trip to Japan in 1940, for example, when questioned about her life, she responded: "My life? What should I say? The false one, or the genuine one?" This was not, Yamaguchi explains, the sort of equivocal answer aimed at evoking mystery and thus more media interest. "It was just that, because I couldn't lie, but I also couldn't tell the truth, I could only hem and haw like that."[31]

Later, convinced that by maintaining the illusion of her Chineseness she was "cheating" the Chinese people, she reports feeling oppressed by guilt.[32] She narrates a significant moment that could have proved a turning point, but was not. Immediately before a Beijing press conference celebrating the success of *Eternity*, she asked the organizer of the conference, a friend of her father's by the name of Li Mou, if she might use the occasion to reveal the secret that she was, in fact, Japanese. Mr. Li responded vehemently: "Absolutely not. Among these reporters there are perhaps those who know you are Japanese. But they are also unwilling to acknowledge this fact. If you are Chinese, then you are Beijing's own movie star. Don't destroy our dream."[33] Leaving aside for a moment Mr. Li's interesting double positioning here (he acknowledges the ruse as a "dream," yet includes himself among its believers), I will continue Yamaguchi's own narrative: As it turns out, at the conference Li was interrogated by one severe young reporter wanting to know how, as a Chinese, she could possibly have made films so embarrassing to the nation as her early *Song of the White Orchid* and

Night in China? Is she, after all, *not* Chinese? Aching to reveal her true identity, she instead resorted to a half-truth: being young at the time, she said, she didn't understand things, and she now owes the Chinese people an apology. Thereupon, by Yamaguchi's account (which remains, as far as I know, the only one), she received a standing ovation from the reporters, most of whom, as she reflected upon it later, must have suspected that she was Japanese.

Yet Yamaguchi seems convinced, at least in her retrospective autobiography, that her success as a movie star was predicated on maintaining the secret of her identity. In 1944 when, chafing under the weight of deception, she finally resolved to reveal her identity, she apparently gave no thought to continuing her life as an actress. Fifty years later, she wrote of her feelings following the aforementioned press conference: "I thought, I'll cast away Li Xianglan; in short, I'll resign from Man'ei. This is what I resolved to do."[34] By her own account, giving up the name Li Xianglan meant giving up acting, or at the very least giving up acting with Man'ei. Yamaguchi explains this now by pointing to the fact that she became popular in China only after the success of *Eternity*, which was also the first film she made with an all-Chinese cast. She could, thus, hardly presume that anyone would want to see her films if she were represented as anything other than Chinese.[35]

For Yamaguchi, then, there continues to exist a strong correlation between her wartime fame and the "pretense" of her ethnic Chineseness.[36] For contemporary Japanese scholars of occupation film, critical of Japanese militaristic policy in the names of its countless Asian victims, it is much the same story. Shimizu Akira, for example, writes that Li was "offered for sale" as Chinese to the Chinese audience, and notes that even after a Japanese newspaper published a scoop in 1941 exposing her as Japanese, other newspapers obediently ignored the news, thus preventing its spread to China.[37] Sato Tadao's opinion does not differ from this, although he does suggest that the secret of Li's identity was protected, at least initially, more as a way of retaining Japanese, rather than Chinese, interest in the star.[38]

What I have found in contemporary texts, however, suggests that while many were perhaps content to assume that Li was Chinese, and while the star herself is convinced that her success lay therein, there also existed ample clues to suggest otherwise, clues that in fact enhanced her role as emblem of an assimilated Asia. She may well have been, as she claims and as my informants contend, deceptively introduced to Shanghai moviegoers as ethnically Chinese. But what I have found in these publications suggests that as she became more famous throughout the early 1940s, she was represented by the print media in such conflicting terms that she emerged within the Shanghai star system not as ethnically Chinese but rather as vaguely and ambiguously pan-Asian.

While depicted as ethnically Chinese in *Eternity*, for example, her name stands out in early magazine and newspaper advertisements of the film through its vertical positioning, separate from the names of the Chinese cast, a marking of her outsider status as well, perhaps, as of her ethnic singularity.[39] The star's Japaneseness is revealed much more overtly in the September 1943 issue of *Riben yingxun* (Japanese film report). In a two-page photo spread entitled "Brilliant Flowers of the Japanese Silver Forum," Li Xianglan appears on an equal standing with 11 other Japanese actresses, in this publication apparently intended to foster a Chinese fandom for Japanese films and film stars.[40] Similarly, there is no attempt to hide the star's background in *Shanghai Film Forum*'s November 1944 feature, "Study of the Stars." This two-page spread contains photographs of 23 Chinese female stars, each listed with items of information such as original name, age, native place, representative work, and current address. Li Xianglan's original name is listed clearly and unapologetically as "Yamaguchi Yoshiko," and her address (although noted to be temporary) as, appropriately enough, "Empire Apartment House, Tokyo, Japan." So as not to erase all mystery about her, however, at the space for the listing of "native place" is printed only a question mark—the only one of the featured stars listed in this manner.[41]

More significantly, Li herself sends different messages when she is referring to herself in the context of China, Manchuria, and Japan. She frequently includes herself in references to the Chinese people, especially when apologizing for the insensitivity of her early films. In the midst of the two-part *Shanghai Film Forum* interview, she offers: "Really, speaking honestly, because of these [films] I have always felt that I have let us, Chinese people, down" (*duibuqi women zhongguoren*).[42] But at the same time, she divulges more candid clues as to her nationality. For example, when asked by a *New Film Forum* reporter what she most desires in the future, she replies that she would most like her *Eternity* co-stars to come and visit "our place" (*women nar*) in Japan and Manchuria.[43]

These brief and scattered revelations as to the background of the star Li Xianglan are not inadvertent slips so much as clues that, read against the background of occupied Shanghai cinema, contribute to a complex star persona. The different ways in which she was represented in the Chinese press suggest a degree of slippage complicating the package in which she was initially presented to occupied Shanghai cinema audiences. In the Chinese journalistic imagination, it seems, Li represents not so much the quintessentially Chinese repository of femininity idealized by Japanese audiences (there were plenty of home-grown Chinese stars to serve this function among China's filmgoers) as, rather, a femininity vaguely pan-Asian in nature. Far from detracting from her effectiveness for the Japanese, however, this slippage can be seen as an augmentation of her image as star representative of Co-Prosperity Sphere ideology.

It is probably the case, as Sato suggests above, that in Li's earlier days as a star whose popularity was more narrowly circumscribed to the Manchurian and Japanese audiences, her image was also more heavily invested in a popular perception of her ethnic Chineseness. (I would favor the notion of her popularity taking on a life and authority of its own, thus increasing studio investment in the name Li Xianglan, rather than a theory supporting some grand manipulators at Man'ei, creating and maintaining use of the name as a politically advantageous deception.) Especially given the plots of her first films, those for which she was later to apologize to "us, Chinese people," it was probably preferable, from the point of view of attracting a Manchurian and Japanese film audience, for her to be seen as ethnically Chinese. Her masquerade as Chinese in the Japanese imagination clearly functions to confirm the Japanese propagandistic notion, expressed repeatedly in these films, that the Chinese not only need but also desire a Japanese presence in the mainland.[44]

For the nationalistic Chinese audience, though, the image of a Chinese star so closely allied to the Japanese would only evoke the sort of hatred due a national traitor. (It is probably for this reason that the early films, even when rescreened following Li's success in *Eternity*, did not prove popular with Chinese audiences.) Thus as Li Xianglan's fame spread outside of Manchuria, and with the wide release of *Eternity*, it became less important that she be seen as ethnically Chinese. Indeed, from this distance, she would appear to be a more effective symbol of Co-Prosperity Sphere ideology if she is seen for what she is: a child of Japanese parents, born in Manchuria but educated in and with a great love for China. What figure could better represent the ideology of Asian unity?

Increasingly, then, in her treatment by the press, Li is not tied to any specific place or to any specific identity, Chinese or otherwise. In these later years her name is introduced more often modified by the route she has taken from the far reaches of the Asian continent; or she is more generally referred to as simply "Asian." This ambiguous marker is used, for example, in a 1945 interview reported by the publication *Zazhi yuekan* (Miscellany monthly). Here she is introduced to the readers as an "East Asian female star" (*Dongya nü mingxing*), while Zhang Ailing (1920–96), who also participates in the interview, is introduced more specifically as a "Chinese female author" (*Zhongguo nü zuojia*).[45] At the hands of the Shanghai press, the specific origin and background of the star Li Xianglan become immaterial: it is more important that she be seen as coming from everywhere, or perhaps nowhere at all. Like the question mark, Li Xianglan is, precisely, an emblem signifying equally no place and every place.

"[They] Just Take Me to Be One of Their Own": Li Xianglan and Universalizability

Tsuji Hisakazu, in his 1987 book *Chuka den'ei shiwa* (A narrative history of Chinese cinema), discusses the enthusiastic Chinese response to *Eternity*, linking it to questions of Li's perceived nationality.

> Was Li Xianglan Japanese? Truly, there were a lot of rumors. But as far as the audience was concerned, captivated as they were by her acting and singing in *Eternity*, they didn't want to fuss over this [question] anymore. Such a thing as this, beautiful and remarkable and bringing joy to people, prompts people to clap and cheer without reserve. In this respect, within the disposition of the Chinese people there seems to be a great magnanimity.[46]

Judging from the responses of most of my informants, it is not true that the Chinese were so enamored of Li Xianglan as to generously and eagerly overlook the question of her nationality. The question was one that occupied all of my informants, if only retrospectively.[47] But insofar as the Chinese audience embraced her, I believe this had less to do with any sort of "magnanimity" and more with a willful overlooking of what, given the rumors and various clues facing them in the press, individuals may have suspected to be the case.

In this respect, Yamaguchi's recounting of the 1943 Beijing press conference at which she received a standing ovation from reporters even as they suspected that she was Japanese, is critical. As the conference organizer Mr. Li suggested to her, these reporters (indeed, Mr. Li himself) maintained an investment in the belief of her ethnic Chineseness. To relinquish this belief would entail, for them, a relinquishment of their pride in this hometown success story. On a larger scale, Yamaguchi suggests that her post-*Eternity* popularity among Chinese audiences rests on the inspirational nature of one of the film's songs. This song, "Jieyan ge" (Stop smoking song), with its lyrics describing the dangers of opium and the benefits of kicking the habit, motivated nationalistic young people in China to stand firm, according to Yamaguchi. She remembers that her sister, who attended a film screening in Beijing, reported that the audience broke into applause following the song.[48] What Li Xianglan represented to the Chinese people, Yamaguchi believes, was a source of national pride. As such, they would surely not be eager to acknowledge a non-Chinese nationality.

There is in audience identification with Li Xianglan, however, something more than hometown or nationalistic pride. It was the very ambiguity of the star Li Xianglan, the multiple nature of her identities, which allowed audiences to see in her whatever they wanted to see. This is suggested most tellingly in regards to the simple matter of her appearance. In a June 1944 *New Film Forum* interview, Li describes her experience of going to the Taiwanese countryside to film the exterior shots for the film *Mannü qingge* (Love song of the barbarian girl, 1943):[49]

> When the [Taiwanese] people opened their eyes wide and stared directly at me, they saw that my eyes are just as big as theirs, and they all assumed that I am of the same stock. It was the same in Harbin, while filming *Harbin genü* (Songstress of Harbin). The Russian people there unexpectedly said that of my father and mother, one must definitely be Russian and the other Chinese. It's really interesting: it's as if wherever I go, the people there just take me to be one of their own.[50]

Such ready identification with the star takes on even more extreme form in a story Yamaguchi tells of a visit to Korea during the early 1940s. An old Korean couple, whose daughter had been kidnapped as a child, insisted that Li was that daughter, finally returned home to them. According to Yamaguchi's rendering of the story, it seems that she never really managed to convince them that they were wrong.[51]

The notion of a universal identification in Li's looks certainly goes some way toward explaining her popularity among various Asian audiences, and furthermore indicates why she may have been a particularly apt spokeswoman for the notion of a future unified and assimilated Asian community. More profoundly, however, it is perhaps suggestive of the way in which audiences take up stars in general. Psychoanalytic approaches to the study of cinema afford a possible way of understanding the phenomenon. As in Lacanian psychoanalysis the gendered human subject is formed through an identification with the parental figure, so too is the cinematic spectator constructed through an identification with cinema's "authority figure," the star. In both cases, the promise of a coherent and fixed identity, embodied in the star, is sought out by the spectator through a denial of difference. While aware of the cultural differences which make the direct importation of Western theory into the Chinese context problematic, the notion that we identify with stars by disavowing difference does suggest to me a useful way of thinking about the apparent wholesale appeal of the star Li Xianglan. The spectator locates in the star whatever it is that she needs to find in herself; the star thus inevitably represents something different to each fan.

In a 1992 review of Yamaguchi's autobiography entitled "People—History—Li Xianglan," Wang Meng (b. 1934) uses the book as a springboard for an analysis of the multifaceted nature of history.[52] He praises Yamaguchi for offering different views of the occupation period, a particularly sensitive subject which all too often is construed in a blindly nationalistic manner or, as in mainland China's canonical film history text, is dismissed entirely.[53] Wang writes that, while there is only one history, each person has his or her own version of that history; indeed, one person, notably Yamaguchi, can even contain different versions within herself.

While I question Wang's assumption that there is one history and that it is possible, in his words, to look it straight in the eye, his analysis does suggest an interesting way of thinking about Li Xianglan's popular appeal.[54] Precisely because each person carries a different view of history, it is impossible to speak of the existence of only one; the "real" history is thus always absent. Similarly, each of Li Xianglan's spectators takes away a different view of her. The "real" star is absent; indeed, because this particular star possesses so many different names, there exists a lack of even nominal unity.

The recollection of one of my informants is especially suggestive of this. A high school student at the time of Li Xianglan's apex of popularity, he remembers buying a photo of the star from one of the many stores which at that time traded in celebrity photos. He took the photo home and, using charcoal, painstakingly created his own likeness of her likeness. He doesn't remember what he did with the photo, he says, but he took great pride in his own creation. He tacked it to his bedroom wall, where for some time afterwards he reflected upon the loveliness of the star (or, at the very least, the loveliness of his own conception of her). Like the star's photo which, admits the informant, was likely discarded, the original "real" image is absent, while what lingers for the fan is his or her own personal rendering.

"Work Diligently, Diligently, Diligently": *Li Xianglan and Industry*

A June 1944 *New Film Forum* piece describes Li Xianglan in the following way: "Li Xianglan, on the run for [or "toiling for"] the Greater East Asia Film Sphere" (*benbo yu Dadongya dianyingquan de Li Xianglan*).[55] Once again the star's name is linked to the notion of the Film Sphere, and is modified by a verb of motion. It is doubly significant, however, that the verb used here, *benbo*, can be taken to mean either motion or exertion, since it is with the latter that the star is also commonly associated in the occupied Shanghai press. Implicit in the travel that keeps her busy and away from Shanghai, Li Xianglan's industry is also showcased in press accounts of her more stationary activities.

The values of diligence are most often linked to Li's persona as singer. As opposed to other film stars who, in the words of one *Female Voice* critic, "use the primitive method of just casually singing a bit, [Li] has put an extensive amount of labor into vocal music; she has received a long training, and she uses the correct vocal techniques in singing her songs. We can't expect every film artist to be able to sing like her...."[56] In a review of *Eternity* published in the magazine *Miscellany Monthly*, reviewer Chi Qing, while decidedly reserved about Li's acting, comments on the hard-earned nature of her musical ability: "What impresses most deeply is her surprising degree of singing ability. In terms of music, the perfection she has attained through years of training is very deep; she is really an outstanding talent in Asia."[57] In interviews Li routinely discusses at length the current status of her study, as well as the name and preferred pedagogy of her latest teacher. Praised in *Shanghai Film Forum* for her study of Italian opera, she is cited in a report in *New Film Forum* for her natural endowments, which are developed by "open-minded study."[58] Many of the songs for which she is most widely known appear to have been written specially to showcase her virtuosity. For example, "Haiyan" (Ocean swallow) and "Watashi no uguisu" both contain passages highlighting the sort of vocal acrobatics more suited for a practice room than a concert hall, thus reinforcing Li's image as serious student rather than melodic entertainer.

The emphasis in the press on "diligent artist Li Xianglan" makes for an interesting confluence in these writings of work, art, and love. Having lauded her attitude equating art with work, one interview concludes: "Well, we respectfully wish Miss Li Xianglan good health, [so that she may] eternally work diligently for art."[59] Similarly, a *Shanghai Film Forum* interview portrays Li as interested not in fame, but rather in improving her own performance skills. This constitutes, for her, a duty: "At my post, I must eternally study, study!"[60] Li is also represented as interested in little else but this duty. With the exception of the two-part *Shanghai Film Forum* interview, which attempts in vain to delve into her love life, press accounts almost invariably suggest that Li is more in love with her work than with anything or anyone else. In contrast to the unflagging investigations into the various love affairs, marriages, and divorces of other Shanghai stars,[61] Li Xianglan is summed up in a *Shanghai Film Forum* article entitled "Secrets of the female stars" in one sentence: "Li Xianglan says: 'I don't want a lover; I like art, and art is my lover.'"[62] In this respect Li's treatment at the hands of the Shanghai fan press provides an interesting contrast to Hollywood fan magazines, which, according to Richard Dyer, present an emphasis on love issues and thus a "suppression of film-making as work."[63] For Li Xianglan, film-making and art alike are work. Behind the outward sign of her industry there exists no love (the signifier of a private life) for the reporters to probe.

Alongside press representation of Li Xianglan as serious artist is Li Xianglan as polyglot. It is the rare reporter who does not comment upon her impressive abilities in Japanese, Chinese, and Manchu—though, significantly, it is never specified which is her mother tongue. As with her musical abilities, her facility in foreign languages is said to be the result of hard work (and the fact that we never know for sure which languages count as foreign and which as native speaks even more to her success). In her autobiography, Li quotes a piece of Japanese propaganda produced at the time of her first visit to Japan: "She speaks Japanese very fluently; you could also say that she speaks Japanese, Manchu, and Chinese—all three languages—and is [thus] a representative worthy of the name 'Happy Asia' (*Xing Ya*)."⁶⁴ She is praised as well for her industrious study of English, Russian, and Cantonese, and she surprises one reporter by showing up, literally on the doorstep, suddenly conversing "beautifully" in the Shanghainese dialect.⁶⁵ In fact, her facility in languages proves disconcerting to some reporters who witness it. When on the *Eternity* set Li, surrounded by reporters, "used English, Chinese and Japanese to deal with each person, one young foreign girl whispered to another: 'How is it that *everybody* is able to talk to her?' "⁶⁶ The confusion of languages surrounding her takes on comic proportions in a gossip column item that reports: "There is a Japanese fan who used Chinese to write a letter to Li Xianglan. He wrote: 'Xianglan, my dear mother [*niang*]!' " The columnist adds in explanation that the word *niang* in Japanese is the equivalent of the Chinese *guniang* (girl).⁶⁷

The languages, of course, are merely tools enabling Li Xianglan to fulfill, on concrete and abstract levels alike, her role as representative of a united Asia through film. This work she carries out most directly through her screen roles, though, as evidenced in her many interviews and appearances at studio functions, she was kept perhaps even more busy off-camera. In both capacities she is represented as embodying the values of hard work. A reporter visiting the set of *Eternity* writes, in language similar to that used to describe her musical study, that what was most impressive about Li was the "open-mindedness and diligence" with which she went about her work: "She accepted the director's notes very open-mindedly, and during breaks she would retreat into the corner, carefully studying her dialogue and blocking."⁶⁸ Indeed, Li's industry seems taken to extremes at times: while she discusses her fifteen- to sixteen-hour work days, reporters note with concern that after her latest trip she appears "haggard" and "pallid," and report that she worked so hurriedly on the filming of *Eternity* that she became sick.⁶⁹ She is also represented at times with pity, as in the case of a photo captioned "Ms. Li Xianglan—the bird, exhausted from flight, which longs for home?"⁷⁰

Regardless of the reporters' apparent misgivings about the demands of her schedule, however, Li Xianglan continues to be associated with the rewards of hard work. The message is presented by her own pen in a *New Film Forum* piece, in which Li exhorts all people of Asia—Japanese, Chinese, and Manchurian alike—to work together so as to enjoy future happiness. She closes the piece with a personal witness:

> When at work I have encountered matters that are arduous and distressing, and when I face the clumsiness of my own efforts, sometimes I simply want to cry. But at these times, I also strengthen my firm resolve to work even harder.
>
>   And now in my heart I can see: work diligently, diligently, diligently—for the art of film, and even more for the future peace and comfort of Greater East Asia!⁷¹

Perhaps because this piece is presented in Li's own voice, it indicates in especially stark terms the close association between the movie star and the Sphere ideology that, throughout the five years of its life, she came to represent in cinematic circles.[72] She alludes to the Sphere with her reference to a future Greater East Asia, and suggests as well a place for the "art of film" within this future. But it is in her invocation of diligence that Li points to the means for a successful implementation of that ideology: it is only through hard work that a Greater East Asia can be achieved. More specifically, the nature of Li's own industry as a movie star mirrors nicely that required by the Sphere: what characterizes both is a superseding of national and indeed even "natural" limits.

This is achieved first as a result of the constant mobility with which Li Xianglan goes about fulfilling her role as a pan-Asian movie star. The blurring of her movements represents, on a personal level, the continual crossing of boundaries in her own identity and, on a global scale, an attempted obscuring of the boundaries separating the Asian nations.[73] More than physical national boundaries, though, Li Xianglan's industry represents an attempt to overcome the more "natural" ethnic or linguistic markings associated with these boundaries. The actress not only uses industry to overcome her own "clumsiness"; through industry, she even dissolves differences between languages and ethnicities. Each expression of confusion from the press regarding her native language or her ethnic identity represents one more promise that in the future Greater East Asia, such markings need not exist at all. Rather, Li Xianglan is fashioned as a model whereby work overcomes distinctions: she suggests to her fans that even languages and ethnicities need not prove insurmountable in the quest for Asian assimilation.

Richard Dyer writes, "What is interesting about [stars] is not the character they have constructed (the traditional role of the actor) but rather the business of constructing/performing/being (depending on the particular star involved) a 'character.'"[74] As illustrated graphically in the cartoon depicting a Li Xianglan globetrotting over the Asian continent, the most important of Li's "characters" is not any on-screen role she may have played, but rather the more encompassing one of spokeswoman and star representative of a unified Asia. Further, as suggested by Dyer's comment, what is more significant from our point of view as spectators of Li Xianglan is watching not her performance of this role, but rather her production of it. Another way of putting it might be: the performance is, precisely, the construction.

Construction is also, of course, at the heart of the Greater East Asia Co-Prosperity Sphere ideology which Li Xianglan represented. The creation of Li's character entailed the study of languages, the study of music, travel. For each citizen, for each "character," the tasks would be different, but each would invariably be called upon to contribute his or her appropriate industry for the sake of the Asian collective community. At its idealistic core, Sphere ideology represented the utopian notion of reshaping the individual through a superseding of the boundaries of national and linguistic distinction.

It is the process of construction of the Greater East Asia Co-Prosperity Sphere that, similarly, seems to have taken precedence over the actual achievement of any sort of pan-Asian identity. Mirroring Li Xianglan's arrival in Shanghai—perpetually discussed, often deferred, and always imminent—the ideology of the Sphere was much discussed and never realized. Like the famous movie star herself, the Sphere future of equality among the nations of Asia was an absent sign, existing not in Shanghai but rather out there and perhaps anywhere but here. And just as Li Xianglan never quite makes her appearance in Shanghai, this Sphere ideal of a pan-Asian identity is never quite achieved and is, perhaps, not even meant to be achieved. Like the love affairs between Chinese woman and Japanese man that conspicuously fail to be consummated on screen, Li Xianglan as representative of assimilationist utopia is the harbinger of a future that never came to pass and was perhaps designed never to come to pass.

The August 1945 issue of *Miscellany Monthly* contains the transcript of a discussion in which Li Xianglan participated along with the writer Zhang Ailing. Throughout the interview, Li appears extremely reluctant to answer questions.[75] She relies once on Kawakita Nagamasa (1903–81), head of Huaying, to formulate a reply for her,[76] and at another time converses behind her paper fan with Zhang Ailing, before letting Zhang voice her opinion. (The unnamed journalist reporting the interview interprets the fan as representing both riddle and symbol: the young girl who can bring herself to say what's in her heart only in the presence of another girl.) Zhang praises Li at one point in the discussion, noting that after hearing Li sing, Zhang could only feel that she's not human but rather some kind of fairy (*xiannü*). Later, one of the reporters asks Li if she has made any new discoveries. This question Li chooses to respond to in her own words and, for the first time, at great length:

> *Li Xianglan*: You ask me if I've made any new discoveries . . . ah, I . . . (she lowers her head, thinks again, and then raises her head, her long-lashed eyes opening wide, intoning heavily the following sentence) I wish to discover how to be a person [*zenyang zuo ge ren*]! . . . My ideal, I should be a healthy person—having a healthy physique, a healthy life, healthy love. To be a person without having a healthy life, to me is like not being a person . . . How to do it, how to be a person? (she stops a moment, then continues to speak) Of course, every day I sing, every day I have teachers teaching me English, Russian, and music. This is study, this is training, but it's not the basic principle behind being a person . . . I don't know how to go about being a person . . . (saying this, she makes one think that, although moving

about in crowds of people, her heart is laden with emptiness, dejection, and loneliness) A girl's blessing doesn't lie in fame and fortune, . . . of what does it consist? . . . I don't know . . . Coming home from [my] concert at Daguangming Theater, all at once I cried, I cried like anything. I feel lonely! . . .

Reporter: She lives her life without the pleasures of humans.

Kawakita: Lives her life for others.

Reporter: Miss Zhang, writing her short stories, can express her own thoughts and feelings, but in film, Miss Li can't derive this sort of comfort.

Li Xianglan: My philosophy of life and what I express in films are two different things.

Reporter: She has two types of personality.

Li Xianglan: Sometimes, I really want to do something bad [*zuo huaishi*] . . . What do you all say? . . . I know that it's dangerous to have this kind of idea.

Reporter: Maybe what you call something bad, is nothing other than the way to go about being a person.[77]

In this excerpt Li Xianglan, while admitting to a busyness about her life which may by most standards represent success, reveals that behind such activity she finds a fundamental emptiness at her core. As accomplished as she is, she feels she still has not completed what she considers to be the most basic task: being a human being. Without the unceasing process of construction of that "character"—that is, without travel and language study and music lessons—there exists in her nothing else.[78] Any attempt to create a core would entail "doing something bad"—something that is, in other words, contrary to character. The construction of character through the blurring of boundaries may be utopian but it is also, by her formulation, deeply dehumanizing.

It is, moreover, from indications in these magazines and among filmgoers in occupied Shanghai, a failed construction. Li Xianglan appears to have been taken up by most viewers as either a Chinese star or as a Japanese star masquerading as Chinese: in either case, she is read as a woman identified by rigid national distinctions. While journalistic accounts tended to emphasize Li's pan-Asianness, even enthusiastic reporters were not above couching her praise in competitively nationalistic language, as evidenced in the quote that began this chapter. What's more, the star herself, in her autobiography, constantly gives the lie to the ideal of surpassing national boundaries: her focus on the secret of her identity, and on the treachery with which she went about posing as Chinese, reveal a deep awareness of those national boundaries she was publicly represented as having surpassed. Indeed, when I mentioned to her my own impressions of contemporary press treatment of Li Xianglan—that is, that she was portrayed on the whole as vaguely Asian—Yamaguchi read it, to my surprise, as a kindness: how charitable it was of the press not to divulge the deception, and how kind it was of me to tell her this, and thus lighten her load of guilt. In Yamaguchi's guilt, and in the remorse that followed it, lies a reinforcement of the racial and ethnic distinctions a united Asia was meant to erase. Li Xianglan crossed boundaries but did not, perhaps, succeed in blurring them: in her they are, rather, constantly confirmed.

The failure of the ideology is also evident in Li's outburst in the above interview. Gledhill, while maintaining that stars tend to be taken as emblems of a particular value or values, emphasizes equally the contradictions and ambiguity that go into the construction of their personae. As essentially ambiguous figures who can represent something to everyone, stars become "figures whose fragmentation can make them sites of ideological contestation."[79] The workings of such contestation are manifest in the anguish displayed by Li Xianglan in this interview. More than a traveler between the distinct identities of Japanese and Chinese, as Li describes herself in her autobiography, she was portrayed by the bulk of the contemporary Shanghai press as nonfixed to the point of emptiness. In the despair she expresses at the loss of her "humanness," we see the failure of the Sphere attempt to reshape the individual, and the impossibility of superseding "natural" boundaries. Behind the activity of her self-construction as the model of an assimilated Asia, there lies nothing else; her traces, scattered everywhere, mask an absence.

REFERENCE MATTER

Filmography

This filmography contains a chronological list of all films mentioned in the book, including Western titles. Chinese titles are listed first in pinyin and then in English translations. Under each year, films are listed alphabetically; d = director and s = screenwriter. Films with uncertain dates are grouped at the end. The reader may also consult the index, where film titles in both pinyin and English are listed in alphabetic order.

1905
Dingjun shan (Dingjun mountain), Beijing: Fengtai

1907
Ben-Hur, U.S.: Kalem

1909
Faust, U.S.: Edison
Les Miserables, U.S.: Vitagraph
Tou shaoya (Stealing the roast duck), d: Liang Shaopo, Hong Kong: Asia
Wapen shenyuan (Righting a wrong with earthenware dish), d: Liang Shaopo, Hong Kong: Asia
Xi taihou (The empress dowager), d: Benjamin Polaski, Hong Kong: Asia

1911
Dante's Inferno, Italy/U. S.
Faust, Italy/U.S.
A Tale of Two Cities, U.S.: Vitagraph

1912
Homer's Odyssey, U. S.

1913
Da chenghuang (Beating the town god), d: Zhang Shichuan, Shanghai: Asia
Erbaiwu baixiang chenghuangmiao (The blockhead roams round the temple of the town god), d: Zhang Shichuan, Shanghai: Asia
Huo Wuchang (A living Wuchang), d: Zhang Shichuan, Shanghai: Asia
Nanfu nanqi (The difficult couple), or *Dongfang huazhu* (Wedding festivities), d: Zhang Shichuan, s: Zheng Zhengqiu, Shanghai: Asia
Wufu linmeng (Five blessings at the threshold), d: Zhang Shichuan, Shanghai: Asia

1915

The Birth of a Nation, d: D. W. Griffith, s: D. W. Griffith, Frank Woods, U.S.: Epoch

1916

Heiji yuanhun (Wronged souls in an opium den), d: Zhang Shichuan, Guan Haifeng, Shanghai: Huanxian

1919

The Cabinet of Dr. Caligari, d: Robert Wiene, s: Carl Mayer, Hans Janowitz, Germany: Decla-Bioscop

1920

Way Down East, d: D. W. Griffith, s: Anthony P. Kelly, U. S.: D. W. Griffith, Inc.

1921

The Four Horsemen of the Apocalypse, d: Rex Ingram, U. S.
Haishi (Sea oath), d: Dan Duyu, Shanghai: Shanghai yingxi
Hongfen kulou (Beauty and the skeleton), d/s: Guan Haifeng, Shanghai: Xinya
Yan Ruisheng (Yan Ruisheng), d: Ren Pengnian, s: Yang Xiaozhong, Shanghai: Zhongguo yingxi

1922

Danao guai juchang (Strange happenings at the theater), d: Zhang Shichuan, s: Zheng Zhengqiu, Shanghai: Mingxing
Huaji dawang you hua ji (The king of comedy's journey to China), d: Zhang Shichuan, s: Zheng Zhengqiu, Shanghai: Mingxing
Laogong zhi aiqing (Laborer's love), or *Zhiguo yuan* (Romance of the fruit seller), d: Zhang Shichuan, s: Zheng Zhengqiu, Shanghai: Mingxing
My American Wife, d: Jesse L. Larsky, s: Monte M. Katterjohn, U. S.: Famous Players-Lasky
Zhang Xinsheng (Zhang Xinsheng), d: Zhang Shichuan, s: Zheng Zhengqiu, Shanghai: Mingxing

1923

The Girl I Loved, d: Joseph DeGrasse, U. S.: Charles Ray Productions
Guer jiuzu ji (The orphan rescues grandfather), d: Zhang Shichuan, s: Zheng Zhengqiu, Shanghai: Mingxing
Second Fiddle, d: Frank Tuttle, U. S.: Film Guild
The Ten Commandments, d: Cecil DeMille, s: Jeanie MacPherson, U. S.: Famous Players-Lasky

1924

Hong meigui (Red rose), d: Xu Zhuodai, Shanghai: Kaixin/Xin wutai
Lingbo xianzi (Fairy maiden), d: Xu Zhuodai, Shanghai: Kaixin/Xin wutai
Qifu (The abandoned wife), d: Li Zeyuan, Hou Yao, s: Hou Yao, Shanghai: Changcheng
Youhun (Seductive marriage), d: Zhang Shichuan, s: Zhou Jianyun, Shanghai: Mingxing

Yuli hun (Spirit of the jade pear), d: Zhang Shichuan, Xu Hu, s: Zheng Zhengqiu, Shanghai: Mingxing

1925

Battleship Potemkin, d/s: Sergei Eisenstein, Russia: First Studio of Goskino
Ben-Hur, d: Fred Niblo, s: Bess Meredyth, Carey Wilson, U. S.: MGM
Chungui mengli ren (The person in the spring boudoir dream), d: Li Zeyuan, Mei Xuechou, s: Hou Yao, Shanghai: Changcheng
The Joyless Street, d: G. W. Pabst, s: Willy Haas, Germany: Sofar Film
Konggu lan (Orchid in a deep valley), d: Zhang Shichuan, s: Bao Tianxiao, Shanghai: Mingxing
Lianhua gongzhu (Princess lotus flower), d: Gu Wuwei, Shanghai: Gong wutai
Shanghai yi furen (A woman in Shanghai), d: Zhang Shichuan, s: Zheng Zhengqiu, Shanghai: Mingxing
The Unchastened Woman, d: James Young, s: Douglas Doty, U. S.: Chadwick Pictures
Xiao pengyou (Little friend), d: Zhang Shichuan, s: Zheng Zhengqiu, Shanghai: Mingxing
Yichuan zhenzhu (A string of pearls), d: Li Zeyuan, s: Hou Yao, Shanghai: Changcheng
Zhaixing zhi nü (The woman who plucked stars), d: Li Zeyuan, Mei Xuechou, s: Hou Yao, Shanghai: Changcheng
Zhan'gong (Victory), d: Lu Jie, Xu Xinfu, s: Lu Jie, Shanghai: Da Zhonghua
Zuihou zhi liangxin (The last trace of conscience), d: Zhang Shichuan, s: Zheng Zhengqiu, Shanghai: Mingxing

1926

Dianying nü mingxing (Movie actresses), d: Shao Zuiweng, s: Shao Cunren, Shao Shanke, Shanghai: Tianyi
Heping zhishen (Spirit of peace), d/s: Hou Yao, Shanghai: Minxin
Huanjin ji (Returning of gold), d: Dan Duyu, s: Zhou Shoujuan, Shanghai: Shanghai yingxi
Liangxin de fuhuo (Rekindling of conscience), d: Bu Wancang, s: Bao Tianxiao, Shanghai: Mingxing
Metropolis, d: Fritz Lang, s: Thea von Harbou, Germany: UFA
Zhibian waishi (Migration to the borders), d/s: Lu Jie, Shanghai: Da Zhonghua-Baihe

1927

Dirnentragödie (Tragedy of the whore), Germany
Fuhuo de meigui (Revived rose), d: Hou Yao, Li Minwei, s: Hou Yao, Shanghai: Minxin
Haijiao shiren (The poet at the end of the seas), d/s: Hou Yao, Shanghai: Minxin
Hongloumeng (Dream of the red chamber), d: Ren Pengnian, Yu Boyan, Shanghai: Fudan
Hongniang xianxing ji (Hongniang reveals her true colors), d: Xu Wenrong, s: Zhu Xuehua, Shanghai: Kuaihuolin
Hubian chunmeng (Spring dream by the lakeside), d: Bu Wancang, s: Tian Han, Shanghai: Mingxing
The Jazz Singer, d: Alan Crosland, s: Al Cohn, U. S: Warner Brothers

Napoleon, d/s: Abel Gance, France: Westi
Nezha chushi (The coming of Nezha), d: Li Zeyuan, s: Sun Shiyi, Shanghai: Changcheng
Pansi dong (The spider queen), d: Dan Duyu, s: Guan Ji'an, Shanghai: Shanghai yingxi
Sanguo zhi Caocao bigong (Romance of the three kingdoms: Caocao closes in on the palace), d: Xia Chifeng, s: Wu Hanyi, Shanghai: Da Zhongguo
Sanguo zhi meiren ji (Romance of the three kingdoms: Beauty's strategy), d: Lu Jie, s: Zhu Shouju, Shanghai: Da Zhonghua-Baihe
Seventh Heaven, d: Frank Borzage, s: Benjamin Glazer, U.S.: Fox
Tieshan gongzhu (Princess iron fan), d: Shao Zuiweng, Li Pingqian, s: Shao Cunren, Shanghai: Tianyi
Xixiang ji (The romance of the western chamber), d/s: Hou Yao, Shanghai: Minxin
Xiyou ji (Journey to the west), d: Qiu Sixiang, Li Pingqian, s: Shao Cunren, Shanghai: Tianyi

1928

Huoshao honglian si (Burning of the Red Lotus Temple), d: Zhang Shichuan, s: Zheng Zhengqiu, Shanghai: Mingxing
Mangmu de aiqing (Blind love), d: Bu Wancang, s: Bao Tianxiao, Shanghai: Hanlun
Qi nüzi (Extraordinary girl), d: Shi Dongshan, s: Zheng Yingshi, Shanghai: Naimei
Street Angel, d: Frank Borzage, s: Marion Orth, U.S.: Fox

1929

Hongxia (The red heroine), d: Wen Yimin, Shanghai: Youlian
Welcome Danger, d/s: Clyde Bruckman, U. S.: Harold Lloyd Corp.

1931

Frankenstein, d: James Whale, s: Garrett Fort, Francis E. Faragoh, U. S.: Universal
Genü hongmudan (Sing-song girl Red Peony), d: Zhang Shichuan, assisted by Cheng Bugao, s: Hong Shen, Shanghai: Mingxing
Taohua qixue ji (Peach blossom weeps tears of blood), d/s: Bu Wancang, Shanghai: Lianhua

1932

Shanghai Express, d: Josef von Sternberg, s: Jules Furthman, U.S.: Paramount
Tianming (Daybreak), d/s: Sun Yu, Shanghai: Lianhua
Ye meigui (Wild rose), d/s: Sun Yu, Shanghai: Lianhua

1933

Alice in Wonderland, d: Norman McLeod, s: Joseph Mankiewicz, William C. Menzies, U. S: Paramount
Beauty for Sale, d: Richard Boleslavsky, s: Zelda Sears, Eve Green, U. S.: MGM
Chuncan (Spring silkworms), d: Cheng Bugao, s: Xia Yan, Shanghai: Mingxing
Ecstasy, d: Gustav Machaty, Czech; Chinese titles: *Ai de xietiao* (harmony of love), *Yuyan* (Flames of desire)
42nd Street, d: Lloyd Bacon, s: Rian James, James Seymour, U. S.: Warner Brothers

Gold Diggers of 1933, d: Merryn LeRoy, s: Erwin Gelsey, James Seymour, U. S.: Warner
  Brothers
Golden Harvest, d: Ralph Murphy, s: Casey Robinson, U. S.: Paramount
Kuangliu (Wild torrents), d: Cheng Bugao, s: Xia Yan, Shanghai: Mingxing
Muxing zhiguang (Light of motherhood), d: Bu Wancang, s: Tian Han, Shanghai:
  Lianhua
My Weakness, d: David Butler, U. S.: Fox
Nüxing de nahan (The protest of women), d/s: Shen Xiling, Shanghai: Mingxing
One Sunday Afternoon, d: Stephen Roberts, s: Grover Jones, William S. McNutt, U. S.:
  Paramount
San'ge modeng nüxing (Three modern women), d: Bu Wancang, s: Tian Han, Shanghai:
  Lianhua
Sweepings, d: John Cromwell, s: Lester Cohen, U. S.: RKO Radio
Torch Singer, d: Alexander Hall, George Somnes, s: Lenore Coffee, Lynn Starling, U. S.:
  Paramount
Xiangcao meiren (A native beauty), d: Chen Kengran, s: Ma Wenyuan, Hong Shen,
  Shanghai: Mingxing
Xiao wanyi (Little toys), d/s: Sun Yu, Shanghai: Lianhua
Zaisheng (Resurrection), d: Chen Tiansuo, Shanghai: Da Changcheng

1934

Little Man, What Now? d: Frank Borzage, s: Wiliam McGuire, U.S.: Universal
Renjian xianzi (The worldly immortals), d: Dan Duyu, s: Jiang Hongjiao, Shanghai:
  Yihua
Shanghai ershisi xiaoshi (Twenty-four hours in Shanghai), d: Shen Xiling, s: Xia Yan,
  Shanghai: Mingxing
Shennü (Goddess), d/s: Wu Yonggang, Shanghai: Lianhua
Taoli jie (The plunder of peach and plum), d: Ying Yunwei, s: Yuan Muzhi, Shanghai:
  Diantong
Tiyu huanghou (Queen of sports), d/s: Sun Yu, Shanghai: Lianhua
Xiangchou (Homesick), d/s: Shen Xiling, Shanghai: Mingxing
Xin nüxing (New woman), d: Cai Chusheng, s: Sun Shiyi, Shanghai: Lianhua
Yuguang qu (Song of the fishermen), d/s: Cai Chusheng, Shanghai: Lianhua
Zaihui ba Shanghai (Farewell, Shanghai), d/s: Zheng Yunbo, Shanghai: Xinhua
Zimei hua (Twin sisters), d/s: Zheng Zhengqiu, Shanghai: Mingxing

1935

Chuanjia nü (Boatman's daughter), d/s: Shen Xiling, Shanghai: Mingxing
Dalu (Big road), d/s: Sun Yu, Shanghai: Lianhua
Dushi fengguang (City scenes), d/s: Yuan Muzhi, Shanghai: Diantong
Fengyun ernü (Children of troubled times), d: Xu Xingzhi, s: Tian Han, Shanghai:
  Diantong
Kaige (Song of triumph), d: Bu Wancang, s: Tian Han, Shanghai: Yihua
Taowang (Fugitive), d: Yue Feng, s: Yang Hanshen, Shanghai: Yihua
Top Hat, d: Mark Sandrich, s: Dwight Taylor, Allan Scott, U. S.: RKO Radio

Wuchou junzi (Unworried gentleman), d: Shen Fu, Zhuang Guojun, s: Shen Fu, Shanghai: Lianhua

Xiao tianshi (Little angel), d: Wu Yonggang, s: Jiang Xingde, Shanghai: Lianhua

Ziyou shen (Goddess of freedom), d: Situ Huimin, s: Xia Yan, Shanghai: Diantong

1936

Dao ziran qu (Back to nature), d/s: Sun Yu, Shanghai: Lianhua

Gucheng lienü (The heroine of the besieged city), d: Wang Cilong, Shanghai: Lianhua

Huashen guniang I–II (The disguised girl), d: Fang Peilin, s: Huang Jiamo, Shanghai: Yihua

Lang taosha (Desert island), d/s: Wu Yonggang, Shanghai: Lianhua

Polo Joe, d: William McGann, s: Peter Milne, Hugh Cummings, U.S.: Warner Brothers

Three Smart Girls, d: Henry Koster, s: Adele Comandini, U.S.: Universal

Xiao Lingzi (Little Lingzi), d: Cheng Bugao, s: Ouyang Yuqian, Shanghai: Mingxing

Yeban gesheng (Singing at midnight), d/s: Ma-Xu Weibang, Shanghai: Xinhua

1937

Chungui duanmeng (Young women's short dream), episode two of *Lianhua jiaoxiangqu* (Lianhua symphony), d: Fei Mu, Shanghai: Lianhua

Fengren kuangxiang qu (Madman's rhapsody), episode seven of *Lianhua jiaoxiangqu* (Lianhua symphony), d: Sun Yu, Shanghai: Lianhua

Guta qi'an (The strange case of the ancient tower), information unknown

Malu tianshi (Street angel), d/s: Yuan Muzhi, Shanghai: Mingxing

Qingnian jinxing qu (March of the youth), d: Shi Dongshan, s: Tian Han, Xia Yan, Shanghai: Xinhua

Sanren xing (Three traveling together), episode four of *Lianhua jiaoxiangqu* (Lianhua symphony), d: Shen Fu, Shanghai: Lianhua

Shizi jietou (Crossroads), d/s: Shen Xiling, Shanghai: Lianhua

Tanxing nüer (A flexible girl), d: Chen Kengran, s: Pan Jienong, Shanghai: Yihua

Yasui qian (A new year's coin), d: Zhang Shichuan, s: Xia Yan, Shanghai: Mingxing

1939

Bailan zhige (Song of the white orchid), d: Watanabe Kunio, Xinjing/Tokyo: Man'ei/Toho

Huashen guniang III–IV (The disguised girl), d: Fang Peilin, s: Huang Jiamo, Shanghai: Yihua

1940

Shamo zhishi (Vow in the desert), d: Watanabe Kunio, Tokyo: Toho

Xixiang ji (The romance of the western chamber), d: Zhang Shichuan, s: Fan Yanqiao, Shanghai: Guohua

Zhina zhiye (Night in China), d: Fushimizu Osamu, s: Oguni Hideo, Tokyo: Toho

1941

The Shanghai Gesture, d: Josef von Sternberg, s: von Sternberg, Karl Vollmoeller, Geza Herczeg, Jules Furthman, U.S.: United Artists

1943

Mannü qingge (Love song of the barbarian girl, or Bell of Sayon), d: Shimizu Hiroshi, Xinjing/Tokyo: Man'ei/Shochiku

Wanshi liufang (Eternity), d: Bu Wancang, Ma-Xu Weibang, Yang Xiaozhong, Zhu Shilin, s: Zhu Shilin, Shanghai: Zhonglian

1948

Xiaocheng zhichun (Spring in a small town), d. Fei Mu, s: Li Tianji, Shanghai: Wenhua

1956

Huashen gunian (A disguised girl), d: Chen Huanwen, Hong Kong: Yihua

1959

Lin Zexu (Lin Zexu), d: Zheng Junli, Cen Fan, s: Lü Dang, Ye Yuan, Shanghai: Haiyan

Nie Er (Nie Er), d: Zheng Junli, s: Yu Ling, Meng Bo, Shanghai: Haiyan

1961

Kumu fengchun (Spring comes to the withered tree), d: Zheng Junli, s: Wang Lian, Zheng Junli, Shanghai: Haiyan

1964

Wutai jiemei (Stage sisters), d: Xie Jin, s: Lin Gu, Xu Jin, Xie Jin, Shanghai: Tianma

1981

Zhiyin (Intimate friends), d: Xie Tieli, Chen Huaiai, Ba Hong, s: Hua Ershi, Beijing: Beijing

1984

Huang tudi (Yellow earth), d: Chen Kaige, s: Zhang Ziliang, Nanning: Guangxi

1986

Daoma dan (Peking opera blue), d/s: Tsui Hark, Hong Kong: Cinema City

Kongbu fenzi (Terrorizer), d: Edward Yang, s: Xiao Ye, Edward Yang, Taipei: Central Motion Picture

1987

Yanzhi kou (Rouge), d: Stanley Kwan, s: Li Bihua, Qiu-Dai Anping, Hong Kong: Golden Harvest

1988

Hong gaoliang (Red sorghum), d: Zhang Yimou, s: Chen Jianyu, Zhu Wei, Xi'an: Xi'an

1989

Niupeng (China, my sorrow), d: Dai Sijie, s: Dai Sijie, Shan Yuanzhu, France: Titane Production / Flach Film

Ren gui qing (Woman demon human), d/s: Huang Shuqin, Shanghai: Shanghai

1991

Dahong denglong gaogao gua (Raise the red lantern), d: Zhang Yimou, s: Ni Zhen, Hong Kong: Era

Ruan Lingyu (Center stage), d/s: Stanley Kwan, Hong Kong: Golden Harvest

1992

Xinxiang (True-hearted), d: Sun Zhou, s: Miao Yue, Sun Zhou, Guangzhou: Pearl River

1993

Anlian taohuayuan (The peach blossom land), d/s: Stan Lai, Taipei: Central Motion Picture

Bawang bieji (Farewell my concubine), d: Chen Kaige, s: Li Bihua, Hong Kong: Tomson

1994

Hongfen (Blush), d: Li Shaohong, s: Ni Zhen, Beijing: Shalong

Huahun (Soul of the painter), d/s: Huang Shuqin, Shanghai: Shanghai

Huozhe (To live), d: Zhang Yimou, s: Lu Wei, Yu Hua, Hong Kong: Era

1995

Fengyue (Temptress moon), d: Chen Kaige, s: Shu Kei, Hong Kong: Tomson

Yao a yao, yao dao waipo qiao (Shanghai triad), d: Zhang Yimou, s: Bi Feiyu, Hong Kong: Era / Shanghai: Shanghai

UNCERTAIN DATES

Harbin genü (Songstress of Harbin), d: Daibutsu Jiro

Mofan qingnian (A model youth), banned

The Oriental Secret, Germany: UFA

Notes

CHAPTER ONE

Condensed versions of this chapter were presented to the East Asian Colloquium of Indiana University in October 1996 and to the Film Studies Program at University of California–Berkeley in November 1997. My thanks to Anton Kaes, Kaja Silverman, and George Wilson for their invitations; to the audiences for their comments; and to Sue Touhy for reading an earlier draft of this introduction.

1. For a brief discussion of the problematic term "Fifth Generation," see Yingjin Zhang, "From 'Minority Film' to 'Minority Discourse': Questions of Nationhood and Ethnicity in Chinese Film Studies," *Cinema Journal* 36, no. 3 (Spring 1997): 88.

2. In chronological order, these five books are Wimal Dissanayake, ed., *Melodrama and Asian Cinema* (New York: Cambridge University Press, 1993); George Semsel, Chen Xihe, and Xia Hong, eds., *Film in Contemporary China* (New York: Praeger, 1993); Nick Browne, Paul G. Pickowicz, Vivian Sobchack, and Esther Yau, eds., *New Chinese Cinemas: Forms, Identities, Politics* (New York: Cambridge University Press, 1994); Linda Erhlich and David Desser, eds., *Cinematic Landscapes: Observations on the Visual Arts and Cinema of China and Japan* (Austin: University of Texas Press, 1994); Rey Chow, *Primitive Passions: Visuality, Sexuality, Ethnography, and Contemporary Chinese Cinema* (New York: Columbia University Press, 1995). For a review of these books, see Yingjin Zhang, "Review Essay: Screening China—Recent Studies of Chinese Cinema in English," *Bulletin of Concerned Asian Scholars* 29, no. 3 (June-Sept. 1997): 59–66. Works on contemporary Chinese cinema have appeared in greater numbers than ever before, in film magazines (e.g., *Cineaction, Cineaste, Cinemaya, Film Comment, Film Note, Post Script, Sight and Sound, Variety,* and the *Village Voice*) as well as in academic journals (e.g., *Asian Cinema, Camera Obscura, Cinema Journal, Cultural Studies, Discourse, East-West Film Journal, Film Quarterly, Framework, Journal of Film and Video, Jump Cut, Modern Chinese Literature, Public Culture, Quarterly Review of Film and Video, Screen, The Velvet Light Trap,* and *Wide Angle*). For bibliographic sources, see H. C. Li, "Chinese Electric Shadows: A Selected Bibliography of Materials in English," *Modern Chinese Literature* 7, no. 2 (Fall 1993): 117–53; "More Chinese Electric Shadows: A Supplementary List," ibid., 8 (1994): 237–50; and "Chinese Electric Shadows III: And the Ship Sails On," ibid., 10, nos. 1–2 (1998): 207–68.

3. Aside from a brief discussion of early Chinese cinema in Paul Clark's *Chinese Cinema: Culture and Politics Since 1949* (New York: Cambridge University Press, 1987) and two essays on pre-1949 films in a most recent collection edited by Sheldon Lu, *Transna-*

tional Chinese Cinemas: Identity, Nationhood, Gender (Honolulu: University of Hawaii, 1997), a few recent studies are scattered in various journals. See, for instance, Chris Berry's "The Sublimative Text: Sex and Revolution in *Big Road*," *East-West Film Journal* 2, no. 2 (1988): 66–86, and "Poisonous Weeds or National Treasures: Chinese Left Films in the 30s," *Jump Cut* 34 (Mar. 1989): 87–94; Kristine Harris, "*The New Woman*: Image, Subject, and Dissent in 1930s Shanghai Film Culture," *Republican China* 20, no. 2 (Apr. 1995): 55–79; Ma Ning, "The Textual and Critical Difference of Being Radical: Reconstructing Chinese Leftist Films in the 1930s," *Wide Angle* 11, no. 2 (1989): 22–31; Paul G. Pickowicz, "The Theme of Spiritual Pollution in Chinese Films of the 1930s," *Modern China* 17, no. 1 (Jan. 1991): 38–75, and "Sinifying and Popularizing Foreign Culture: From Maxim Gorky's *The Lower Depths* to Huang Zuolin's *Ye dian*," *Modern Chinese Literature* 7, no. 2 (Fall 1993): 7–31; Zhiwei Xiao, "Wu Yonggang and the Ambivalence in the Chinese Experience of Modernity: A Study of His Three Films of the Mid-1930s," *Asian Cinema* 9, no. 2 (Spring 1998): 3–15; Yingjin Zhang, "Engendering Chinese Filmic Discourse of the 1930s: Configurations of Modern Women in Shanghai in Three Silent Films," *Positions* 2, no. 3 (Winter 1994): 603–28; Dafeng Zhong, Zhen Zhang, and Yingjin Zhang, "From *Wenmingxi* (Civilized Play) to *Yingxi* (Shadowplay): The Foundation of Shanghai Film Industry in the 1920s," *Asian Cinema* 9, no. 1 (Summer 1997): 46–64. One earlier book, Jay Leyda's *Dianying: An Account of Films and the Film Audience in China* (Cambridge, Mass.: MIT Press, 1972), devotes substantial space to the early period. Yet, as Leo Ou-fan Lee points out, "The book unfortunately is marred by errors due to Leyda's unfamiliarity with the Chinese language"; see Lee, "The Tradition of Modern Chinese Cinema: Some Preliminary Explorations and Hypotheses," in Chris Berry, ed., *Perspectives on Chinese Cinema* (London: BFI Publishing, 1991), p. 18.

4. See, for instance, Frederic Wakeman, Jr., *Policing Shanghai* (Berkeley: University of California Press, 1995), and "Licensing Leisure: The Chinese Nationalist Attempt to Regulate Shanghai, 1927–49," *Journal of Asian Studies* 54, no. 1 (Feb. 1995): 19–42; Frederic Wakeman, Jr., and Yeh Wen-hsin, eds., *Shanghai Sojourners* (Berkeley: University of California–Berkeley, Institute of East Asian Studies, 1992). Other recent works on Shanghai culture include Robert A. Bickers, *Changing Shanghai's "Mind": Publicity, Reform and the British in Shanghai, 1927–1931* (London: China Society, 1992); Poshek Fu, *Passivity, Resistance, and Collaboration: Intellectual Choices in Occupied Shanghai, 1937–1945* (Stanford: Stanford University Press, 1993); Harriet Sergeant, *Shanghai: Collision Point of Cultures, 1918–1939* (New York: Crown Publishers, 1990); Randolph Trumbull, "The Shanghai Modernists," Ph.D. diss. (Stanford University, 1989); Wang-chi Wong, *Politics and Literature in Shanghai: The Chinese League of Left-Wing Writers, 1930–36* (Manchester, Eng.: Manchester University Press, 1991); Yingjin Zhang, *The City in Modern Chinese Literature and Film: Configurations of Space, Time, and Gender* (Stanford: Stanford University Press, 1996). Individual essays and Chinese publications are too numerous to be adequately represented here; see Bibliography for relevant items.

5. These film plot sheets, written in both English and literary Chinese, were usually distributed free of charge by first-run theaters in Shanghai, such as the Grand (Daguangming), Cathay (Guotai), Nanking (Nanjing), and Metropole (Da Shanghai). Because they could be read as short stories or used as supplementary English readings, these programs soon became collectors' items, especially among college students. One such collector, who had gathered about a thousand programs in eight years, deplored that movie

theaters were forced to end free distribution by the early 1940s due to the increased price of paper. See *Shanghai shenghuo* (Shanghai guide) 1941, no. 5 (May): 44. For further discussion of film plot sheets, see Leo Lee's essay (Chapter 4) in this volume.

6. Michel Foucault used "the archaeology of knowledge" as the title for one of his early books (*L'Archéologies du savoir*), originally published in France in 1969; see the English version, *The Archaeology of Knowledge and the Discourse on Language*, trans. A. M. Sheridan Smith (New York: Pantheon Books, 1972), esp. pp. 126–40. For sample discussions of Foucault's notions of archeology, knowledge, and power, see Hubert L. Dreyfus and Paul Rabinow, *Michel Foucault: Beyond Structuralism and Hermeneutics*, 2d ed. (Chicago: University of Chicago Press, 1983); David Couzens Hoy, ed., *Foucault: A Critical Reader* (New York: Basil Blackwell, 1986).

7. Foucault, *The Archaeology of Knowledge*, p. 130. He continues to write, "The never completed, never wholly achieved uncovering of the archive forms the general horizon to which the description of discursive formations, the analysis of positivities, the mapping of the enunciative field belong"; these types of research constitute what he terms "archaeology" (p. 131).

8. This centennial occasion saw the publication of several long-awaited, substantial volumes on Chinese cinema in mainland China: Dai Xiaolan, ed., *Zhongguo wusheng dianying* (Chinese silent films) (Beijing: Zhongguo dianying chubanshe, 1996); Li Suyuan and Hu Jubin, *Zhongguo wusheng dianying shi* (A history of Chinese silent film) (Beijing: Zhongguo dianying chubanshe, 1996); Zhang Junxiang and Cheng Jihua, eds., *Zhongguo dianying dacidian* (China cinema encyclopedia) (Shanghai: Shanghai cishu chubanshe, 1995); and the following compilations by the China Film Archive or other agencies: *Zhongguo dianying dadian* (Encyclopedia of Chinese films), 4 vols. (Beijing: Zhongguo dianying chubanshe, 1996–98); *Zhongguo dianying haibao yishu jingcui* (Selections of poster art in Chinese film) (Guangzhou: Guangzhou chubanshe, 1996); *Zhongguo dianying tuzhi* (Illustrated annals of Chinese film) (Guangxi: Zhuhai chubanshe, 1995); *Zhongguo wusheng dianying juben* (Screenplays of Chinese silent films), 3 vols. (Beijing: Zhongguo dianying chubanshe, 1997); *Zhonghua yingxing* (Chinese film stars) (Nanjing: Xinhua chubanshe, 1997).

9. See Cheng Bugao, *Yingtan yijiu* (Reminiscences of the film circles) (Beijing: Zhongguo dianying chubanshe, 1983), pp. 35–120.

10. See *Zhibian waishi tekan* (a special issue on *Migration to the Borders*) (Shanghai: Da Zhonghua Baihe, 1926), pp. 1–2.

11. See Chen Wei, ed., *Ke Ling dianying wencun* (Ke Ling's film essays) (Beijing: Zhongguo dianying chubanshe, 1992), p. 297. For the historical background, see Tang Chunfa, *Kai yidai xianhe—Zhongguo dianying zhifu Zheng Zhengqiu* (Opening a new road—Zheng Zhengqiu, the father of Chinese cinema) (Beijing: Guoji wenhua chuban gongsi, 1992), pp. 338–45.

12. For a discussion of commercial films in the late 1920s, see Hong Shi, "Diyici langchao: mopian qi Zhongguo shangye dianying xianxiang shuping" (The first wave: a discussion of commercial films in the silent era of Chinese cinema), *Dangdai dianying* 1995, no. 2: 5–12; Li Suyuan and Hu Jubin, *Zhongguo wusheng dianying*, pp. 209–44.

13. In addition to Xia Yan (or Huang Zibu), the active participants—many of them underground Communists—in leftist film criticism at the time include Chen Liting (b. 1910), Hong Shen, Ke Ling (b. 1909), Ling He (or Shi Linghe, b. 1906), Lu Si (b. 1912),

Qian Xingcun (A Ying, or Zhang Fengwu, 1900–1977), Tang Na (1914–88), Wang Chenwu (or Chen Wu, 1911–37), Yu Ling (or You Jing, b. 1907), Zheng Boqi (or Xi Naifang, 1895–1979), Zheng Junli, and others. See Lu Si, *Yingping yijiu* (Film criticism in recollection) (Beijing: Zhongguo dianying chubanshe, 1962); Chen Bo, ed., *Zhongguo zuoyi dianying yundong* (The leftist film movement in China) (Beijing: Zhongguo dianying chubanshe, 1993), esp. pp. 60–225.

14. These people include writers Yao Sufeng (1905–74) and Ye Lingfeng (1904–1975), film directors Fei Mu (1906–51) and Ying Yunwei (1904–1967), and many others. See Shu Yan, "Dianying de 'lunhui'—jinian zuoyi dianying yundong 60 zhounian" (The cycles of film—in commemoration of the sixtieth anniversary of the leftist film movement), *Xin wenxue shiliao* 1994, no. 1: 72–93. Shu's article is a significant revisionist account of leftist film criticism in the early 1930s. A decade earlier, Xia Yan also acknowledged the guiding principle of "leftist doctrinairism" (*zuoqing jiaotiao zhuyi*) in the leftist film movement in the 1930s; see his "Zai 'ershi-sishi niandai Zhongguo dianying huigu' kaimu shi shangde jianghua" (Speech at the opening ceremony of "Retrospective of Chinese cinema of the 1920s–1940s"), *Xin wenxue shiliao* 1984, no. 1: 21–29.

15. Huang Jiamo wrote all four episodes of *The Disguised Girl*, which were directed by Fang Peilin (?–1949) and produced by Yihua Film Company in Shanghai. The first episode was immensely popular and made the female lead Yuan Meiyun (b. 1917) a movie star; it also reportedly saved Yihua from bankruptcy (with U.S. $600,000 in debt) and miraculously "cured" the owner of Xinguang Theater of his illness caused by high blood pressure. See Gongsun Lu, *Zhongguo dianying shihua* (A history of Chinese cinema) (Hong Kong: Nantian shuye gongsi, 1977), 2: 86–88. The 1956 remake of *The Disguised Girl*, directed by Chen Huanwen and featuring Lin Cui (1936–95), was released by Hong Kong's Yihua; a production still can be found in Hsieh Shu-fen, "A Nostalgic Look at Classic Chinese Films," *Sinorama* (Guanghua) 18, no. 5 (May 1993): 44.

16. For discussions of the debate between the leftists and the promoters of soft film, see Chen Bo, *Zhongguo zuoyi dianying*, pp. 142–74; Cheng Jihua, Li Shaobai, and Xing Zuwen, *Zhongguo dianying fazhan shi* (A history of the development of Chinese cinema) (Beijing: Zhongguo dianying chubanshe, 1963; 1981), 1: 494–501; Lu Si, *Yingping yijiu*, pp. 16–26; Shu Yan, "Dianying de 'lunhui,' " pp. 84–88; Luo Yijun, ed., *Zhongguo dianying lilun wenxuan 1920–1989* (Chinese film theory: an anthology) (Beijing: Wenhua yishu chubanshe, 1992), 1: 256–84; Yi Ming, ed., *Sanshi niandai Zhongguo dianying pinglun wenxuan* (Selections of Chinese film criticism in the 1930s) (Beijing: Zhongguo dianying chubanshe, 1993), pp. 744–866. Film books published in Hong Kong and Taiwan since the 1950s generally ignore the debate and carry favorable accounts of people such as Liu Na'ou and Fang Peilin. See, for instance, Du Yunzhi, *Zhongguo dianying shi* (A history of Chinese cinema) (Taibei: Taiwan shangwu yinshuguan, 1972), 1: 179–82.

17. See Gan Yazi (Atsu Kann), Cheng Shuren, and Chen Dingxiu (D. S. Chen), eds., *1927 Zhonghua yingye nianjian* (1927 China cinema yearbook) (Shanghai: Zhonghua yingye nianjian she, 1927), chap. 2. Jiang Gubai's article appeared in *Lingxing zazhi erzhounian zhuanji* (The second anniversary issue of the *Stars Magazine*) (Hong Kong: Lingxing, 1933), pp. 99–124. Other short articles on Chinese film history published in the 1920s–30s are collected in Dai Xiaolan, *Zhongguo wusheng dianying*, pp. 1311–54, 1381–84.

18. Gu Jianchen, "Zhongguo dianying fada shi" (A history of the development of Chinese cinema), first published in *Zhongguo dianying nianjian* (Yearbook of Chinese

cinema) in 1934, is reprinted in Dai Xiaolan, *Zhongguo wusheng dianying*, pp. 1349–54. A drama expert and author of *Jutuan zuzhi ji wutai guanli* (Drama organization and stage management) (Changsha: Shangwu, 1940), Gu Jianchen also made references to film in his *Minzhong xiju gailun* (Introduction to popular drama) (n.p./n.d.). Zheng Junli's "Xiandai Zhongguo dianying shilüe" (A concise history of modern Chinese film) was originally published in *Jindai Zhongguo yishu fazhan shi* (A history of the development of art in modern China) (Shanghai: Liangyou, 1936), rediscovered by Yu Ji and Yang Kunxu in the 1980s, first reissued in nine installments in *Dianying chuangzuo* during 1989, and then reprinted in Dai Xiaolan, *Zhongguo wusheng dianying*, pp. 1385–1432. The circumstances surrounding the "loss" of Zheng's work are highly suspicious. Given the fact that he was treated favorably by the Communist regime after 1949 and continued to direct important films such as *Lin Zexu* (Lin Zexu, 1959), *Nie Er* (Nie Er, 1959), and *Kumu fengchun* (Spring comes to the withered tree, 1961), his earlier contribution to Chinese film historiography should have been acknowledged somewhere, even if it was presumed lost after the war. For whatever reasons, *Dianying chuangzuo*'s editorial preface still claims Cheng Jihua's 1961 history to be "the first specialized book on Chinese cinema" (see *Dianying chuangzuo* 1989, no. 2: 70).

19. Cheng et al., *Zhongguo dianying*, 1: xi.

20. Ibid., 2: 271–72.

21. Numerous recent film histories are adaptations of Cheng's work in one way or another; for example, see Xu Daoming and Sha Sipeng, *Zhongguo dianying jianshi* (A brief history of Chinese cinema) (Beijing: Zhongguo qingnian chubanshe, 1990). Cheng Jihua told me in his Beijing residence in October 1995 that his history has been translated, in part or in full, into English, French, and German, but none of the translations has appeared so far, presumably due to a lack of funding. For a French book on pre-1949 Chinese film, see Régis Bergeron, *Le Cinema chinois, 1905–1949* (Lausanne: Alfred Eibel, 1977). In addition, information regarding early Chinese cinema can be found in those illustrated volumes designed for or issued after major Chinese film retrospectives in Europe in the early 1980s: Tony Rayns and Scott Meek, eds., *Electric Shadows: 45 Years of Chinese Cinema*, Dossier No. 3 (London: British Film Institute, 1980); *Ombre elettriche: Saggi e ricerche sul cinema cinese* (Milan: Regione Piemonte/Electa, 1982); *Ombres électriques: Panorama du cinéma chinois 1925–1982* (Paris: Centre de Documentation sur le Cinéma Chinois, 1982); Marie-Claire Quiquemelle and Jean-Loup Passek, eds., *Le Cinéma chinois* (Paris: Centre Georges Pompidou, 1985).

22. Du Yunzhi, *Zhonghua minguo dianying shi* (A history of cinema in the Republic of China) (Taibei: Xingzhengyuan wenhua jianshe weiyuanhui, 1988), 2 vols. This book is a revised and enlarged edition of his earlier three-volume *Zhongguo dianying shi* cited in note 16 above. Du also published *Zhongguo de dianying* (Film in China) (Taibei: Huangguan, 1978) and other film books.

23. Du Yunzhi, *Zhongguo dianying shi*, 3: 187. Instead, he included reports—some obviously exaggerated—of the Communist persecution of the veteran filmmakers during the 1950s–1970s (3: 187–210).

24. Zhong Lei, *Wushinian laide Zhongguo dianying* (Chinese cinema in the past fifty years) (Taibei: Zhengzhong shuju, 1965).

25. Du Yunzhi, *Zhonghua minguo*, 1: 173–262. This represents a discrepancy from Du's earlier book, where Cai and Shi are among the leftists, while Cheng and Shen are

among the emerging directors (see Du, *Zhongguo dianying shi*, 1: 160–88). Other leftist directors mentioned in passing in both books are Ying Yunwei, Situ Huimin (1910–87), and Yuan Muzhi (1909–78).

26. Cheng et al., *Zhongguo dianying*, 1: 342–45, 459–61, 468–70.

27. Wang Yunman's book is excluded from discussion here because it is a brief overview of Chinese film history (a little over 140 pages, with an emphasis on the 1950s–60s) and does not specifically deal with film art; see Wang Yunman, *Zhongguo dianying yishu shilüe* (An outline history of Chinese film art) (Beijing: Zhongguo guoji guangbo chubanshe, 1989).

28. Zhou Xiaoming, *Zhongguo xiandai dianying wenxue shi* (A history of film literature in modern China) (Beijing: Gaodeng jiaoyu chubanshe, 1985), 2 vols.

29. Feng Min, Shao Zhou, and Jin Fenglan, *Zhongguo dianying yishu shigang* (An outline history of Chinese film art) (Tianjin: Nankai daxue chubanshe, 1992), pp. 31, 85, 127–28.

30. Zhong Dafeng and Shu Xiaoming, *Zhongguo dianying shi* (History of Chinese cinema) (Beijing: Zhongguo guangbo dianshi chubanshe, 1995), pp. 1–83. Zhong wrote the introduction and the first three chapters that cover up to 1949.

31. See Li and Hu, *Zhongguo wusheng dianying shi*, pp. 69–70, 118–19, 216, 218.

32. Li Shaobai, a senior film historian who participated in Cheng Jihua's project in the 1960s, has been compiling a history of Chinese film art for some years, but the book has not been released as this volume is in press.

33. Yang Cun, *Zhongguo dianying sanshinian* (Thirty years of Chinese cinema) (Hong Kong: Shijie chubanshe, 1954), p. ii–iii. However, Yang gathered materials and compiled a book on Chinese film stars, *Zhongguo dianying yanyuan cangsang lu* (The vicissitudes of Chinese movie actors and actresses) (Hong Kong: Shijie chubanshe, 1954–55), 2 vols. See also Yang Cun, *Dianying yu dianying yishu* (Film and film art) (Hong Kong: Chuangken, 1953).

34. Gongsun Lu, *Zhongguo dianying*, 1: i–vii.

35. One extreme example is a work by Sima Fen (Wan Bin), *Zhongguo dianying wushinian* (Fifty years of Chinese film) (Taibei: Huangding wenhua chubanshe, 1983). It is not a film history per se, but a collection of miscellaneous journalistic articles the author wrote over the years.

36. See *Yong yanjing kan de Zhongguo dianying shi* (A history of Chinese cinema seen through the eyes) (Taibei: Longjiang, 1979), p. 27. Du Yunzhi, Wei Qiren, and Wu Cheng served on the advisory board on this pictorial history. For another contemporary, perhaps more famous, actress, "Miss S S" Wang Hanlun, see Michael Chang's essay (Chap. 6) in this volume.

37. Wang Zilong, *Zhongguo yingju shi* (A history of Chinese film theater) (Taibei: Jianguo chubanshe, 1960).

38. Zhong has written numerous Chinese articles on the subject. For an English exposition, see Dafeng Zhong et al., "From *Wenmingxi* (Civilized Play) to *Yingxi* (Shadow-play)."

39. See He Ma, *Shanghai jiuhua* (Old stories from Shanghai) (Shanghai: Shanghai wenhua chubanshe, 1956), pp. 49–50. According to Gu Jianchen, Shanghai's Gong wutai (Shared stage) also made a *lianhuan xi* named *Lianhua gongzhu* (Princess lotus flower)

in 1925, which later led to the formation of Da Zhongguo (Great China) Film Company under Gu Wuwei (b. 1892); see Dai Xiaolan, ed., *Zhongguo wusheng dianying*, pp. 1365–66.

40. Here are a few examples: in mainland China, Xie Jin's (b. 1923) *Wutai jiemei* (Stage sisters, 1964), Huang Shuqin's (b. 1940) *Ren gui qing* (Woman demon human, 1989), Sun Zhou's (b. 1954) *Xinxiang* (True-hearted, 1992); in Hong Kong, Tsui Hark's (Xu Ke, b. 1952) *Daoma dan* (Peking opera blue, 1986); in Taiwan, Stan Lai's (Lai Chuansheng) *Anlian taohuayuan* (The peach blossom land, 1993).

41. For Huang Jichi's original formulation of *xiren dianying* and its two companion terms, *wenren dianying* (film produced by literature people) and *yingren dianying* (film produced by film people), see the report on a 1983 roundtable discussion in *Tansuo de niandai* (Early Chinese cinema: the era of exploration), a film program for the Hong Kong Arts Festival 1984, jointly published by Hong Kong Arts Center and Hong Kong Chinese Film Association, without pagination. Later, Zhang Chengshan expands on these two terms and sketches the development of three distinct types of films in China: (1) *xiren dianying* of the First Generation, which dominated in the 1920s and lasted till the early 1930s; (2) *wenren dianying* of the Second, the Third, and the Fourth Generations, which emerged in the early 1930s, flourished in the late 1940s, and matured in the 1950s and 1960s; and (3) *yingren dianying* of the Fifth Generation, which started to attract attention in the mid-1980s. See his *Zhongguo dianying wenhua toushi* (Cultural perspectives on Chinese film) (Shanghai: Xuelin chubanshe, 1989). For a classification of five generations of film directors in China, see Huang Shixian, "Zhongguo dianying daoyan 'xingzuo' jiqi yishu puxi" (The "galaxy" of Chinese film directors and their artistic genealogy), *Dangdai dianying* 1992, no. 6: 77–85.

42. Bao Tianxiao contributed numerous screenplays directly or indirectly in the 1920s, including *Xiao pengyou* (Little friend, 1925), based on his own work, and *Konggu lan* (Orchid in a deep valley, 1925), adapted from a Japanese translation of an English story and reprinted in *Dangdai dianying* 1995, no. 2: 114–22, with a preface by Xing Zuwen (p. 113). An author of more than one hundred novels and stories, Bao edited many magazines, among them *Funü shibao* (Women's times, 1911–17), *Xiaoshuo daguan* (The grand magazine, 1915–21), *Xiaoshuo huabao* (Fiction pictorial, 1917–20), and *Xingqi* (Weeks, 1922–23). Zhou Shoujuan wrote the screenplay for *Huanjin ji* (Returning of gold, 1926) and edited or co-edited some of the most popular magazines in the Republican era, among them *Libailiu* (Saturday, 1914–16, 1921–23), *Banyue* (The half-moon journal, 1921–25), *Ziluolan* (Violet, 1925–30, 1943–45), *Liangyou* (The young companion, 1926–45), and *Leguan* (Optimism, 1943–45, 1947); he also edited two newspaper supplements, "Ziyou tan" (Freedom talks) and "Chunqiu" (Spring and autumn) for *Shen bao* in the 1910s–1920s. See Rui Heshi, Fan Boqun, Zheng Xuetao, Xu Sinian, and Yuan Cangzhou, eds., *Yuanyang hudie pai wenxue ziliao* (Research materials on mandarin ducks and butterflies literature) (Fuzhou: Fujian renmin chubanshe, 1984), 2: 627–36.

43. *Diansheng* 6, no. 16 (Apr. 23, 1937): 725.

44. See the entry on cinemas in *Shanghai zhinan*, 19th ed. (revised), with its own original English title, *Guide to Shanghai: a Chinese Directory of the Port* (Shanghai: Shangwu yinshuguan, 1919), 5: 18. See also Wang Dingjiu, ed., *Shanghai menjing* (Guide to Shanghai), 4th ed. (Shanghai: Zhongyang shuju, 1935), pp. 14–20 (separate pagination under "Guide to seeing" [Kan de menjing]).

45. For a list of movie theaters in major Chinese cities other than Shanghai, see *1927 Zhonghua yingye nianjian*, chap. 33. The editor Cheng Shuren notes with apprehension in his foreword to this listing that there were 156 theaters in the entire country at the time but 90 percent of them were controlled by foreign businessmen. For instance, after successfully building Hongkew (Hongkou), Shanghai's first exclusive movie theater with 250 seats, in 1908, the Spanish showman Antonio Ramos invested in a chain of other theaters: Victoria (Weiduoliya, 750 seats), Olympic (Xialingpeike), Carter (Kate), Empire (Enpaiya), and China (Wanguo). See Zhang Zhongli, ed., *Jindai Shanghai chengshi yanjiu* (Urban studies of modern Shanghai) (Shanghai: Shanghai renmin chubanshe, 1990), pp. 1106–107.

46. See "Kan dianying de 'menkan'" ("Guide" to watching films), *Qingqing dianying* 4, no. 3 (Apr. 18, 1939): 8. Similar but more informed instructions are found in Wang Dingjiu, *Shanghai menjing*, pp. 20–24. For the research article, see Hu Daojing, "Shanghai dianyingyuan de fazhan" (The development of cinemas in Shanghai), in Shanghaitong she (Society of Shanghai experts), ed., *Shanghai yanjiu ziliao xuji* (Sequel to research materials on Shanghai) (Shanghai: Zhonghua shuju, 1939), pp. 532–63.

47. The young woman was arrested once for possessing liquor after midnight and, passing as Carmen, later became well-known in Shanghai and Qingdao for her Spanish-style dances. See Chen Dingshan, *Chunshen jiuwen* (Old tales of Shanghai) (Taibei: Chenguang yuekan she, 1964), 2: 106–9.

48. For an extensive discussion of the modern woman as urban secrecy, see Yingjin Zhang, *The City in Modern Chinese Literature*, pp. 207–23.

49. For instance, a *Diansheng* article defines the subtle relationships between a dancing hostess and her customers in terms of as many as fourteen variations of the slang *tuoche* (for a discussion of this term, see Andrew Field's essay [Chap. 5] in this volume); another article reported the suicide of a sixteen-year-old dancing hostess, Yao Aina. See *Diansheng* 6, no. 16 (Apr. 23, 1937): 744; 6, no. 22 (June 4, 1937): 986.

50. I am indebted to Sue Tuohy for suggesting identity as a unifying theme for this group of essays.

51. For investigations along these lines, see Poshek Fu, "Framing History: Popular Film Culture in Wartime Shanghai," and Paul Pickowicz, "Unpacking China's Wartime Baggage: The Early Postwar Films of Shi Dongshan, Cai Chusheng, and Zheng Junli," both papers delivered at the annual meeting of the Association for Asian Studies in Washington, D. C., Apr. 1995.

52. One of the few recent examples is Marie Cambon's "The Dream Palaces of Shanghai: American Films in China's Largest Metropolis Prior to 1949," *Asian Cinema* 7, no. 2 (Winter 1995): 34–45.

53. See *Xiaoshuo shijie* (The story world) 3, no. 5 (Aug. 1923)–4, no. 1 (Oct. 5, 1923). Some issues also include comments on Chinese films.

54. See *Beiyang huabao* no. 972 (Aug. 15, 1933)–no. 1586 (July 27, 1937). This weekly feature testifies to the sustained interest of the Chinese reading public in film news during the 1930s. Earlier, the pictorial devoted a special page to *The Secrets of the East*, an UFA production shown in Tianjin; see ibid., no. 406 (Dec. 5, 1929): 3.

55. *Dianying jiancha weiyuanhui jiancha dianying baogao* (Report on film censorship by the Film Censorship Committee, 1934) published these three catalogues: domestic films permitted for screening, June 1931–June 1933 (22 pages); domestic films banned

from screening, June 1931–Feb. 1934, specific violations cited (4 pages); and foreign films permitted for screening, June 1931–June 1933, with Chinese and English titles (259 pages). The striking imbalance in market shares held by domestic and foreign films in the early 1930s is self-evident in the report.

56. See *Shanghai shenghuo* 1941, no. 12 (Dec.): 70, 76–79.

57. See *Dianying zazhi* (Picture news) nos. 1–35 (Oct. 1947–Mar. 1949). To be sure, the magazine also reported news of Chinese productions, the most attractive of which were synopses done in the fashion of "serial-picture book" (*lianhuan dianying tuhua*).

58. As Zhong Dafeng speculates, since Soviet films were not widely available in China at the time, the Chinese "borrowed" the Soviet theory of montage on the basis of its own film tradition and its understanding of Hollywood film experience (see Zhong Dafeng and Shu, *Zhongguo dianying shi*, p. 48).

59. Lu Si mentioned several translations of Soviet film publications among the achievements of leftist film criticism in the 1930s (see his *Yingping yijiu*, pp. 4–5, 13–14).

60. For sample memoirs by directors and screen writers, see Cheng Bugao, *Yingtan yijiu*; Sun Yu, *Yinhai fanzhou—huiyi wode yisheng* (Sailing across the sea of the silver screen—my life in recollection) (Shanghai: Shanghai wenyi chubanshe, 1987); Ouyang Yuqian, *Dianying banlu chujia ji* (Entering the film world in my mid-career) (Beijing: Zhongguo dianying chubanshe, 1984); Tian Han, *Yingshi zhuihuai lu* (Recollections of film activities) (Beijing: Zhongguo dianying chubanshe, 1981); Wu Yonggang, *Wode tansuo he zhuiqiu* (My explorations and quests) (Beijing: Zhongguo dianying chubanshe, 1986); Xia Yan, *Lanxun jiumeng lu* (Too lazy to seek old dreams) (Beijing: Sanlian shudian, 1985); Zheng Junli, *Huawai yin* (Off-screen sound) (Beijing: Zhongguo dianying chubanshe, 1979). For memoirs by actors and actresses, see Hu Die, with Liu Huiqin, *Hu Die huiyi lu* (Hu Die's memoirs) (Beijing: Wenhua yishu chubanshe, 1988); Gong Jianong (Robert Kung), *Gong Jianong congying huiyi lu* (Gong Jianong's memoirs of his film activities) (Taibei: Wenxing shudian, 1967), vols. 1–3; Guan Wenqing (Moon Kwan), *Zhongguo yintan waishi* (Stories of Chinese film) (Hong Kong: Guangjiaojing chubanshe, 1976); Wang Hanlun, "Wo de congying jingguo" (My experience in the film industry), in *Gankai hua dangnian* (Sighing about those years) (Beijing: Zhongguo dianying chubanshe, 1962), pp. 50–59; Wang Renmei, with Xie Bo, *Wode chengming yu buxing: Wang Renmei huiyi lu* (My rise to fame and unhappiness: the reminiscences of Wang Renmei) (Shanghai: Shanghai wenyi chubanshe, 1985); Wu Yin, *Huishou yi dangnian* (Remembering the past) (Beijing: Zhongguo dianying chubanshe, 1993); Zhao Dan, *Diyu zhimen* (The gate of hell) (Shanghai: Shanghai wenyi chubanshe, 1980).

61. Among other chapter headings, *1927 Zhonghua yingye nianjian* includes Chinese and foreign studios, their officials and their productions, screenplay writers, writers of Chinese and English titles, translators of foreign films, film directors, cinematographers, art designers, make-up artists, actors and actresses, projectionists, movie theaters under Chinese and foreign management, film distribution companies, reports on Chinese films from foreign markets, film organizations, film schools, film publications, film censorship, local government and police regulations, legal representatives for producers, as well as dealers in film equipment.

62. Research on these topics has started. See, for example, Carlton Benson, "The Manipulation of *Tanci* in Radio Shanghai During the 1930s," *Republican China* 20, no. 2 (Apr. 1995): 117–46; Joan Judge, *Print and Politics: "Shibao" and the Culture of Reform in*

Late Qing China (Stanford: Stanford University Press, 1996); Christopher Reed, "Guten-berg in Shanghai: Mechanized Printing, Modern Publishing, and Their Effects on the City, 1876–1937," Ph.D. diss. (University of California–Berkeley, 1997). The following pa-pers related to visual culture were presented at the annual meeting of the Association for Asian Studies in Chicago in March 1997: Julia F. Andrew, "Judging a Book by Its Cover: Book Cover Design in Shanghai"; Ellen J. Laing, "Commodification of Art Through Ex-hibition and Advertisement"; Kuiyi Shen, "Comics, Illustrations, and the Cartoonist in Republican Shanghai"; Yingjin Zhang, "The Corporeality of Erotic Imagination: A Study of Shanghai Pictorials and Fan Magazines of the 1930s."

63. For a historical overview of cultural history in the West, see Peter Burke, "Reflec-tions on the Origins of Cultural History," in Joan H. Pittock and Andrew Wear, eds., *In-terpretation and Cultural History* (New York: St. Martin's Press, 1991), pp. 5–24.

64. Roger Chartier, *Cultural History: Between Practices and Representations* (Oxford: Polity Press, 1988), pp. 13–14.

65. Ibid., p. 6.

66. Jacques Le Goff, "Mentalities: a History of Ambiguities," in Jacques Le Goff and Pierre Nora, eds., *Constructing the Past: Essays in Historical Methodology* (Cambridge: Cambridge University Press, 1985), pp. 167–69. The book contains English translations of selected essays from the same editors' three-volume *Faire de l'histoire: nouveaux prob-lèmes* (Paris: Gallimard, 1974). Except for bibliographic data, I have followed the example of Roger Chartier, who believes that "the *histoire des mentalités* has proved difficult to ex-port" and has thereby decided to "leave the expression untranslated, recognizing the in-evitable specificity of each nation's way of considering historical questions" (*Cultural History*, p. 19).

67. Le Goff, "Mentalities," p. 169.

68. Ibid., pp. 173–75.

69. Siegfried Kracauer, *From Caligari to Hitler: A Psychological History of German Film* (Princeton: Princeton University Press, 1947), p. 6.

70. For more examples, see Anton Kaes, "German Cultural History and the Study of Film: Ten Theses and a Postscript," *New German Critique* 65 (Spring–Summer 1995): 47–58.

71. Colin Lucas, "Introduction," in Le Goff and Nora, *Constructing the Past*, p. 8.

72. For a discussion of this film sequence, see Yingjin Zhang's essay (Chap. 7) in this volume.

73. The connection between urban history and the *histoire des mentalités* in the Shanghai context has also attracted attention of Chinese historians. See, for example, Le Zheng, *Jindai Shanghairen shehui xintai, 1860–1910* (The social *mentalités* of Shanghai people in the early modern period) (Shanghai: Shanghai renmin chubanshe, 1991).

74. For a general picture of the contemporary cultural scenes in China, see Orville Schell, "China—the End of an Era," *The Nation*, July 17–24, 1995: 84–98; Jianying Zha, *China Pop: How Soap Operas, Tabloids, and Bestsellers Are Transforming a Culture* (New York: New Press, 1995). For critical discussions, see Andrew F. Jones, *Like a Knife* (Ithaca: East Asia Program, Cornell University, 1992); Sheldon Hsiao-peng Lu, "Postmodernity, Popular Culture, and the Intellectual: A Report on Post-Tiananmen China," *Boundary 2* 23, no. 2 (Summer 1996): 139–69.

75. This controversial statement was used by Shao Mujun (b. 1928), a leading film

theorist in contemporary China, as a title for his article, "Dianying shouxian shi yimen gongye, qici caishi yimen yishu" (Cinema is primarily an industry and only secondarily an art form), *Dianying yishu* 1996, no. 2: 4–5. It is "controversial" because it generated a debate in Chinese film circles. For a counter-example, see Yin Hong, "Shangpin baiwujiao yu dianying guannian bianxi" (Differentiating commodity fetishism and film concepts), ibid., pp. 6–10.

76. This title is all the more ironic because Su Yan's article was written in commemoration of the 60th anniversary of the leftist film movement; see his "Dianying de 'lunhui.'"

77. For a discussion of pressing issues in Chinese film studies, see Yingjin Zhang, "Chinese Cinema and Transnational Cultural Politics: Reflections on Film Festivals, Film Productions, and Film Studies," *Journal of Modern Literature in Chinese* 2, no. 1 (July 1998): 105–32.

CHAPTER TWO

I wish to thank Miriam Hansen for a careful reading of the first draft of the essay and her very helpful suggestions for the revision. Yingjin Zhang provided constructive comments and editorial assistance.

1. These terms were still relatively new to Chinese filmmakers as they had only been translated recently. According to Cheng Bugao's account, Zhang and Zheng's early filming experience was largely improvisational and collaborative. A detailed shooting script was an unknown concept until much later. Zheng's scripts, based on the models of Peking opera and modern urban drama (*wenmingxi*), would usually consist of rough outlines of main scenarios (*mubiao*), allowing much room for actors' improvisation. See Cheng Bugao, *Yingtan yijiu* (Reminiscences of the film circles) (Beijing: Zhongguo dianying chubanshe, 1983), pp. 108–10. See also Kou Tianwu, "The 'Firsts' in Chinese Film History," *Yingshi wenhua* 1989, no. 2: 267. Cheng and Kou give different dates for the "first" full-fledged film script. Cheng recalls Xia Yan's *Kuangliu* (Wild torrents, 1933) as the first instance of a real film script, whereas Kou attributes the "first" to Hong Shen's *Shen Tu shi* published in 1925. It should be noted, however, that a "film script" as such was also quite a recent development in American film production, and Zhang was made aware of this through his conversations with a film professor from Columbia University who visited Zhang's film company in the early twenties. See Wang Suping, comp., "Zhongguo dianying tuohuangzhede zuji—zaoqi dianying daoyan tanyilu" (Footprints of the pioneers of Chinese cinema—early film directors on their art), *Yingshi wenhua* 1989, no. 2: 308.

2. Gongsun Lu, *Zhongguo dianying shihua* (A historical account of Chinese cinema) (Hong Kong: Nantian shuye gongsi, n.d.), 1: 46–48.

3. See Cheng Jihua, Li Shaobai, and Xing Zuwen, *Zhongguo dianying fazhanshi* (A history of the development of Chinese cinema) (Beijing: Zhongguo dianying chubanshe, 1963), 1: 59. This work is to date the most comprehensive survey of Chinese cinema up until 1949, but with obvious ideological biases.

4. See, for instance, *Early Chinese Cinema: The Era of Exploration* (Programme for Hong Kong Arts Festival, 1984), no pagination.

5. "Chronotope" is a key concept of Bakhtin's historical poetics. Literally meaning

"time space," it refers to the "intrinsic connectedness of temporal and spatial relationships that are artistically expressed in literature." See M. M. Bakhtin, *The Dialogical Imagination: Four Essays*, ed. Michael Holquist, trans. Caryl Emerson and Michael Holquist (Austin: University of Texas Press, 1981), p. 84. Although Bakhtin's original essay primarily discusses the novel, the concept has been widely adopted in critical interpretations of other cultural texts and their relationships to dynamic cultural systems.

6. See Cheng Jihua et al., *Zhongguo dianying*, 1: 13–49; 1: 50–161.

7. Jay Leyda, *Dianying / Electric Shadows: An Account of Films and the Film Audience in China* (Cambridge, Mass.: MIT Press, 1972).

8. Paul Clark, *Chinese Cinema: Culture and Politics Since 1949* (New York: Cambridge University Press, 1987): pp. 4–19.

9. Chris Berry, ed., *Perspectives on Chinese Cinema* (London: British Film Institute, 1991).

10. Back cover of *To the Distant Observer* (Berkeley: University of California Press, 1979).

11. Ibid., p. 27.

12. Homi K. Bhabha, "Signs Taken for Wonders: Questions of Ambivalence and Authority Under a Tree Outside Delhi, May 1817," in Henry Louis Gates, Jr., ed., *"Race," Writing, and Difference* (Chicago: University of Chicago Press, 1986), pp. 163–84.

13. Ibid., p. 175.

14. The term is borrowed from Tom Gunning, "The Cinema of Attractions: Early Film, Its Spectator and the Avant-Garde," *Wide Angle* 8, nos. 3–4 (1986): 63–70. Gunning identifies "the cinema of attractions" primarily in films by early filmmakers such as Meliés, Lumière, Smith, and Porter, before the onset of narrative cinema around 1906–7. It is a cinema that addresses itself directly to spectators who are chiefly fascinated by the cinema's power to "show" something. Such an emphasis on visibility and audience involvement constitutes an "exhibitionist cinema." One significant marker of this cinema is the "recurring look at the camera by actors," which is radically different from the realistic illusion so central to later narrative cinema (p. 64). I will return to this point later in my discussion of the institutional transition the Mingxing Company was undergoing at the time when *Laborer's Love* was produced and released.

15. Han Chenliu, "Ersanshi niandai Zhongguo dianyingde dian he xian" (Points and threads of Chinese cinema in the twenties and thirties), in *Early Chinese Cinema*, no pagination.

16. Zhang Zhenhua, "'Shanghai dianyingde, dansheng jiqi meixue tezheng" (The birth of 'Shanghai cinema' and its aesthetic traits), *Dianying yishu* 1992, no. 3: 62.

17. Cheng Jihua et al., *Zhongguo dianying*, 1: 53–54.

18. Tom Gunning, "Film History and Film Analysis: The Individual Film in the Course of Time," *Wide Angle* 12, no. 3 (July 1990): 5.

19. Ibid., p. 6.

20. Ibid., pp. 13–14.

21. Cheng Jihua et al., *Zhongguo dianying*, 1: 8–9.

22. See Yong Li, "Woguo diyizuo yingyuan jin hezai?" (Where is China's first movie theater today?), *Shanghai dianying shiliao* (Historical materials on Shanghai cinema) (Shanghai dianyingju shizhi bangongshi, n.d.), 5: 99–100. The theater was also called

"Hongkou huodong yingxiyuan" (Hongkou moving shadowplay theater). Years later, Ramos rebuilt it into a concrete structure, expanding the space to hold 710 seats.

23. See, for instance, the section on entertainment in Liu Peiqian, ed., *Da Shanghai zhinan* (A guide for greater Shanghai) (Shanghai: Guoguang shudian, 1936), esp. pp. 118–33.

24. Cheng Bugao, *Yingtan yijiu*, pp. 84–87.

25. "Chaguan yu yinyue chalou" (Teahouse and music tearoom), in Tu Shiping, ed., *Shanghai chunqiu* (Vicissitudes of Shanghai) (Hong Kong: Zhongguo tushu jicheng gongsi, 1968). The book appears to be a reprint of *Shanghai daguan* (An overview of Shanghai) published in Shanghai in the 1940s.

26. This sketch of the atmosphere of the Shanghai "teahouse culture" is based on a reading of *Tuhua ribao* (The illustrated daily), July 1908–Feb. 1909.

27. For a rather comprehensive genealogy and stylistic analysis of shadowplay in China and its export to foreign countries, see Dong Jingxin, "Zhongguo yingxi kao" (An examination of Chinese shadowplay), *Juxue yuekan* 3, no. 11 (1934): 1–19.

28. For visual illustrations of the "leather shadowplay," see A Wei, ed., *Pi yingxi* (Shadowplay) (Beijing: Zhaohua meishu chubanshe, 1955). Zhang Yimou's recent film, *To Live* (1994), contains vivid scenes of the milieu and of shadowplay.

29. Dong Jingxin, "Zhongguo yingxi kao," pp. 5–8. Dong's article also included a list of some major titles of shadowplay programs, p. 18.

30. "Cong yingxi dao dianying" (From shadowplay to cinema), Wu Qiufang, ed., *Shanghai fengwu zhi* (Gazetteer of Shanghai lore) (Shanghai: Shanghai wenhua chubanshe, 1982), p. 256.

31. Zhong Dafeng, "Lun 'yingxi'" (On "shadowplay"), *Beijing dianying xueyuan xuebao* 1985, no. 2: 54–92, and "Zhongguo dianyingde lishi jiqi gengyuan: zailun 'yingxi'" (The history of Chinese cinema and its sources: again on "shadowplay"), *Dianying yishu* 1994, no. 1: 29–35; 1994, no. 2: 9–14.

32. For a concise history of *wenmingxi*, see Ouyang Yuqian's memoir "Tan wenmingxi," in *Zhongguo huaju yundong wushinian shiliaoji* (Collection of historical materials on fifty years of Chinese spoken drama movement) (Beijing: Zhongguo xiju chubanshe, 1958), 1: 48–108. It is noteworthy that many pioneers of modern spoken drama, like Ouyang Yuqian himself, had a background in Peking opera. While studying in Japan, they were inspired by the Japanese version of Western drama, *shinpaigekki*, and began to perform it in Chinese. *Wenmingxi* is a folk term for this new type of drama, *xinju*. But advocates and practitioners of a truly "modern" and progressive spoken drama (*huaju*) distanced themselves from *wenmingxi*, as the latter retained many vestiges of traditional theater and catered to an urban audience who sought pleasure and entertainment more than didacticism. Though it departed significantly from the traditional opera in that it is mainly "spoken" in the vernacular, it retained many features of Chinese old drama. See Wang Zilong, *Zhongguo yingju shi* (A history of Chinese film theater) (Taibei: Jianguo chubanshe, 1950), pp. 1–5.

33. Lin Niantong, "Zhongguo dianyingde kongjian yishi" (The sense of space in Chinese cinema), *Zhongguo dianying yanjiu* (Dianying: an interdisciplinary journal of Chinese film studies) (Hong Kong: Hong Kong Chinese film association, 1984), 1: 58–78.

34. Zheng Yimei and Xu Zhodai, *Shanghai jiuhua* (Reminiscences of old Shanghai) (Shanghai: Shanghai wenhua chubanshe, 1986), p. 112. Zhang was also behind an inge-

nious, but failed, plan to build an underground tunnel linking the complex to its branch on the other end of the area. The entertainment complex was turned into a department store during the Communist era, but one film theater, renamed the Red Flag Theater, continued to operate. When I visited Shanghai in the summer of 1993, the building had just been demolished so that a high-rise commercial center, also called the New World, could be constructed on its expensive site.

35. *Yinshi wenhua* 2 (1989): 302.

36. Gongsun Lu, *Zhongguo dianying*, 1: 13. The first filming done in China was footage of a performance by a Peking opera singer, shot by a Peking photographer in 1905 outside of his shop. Zhang and Zheng's enterprise is the first commercial cinematic effort in China.

37. For a history and a genre analysis of this literature, see Perry Link, *Mandarin Ducks and Butterflies: Popular Fiction in Early-Twentieth Century Chinese Cities* (Berkeley: University of California Press, 1981). See also Rey Chow, *Woman and Chinese Modernity: The Politics of Reading between West and East* (Minnesota: University of Minnesota Press, 1991), pp. 34–83.

38. Zhong Dafeng, "Lun 'yingxi,'" p. 63.

39. Cheng Jihua et al., *Zhongguo dianying*, 1: 58.

40. Gunning, "Cinema of Attractions," p. 64.

41. Cheng Jihua et al., *Zhongguo dianying*, 1: 59.

42. Thomas Elsaesser, Introduction to *Early Cinema: Space, Frame, Narrative* (London: BFI, 1990), pp. 167–68.

43. For more on this particular Shanghai urban spatial feature and public space in general, see Lu Hanchao's informative article, "Away from Nanking Road: Small Stores and Neighborhood Life in Modern Shanghai," *Journal of Asian Studies* 54, no. 1 (1995): 93–123. The hot-water shops are called "tiger stoves" (*laohuzhao*) in local parlance. Though on the brink of extinction, they can still be found in some typical *lilong* (alleyway) neighborhoods. For a more detailed description of the tea shop in the Republican period, see Bao Jing, ed., *Lao Shanghai jianwen* (Impressions of old Shanghai) (Shanghai: Shanghai guoguang shudian, 1947), 2: 52–53. Bao depicts the tea shop as a public space patronized mainly by people from the lower social strata. It functioned as a bathroom in the summer and cheap hotel for the homeless in the winter. But hooligans and thieves also constituted a major clientele.

44. Hong Shi et al., "Zhongguo zaoqi gushipiande chuangzuo tansuo" (Explorations on the creation of early Chinese narrative cinema), *Dianying yishu* 1990, no. 1: 39.

45. For lack of a more pertinent term, the "leisure class" used here refers to a particular urban social group emerging in the Chinese cities around the turn of last century. They include gangsters, dandies, gamblers, high-class prostitutes, and those who run the mass entertainment establishments. Shanghai dialect has a particular word for this group: *baixiangren* (person who plays).

46. My reading of the theme of social mobility here is also partly inspired by Thomas Elsaesser's perceptive analysis of the early German films such as *Student of Prague* and *The Cabinet of Dr. Caligari* (1919); see his "Social Mobility and the Fantastic: German Silent Cinema," in Mike Budd, ed., *The Cabinet of Dr. Caligari: Texts, Contexts, Histories* (New Brunswick: Rutgers University Press, 1990), pp. 171–89.

47. For the original use of the concept *bricoleur* in anthropological theory, see

Claude Lévi-Strauss, *The Savage Mind* (Chicago: University of Chicago Press, 1966), pp. 16–33. The term is first used in film history by Alan Williams, to describe the heterogeneity of the origins of cinema as a cultural and technological medium. See his *Republic of Images: A History of French Filmmaking* (Cambridge, Mass.: Harvard University Press, 1992), pp. 8–9.

48. Thomas Elsaesser, "Film History and Visual Pleasure: Weimar Cinema," in Patricia Mellencamp, ed., *Cinema Histories / Cinema Practices* (Los Angeles: AFI, 1984), pp. 76–78.

49. In addition, Zheng Zhengqiu's role as the doctor is also suggestive of his family background in the pharmaceutical (and sometimes opium) business; his other given name is Yaofeng, which has a reference to medicine (*yao*). Such self-referential practice (characters assuming the same last names of the actors) continued well into the 1930s, as with *Big Road*.

50. For a historical investigation of the Chinese communities in that region, see Maurice Freedman, "The Chinese in Southeast Asia: A Longer View," in *The Study of Chinese Society: Essays by Maurice Freedman* (Stanford: Stanford University Press, 1979). For a rich cultural history of the Chinese diaspora as a whole, see Lynn Pan, *Sons of the Yellow Emperor: The Story of the Overseas Chinese* (London: Secker and Warburg, 1990).

51. Wu Xiwen, "Guochan yingpian yu nanyang wenhua" (Chinese film and Nanyang culture), *Zhongnan qingbao* 2, no. 2 (Mar. 1935): 20–22. See also Ma Junxiang, "Zhongguo dianying qingxiede qipaoxian" (The slanting starting line of Chinese cinema), *Dianying yishu* 1990, no. 1: 12.

52. Ma Junxiang, "Qingxiede qipaoxian," p. 9.

53. Miriam Hansen, "Adventures of Goldilocks: Spectatorship, Consumerism and Public Life," *Camera Obscura* 22, no. 2 (Jan. 1990): 57.

54. The controversy that the success of this cinema has sparked is critically commented upon in Rey Chow's recent book, *Primitive Passions: Visuality, Sexuality, Ethnography, and Contemporary Chinese Cinema* (New York: Columbia University Press, 1995).

55. For a perceptive rereading of this group of films, see Ma Ning, "The Textual and Critical Difference of Being Radical: Reconstructing Chinese Leftist Films of the 1930s," *Wide Angle* 11, no. 2 (1989): 22–31. Interestingly, Ma Ning's reading of this cinema, through the example of *Street Angel* (1937), which, incidentally, contains a scene of "shadowplay," points to its complex genre composition, which negotiates between Soviet montage and Hollywood continuity editing. It also involved the inscribing of "a theatrical mode of spectatorship which comes into a dialectical relationship with that of the cinematic mode" (p. 29). Clearly, the ambivalence concerning the cinema that informed the making of *Laborer's Love* was never resolved with the emergence of a more narratively integrated cinema, and even the sound cinema. Given that the film directors and actors of the 1930s also worked actively in spoken drama theaters, Ma's observation adds a further historical dimension to my present discussion of a much earlier film. Chris Berry also notices some nonnarrative strains in this late silent film (with partial sound effects and some songs); see his "The Sublime Text: Sex and Revolution in *Big Road*," *East-West Film Journal* 2, no. 2 (June 1988): 66–86.

56. For a discussion on the link between the melodramatic tradition of the Republican cinema and post–Cultural Revolution melodrama, in particular those directed by Xie Jin, see Paul G. Pickowicz, "Melodramatic Representation and The 'May Fourth' Tra-

dition of Chinese Cinema," in Ellen Widmer and David Der-wei Wang, eds., *From May Fourth to June Fourth: Fiction and Film in Twentieth-Century China* (Cambridge, Mass.: Harvard University Press, 1993), pp. 295–326.

57. These debates were carried out in some major film journals in China in the 1980s. Some of the debaters are themselves filmmakers. Unlike the often academicized film criticism in the United States, film criticism in China is a public sphere involving critics, scriptwriters, directors, actors, and the audience. Some of the key texts of these debates are translated and collected in George Semsel et al., eds., *Chinese Film Theory: A Guide to the New Era* (New York: Praeger, 1990).

58. Luo Yijun, "Wenhua chuantong yu zhongguo dianying lilun" (Cultural tradition and Chinese film theory), *Dianying yishu* 1992, no. 2: 26.

59. Leo Ou-fan Lee, "The Tradition of Modern Chinese Cinema: Some Preliminary Explorations and Hypotheses," in Chris Berry, *Perspectives*, p. 16.

60. I am grateful to Yingjin Zhang for reminding me that Dai Sijie's *Niupeng* (China, My Sorrow, 1989) also contains references to the traditional shadowplay.

61. For a selection of the articles on this debate in English, see Part 4, "The Entertainment Film," in George S. Semsel et al., eds., *Film in Contemporary China: Critical Debates, 1979–1989* (Westport, Conn.: Praeger, 1993), pp. 83–139.

62. For a critique of this kind of interpretation of the "left-wing" film, see Ma Ning's article, "The Textual and Critical Difference of Being Radical."

63. As I mentioned earlier, Zhong Dafeng has written extensively on the theory of shadowplay. See also Chen Xihe's "Shadowplay: Chinese Film Aesthetics and Their Philosophical and Cultural Fundamentals," in Semsel, *Chinese Film Theory*, pp. 193–201.

64. See, among other things, articles by Ma Junxiang and Hong Shi et al. quoted earlier. For a study of the martial arts cinema, see Jia Leilei's "Zhongguo wuxia dianying yuanliu lun" (On the genesis and development of the Chinese martial arts film), *Yingshi wenhua* 1992, no. 5: 204–24.

65. Ma Junxiang, "Zhongguo dianying," pp. 14–15.

66. Li Shaobai, *Dianying lishi ji lilun* (Film history and theory) (Beijing: Wenhua yishu chubanshe, 1991). See especially "Zhongshi dianying shichangxue yanjiu" (Pay attention to the study of the film market), pp. 15–21, and "Guanyu zhongguo shangyepian" (On Chinese commercial cinema), pp. 86–105. As one of the main writers of the official *Zhongguo dianying fazhanshi*, Li told me in a conversation in the summer of 1995 that he had revised many of his earlier views on early Chinese cinema. He is currently one of the main editors of a new film history, *Zhongguo dianying yishu shi* (A history of Chinese film art), soon due for publication.

67. Miriam Hansen's article "Early Cinema, Late Cinema: Permutations of the Public Sphere," *Screen* 34, no. 3 (Autumn 1993): 192–210, on the comparison between preclassical cinema and postmodern media culture, has been very helpful in shaping my ideas here. In portraying the Chinese postmodern scenario, I am primarily referring to the coastal areas and big cities.

CHAPTER THREE

1. See Tom Gunning, "The Cinema of Attractions: Early Film, Its Spectator, and the Avant-Garde," *Wide Angle* 8, nos. 3–4 (Fall 1986): 63–70, and "An Aesthetic of Aston-

ishment: Early Film and the (In)Credulous Spectator," *Art and Text* 34 (Spring 1989): 31–45.

2. Tung Chieh-yuan [Dong Jieyuan], *Master Tung's Western Chamber Romance (Tung Hsi-hsiang chu-kung-tiao): A Chinese Chantefable*, trans. Li-li Chen (London: Cambridge University Press, 1976), pp. ix-xi. When referring to prior versions of *The Romance*, I have generally selected quotations from Li-Li Chen's translation of Dong Jieyuan's *zhugongdiao*, along with my own adaptations based on the Chinese original, *Xixiang ji zhugongdiao zhuyi* (The romance of the western chamber: chantefable with annotations), annotated by Zhu Pingchu (Lanzhou: Gansu Renmin chubanshe, 1982). For the Tang *chuanqi* by Yuan Zhen and the Yuan drama by Wang Shifu, I have referred to *The Romance of the Western Chamber* (Xixiang ji), trans. S. I. Hsiung, introduction by C. T. Hsia (New York: Columbia University Press, 1968 [1936]). Readers may also wish to consult *The Moon and the Zither: The Story of the Western Wing* (Xixiang ji), trans. Stephen H. West and Wilt L. Idema (Berkeley: University of California Press, 1991). The various versions of *The Romance* are considered in Jiang Xingyu, *Xixiang ji kaozheng* (The romance of the western chamber: textual verification) (Shanghai: Shanghai guji chubanshe, 1988).

3. The protagonist is also referred to as Zhang Junrui or simply Zhang Sheng.

4. Incidentally, the "happy ending" is characteristic of all but the earliest *chuanqi* version, where the young scholar is a cad who forsakes Yingying and never returns. In the popular Yuan drama, Madam Cui is reluctant to allow Zhang to marry Yingying when she discovers their affair, and only concedes to the marriage to save the Cui family from a scandal—*if* he passes the examination.

5. Wei Shaochang, ed., *Wu Jianren yanjiu ziliao* (Sources for research on Wu Jianren) (Shanghai: Shanghai guji chubanshe, 1980), pp. 200–206. Characteristically, Wu's novel opens with an amusing scenario "explaining" his revival of *The Romance*: Wang Shifu and Cao Xueqin are in heaven. Wang hears the smug vernacular novelist brag to the Jade God that *Honglou meng* (Dream of the red chamber) is the first and best vernacular *yanqing xiaoshuo* (love story). Wang secretly vows to prove him wrong, and persuades an earthly writer—Wu Jianren, of course—to resuscitate *The Romance* in the vernacular.

6. *Hongniang* premiered in Beijing on October 22, 1936, and is a popular piece in repertoires even today. See *Xun Huisheng yanchu juben xuan* (Selected scripts of Xun Huisheng's performances) (Shanghai: Shanghai wenyi chubanshe, 1982), pp. 453–96; Wei Shaochang, *Yiyuan shiyi* (Recollections from the world of art and literature) (Shanghai: Sanlian shudian, 1991), pp. 38–41.

7. See Cheng Jihua et al., *Zhongguo dianying fazhanshi*, 1: 91–95, 108–111. To account for the early careers of Hou and Pu, I have also searched through film publicity, credits, and publications from 1924 to 1928, of which the key relevant sources are listed in notes below.

8. Dongnan daxue (Southeastern University) was still known as Nanjing gaodeng shifan xuexiao (Nanjing higher normal school) when Hou Yao and Pu Shuqing began their studies. Dongnan was an early incarnation of the present Nanjing University. See Wen-hsin Yeh, *The Alienated Academy: Culture and Politics in Republican China 1919–1937* (Cambridge, Mass.: Harvard University Press, 1990).

9. The initial Beijing group included Xu Dishan (1893–1941), Ye Shaojun (b. 1893), Zhu Ziqing (1898–1948), and Wang Tongzhao (1897–1957). Later editors of *Xiaoshuo*

yuebao included Zheng Zhenduo and Ye Shaojun. See Li Baotan, ed., *Wenxue yanjiu hui xiaoshuo xuan* (Selected stories by the Literary Association) (Beijing: Renmin wenxue chubanshe, 1991), 1: 3.

10. The competing aims of the Literary Association and the Creation Society were staked out in series of essays by Mao Dun and Guo Moruo from 1920–24, reprinted in Zhang Ruoying, ed., *Zhongguo xinwenxue yundongshi ziliao* (Sources on the history of China's new literature movement) (Shanghai: Guangming shuju, 1934; Shanghai shudian facsimile ed., 1982), pp. 291–352. See also C. T. Hsia, *A History of Modern Chinese Fiction* (New Haven: Yale University Press, 1971), pp. 55–111; Vera Schwarcz, *The Chinese Enlightenment: Intellectuals and the Legacy of the May Fourth Movement of 1919* (Berkeley: University of California Press, 1986), pp. 152–53; Chow Tse-tsung, *The May Fourth Movement: Intellectual Revolution in Modern China* (Cambridge, Mass.: Harvard University Press, 1960), pp. 283–88.

11. Shen Yanbing (Mao Dun), "Xinwenxue yanjiuzhe de zeren yu nuli" (The responsibilities and efforts of researchers in new literature), from the same series of 1920–24 essays reprinted in Zhang Ruoying, *Zhongguo xinwenxue*, p. 298.

12. Hou Yao, *Qifu* (Abandoned wife) (Shanghai: Shangwu yinshuguan, 1925, 1929), pp. 63, 70.

13. The 1922 preface to Hou Yao, *Fuhuo de meigui* (Revived rose) (Shanghai: Shangwu yinshuguan, 1924, 1929).

14. Some unclarity has surrounded the various release prints of *The Romance*. Cheng Jihua's filmography of 1963 lists it as a ten-reel black-and-white film; see Cheng Jihua, Li Shaobai, and Xing Zuwen, eds., *Zhongguo dianying fazhanshi* (A history of the development of Chinese cinema) (Beijing: Zhongguo dianying chubanshe, 1963, 1980), 1: 555. However, the extant version is a coherent, partially tinted narrative which measures half that length. Some archivists have assumed that the extant print is shorter because it was abridged for export. I have located a news item in *Shibao* that may help untangle the issue. It reports that while "response was extremely praiseworthy" at the test screening, the film was rather long and so it underwent "drastic cutting and tinting, done personally by the head of the Minxin studio, Li Minwei, to increase its beauty" before its commercial release. Therefore, the shorter five-reel version extant today may well represent the version Minxin ultimately released in China on September 21, 1927, and also for export the following spring. See *Shibao* (Shanghai), Sept. 18–21, 1927.

15. Between 1926 and 1929, Guo Moruo and other writers affiliated with groups such as the Creation Society and the Sun Society reworked the romantic ideals of their "art for art's sake" position into a strident campaign for revolutionary literature. In one key essay, "Geming yu wenxue" (Revolution and literature), dated April 13, 1926, Guo Moruo stated that "literature is the frontrunner for revolution" and that the writer "must go to the soldiers, the people, the factories, the whirlpool of revolution; you must know that the literature we demand is a socialist literature that expresses sympathy with the proletariat, and that our demands are in line with the rest of the world's demands." Reprinted in Zhang Ruoying, *Zhongguo xinwenxue*, pp. 374–75. From this new position, Guo continued his offensive on the humanistic realism of Mao Dun and Lu Xun. By February 1930 the attacks were somewhat defused by the founding of the Zhongguo zuoyi zuojia lianmeng (League of left-wing writers), with its slightly broader interpretation of realism and revolutionary literature.

16. Qu Qiubai [Shi Tie'er], "Puluo dazhong wenyi de xianshi wenti" (The problem of reality in proletariat popular art), *Wenxue* (Literature, 1932); reprinted in *Qu Qiubai wenji: wenyi* (Collected writings of Qu Qiubai: arts and literature) (Beijing: Renmin wenxue chubanshe, 1985), 1: 463. Original essay dated Oct. 25, 1931.

17. Wang Zilong, *Zhongguo yingju shi* (History of Chinese film theater) (Taibei: Jianguo chubanshe, 1960), pp. 31–34; Du Yunzhi, *Zhongguo dianyingshi* (A history of Chinese cinema) (Taibei: Shangwu yinshuguan, 1972), p. 123.

18. Cheng Jihua et al., *Zhongguo dianying fazhanshi*, 1: 95, 1: 109–11. Qu's critique is invoked on pp. 133, 177. Similarly, Zhang Shichuan's 1940 remake of *The Romance* starring Zhou Xuan is relegated to a long list of costume dramas that proliferated in "Orphan Island" Shanghai only because of their popularity among "landlords escaping hardship" and "backward petty urbanites." Ibid., 2: 103–104; Du Yunzhi, *Zhonghua minguo dianyingshi* (A history of film in the Republic of China) (Taipei: Xingzheng yuan wenhua jianshe weiyuan hui, 1988), 1: 109.

19. David Bordwell, Janet Staiger, and Kristin Thompson, *The Classical Hollywood Cinema: Film Style and Mode of Production to 1960* (New York: Columbia University Press, 1985), pp. 130–33. On this phenomenon in theater, see Lawrence W. Levine, *Highbrow/Lowbrow: The Emergence of Cultural Hierarchy in America* (Cambridge, Mass.: Harvard University Press, 1988).

20. Official estimates from the China Film Archive and Cheng Jihua et al. Also see Marie-Claire Quiquemelle and Jean-Loup Passek, eds., *Le Cinema Chinois* (Paris: Centre national d'art et de culture Georges Pompidou, 1985), pp. 41, 61. Future research may of course reveal further information.

21. Purely martial arts films based on swordsman legends began appearing in 1925, a year or two earlier than costume dramas (*shidai xi / guzhuang xi*) and films such as *Burning of the Red Lotus Temple* which brought in elements of fantastic legends of ghosts and demons (*shenguai pian*). In this technical sense the earlier films are somewhat distinct from their more eclectic successors, as Huang Ren argues in "Wei zhongguo wuxia dianying tanyuan" (In search of the origins of Chinese martial arts films), *Dianying xinshang* 7, no. 4 (1989): 82–83. Nonetheless, martial arts legends and costume drama films shared the common features of spectacle and traditional native sources, and had merged by 1927, so for our current purposes they may be considered together as a genre of "classical-subject films."

22. See, for example, *Dagong bao* (L'Impartial, Tianjin), Sept. 18, 1927: 5; Oct. 16, 1927: 5.

23. Admittedly there was no shortage of low-budget productions overworking one or two mechanical effects amid otherwise lackluster writing or staging (e.g., certain swordsman films from Fudan, Youlian, or Tianyi). One or two "tricks" would be held off till the end, and then wantonly repeated. In *Hongxia*, the same short piece of footage showing the hero "flying" (on a hidden wire swing, superimposed over a backdrop "sky") was recycled at least three times in the course of fifteen minutes, and ordinary narrative footage was monotonously recapitulated for "flashbacks." One reviewer found Tianyi's *Sanguo zhi* so tedious that he walked out: "The so-called costumes are just one big show (*daxi*): the so-called action is all old theater, . . . [the kings] aren't kingly . . . , and Hu Die is dull as a doorknob . . . The audience shouted for their money back." *Dagong bao*, Sept. 4, 1927: 5.

24. He Xiujun, "Zhang Shichuan he Mingxing yingpian gongsi" (Zhang Shichuan

and Mingxing Film Company), *Wenhua shiliao* 1 (1980 [1965]): 131–32. Agreeing with Qu Qiubai's opinion, however, He Xiujun quickly adds that although *Burning of the Red Lotus Temple* was hugely profitable, "it harmed a part of the lively young audience. One would often hear that so-and-so's child, having seen *Burning of the Red Lotus Temple*, had left home for the mountains to learn how to become a flying immortal or a heroic swordsman."

25. These plot deviations from earlier versions are minor. To summarize: the film excludes the subplot of the Cui family's prior arrangements for Yingying's marriage to her highborn cousin Zheng Heng. There are also certain changes in the depth of characterization and the sequence or length of events. In Wang Shifu's play, Zhang departs for his examination and stays away for a longer period, during which he dreams of Yingying; but in the film, Zhang dreams of Yingying before he even goes away, and the trip itself is collapsed into an "immediate" return. Graphic sexual references are omitted from the film. Note that much of the "cleaning up" of the Yuan drama had already occurred during the early Qing; see C. T. Hsia, introduction to Wang Shifu, *The Romance*, pp. xxvii–xxxi.

26. Mei Lanfang, *Wo de dianying shenghuo* (My life in the movies) (Beijing: Zhongguo dianying chubanshe, 1984 [1962]), p. 5.

27. Ibid., p. 11.

28. Some recent critics go so far as to retroactively identify a "nationalistic style" (*minzu pai*), whose main feature is a flat mise-en-scène that draws on the "multiple" or "parallel" perspective of classical Chinese ink painting. See, for example, Hao Dazheng, "Chinese Visual Representations: Painting and Cinema," in Linda C. Ehrlich and David Desser, eds., *Cinematic Landscapes: Observations on the Visual Arts and Cinema of China and Japan* (Austin: University of Texas Press, 1994), pp. 45–62. I consider the question of nationalism and film style further in my "Silent Speech: Envisioning the Nation in Early Chinese Cinema," Ph.D. diss. (Columbia University, 1997).

29. For recent commentary on the "Orient" imagined by American cinema, see Gina Marchetti, *Romance and the "Yellow Peril": Race, Sex, and Discursive Strategies in Hollywood Fiction* (Berkeley: University of California Press, 1993), pp. 10–45; Kevin Brownlow, *Behind the Mask of Innocence—Sex, Violence, Prejudice, Crime: Films of Social Conscience in the Silent Era* (New York: Knopf, 1990), pp. 320–52.

30. A five-reel print made its way to Paris as *La Rose de Pu-Chui*, and there it ran from April 20 to June 3, 1928—concurrently with *Ben-Hur* (1925) and *Joyless Streets* (1925). Hou Yao's film was exhibited at the experimental Studio 28, just when Abel Gance's "Polyvision" triptych screen had been installed for his four-hour epic-scale *Napoleon* (1927). The daily Paris newspaper *Le Temps*—filled with front-page updates on the National Revolutionary Army's Northern March clashes with Japanese in Shandong's May Third Incident—praised the "new spectacle" at Studio 28 as "a terribly interesting film from the Far East." See Emile Vuillermoz, "Chronique Cinematographique," *Le Temps*, Apr. 28, 1928: 4. One might add that the horseback swordfighting in Hou Yao's film would have rested comfortably alongside Gance's program of elaborate cavalry shots. Note that Pu-Chui in the film's French title designated the temple's name, Pujiu (in pinyin), usually rendered as P'u-chiu in Wade-Giles romanization. Because of the French title *Rose de Pu-Chui*, occasionally *The Romance* has been confused with a different film by Hou Yao, *Fuhuo de meigui* (Revived rose).

31. My emphasis. In Chinese, Zhang's first encounter at the temple is conveyed with a

variegated vocabulary referring to the sense of sight (e.g., *guan, kan, jian, shi, qu, gupan, piejian,* each repeated numerous times). Moreover, the sights directly affect him, alternately bringing torment, salvation, insanity, belief in the divine, sexual desire, and rendering him repetitive or simply speechless. The translations here (and those that follow) of Dong Jieyuan's text are from *Master Tung,* trans. Li-Li Chen (Cambridge: Cambridge University Press, 1976), pp. 14–20; I have adjusted Chen's phrasing in places to convey more precisely the persistent recurrence of vocabulary relating to the visual in the original. Also, the transliteration of names has been converted from Wade-Giles to pinyin for consistency.

32. See Gunning, "Cinema of Attractions."

33. Laura Mulvey, "Visual Pleasure and Narrative Cinema," *Screen* (1975), reprinted in her *Visual and Other Pleasures* (Bloomington: Indiana University Press, 1989), p. 17.

34. As C. T. Hsia points out, the secrecy of their affair in this comparatively neutral space impels the story forward toward exposure and, finally, rectification; see his introduction to Wang Shifu, *The Romance,* p. xix.

35. Ze Ren, "Yingju yu shaonian nannü" (The movies and young men and women), *Shenbao* (Shanghai) Aug. 30, 1927: 3.

36. A static "iris" mask was used consistently in U.S. and European narrative filmmaking from at least 1900, though D. W. Griffith has been credited with the first artistic use of the contracting or dilating "iris" diaphragm in his 1915 epic *The Birth of a Nation*—which incidentally had just had a long run in China in 1924. While today "iris shot" commonly denotes a closing or opening shot, I use the term here to indicate the usually static, circular black mask in *The Romance.*

37. Since *The Romance* was filmed mainly with a static camera, these iris shots provided an economical replica of the zoom-in and also added motion, focus, and visual variety to the film.

38. The characterization of a "male gaze" in classical Hollywood cinema is based on two decades of debates in feminist film studies during the 1970s and 1980s. See, for example, Laura Mulvey, "Visual Pleasure." Note that recent historical studies of spectatorship and cinematic conventions in Hollywood cinema have added new dimensions to the analysis of film and gender which caution against generalizations. See Miriam Hansen, *Babel and Babylon: Spectatorship in American Silent Film* (Cambridge, Mass.: Harvard University Press, 1991); Mary Ann Doane, *The Desire to Desire: The Woman's Film of the 1940s* (Bloomington: Indiana University Press, 1987).

39. Soon after he has met Yingying, Zhang climbs over a wall to spy on her strolling by a lake with her maid. The women literally "spot" the peeping man, isolated atop the wall in an iris shot. Zhang's own iris shot counters the women's, catching sight of them even as they run off in the opposite direction. Elsewhere in the film, the static iris shot is used for a young monk's sight of marauders approaching from afar, and heightens the comedy of a scene where Zhang singles out a reluctant staff member of the monastery to deliver his message to General Du.

40. A detailed discussion of this effect in later films can be found in Harris, "Silent Speech." One classic example that is relevant here: the scene in *Malu tianshi* (Street angel, 1937) where Xiao Hong sings of a girl embroidering mandarin ducks and butterflies as she awaits the return of her beau fighting off invaders at the Great Wall.

41. Cf. Wang Dewei, *Cong Liu E dao Wang Zhenhe* (From Liu E to Wang Zhenhe) (Taibei: Shibao wenhua chubanshe, 1986), pp. 183–208.

42. In other versions of *The Romance*, Hongniang and Yingying both sing and also communicate with Zhang by letter. The solo voice of the maid Hongniang, as intermediary, shares equal time with Zhang's voice. The centrality of the Hongniang figure is also key to opera renditions of *The Romance*: Xun Huisheng explains that he built on "the way the Kunqu opera *Kaohong* had emphasized the character of Hongniang and eulogized her bravery, composure, and resourcefulness." See *Xun Huisheng*, p. 453.

43. It is possible that the original ten-reel version may have included some such scenes inspired by previous editions of the play (such as the Yuan edition)—for example, where Hongniang encourages Yingying into Zhang's bed for a sexual tryst. However, I have found no mention of censorship of this film. The Nationalist Government had not yet drawn up a formal film censorship law, although there may have been self-censorship on the part of the director, the film company, or the distributor.

44. Keith McMahon describes this elevation of women in the "beauty-scholar genre" as a sort of "expedient rebellion" and "rational optimism"—a mode that negotiated, without entirely rejecting, familiar restrictions on the conduct of an unmarried woman. See "The Classic 'Beauty-Scholar' Romance and the Superiority of the Talented Woman," in *Body, Subject and Power in China,* eds. Angela Zito and Tani E. Barlow (Chicago: University of Chicago Press, 1994), p. 246.

45. Dong Jieyuan, *Master Tung's Western Chamber Romance*, p. 1. The original reads: "Xiyu taiping duo xia, / gange dao zai xian bingjia. / Zhe shi wei ren, / baishen bu huan qia!" See *Xixiang ji zhugongdiao zhuyi*, annotated by Zhu Pingchu, p. 1.

46. Wang Shifu, *The Romance*, pp. 6, 269. In the extant film, the character Zheng Heng is effectively collapsed into the figure of Song, as a competitor for Yingying, so that the film consistently retains the sense that literary merit conquers martial force and aristocratic claims. It is also fair to say that the tale was so familiar that contemporary Chinese audiences could read into the film elided narrative elements such as this.

47. Judith Butler, *Gender Trouble: Feminism and the Subversion of Identity* (New York: Routledge, 1990), p. 140.

48. Tian Han, "Yinse de meng" (The silvery dream), *Yinxing* 5–13 (1927); reprinted in *Tian Han wenji* (Collected writings of Tian Han) (Beijing: Zhongguo xiju chubanshe, 1987), 14: 104. Tian selectively refers to Tanizaki's essay "Katsudō shashin no genzai to shōrai" (The present and future of the moving pictures), *Shin shōsetsu* (New fiction) (Sept. 1917), reprinted in *Tanizaki Jun'ichirō zenshū* (Complete works of Tanizaki Jun'ichiro) (Tokyo: Chūō kōron sha, 1957–1959), 14: 91–98. On Tanizaki's seminal essay, see Joanne R. Bernardi, "The Early Development of the Gendaigeki Screenplay: Kaeriyama Norimasa, Kurihara Tomas, Tanizaki Jun'ichiro and the Pure Film Movement," Ph.D. diss. (Columbia University, 1992), pp. 229–44. My thanks to Professor Bernardi for help in locating the Tanizaki reference.

49. Lu Mengshu, ed., *Dianying yu wenyi* (Film and the arts) (Shanghai: Liangyou, 1928), pp. 145–46.

50. Sa Mengwu, "Wenhua jinhua lun" (On the evolution of culture), *Dongfang zazhi* 24, no. 23 (Dec. 10, 1927): 13.

51. See, for example, Tian Han, "Xiju dazhonghua he dazhonghua xiju" (The popularization of theater and the popularized theater), *Beidou* 2, no. 3 (July 20, 1932); reprinted in *Tian Han wenji*, 14: 372–76.

52. Tian Han, "Cong yinse zhi mengli xingzhuan lai" (Awakening from the silvery

dream), *Dianying* (May 1, 1930), reprinted in *Tian Han wenji*, 14: 348–362; Cai Chusheng, "Zhaoguang" (Morning light), *Xiandai dianying* 1 (1933), quoted in Cai Hongsheng, *Cai Chusheng de chuangzuo daolu* (Cai Chusheng's creative path) (Beijing: Wenhua yishu chubanshe, 1982), p. 33.

CHAPTER FOUR

1. I have delineated them in some detail in a chapter called "Remapping Shanghai" in my new book manuscript, *Shanghai Modern*.

2. Ye Shuping and Zheng Zu'an, eds., *Bainian Shanghai tan* (A hundred years of Shanghai) (Shanghai: Shanghai huabao chubanshe, 1990), p. 119. See also Cao Yongfu, "Shanghai Daguangming dianying yuan gaikuang" (General account of Shanghai's Grand movie theater), *Shanghai dianying shiliao* (Shanghai film historical materials) 1 (Oct. 1992): 207–11. I am indebted to Zhang Wei of the Shanghai Municipal Library for this journal.

3. Shanghai yanjiu zhongxin (Shanghai research center), ed., *Shanghai qibainian* (Seven hundred years of Shanghai) (Shanghai: Shanghai renmin chubanshe, 1991), p. 360.

4. Betty Pei-t'i Wei, *Old Shanghai* (Hong Kong: Oxford University Press, 1993), p. 31.

5. See "Shanghai dianying yuan de fazhan" (The development of Shanghai movie theaters), in Shanghaitong she, ed., *Shanghai yanjiu ziliao xuji* (Research materials on Shanghai, sequel collection) (Shanghai: Zhonghua shuju, 1939), p. 532. The article also gives a detailed listing of some fifty theaters and eleven open-air cinemas (pp. 541–51), plus discussion of the architecture and equipment of three leading theaters: Nanking, Grand, and Metropole (pp. 553–54).

6. Yang Cun, *Zhongguo dianying sanshinian* (Thirty years of Chinese cinema) (Hong Kong: Shijie chubanshe, 1954), p. 168. According to Yang, the decline was caused by Japanese bombing of Shanghai in January 1932. He also listed a total of some 40 movie theaters in Shanghai: 8 in the Chinese city, 24 in the International Settlement, 12 in the French concession, not counting the movie theaters within amusement halls.

7. For instance, a "combine" of six companies built new movie theaters in other cities and controlled the Zhongyang chain of five theaters in Shanghai (Palace, Empire, Huguang, Xingguang, Jincheng). See ibid., p. 21. A one-page advertisement of these theaters can be found in the magazine *Xinhua huabao* (New China pictorial), no. 2 (1940). I am indebted to Poshek Fu for this and other movie magazines used in this article.

8. In the 1932–34 period, Lianhua produced 25 films, Mingxing 19, Tianyi 21, Yihua 10, according to Yang Cun, *Zhongguo dianying*, p. 169.

9. Zhang Wei, Ying Xian, and Chen Jing, "Zhongguo xiandai dianying chubanwu zongmu tiyao" (A concise listing of modern Chinese film publications), *Shanghai dianying shiliao* 1 (Oct. 1992): 212–34; 2/3 (May 1993): 289–344.

10. Yang Cun, *Zhongguo dianying*, pp. 9 and 24.

11. I am indebted to Feng Jicai of Tianjin, a famous writer who also has a passion for collecting popular journals of earlier times. This magazine was a personal gift.

12. See *Linglong funü tuhua zazhi* (Lin loon lady's magazine) 3, no. 43 (Dec. 6, 1933): 2425.

13. Wang Dingjiu, *Shanghai menjing* (Guide to Shanghai) (Shanghai: Zhongyang shudian, 1932), p. 14 in the chapter on "seeing" (Kan de menjing).

14. Ibid., p. 20.

15. Ibid., pp. 15–22.

16. According to Gongsun Lu, those who wrote plot sheets for silent films were mostly literary and cultivated, including such butterfly writers as Yao Sufeng, Fan Yanqiao, Zheng Yimei, and Zheng Zhengqiu. Dan Duyu went to excess by writing in an elegant classical style, beyond the comprehension of the average filmgoer. See Gongsun Lu, *Zhongguo dianying shihua* (Historical notes on Chinese cinema) (Hong Kong: Nantian shuye gongsi, 1961), 1: 219–20.

17. Interview on Oct. 22, 1984.

18. See *Xiandai dianying* (Modern cinema) 1, nos. 2 and 5–7 (1933–34). Those are some of the issues I was able to locate in my research in Shanghai. Liu's praise of Garbo and Crawford can be found in *Furen huabao* (Women's pictorial), no. 18 (May 1934): 16.

19. *Xiandai dianying* 1, no. 2 (1934).

20. Liu Na'ou, "Dianying xingshi mei de tanqiu" (The search for the formal aesthetics of film), *Wanxiang* (Kaleidoscope) 1 (1934). Expectedly, Liu's views received scathing criticism from leftist critics of the time. For a typical sample, see Chen Wu, "Qingsuan Liu Na'ou de lilun" (Liquidating Liu Na'ou's theory), in Zhongguo dianying yishu yanjiu zhongxin (Center for the study of Chinese film art), ed., *Zhongguo zuoyi dianying yundong* (The leftist film movement in China) (Beijing: Zhongguo dianying chubanshe, 1993), pp. 162–67.

21. For a detailed analysis of this and other issues, see Yingjin Zhang, *The City in Modern Chinese Literature and Film: Configurations of Space, Time, and Gender* (Stanford: Stanford University Press, 1996), pp. 154–231.

22. The traffic of books and journals as a new phenomenon of cultural production which contributed significantly to the imaginary of urban modernity is discussed in a chapter of my *Shanghai Modern*. I first learned about the accessibility of American magazines from lengthy interviews conducted with two famous writers of the time, Shi Zhicun and Xu Chi, in the early 1980s.

23. Leo Ou-fan Lee, "The Cultural Construction of Modernity in Early Republican China," paper delivered at a conference on "Passages to Modernity in Republican China," held at University of California–Berkeley in September 1995.

24. Miriam Hansen, *Babel and Babylon: Spectatorship in American Silent Film* (Cambridge, Mass.: Harvard University Press, 1991), p. 15.

25. Ibid, p. 123.

26. Ibid., p. 120. Hansen quoted the words of Mary Ryan.

27. The woman in the front cover tradition was established by the late Qing courtesan journals, of which the female star covers in the 1930s can be regarded as a form of commercial and aesthetic displacement. I have discussed this phenomenon in my article, "The Cultural Construction of Modernity." The film historian Jay Leyda also remarked: "Only on Chinese calendars of modern beauties can one find counterparts of the ladies who were 'developed' to attract film audiences of the treaty ports in the 1930s, and these standards have changed little since then." See Jay Leyda, *Dianying: An Account of Films and the Film Audience in China* (Cambridge, Mass.: MIT Press, 1972), p. 86.

28. "Cong modeng shuodao xiandai qingnian funü" (From the modern to the young women of the present era), *Linglong* 3, no. 44 (Dec. 13, 1933): 2439–42.

29. Leyda, *Dianying*, p. 49.

30. Ibid., pp. 49–50.

31. Xu Changlin, "Zaoqi Zhongguo yinmu shang de minzu tese" (The national characteristic in early Chinese cinema), in Hong Kong Society of Chinese Film Studies, ed., *Zhongguo dianying yanjiu* (Studies in Chinese cinema), no. 1 (Dec. 1983): 20–21.

32. Shu Zi, "Fengyu zhai yingxi tan" (Talking about movies from the Wind-and-Rain Studio), *Banyue* 2, no. 4 (1922): 3–4. I am indebted to Chen Jianhua for this source, which shows that Western films were by no means a hobby only for the Westernized upper classes but were eagerly embraced by the authors and readers of this allegedly traditional school as well. In the same issue, the magazine's editor, Zhou Shoujuan, himself a translator of Western fiction, raved about another film, *The Four Horsemen of the Apocalypse* (1921), in an editorial comment; and in a subsequent issue he quibbled about the translation of film titles. See ibid., 3, no. 2 (1923): 13.

33. Hansen, *Babel and Babylon*, pp. 15–16.

34. Ibid., p. 161.

35. Ibid., p. 141. According to Hansen, this is the modern narrative which Griffith had both contributed to and departed from in his films.

36. Paul Pickowicz, "Melodramatic Representation and the 'May Fourth' Tradition of Chinese Cinema," in Ellen Widmer and David Wang, eds., *From May Fourth to June Fourth: Fiction and Film in Twentieth-Century China* (Cambridge, Mass.: Harvard University Press, 1993), p. 298.

37. See *Tansuo de niandai* (Early Chinese cinema: the era of exploration), a catalogue for a festival of films of the 1930s, sponsored by the Hong Kong Arts Center and the Hong Kong Chinese Film Association in 1984. These categories were first developed by the literary scholar Huang Jichi.

38. Cheng Jihua, Li Shaobai, and Xing Zuwen, *Zhongguo dianying fazhan shi* (A history of the development of Chinese cinema) (Beijing: Zhongguo dianying chubanshe, 1963). The thesis is contained in vol. 1, chap. 3, esp. pp. 171–244. For obvious reasons, I have not relied on this book for my analysis.

39. *Xin Shanghai* 1, no. 1 (1933): 67.

40. Ibid., p. 68.

41. Ibid., pp. 67–73.

42. Pickowicz, "Melodramatic Representation," pp. 304–5.

43. Ibid., p. 324.

44. Nick Browne, "Society and Subjectivity: On the Political Economy of Chinese Melodrama," in Nick Browne, Paul G. Pickowicz, Vivian Sobchack, and Esther Yau, eds., *New Chinese Cinemas: Forms, Identities, Politics* (Cambridge: Cambridge University Press, 1994), 40–56.

45. Ibid., p. 41.

46. Pickowicz, "Melodramatic Representation," pp. 301–3. Both Browne and Pickowicz draw from Peter Brooks's book *The Melodramatic Representation* (New York: Columbia University Press, 1985), which is a study of the (written) fiction of Balzac and Henry James.

47. Xia Yan, *Lanxun jiumeng lu* (Too lazy to seek old dreams) (Beijing: Sanlian shudian, 1985), pp. 224–31. Xia's friend Qian Xingcun was a close friend of Zhou Jianyun, the manager of Mingxing; their first meeting with the Mingxing in-house directors, Zhang

Shichuan and Zheng Zhengqiu, took place in the popular DD's Cafe in the French conces-sion. Zhang was old-fashioned, but Zheng admired Hong Shen and had more influence.

48. Ibid., pp. 232–33.

49. Ibid., p. 233.

50. Leo Ou-fan Lee, "The Tradition of Modern Chinese Cinema: Some Preliminary Explorations and Hypotheses," in Chris Berry, ed., *Perspectives on Chinese Cinema* (Lon-don: British Film Institute, 1991), p. 12. Ironically, the scripts of the silent films are slightly more elaborate in technical clues, which include scene-by-scene and even shot-by-shot directions.

51. Lin Niantong, *Jingyou* (Camera work) (Hong Kong: Suye chubanshe, 1985), pp. 3–6.

52. Lee, "The Tradition of Modern Chinese Cinema," p. 14.

53. Hansen, *Babel and Babylon*, pp. 23, 79.

54. Ibid., p. 82; a quote from the critic Frank Woods.

55. Since the celebrated theorizing by Andre Bazin, the long-take aesthetic has been seen as more characteristic of the European tradition, from Italian Neo-Realism to the films of Godard and Chantal Ackerman. For an insightful application of Bazin's theory of "documentary realism" to Chinese films, though not to those of the 1930s, see Li Tuo, "Chang jingtou he dianying de jishixing" (The long take and the film's documentary re-alism), in Zhong Dianfei, ed., *Dianying meixue: 1982* (Film aesthetics: 1982) (Beijing: Zhongguo wenyi lianhe chuban gongsi, 1983), pp. 94–131.

56. Noel Burch, "Narrative/Diegesis—Thresholds, Limits," *Screen* 23 (July–Aug. 1982): 22.

57. Huang Ailing, "Shilun sanshi niandai Zhongguo dianying danjingtou de xingzhi" (On the nature of the single long take in 1930s Chinese cinema), in *Zhongguo dianying yanjiu*, 1: 47.

58. Ibid, pp. 44, 49.

59. Ma Ning, "The Textual and the Critical Difference of Being Radical: Reconstruct-ing Chinese Leftist Films of the 1930s," *Wide Angle* 11, no. 2 (1989): 23.

60. Ibid., p. 26.

61. The film starred Janet Gaynor and was directed by Frank Borzage, whose senti-mental style may have endeared him to Chinese audiences. I was unable to find the video version of the film. The following plot summary and assessment is taken from a current guide to old movies on television: "Italian girl fleeing from police joins traveling circus, meets and falls in love with young painter who finds her an inspiration. Followup to suc-cess of *Seventh Heaven*, is actually much better, a delicate, beautifully photographed ro-mance." Leonard Maltin, ed., *1979–80 TV Movies* (New York: Signet, 1980), p. 669. *Sev-enth Heaven*, translated as *Qichong tian*, was apparently also a box-office hit in Shanghai.

62. Leyda, *Dianying*, p. 106.

63. Ma Ning, "The Textual and the Critical Difference," p. 24.

64. Leyda, *Dianying*, p. 117.

65. *Spring in a Small Town* is an awesome accomplishment which in my view differs from and towers above all the thirties films in its mastery of the form in the service of a deeply psychological drama of ethical conflict and sexual repression. In his short biogra-phy of Fei, Leyda does not even mention this film. Since I saw this film only once in Hong Kong and have not been able to find a video version, I cannot do an extensive analysis.

66. Leyda, *Dianying*, p. 86.

67. Huang Ailing, "Shilun sanshi niandai," p. 42.

68. Ibid., p. 43.

69. *Zhongguo zuoyi dianying yundong*, p. 555.

70. Cai Chusheng, "Bashi siri zhihou—gei *Yukuang qu* de guanzhongmen" (Eighty-four days later—to the audience of *Song of the Fishermen*," ibid., pp. 364–65.

71. Ibid., p. 215.

72. Shen Xiling, "Zenyang zhizuo *Shizi jietou*" (How was *Crossroads* made), ibid., p. 395.

73. The Hong Kong director Tsui Hark (Xu Ke) later made a spoof of this story by making the "menage à deux" situation into a "menage à trois" in one of his own films.

74. We could even compare such sequences intergenerically with the beginning pages of Mao Dun's novel *Ziye* (Midnight), which likewise evokes such a "contradictory" atmosphere of the exhilarating modernity of (as Mao Dun wrote in original English) LIGHT, HEAT, POWER and wanton depravity.

75. For a brief but perceptive analysis, see Rey Chow, *Primitive Passions: Visuality, Sexuality, Ethnography, and Contemporary Chinese Cinema* (New York: Columbia University Press, 1995), pp. 23–26. In this film, as Chow remarks, "words, whenever they are used, are used very sparingly, so that the audience must learn to see the film through the visual composites that we conventionally call images" (p. 25). This is precisely what makes this particular film so exceptional. Chow sees elitist resistance to visuality by both writers and scholars of modern Chinese literature. My own position is to find linkages and mutual mediations between visuality and the written word.

76. Chen Huiyang, *Mengying ji* (Dreaming of movies) (Taipei: Yunchen, 1990), pp. 77–79.

77. This remark and other information are taken from *Tansuo de niandai*, no pagination.

78. The film's popularity also "benefited a lot from the producer's aggressive promotion in the newspaper as 'the first horror film' and outside the theaters with giant posters and eery lights that scared the passers-by." I am grateful to Yingjin Zhang for the above reminder in his editorial review of the first draft of this chapter. See also, Jin Shan, "Yi wangshi nian wangyou" (Reminiscing about the past, thinking of my deceased friends), *Dazhong dianying*, no. 139 (1956), p. 25; Cao Maotang and Wu Lun, *Shanghai yingtan huajiu* (Reminiscences of the Shanghai film scene) (Shanghai: Shanghai wenyi chubanshe, 1987), pp. 184–85.

79. *The Desert Island* is considered reactionary, and one of the faults Cheng finds in *Singing at Midnight* is the director's "direct copying" of *Phantom of the Opera*. See Cheng Jihua et al., *Zhongguo dianying fazhan shi*, 1: 460–61, 1: 490.

CHAPTER FIVE

1. Frederic Wakeman, Jr., puts it more eloquently, arguing that "Shanghai changed from a pre-electric city of pleasure, centered on teashops and courtesans' quarters, to a garishly illuminated metropolis of night-life vice in cabarets, dance halls, and bordellos," in which public policy played a much stronger role than before. See his "Licensing Leisure: The Chinese Nationalists' Attempt to Regulate Shanghai, 1927–49," *Journal of Asian Studies* 54, no. 1 (Feb. 1995): 19.

2. Following its usage in most non-Chinese Shanghai guidebooks, this essay employs

a broad definition of the term "cabaret" to include any public space that involved drinking, eating, and dancing as the primary social activities. It is also understood to mean an establishment where women were hired to accompany patrons both at the table and on the dance floor, thus excluding clubs such as the Cercle Sportif FranÁais which offered drinks and dancing but not professional dancing partners. In contrast, Peter Jelavich, in his study of cabaret in Berlin during the first half of the twentieth century, defines cabaret more strictly as public entertainment in which performers engaged their audience in variety shows of an often satirical nature. Such performances did indeed occur in many of the establishments discussed here, but are not an essential part of this study. For Jelavich's definition of cabaret, see his *Berlin Cabaret* (Cambridge, Mass.: Harvard University Press, 1993), p. 2.

3. For a brief secondary account of clubs and nightlife in prerevolution Shanghai, see Nicholas Clifford, *Spoilt Children of Empire: Westerners in Shanghai and the Chinese Revolution of the 1920s* (Hanover: University Press of New England, 1991), pp. 73–76.

4. "Shanghai Boom," *Fortune* 11, no. 1 (Jan. 1935): 106.

5. Many cabarets were located just outside of settlement boundaries, placing them outside the purview of the Shanghai Municipal Police. See "Shanghai at Play," *China Journal* (May 1935): 231.

6. A translation by Eileen Chang of the first two chapters of this sprawling novel appears in Liu Ts'un-yan, ed., *Chinese Middlebrow Fiction* (Hong Kong: Chinese University Press, 1984), pp. 95–110.

7. See Perry Link, Jr., *Mandarin Ducks and Butterflies: Popular Fiction in Early Twentieth-Century Chinese Cities* (Berkeley: University of California Press, 1981), pp. 118–24.

8. Francesca Dal Lago, a student at New York University, has written a master's thesis on this subject (personal correspondence).

9. Hershatter offers the most complete account to date of the historical factors that led to the decline of courtesan culture and changing elite perceptions of prostitution in the 1920s and 1930s. See Gail Hershatter, "Courtesans and Streetwalkers: The Changing Discourses on Shanghai Prostitution, 1890–1949," *Journal of the History of Sexuality* 3, no. 2 (1992): 245–69.

10. Yao Hsin-nung, "When Sing-Song Girls Were Muses," *T'ien-Hsia Monthly* (May 1937): 482; my emphasis.

11. This is the result of a personal survey of *Jingbao*, during which I counted over 1,000 articles concerning dancing hostesses over this period.

12. Perry Link claims that the paper had a circulation of around 10,000 in the twenties; see his *Mandarin Ducks and Butterflies*, p. 120.

13. For more information on the changes in *Jingbao*'s management and ownership in 1939, see Shanghai Municipal Police (SMP) Files, reel 43, D-8149/c484.

14. *Jingbao*, Dec. 3, 1939.

15. Edna Lee Booker, *News Is My Job: A Correspondent in War-Torn China* (New York: Macmillan, 1940), p. 322.

16. *Linglong* 1936: 3311. The interview subsequently mentioned in the text appears on this page as well.

17. For a more complete description of this class of women, and a discussion of the etymological derivation of the word (*changsan* comes from the name of a mahjong tile), see Hershatter, "Courtesans and Streetwalkers," pp. 249–50.

18. The resemblance between Chinese elite attitudes towards dancing in the twenties and those of American elite society several decades earlier is quite remarkable, though perhaps less so when one considers that the tendency of high culture to vulgarize and thus separate itself from popular culture seems to be universal. See Lewis A. Erenberg, *Steppin' Out: New York Nightlife and the Transformation of American Culture, 1890–1930* (Chicago: University of Chicago Press, 1981), pp. 22–25.

19. *Beiyang huabao*, Oct. 18, 1932.

20. SMP Files, reel 6, D-2344.

21. For some other examples of exclusionary practices based on race, see Edgar Snow, "The Americans in Shanghai," *American Mercury* (Aug. 1930): 437–45; Randall Gould, "Where Races Mingle but Never Merge," *Christian Science Monitor* (June 24, 1936): 4. For a secondary account of such practices, see Robert A. Bickers and Jeffrey N. Wasserstrom, "Shanghai's 'Dogs and Chinese Not Admitted' Sign: Legend, History and Contemporary Symbol," *China Quarterly*, no. 142 (June 1995): 444–66.

22. Si Tui, "Wo henjile shishi chongbai waiguoren de xinli!" (I hate the psychology of worshipping everything about foreigners!), *Shenghuo*, Mar. 13, 1927: 55.

23. "Shanghai Boom," pp. 104–6.

24. For gangster politics in Shanghai in the 1930s, see Brian G. Martin, " 'The Pact with the Devil': The Relationship between the Green Gang and the Shanghai French Concession Authorities, 1925–1935," in Frederic Wakeman, Jr., and Wen-hsin Yeh, eds., *Shanghai Sojourners* (Institute of East Asian Studies, University of California, Berkeley, 1992), pp. 266–304; Brian Martin, "The Green Gang and the Guomindang State: Du Yuesheng and the Politics of Shanghai, 1927–37," *Journal of Asian Studies* 54, no. 1 (Feb. 1995): 64–92. See also Wakeman, *Policing Shanghai, 1927–1937* (Berkeley: University of California Press, 1995), pp. 244–76.

25. John Pal, *Shanghai Saga* (London: Jarrolds, 1963), p. 89.

26. Heinrich Freuhauf, "Urban Exoticism in Modern Chinese Literature, 1910–1933," Ph.D. diss. (University of Chicago, 1990), p. 242.

27. Pal, *Shanghai Saga* , p. 112.

28. Ibid.

29. The vast majority of America's first "talkies"—films that included soundtracks—were song-and-dance extravaganzas modeled on the successful institution of the Broadway musical. See Richard Barrios, *A Song in the Dark: The Birth of the Musical Film* (New York: Oxford University Press, 1995), pp. 41–70.

30. See, for example, Pan Gongzhan, *Xuesheng de xinshenghuo* (Nanjing, 1935), p. 68, quoted in Wen-hsin Yeh, *The Alienated Academy: Culture and Politics in Republican China, 1919–1937* (Cambridge, Mass.: Harvard University Press, 1990), p. 191; see also Gu Fan, "Cong jin wu tandao jin guan buliang dianying" (From prohibiting dance let's speak of prohibiting watching bad films), *Libailiu*, Dec. 1, 1934: 628.

31. "Shanghai at Play," *China Journal* (May 1935): 231.

32. *All About Shanghai* (Shanghai: University Press, 1934–35; reprinted by Oxford University Press, 1983), p. 77.

33. Langman Shusheng, "Wuchang manhua" (Dance hall slow-talk), *Libailiu*, July 1935: 938.

34. "Shanghai Boom," p. 106.

35. Ruth Day mentions meeting several Chinese and foreign notables during a visit

to the Park Hotel ballroom in 1935. Ruth Day, *Shanghai 1935* (Claremont, Calif.: The Saunders Studio Press, 1936), p. 12. John Pal claims that Du Yuesheng was a regular cabaret-goer and always got red-carpet treatment from the management. See his *Shanghai Saga* (London: Jarrolds, 1963), p. 116.

36. Cabarets were a central part of the American marine experience in Shanghai. For some examples, see *Walla Walla* (Magazine of the Fourth Marines in Shanghai) Apr. 22, 1933: 9; Feb. 17, 1934: 1; May 16, 1936: 22.

37. For a listing of such "third-class" establishments and their clientele in 1928, see SMP Files, reel 1, B-8632.

38. See Nicholas Clifford, *Spoilt Children of Empire*, pp. 194–97, for an account of the social changes wrought by the influx of foreign soldiers and sailors during the revolution.

39. Though numerous accounts of this alley exist, the most sordid by far is Ralph Shaw, *Sin City* (London: Futura, 1986), pp. 80–97. Shaw was a British navy man turned journalist who lived and worked in Shanghai during the Japanese occupation. Detailed eyewitness accounts of a large-scale fight in Blood Alley between British and Italian soldiers appears in SMP Files, reel 32, D-7808. Another interesting account is Jim Marshall, "Sad Sin in Shanghai," *Collier's*, July 10, 1937: 46–47.

40. SMP Files, reel 26, D-7073, an in-depth study of the case following the shooting of Japanese sailor Hideo Nakayama in November 1935, offers numerous details on the efforts of Ye Haisheng, a Red Gang member accused of murdering the Japanese sailor, to set up cabarets with a friend. Ye was the manager of the Moon Palace cabaret on Sichuan Road when the murder occurred. Mention of Green Gang involvement in cabarets appears in various sources, including SMP Files, reel 56, D-9319, a short dossier on Du Yuesheng that includes mention of his associate Gao Xingbao who managed the Lido Cabaret.

41. Tang Youfeng, *Xin Shanghai* (New Shanghai) (Shanghai: Shanghai yinshuguan, 1931), p. 138.

42. Lang Dang, "Qiekan haiyou shenme hao xuetou" (And look at what good gimmicks there are), under heading "Wushi xunyou" (Dance circuit news), *Libailiu*, Sept. 14, 1935: 139.

43. Chang Gong, "Wuchang renwu dian mingbu: jueshi xianshang de jingjizhe" (A roster of dance hall characters: skilled competitors on the jazz circuit), *Libailiu*, Sept. 7, 1935: 118–19.

44. Booker, *News Is My Job*, p. 238.

45. Edna Lee Booker claims that there were around 5,000 dancing hostesses working in Shanghai in the 1930s (*News Is My Job*, p. 238). While it is difficult to determine the exact number of women in the profession, SMP records suggest that by the early 1940s around 1,200 women were registered with licensed dance halls in the International Settlement, while many more worked in cafes, restaurants, bars, and unlicensed fly-by-night establishments. The total number of women fluctuated by year and season. For example, between October 1941 and May 1942, the total number of registered women fell to around 1,100 (Jan.) and then rose to over 1,300 (May). See SMP Files, reel 1, D-8/24.

46. The Chinese encyclopedia *Cihai* (Sea of words) (Taibei: Taiwan Zhonghua Shuju, 1969), 2: 3399, offers three definitions for this term: (1) a leader (*shouling*); (2) the top examination candidate, or *zhuangyuan*; and (3) a vessel for warming wine (*jiu-*

cheng). Perhaps the latter definition is the closest semantic source in this context, since dancing partners also served drinks.

47. Tang Youfen gives two definitions of *tuoche*: (1) patrons who cannot dance but are pushed around on the dance floor by their partners; (2) those who patronize a certain woman, serving as her "protector" and benefactor, and who dance but do not give out tickets. See Tang, *Xin Shanghai*, p. 139.

48. See, for example, SMP Files, reel 1, D-8/24, listing for the Vienna Gardens dance hall. Girls under the age of fifteen were prohibited from working in dance halls. See SMP regulations in SMP Files, reel 22, D-6583.

49. For example, Del Monte's and the Majestic, two well-known cabarets, required women to return home by appointed buses or lose their jobs. See Day, *Shanghai 1935*, p. 51.

50. "Shanghaitan zhi wunü" (Shanghai dancing hostesses), in Ke Zhaoyin and Zhuang Zhenxiang, eds., *Shanghaitan yeshi* (Shanghai unofficial history) (Nanjing: Jiangsu wenyi chubanshe, 1993), pp. 186–88.

51. [Bao] Tianxiao, "Tiaowu xuexiao" (The dancing school), *San wunü* (Three dancing hostesses), nos. 31–53, *Libao*, June 1–22, 1936.

52. *Libailiu*, Sept. 7, 1935: 119.

53. Percy Finch, *Shanghai and Beyond* (New York: Charles Scribner's Sons, 1953), pp. 303–4.

54. For example, see Booker, *News Is My Job*, pp. 236–38.

55. *Linglong* 1936: 163–67.

56. "Wan tiaowu menjing" (Guide to dancing) in "Wan de menjing" (Guide to playing), Wang Dingjiu, ed., *Shanghai menjing* (Guide to Shanghai) (Shanghai: Zhongyang shudian, 1932), pp. 9–17.

57. For an account of the bargaining powers and self-determination of courtesans, see Virgil Hit-yiu Ho, "Selling Smiles in Canton: Prostitution in the Early Republic," *East Asian History*, no. 5 (June 1993): 110–27.

58. Frederic Wakeman's analysis of the emergence of a new civic culture in modern Shanghai, in his "Licensing Leisure" and further elaborated in his book *Policing Shanghai*, has led me to rethink some of the views originally presented here. Nevertheless, although I agree with Wakeman's argument that government through the institution of the police exerted greater regulative capacities than ever before, I still believe that private and informal social dictums continued to serve important social functions in the public amusement sphere. For a similar study of the case of Canton, see Ho, "Selling Smiles," pp. 101–1.

59. The Shanghai Municipal Council in the 1920s made a series of attempts to curtail prostitution in the concessions. However, the government acts merely obscured the lines drawn between legitimate singing and dance halls and brothels. Several years of reforms and regulations banning organized prostitution only served to force such activities underground, making them more widespread and less easy to regulate. In the mid-1920s the municipal government finally admitted the failure of these policies, and again permitted brothels to operate. However, to save face the government required that such establishments call themselves "sing-song" houses, and licensed them upon the provision that they not allow their employees and patrons to remain on the premises overnight. See Gail Hershatter, "Regulating Sex in Shanghai: The Reform of Prostitution in 1920 and 1951," in Wakeman and Yeh, *Shanghai Sojourners*, pp. 151–66.

60. For a discussion of the collaborative attempts of the SMP and the PSB to prevent the spread of Communism in Shanghai through often brutal measures, see Wakeman, *Policing Shanghai*, pp. 132–61.

61. See SMP Files, reel 5, D-1801 for a case involving Russian cabaret girls who were Red agents.

62. See SMP Files, reel 1, D-8/24 for a case involving the Vienna Gardens ballroom, which sent a list containing what were later discovered to be two false addresses of Russian dancing hostesses. Unbeknownst to the police, who for political reasons concentrated on the Russians, several Chinese women also supplied false names and addresses.

63. In the SMP license for "Music Hall, Circus, Fair, Dancing Saloon, or Other Place of Public Entertainment," condition 6B stated that all "dancing saloons" were required to submit monthly lists of professional dancers to the Council. See SMP Files, reel 22, D-6583. For examples of such lists, see SMP Files, reel 1, D-8/24.

64. *Linglong* 1935: 1452.

65. Ibid., 1935: 965.

66. Ibid., 1935: 972–73.

67. Ibid., 1935: 1426–29.

68. According to one source, dancing hostesses put up a great fuss when such rules were instituted. Rules restricting women's leisure time might also reflect attempts by management to prevent ties from forming among the women. Steve Smith notes that social activities among women laborers in St. Petersburg and Shanghai, such as smoking, drinking, and bathroom chats, helped to forge bonds of solidarity against their employers. See Steve Smith, "Class and Gender: Women's Strikes in St. Petersburg, 1895–1917 and in Shanghai, 1895–1927," *Social History* 19, no. 2 (May 1994): 153–54.

69. For a discussion of the latter, see Wen-hsin Yeh, "Corporate Space, Communal Time: Everyday Life in Shanghai's Bank of China," *American Historical Review* 100, no. 1 (Feb. 1995): 97–122.

70. *Linglong* 1936: 3247.

71. Ke and Zhuang, *Shanghaitan yeshi*, p. 168.

72. A similar story appears in Booker, *News Is My Job*, pp. 236–38, in which the father of a country girl prevents her from going to Shanghai to become a dancing hostess by marrying her off to a gardener.

73. *Linglong* 1935: 831.

74. Ibid., 1935: 965–67.

75. Ibid., 1936: 3248.

76. Lei Zhusheng's *Shanghai huo diyu* (Shanghai: a living hell, 1929) is another example of a popular novel that revolves around the cabaret set. For an analysis of this novel, which fits somewhere in between the genres of butterfly novel and pornography, see Mark Elvin, "Tales of Shen and Xin: Body-Person and Heart-Mind in China During the Last 150 Years," *Zone: Fragments for a History of the Human Body*, no. 2 (1991): pp. 289–315.

77. Freuhauf, "Urban Exoticism," pp. 242–55. The following two stories are also from this source. For other analyses of these writers, presented in different groupings and analytic formats, see Randolph Trumbull, "The Shanghai Modernists," Ph.D. diss. (Stanford University, 1989); Yingjin Zhang, *The City in Modern Chinese Literature and Film: Configurations of Space, Time, and Gender* (Stanford: Stanford University Press, 1996). The first modern scholar to assess these writers as a whole is Yan Jiayan, who lays out a framework

for discussion and analysis upon which subsequent scholars have drawn; see his *Xin gan-jue pai xiaoshuo xuan* (A selection of new perceptionist writings) (Beijing: Renmin wenxue chubanshe, 1985), pp. 1–38.

78. For a discussion of the flaneur in the Chinese context, see Yingjin Zhang, "The Texture of the Metropolis: Modernist Inscriptions of Shanghai in the 1930s," and Yomi Braester, "Shanghai's Economy of the Spectacle: The Shanghai Race Club in Liu Na'ou's and Mu Shiying's Stories," *Modern Chinese Literature* 9 (1995): 19–20 and 46–47.

79. Mu Shiying, "Hei Mudan," *Liangyou*, no. 74 (Feb. 1933): 10–12, 28; reprinted in Mu Shiying, *Hei mudan* (Black peony) (Shanghai: Liangyou, 1934).

80. See Zhang Yingjin, *The City*, for a more involved discussion of the urban-rural dichotomy and its functions in modern Chinese literature and film.

81. See Bao Shiying, *Shanghai shi hang hao tutu lu* (Shanghai city business road map and record) (Shanghai: Fuli yingye gufen youxian gongsi, 1947), 1: 70, 86.

82. The film script for *A New Year's Coin*, complete with song lyrics, is published in *Zhongguo xin wenxue daxi, 1927–1937* (Anthology of modern Chinese literature) (Shanghai: Shanghai wenyi chubanshe, 1984), 18: 541–601. The song appears on p. 551.

83. Ibid., 18: 598.

84. *Liangyou*, no. 1 (Feb. 1926): 17.

85. Tian Ma, "Tiaowu shi yeman canhen" (Dancing is a scar left by barbarians), *Jingbao*, July 15, 1930, quoted in Tang, *Xin Shanghai*, pp. 140–41.

86. *Liangyou*, no. 64 (Dec. 1931): 42.

87. *Libailiu*, Sept. 4, 1935: 139.

88. Lu, "Gems from the Mosquito Press," p. 16.

89. Four of Xiao Jianqing's cartoons, taken from *Manhua Shanghai* (Shanghai: Jingwei shuju, 1935), appear in Wakeman, "Licensing Leisure," pp. 26–27.

90. Xiao Jianqing, *Shanghai xiangdao* (Shanghai guide) (Shanghai: Jingwei shuju, 1937), pp. 88–89.

91. Langman Shusheng, "Wuchang manhua (xia): Shanghai shehui texie zhi er" (Dance hall slow talk [cont.]: special writings on Shanghai society, number two), *Libailiu*, July 6, 1935: 958.

92. *New York Times*, Sept. 3, 1933: 6; Dec. 2, 1934: IV 8; Sept. 2, 1937: 3–5.

93. SMP Files, reel 13, D-4422.

94. Ibid., reel 48, D-8298/45.

95. Ibid., reel 62, N-615.

96. Joseph Levenson, *Confucian China and Its Modern Fate* (Berkeley: University of California Press, 1965).

97. See "Wunü tongda shehui ju" (Dancing hostesses attack the bureau of social affairs), in Ke and Zhuang, *Shanghai yeshi*, pp. 325–26.

CHAPTER SIX

I would like to thank my colleagues at the University of California–San Diego for both their support and critical acumen. Paul Pickowicz allowed me to view a number of movies in his collection and was pivotal in obtaining key sources. Zhiwei Xiao generously shared documents cited in his dissertation. Josh Goldstein and Madeline Yue Dong deserve thanks for nourishing my body, my sanity, and my intellect with fine food and even better dinner table conversations. Thanks to Perry Link, Carlton Benson, and Susan Fernsebner for helpful comments and suggestions on earlier versions of this essay. Finally, Dorothy Ko has been a constant source of criticism, inspiration, and encouragement. Of course, I alone bear full responsibility for all errors of fact or interpretation which remain.

1. The story of China's earliest film history is a well-worn one and needs no recounting here. See Jay Leyda, *Dianying / Electric Shadows: An Account of Films and the Film Audience in China* (Cambridge, Mass.: MIT Press, 1972); Cheng Jihua, Li Shaobai, and Xing Zuwen, *Zhongguo dianying fazhan shi* (A history of the development of Chinese cinema) (Beijing: Zhongguo dianying chuban she, 1980), 2 vols.; Du Yunzhi, *Zhonghua minguo dianying shi* (A history of film in the Republic of China) (Taibei: Xingzheng yuan wenhua jianshe weiyuanhui, 1988), 2 vols.; Bao Minglian, *Dongfang Haolaiwu: Zhongguo dianying shiye de jueqi yu fazhan* (The Hollywood of the East: the rise and development of the Chinese film industry) (Shanghai: Shanghai renmin chubanshe, 1991). On film censorship, see Xiao Zhiwei, "Film Censorship in China, 1927–1937," Ph.D. diss. (University of California–San Diego, 1994).

The most important developments were the introduction of lithographic printing technology and the proliferation of the pictorial format. See Perry Link, *Mandarin Ducks and Butterflies: Popular Fiction in Early Twentieth-Century Chinese Cities* (Berkeley: University of California Press, 1981), pp. 79–124; cf. also Ma Yunzeng et al., eds., *Zhongguo sheying shi, 1840–1937* (A history of Chinese photography) (Beijing: Zhongguo sheying chubanshe, 1987), pp. 282–88.

2. Cheng Weikun, "The Challenge of the Actresses: Female Performers and Cultural Alternatives in Early Twentieth Century Beijing and Tianjin," *Modern China* 22, no. 2 (Apr. 1996): 199; cf. also Dorothy Ko, *Teachers of the Inner Chambers: Women and Culture in Seventeenth-Century China* (Stanford: Stanford University Press, 1994), p. 77.

3. Feng Ge, "Funü yu dianying zhiye" (Women and the movie industry), *Funü zazhi* 13, no. 6 (June 1927): 9.

4. Ibid.

5. *Beiyang huabao*, Nov. 6, 1926: 3; Nov. 13, 1926: 3.

6. Hayden White, *Tropics of Discourse: Essays in Cultural Criticism* (Baltimore: Johns Hopkins University Press, 1978), p. 3. Emphasis in original.

7. Christian Henriot has argued, "a status-dominated society was increasingly replaced by a money-dominated society. The growing commercialization of the local economy combined with the restructuring of the various social strata—in particular the emergence of middle-class urbanites—caused a general decline of the role and status of courtesans. It generated the development of more original forms of prostitution, even if all became more homogeneous in their function. They merely provided sexual services. Whereas sex continued to be a marketable commodity, the kind of female companionship courtesans once provided did not." See her "'From a Throne of Glory to a Seat of Ignominy': Shanghai Prostitution Revisited (1849–1949)," *Modern China* 22, no. 2 (Apr. 1996): 134.

8. Gong Jia'nong, *Gong Jia'nong congying huiyi lu* (Gong Jia'nong's recollections of his film career) (Taibei: Zhuanji wenxue zazhi she, 1980), 1: 13.

9. By identifying Wang Hanlun and Yang Naimei as two of China's "first generation"

actresses, I am making a simple claim of *representativeness* and am in no way making any claims to full *comprehensiveness*. Wang Hanlun and Yang Naimei do not define, but merely represent, China's "first generation" of female movie stars. Nor can either of them be called *the* first female film star in China. As mentioned earlier in this volume, Zhong Dafeng identifies Yin Mingzhu as China's *first* female film star. This issue of singular origins, however, is not a concern of mine in writing this essay.

10. Wang was born into a well-to-do family from Suzhou in 1903 as Peng Jianqing. Her father was well educated and had once served as the superintendent of the Manufacturing Bureau (*zhizao ju*) in Anhui province's Bureau of Commerce (*zhaoshang ju*). She attended St. Mary's School in Shanghai until the age of sixteen, when her father died. At this point she was forced to abandon her studies due to financial difficulties, and her sister-in-law arranged for her to marry. Later, Peng Jianqing followed her new husband to Shanghai where he worked as a comprador for a Japanese *hong*. Soon afterwards, he began to hit her and she quickly divorced him. Her brother and sister-in-law disapproved of her divorce and offered no moral or financial support. Left to her own wits, Peng studied typing and English at night for three months and eventually took a typist's job at the "Four Brights" *hong*. See Wang Hanlun, "Yingtan huiyi lu" (Recollections of the film world), *Liangyou* (The young companion), no. 64 (Dec. 1931): 32–33, and "Wo de congying jingguo" (My experience in the film industry), in *Gankai hua dangnian* (Sighing about those years) (Beijing: Zhongguo dianying chubanshe, 1962), pp. 50–59; Yang Cun, *Zhongguo dianying yanyuan cangsang lu* (Biographic sketches of Chinese film actors and actresses) (Hong Kong: Shijie chubanshe, 1955); Gong Jia'nong, *Gong Jia'nong*, 1: 13–15.

11. Like Wang Hanlun, Yang Naimei came from a well-to-do family. She was the daughter of a wealthy Cantonese businessman and attended Shanghai's elite Wuben Girls' School (Wuben nü zhongxue) where she was a paragon of popularity. She met the Mingxing founder and screenwriter Zheng Zhengqiu through the school's drama group. See Gong Jia'nong, *Gong Jia'nong*, 1: 109–126; Yang Cun, *Zhongguo dianying sanian* (Thirty years of Chinese film) (Hong Kong: Shijie chubanshe, 1954), pp. 31–34.

12. Gong Jia'nong, *Gong Jia'nong*, 1: 89–90.

13. Alvin Kernan, *The Death of Literature* (New Haven: Yale University Press, 1990), pp. 170–71.

14. Wang Hanlun, "Yingtan huiyi lu," p. 32.

15. An exact replica of the movie's set was built, and Yang donned the same costume that she wore in the film. When the designated scene appeared on screen, the lights of the Central Theater came on, the screen was raised, and Yang sang "Song of the Floating Girl" (Funiang qü). After her performance, the screen was lowered, the lights dimmed, and the silent movie would run to its end. See Gong Jia'nong, *Gong Jia'nong*, 1: 113–14.

16. Ibid., p. 116. In the early days of Chinese films, there were no credits for the actresses. It was difficult for fans to write letters to an actress they saw in a movie. Usually someone would send a letter to the studio asking them to forward it on to "that woman who wore XX in this movie." Rarely would the studio pass on the letters, for fear that actresses would ask for a raise given these extra duties of tending to fan mail. See Liu Guojun, *Cong xiao yatou dao da mingxing: Ruan Lingyu zhuan* (From maid to star: the biography of Ruan Lingyu) (Chengdu: Sichuan wenyi chubanshe, 1986), p. 80.

17. Yang Cun, *Zhongguo dianying sanian*, pp. 32–33.

18. Gong Jia'nong, *Gong Jia'nong*, 1: 121–23.

19. Ibid., p. 111.

20. Ibid.

21. These initial views are tentative as I have not been able to see any fan magazines from the 1920s. See note 47.

22. Elizabeth Wilson, *The Sphinx in the City: Urban Life, the Control of Disorder and Women* (Berkeley: University of California Press, 1991), pp. 3–7.

23. Such notions were also based upon demographic realities. Far more men than women migrated to Shanghai, and the ratio of men to women in the Chinese-governed sectors of the city during the early 1930s ran somewhere around 135:100. And as Gail Hershatter has noted, "Republican-period social reformers were fond of pointing out that the predominance of unattached men in the urban population increased the demand for commercial sexual services." See her "The Hierarchy of Shanghai Prostitution, 1870–1949," *Modern China* 15, no. 4 (Oct. 1989): 465.

24. Yingjin Zhang, "Engendering Chinese Filmic Discourse of the 1930s: Configurations of Modern Women in Shanghai in Three Silent Films," *Positions* 2, no. 3 (Winter 1994): 603–28.

25. Rao Yu, *Shi Zhecun, Mu Shiying, Liu Na'ou xiaoshuo xinxiang* (Appreciating the fiction of Shi Zhecun, Mu Shiying, and Liu Na'ou) (Nanning: Guangxi jiaoyu chubanshe, 1992).

26. "Shanghai Foxtrot" was published in 1932 as the first segment of a larger but unfinished novel entitled *China, 1931* (*Zhongguo 1931*). See Rao Yu, *Shi Zhecun*, pp. 171–83; cf. also Yomi Braester, "Shanghai's Economy of the Spectacle: The Shanghai Race Club in Liu Na'ou's and Mu Shiying's Stories," *Modern Chinese Literature* 9, no. 1 (Spring 1995): 37.

27. Zhu Qiang, "Dianju yuanzhong" (In the movie theater), *Xin Shanghai* 1, no. 8 (Dec. 1925): 95–100.

28. These were called *shuoming shu* and were usually written in classical Chinese.

29. Huo Xueyin, "Dianying mingxing" (Movie star), *Xin Shanghai* 1, no. 9 (Jan. 1926): 9–13.

30. Ding Ling, "Mengke" (Mengke), *Xiaoshuo yuebao* (Fiction monthly) 18, no. 12 (Dec. 1927): 11–35.

31. Feng Ge, "Funü yu dianying zhiye," p. 10.

32. Wang Hanlun, "Wo de congying jingguo," p. 53.

33. Feng Ge, "Funü yu dianying zhiye," p. 10.

34. Emily Honig, *Sisters and Strangers: Women in the Shanghai Cotton Mills, 1919–1949* (Stanford: Stanford University Press, 1986), pp. 76–77.

35. *Liangyou*, no. 2 (Mar. 1926), no. 30 (Sept. 1928), no. 31 (Oct. 1928), no. 40 (Dec. 1929), no. 44 (Apr. 1930), no. 60 (Aug. 1931).

36. *Liangyou*, no. 30 (Sept. 1928): 24–25, no. 56 (Apr. 1931): 30, no. 62 (Oct. 1931): 36.

37. Leyda, *Dianying*, pp. 29–36. For the influence of the Commercial Press on publishing, see Link, *Mandarin Ducks*, pp. 85–88; Christopher Reed, "Gutenberg in Shanghai: Mechanized Printing, Modern Publishing, and Their Effects on the City, 1876–1937," Ph.D. diss. (University of California–Berkeley, 1997).

38. Xi Shen, "Shanghai zhi dianying shiye" (The Shanghai film industry), *Xin Shanghai* 1, no. 1 (May 1925): 71; cf. also Yang Cun, *Zhongguo dianying sanian*, p. 15.

39. For a complete list, see Gan Yazi (Atsu Kann) and Chen Dingxiu (D. S. Chen),

eds., *Zhonghua yingye nianjian 1927* (China cinema yearbook) (Shanghai: Zhonghua yingye nianjian she, 1927), pp. 3–25.

40. Xiao Zhiwei, "Film Censorship," p. 42.

41. Wang Hanlun retired in 1928 at the age of 26 after five years of making movies. She married a Frenchman and opened the Hanlun Beauty Salon (Hanlun meirong yuan) in the French Concession. See Gong Jia'nong, *Gong Jia'nong*, 1: 14; Wang Hanlun, "Wo de congying jingguo," p. 58. The end of Yang Naimei's acting career was much less decisive than that of Wang Hanlun. Soon after establishing the Naimei Film Company in 1928, Yang Naimei became addicted to opium. Within two years she lost hundreds of thousands of yuan. Finally, no studio would hire her, and she was reduced to joining Gu Wuwei's "Great China Drama Troupe" in Nanjing, where she was paid a few hundred yuan for her choppy Mandarin performances. This was hardly enough to support the lifestyle Yang Naimei was used to living. After Gu turned down her request for a raise, Yang returned to Shanghai and married a wealthy Cantonese businessman. They fled to Hong Kong during the war and then to Taibei where she died in 1949. See Gong Jia'nong, *Gong Jia'nong*, 1: 123–26.

42. Hu Die was born in 1907 as Hu Ruihua to a well-to-do Cantonese family living in Shanghai. After Hu's father became the general inspector (*zong jicha*) for the Beiping-Fengtian Railroad, the family moved north, first to Beiping where Hu Ruihua attended two or three years of elementary school, then to Tianjin in 1915 where Hu attended the Shenggong Catholic school. In 1924 the Hu family moved once again, this time back to Shanghai where Hu Ruihua entered the Wuben Girls' School, which Yang Naimei had also attended. Soon after returning to Shanghai, Hu left school due to financial difficulties. See Cheng Shu'an, ed., *Zhongguo dianying yanyuan cidian* (Dictionary of Chinese movie actors and actresses) (Beijing: Zhongguo guangbo dianshi chubanshe, 1992), pp. 344–46; cf. also Hu Die with Liu Huiqin, *Hu Die huiyi lu* (The reminiscences of Hu Die) (Taibei: Lianhe bao chubanshe, 1986).

43. The China Film Academy, located on Prince Edward Road, was founded by Zeng Huantang and financed by Huang Chujiu. The school only graduated one class before closing due to financial difficulties. The six-month curriculum included watching two foreign films per week. Three hours of classes were held every day (including the history of modern Western drama, general cinematographic knowledge, directing, general screenwriting, song and dance training, and so on). See Hu Die, *Hu Die huiyi lu*, pp. 9–13.

44. Ruan Lingyu was born in April 1910 as Ruan Fenggeng into a working-class Cantonese household in Shanghai. Her father, Ruan Yongrong, was a machinist. He died in 1916, leaving the family in financial straits. Ruan's young mother went to work as a domestic. In 1918 Ruan entered the Chongde Girls' School (Chongde nü xuexiao). In 1925, at the age of sixteen, Ruan, who had now changed her name to Lingyü, met Zhang Damin, the sixth scion of Shanghai's wealthy Zhang family on Haining Road. Within months Ruan had left school and was living with Zhang in an apartment on North Sichuan Road. See Cheng Shu'an, *Zhongguo dianying*, pp. 97–98; Shu Qi et al., *Ruan Lingyu shenhua* (The legend of Ruan Lingyu) (Hong Kong: Chuangjian chuban gongsi, 1992), pp. 33–48; cf. also Liu Guojun, *Cong xiao yatou*.

45. These included *San'ge modeng nüxing* (Three modern women, 1933), *Little Toys* (1933), *Goddess* (1934), and *New Woman* (1935).

46. See Cheng Jihua, et al., *Zhongguo dianying fazhan shi*.

47. The earliest film magazines were overwhelmingly sponsored and published by movie studios themselves. Thus many of these early magazines were simply straightforward advertising. However, by the 1930s film magazines were becoming more and more autonomous. See Xiao Zhiwei, "Film Censorship," pp. 23–24. The bulk of my evidence in the following sections is drawn from the 1934 and 1935 editions of *Qingqing dianying*, which was published from 1934–48 in Shanghai. I would like to thank Paul Pickowicz for providing me with microfilmed copies of *Qingqing dianying*. Unfortunately, I was unable to view copies of a 1926–27 fan magazine called *Xin yinxing yü tiyu* (Silverland) held in Cornell University's Wason Collection.

48. Approximately 400 knight-errant–style movies were produced by some 50 or so Shanghai movie studios between 1928 and 1930. See Hu Die, *Hu Die huiyi lu*, p. 51.

49. Li Jinhui was a music teacher from Changsha, Hunan. He went to work for Shanghai's China Bookstore (Zhonghua shuju) in 1921 as an editor in the textbook department. In 1922 he became the head of the newly established "national language" literature department (*guoyu wenxue bu*) and was the editor-in-chief of a popular children's magazine called *Small Friends* (*Xiao pengyou*), which was meant to promote the national language. It was through his work at the China Bookstore that Li became involved in the movement to promote a "national language" (*guoyu*) and began to teach at Shanghai's School for Training in National Language (Guoyu zhuanxiu xuexiao). See Wang Renmei with Xie Bo, *Wode chengming yu buxing: Wang Renmei huiyi lu* (My rise to fame and misfortune: the reminiscences of Wang Renmei) (Shanghai: Shanghai wenyi chubanshe, 1985), pp. 24, 42–44.

50. Ibid., p. 46. After Li organized the China Song and Dance Society in May 1927, Gezhuan students spent half of their day on studies, and the other half on rehearsals for performances. While it would be easy to label these arrangements as exploitative, those who were part of Gezhuan and the troupes that were later organized by Li Jinhui did not seem to feel that they were being victimized. See "Mingyue gewu tuan yu bense pai yanji—Wang Renmei, Li Lili fanwen ji" (The Mingyue song and dance troupe and the *bense pai* acting technique—an interview with Wang Renmei and Li Lili), *Zhongguo dianying yanjiu* 1 (Dec. 1983): 131.

51. Wang Renmei, *Wode chengming*, pp. 42–46. The China Song and Dance Troupe left for a ten-month tour of Southeast Asia in May 1928. Cf. also "Mingyue gewu tuan yu bense pai yanji—Wang Renmei, Li Lili fanwen ji," p. 131.

52. Zhao Shihui, "Mingyue zhaxian yue xingguang, gewu bianping zhuan yankong," *Shijie zhoukan*, Dec. 18, 1994: S9.

53. Wang Renmei, *Wode chengming*, pp. 84–85.

54. Ibid., p. 102.

55. Hu Die won in a landslide, garnering 21,334 votes. The first and second runners-up were Chen Yumei and Ruan Lingyu, who respectively received 10,028 and 7,290 votes. See Shen Feide, "1933 nian Hu Die dangxuan 'Dianying huanghou' shengkuang" (The grand spectacle of Hu Die's election as "Movie Queen"), *Minguo chunqiu* (Mar. 1993): 16. As for the election process, one ballot slip would be included in every copy of *Mingxing Daily* for one month from January 1–30, 1933; thus, one had to buy a paper in order to cast a vote. The organizers of the gala coronation ceremony held on March 28, 1933, at the Grand Shanghai Ballroom (Da Hu wuting) on West Nanjing Road, were the editor Feng Mengyun; the publisher/songwriter Chen Dieyi; and the publisher Mao Zipei. In addi-

tion to film world glitterati and papparazzi, the star-studded guest list also included the mayor of Shanghai, Wu Tiecheng; the head of Shanghai's social bureau, Pan Gongzhan; and, of course, a representative of Du Yuesheng, head of Shanghai's Green Gang. Tickets cost one yuan each and all proceeds went to the Chinese Air Force Defense Movement. See Mao Zipei, "Wei yinghou Hu Die 'jia mian'" (A crowning for the movie queen Hu Die), *Shanghai wenshi* 3 (Apr. 1990): 33. I'd like to thank Zhiwei Xiao for making me aware of these materials.

56. Hu attended a Nazi-sponsored event while in Berlin and refused to proceed until a Chinese national flag was raised alongside the NSDAP flag. Hu also refused to buy any clothes or cosmetics while in Paris in order to show her support for Chinese products. See Zhang Ruoyu, "Hu Die koushu Ouzhou youzong" (Hu Die recounts her footsteps through Europe), *Shidai huabao* 8, no. 3 (July 20, 1935): 5–6.

57. For an account of her return to Shanghai, see "Ying Hu Die Zhou Jianyun guiguo" (Welcoming Hu Die and Zhou Jianyun back from abroad) and "Hu Die huiguo huaxu" (Tidbits on Hu Die's homecoming), *Qingqing dianying* 2, no. 4 (June 1935): no pagination. Only one day after her return, Shanghai's *Shidai huabao* (Times pictorial) hustled Hu away for an exclusive interview. See Zhang Ruoyu, "Hu Die koushu," pp. 5–6.

58. "Hu Die huiguo huaxu."

59. Hu Die, *Ou you zaji* (Miscellaneous notes on a European journey) (Shanghai: Liangyou, 1936). The book was a best-seller and went into a second printing within four months (see the imprint of the 1936 edition). This book was actually put down on paper after Hu Die had dictated her recollections to a ghostwriter (see William Tay, personal communication, Spring 1995).

60. A Ling, "Nü mingxing de xingyun" (The lucky female stars), *Dianying yuekan* 26 (1933): 31.

61. *Qingqing dianying* 2, no. 2 (Apr. 1935): no pagination. At the time of her death, Ruan was studying Mandarin every day from 2–6 P.M. with Professor Du Huamin. See Liu Guojun, *Cong xiao yatou*, p. 71.

62. A Ling, "Nü mingxing de xingyun," p. 31.

63. *Qingqing dianying* 1, no. 7 (Sept. 1934): no pagination.

64. *Qingqing dianying* 1, no. 12 (Feb. 1935): no pagination.

65. "Er ke liang jingjing de mingxing" (Two glittering stars), *Qingqing dianying* 2, no. 2 (Apr. 1935): no pagination.

66. "Mei Lin nüshi de sheying zuopin" (Ms. Mei Lin's photographic artwork), *Qingqing dianying* 2, no. 2 (Apr. 1935): no pagination.

67. Dorothy Ko has noted that during the late Ming "it became customary for female entertainers to appear as guests in parties held at literati homes. There is some indication that the more sophisticated of these women were invited not just as entertainers but as artistic equals." See her *Teachers of the Inner Chambers*, p. 256. Cf. also Katherine Carlitz, "Desire, Danger, and the Body: Stories of Women's Virtue in Late Ming China," in Christina K. Gilmartin et al., eds., *Engendering China: Women, Culture, and the State* (Cambridge, Mass.: Harvard University Press, 1994), p. 117.

68. Henriot, "From a Throne of Glory," p. 138.

69. Wang Hanlun, "Wo de congying jingguo," p. 56.

70. "Mingxing xinxiang" (Mailbox of the stars), *Qingqing dianying* 2, no. 1 (Mar. 1935): no pagination.

71. Ibid.

72. "Yingmi de baichi" (The foolishness of movie fans), *Qingqing dianying* 1, no. 10 (Dec. 1934): no pagination.

73. Liu Guojun, *Cong xiao yatou*, p. 63.

74. Li Sha, "Yingcheng binfen ji" (Movie world miscellany), *Qingqing dianying* 2, no. 2 (Apr. 1935): no pagination.

75. Zhu Ping, "Duzhe lai gao: yingmi suibi" (A reader's contribution: notes of a movie fan), *Qingqing dianying* 2, no. 7 (Sept. 1935): no pagination.

76. "Wo xiang: wo shi renshi le tamen ma?" (Do I think that I know them?), *Qingqing dianying* 1, no. 5 (July 1934): no pagination.

77. Lianhua's famed director Sun Yu would actually accompany the newly named Lianhua Song and Dance Group on their tours to Nanjing in order to become more familiar with the various actresses' personalities. After observing the former Bright Moon actresses closely, Sun would write his scripts with a certain actress in mind and tailor the roles in his screenplays to these actresses' personalities. See Wang Renmei, *Wode chengming*, p. 103. For Sun's discussion of those performers "whose own personalities mesh with characters in the screenplay" and those who were able to "act out and portray" various characters on screen, see Sun Yu, "Dianying daoyan lun" (On movie directors), *Qingqing dianying* 2, no. 1 (Mar. 1935): no pagination.

78. Wang Renmei, *Wode chengming*, pp. 108–9.

79. *Qingqing dianying* 1, no. 7 (Sep. 1934): no pagination.

80. "Yingmi de baichi."

81. *Qingqing dianying* 1, no. 12 (Feb. 1935): no pagination.

82. *Qingqing dianying* 2, no. 2 (Apr. 1935): no pagination.

83. "Zheli dou shi nimen renshi de huaidan—Zhongguo yingtan shang de si ge huaidan" (Here are the villains you all know—the four bastards of Chinese film), *Qingqing dianying* 1, no. 10 (Dec. 1934): no pagination.

84. See "Nü mingxing yitian de shenghuo—cong zaochen dao yewan" (One day in the life of a movie actress from morning until night), *Qingqing dianying* 2, no. 1 (Mar. 1935): no pagination; "Li Lili de si shenghuo" (Li Lili's private life), *Qingqing dianying* 1, no. 12 (Feb. 1935): no pagination.

85. Li Sha, "Zhongguo yintan mingxing dengci biao" (A ranked table of China's silver stars), *Qingqing dianying fu kan hao*, no. 1 (Mar. 1937): no pagination.

86. I have pieced together the following account of Ruan's suicide from a number of sources: *Shenbao*, Mar. 9, 1935: 11, Mar. 10, 1935: 13; *Xin ye bao* (New evening news), Mar. 9, 1935: 1; *Dagong bao* (L'Impartial), Mar. 9, 1935: 1; Liu Guojun, *Cong xiao yatou*, pp. 102, 107–12.

87. Altogether there are two sets of suicide notes attributed to Ruan—one "spurious," one "authentic." Each set contains a letter to Zhang Damin (her estranged husband) and a letter to Tang Jishan. Unfortunately, I do not have the space to include my translations of them here. The "spurious" letters were published in *Lianhua huabao* on Mar. 11 and 13, 1935. For the texts of all four letters, see Liu Guojun, *Cong xiao yatou*, pp. 116–21.

88. Hundreds of people, mostly women, gathered and refused to go home when policemen ordered them to disperse (see *Xin ye bao*, Mar. 9, 1935: 1). On March 11 some

10,000 to 20,000 mourners turned out for Ruan's viewing and caused a traffic jam, to the dismay of the foreign and Chinese policemen who had been sent to keep order. Once again the majority of these mourners were women, especially female students (see *Shenbao*, Mar. 12, 1935: 12). Two thousand mourners attended Ruan's burial on March 14, but a sea of people lined the streets to watch the funeral procession, which again interrupted regular traffic (see *Xin ye bao*, Mar. 14, 1935: 1).

89. "Ruan Lingyü zhi lueli" (A brief history of Ruan Lingyü), *Qingqing dianying* 2, no. 1 (Mar. 1935): no pagination; cf. also *Yiren Ruan Lingyu nushi rong'ai lu* (An elegiac record for the artist Ms. Ruan Lingyü), 1935.

90. "Ruan Lingyü si hou . . . ," *Dagong bao*, Mar. 14, 1935: 4. Various theories held that Ruan was ashamed to appear in court or that she had been influenced by the tragic characters that she played, especially the protagonist of *New Woman*, Wei Ming, who also committed suicide. See Shu Qi et al., *Ruan Lingyu shenhua*, p. 46.

91. *Xin ye bao*, Mar. 9, 1935, p. 1.

92. May-lee Chai, "Urban Divorce and the Divorce Debate in Republican-era China" (M.A. thesis, Yale University, 1992), pp. 1–3.

93. We can be assured of Ruan's and Tang's genuine feelings for each other because Ruan was making 700 to 1,000 yuan a month at the time and did not need Tang's financial support. Moreover, Tang was no longer the dashing young man he used to be. See Liu Guojun, *Cong xiao yatou*, pp. 84, 91.

94. Ibid., p. 92. See also Chai, "Urban Divorce," p. 1.

95. For the complete document, see Liu Guojun, *Cong xiao yatou*, pp. 93–94.

96. Ibid., pp. 101–2.

97. *Qingqing dianying* 1, no. 7 (Sept. 1934): no pagination.

98. Zhao Lingyi (Lu Xun), "Lun renyan kewei" (Gossip is fearful), *Taibai* 2, no. 5 (May 20, 1935).

99. Zhu Ping, "Jiashi de hua" (If . . .), *Qingqing dianying* 2, no. 4 (June 1935): no pagination.

100. Wu Kaisheng, "Die ying huaxiang liu renjian," p. 34.

101. Hershatter, "The Hierarchy of Shanghai Prostitution," p. 467.

102. "Tan Ying da Cheng Bugao yao hao de lai . . . " (Tan Ying meets and seduces Cheng Bugao . . .), *Qingqing dianying* 1, no. 5 (July 1934): no pagination.

103. Ibid.

104. Zhu Ping, "Jiashi de hua."

105. Li Lili, Wang Renmei, Hu Die, and Hu Ping were all rated "first class." Tan Ying, Xu Lai, and Li Minghui were rated "second class." Lan Ping (later known as Jiang Qing or Madame Mao Zedong) was rated "third class." Ruan Lingyü was not included, probably because she was already dead. See Li Sha, "Zhongguo yintan."

CHAPTER SEVEN

An earlier version of this essay was presented at the Faculty Seminar of the Center for Chinese Studies at the University of Michigan, Ann Arbor, in September 1995.

1. Burton Pike, *The Image of the City in Modern Literature* (Princeton: Princeton University Press, 1981), pp. 6–7; see also William Sharpe, *Unreal Cities: Urban Figuration*

in Wordsworth, Baudelaire, Whitman, Eliot, and Williams (Baltimore: Johns Hopkins University Press, 1990), pp. 1–15.

2. Prostitution was noted as early as the Shang dynasty (1523–1028 B.C.). As its Chinese etymology suggests, a *chang* (prostitute) is a female performer skilled in music, singing, and dancing and employed in service for male pleasure. See Xin Ren, "China," in Nanette J. Davis, ed., *Prostitution: An International Handbook on Trends, Problems, and Policies* (Westport, Conn.: Greenwood Press, 1993), p. 88.

3. Gail Hershatter, *Dangerous Pleasures: Prostitution and Modernity in Twentieth-Century Shanghai* (Berkeley: University of California Press, 1997), p. 4.

4. Charles Bernheimer, *Figures of Ill Repute: Representing Prostitution in Nineteenth-Century France* (Cambridge, Mass.: Harvard University Press, 1989), p. 1.

5. For the concept of the public sphere, see Jürgen Habermas, *The Structural Transformation of the Public Sphere: An Inquiry into a Category of Bourgeois Society*, trans. Thomas Burger (Cambridge, Mass.: MIT Press, 1989). On the China side, William Rowe argues that "the urban teahouse and wine shop, in all their varieties, were at least available to serve the same catalytic function in the fostering of popular critical debate of public issues that is routinely attributed to the early modern European cafe and coffee house" ("The Problem of 'Civil Society' in Late Imperial China," *Modern China* 19, no. 2 [Apr. 1993]: 146). For a discussion of late Qing literati gathering in houses of prostitution and commenting on politics, see Yu Xingmin, *Shanghai, 1862 nian* (Shanghai, 1862) (Shanghai: Shanghai renmin chubanshe, 1991), pp. 420–27.

6. For a description of his first experience with the flower boat at the age of eight, see Bao Tianxiao, *Chuanying lou huiyi lu* (Reminiscences of the Bracelet Shadow Chamber) (Hong Kong: Dahua chubanshe, 1971, 1973), 1: 47. In the second volume of his memoir, written at the age of 98, Bao recounts in detail what he calls a trilogy—his three-step sexual experience, for a price of 100 yuan, with a young, blond-haired foreign prostitute in the Eastern Hotel in Beijing (ibid., 2: 144–46).

7. See Yu, *Shanghai*, pp. 426–27. Due to the efforts of Wang Tao and other romantic literati of his type, promoting famous prostitutes became a fashionable practice in late Qing magazines and tabloids. In 1897, for instance, many Shanghai residents were involved in the election of the top-listed prostitutes (*kai huabang*) by way of casting their votes in *Youxi bao* (Play magazine). See Xu Min, "Shi, chang, you—wan Qing Shanghai shehui shenghuo yipie" (Literatus, prostitute, actor: a glimpse of social life in late Qing Shanghai), *Ershiyi shiji* (Twenty-first century), no. 23 (June 1994): 37–38.

8. In addition to Hershatter's *Dangerous Pleasures*, see Sue Gronewold, *Beautiful Merchandise: Prostitution in China, 1860–1936* (New York: Haworth Press, 1982); Christian Henriot, "Chinese Courtesans in Late Qing and Early Republican Shanghai (1849–1925)," *East Asian History* 8 (Dec. 1994): 33–52, and "'From a Throne of Glory to a Seat of Ignominy': Shanghai Prostitution Revisited (1849–1949)," *Modern China* 22, no. 2 (Apr. 1996): 132–63.

9. See Gail Hershatter, "Modernizing Sex, Sexing Modernity: Prostitution in Early Twentieth-Century Shanghai," in Christina K. Gilmartin, Gail Hershatter, Lisa Rofel, and Tyrene White, eds., *Engendering China: Woman, Culture, and the State* (Cambridge, Mass.: Harvard University Press, 1994), pp. 147–74.

10. Gronewold, *Beautiful Merchandise*, p. 36.

11. See Hershatter, "Modernizing Sex," p. 157.

12. Virgil Kit-yiu Ho, "Selling Smiles in Canton: Prostitution in the Early Republic," *East Asian History* no. 5 (June 1993): 107–27. At one point, Ho goes so far as to suggest that, "from the point of view of 'poor' brothel-goers, it was they who were 'exploited' by prostitutes in this long process of financially exhausting courtship" (ibid., p. 112).

13. Ibid., p. 127.

14. Ibid., p. 101.

15. Ibid., p. 120.

16. Henriot, "Chinese Courtesans," p. 51.

17. Henriot, " 'From a Throne of Glory,' " p. 133.

18. Hershatter, "A Response," *Modern China* 22, no. 2 (Apr. 1996): 165. For more elaboration on the historian's self-reflexive strategy of knowing and storytelling, see Hershatter, *Dangerous Pleasures*, esp. pp. 3–39.

19. For example, the December 1915 issue of *The Grand Magazine* featured the photographs of prostitutes in Shanghai, Beijing, Tianjin, Hangzhou, and Jiangshan (see *Xiaoshuo daguan*, ed. Bao Tianxiao [Shanghai: Zhonghua shuju], no. 4, illustration pages). In May 1924, *The Half-Moon Journal* carried a special issue on prostitution, in which practical aspects of prostitution in the cities of Beijing and Jiujiang are enumerated (e.g., Jiujiang's six classes of prostitutes and their market prices), and several literati's couplets based on the prostitutes' professional names (e.g., "Winter Lotus Seed" and "Golden Scent") are printed (see *Banyue*, ed. Zhou Shoujuan [Shanghai: Dadong shuju], 3, no. 16: a special issue on prostitution, no pagination). For more connections between the literati and the prostitute in late Qing Shanghai, see Xu Min, "Shi, chang, you"; for classification of Shanghai prostitutes, see Gail Hershatter, "The Hierarchy of Shanghai Prostitution, 1870–1949," *Modern China* 15, no. 4 (Oct. 1989): 463–98.

20. See *Huitu youli Shanghai zaji* (An illustrated guidebook to Shanghai with miscellaneous notes) (Shanghai: Wenbao shuju, 1906); *Shanghai zhinan* (Guide to Shanghai), 10th and expanded ed. (Shanghai: Shangwu, 1919; first ed. in 1909); Wang Dingjiu, ed., *Shanghai menjing* (Guide to Shanghai), 4th ed. (Shanghai: Zhongyang shuju, 1935; first ed. in 1932). Definitely not a writer of the tabloid type, Wang Dingjiu edited these anthologies of high literary quality: *Dangdai nüzuojia suibi* (Occasional writings by contemporary women writers), *Dangdai nüzuojia sanwen* (Prose essays by contemporary women writers), and *Dangdai nüzuojia shuxin* (Correspondences by contemporary women writers), all published by Shanghai's Zhongyang shuju in 1935.

21. See Shanghaitong she (Society of Shanghai experts), ed., *Shanghai yanjiu ziliao* (Research materials on Shanghai) (Taibei: Zhongguo chubanshe, 1973), pp. 578–608.

22. See Perry Link, *Mandarin Ducks and Butterflies: Popular Fiction in Early Twentieth-Century Chinese Cities* (Berkeley: University of California Press, 1981); Ts'un-yan Liu, ed., *Chinese Middlebrow Fiction: From the Ch'ing and Early Republican Eras* (Hong Kong: Chinese University Press, 1984), pp. 1–40.

23. Han's novel *Haishang hua liezhuan* (Sing-song girls of Shanghai) was written and published in 1892 in installments in a magazine he practically edited in the houses of prostitution (see Liu, *Chinese Middlebrow Fiction*, pp. 11–18). For a reprint of the novel, see *Zhongguo jindai wenxue daxi* (Anthology of early modern Chinese literature) (Shanghai: Shanghai shudian, 1991), 3: 153–648. For sample critical studies, see David Wang, *Fin-de-Siècle Splendor: Repressed Modernities of Late Qing Fiction, 1849–1911* (Stanford: Stanford University Press, 1997), pp. 89–101; Yingjin Zhang, *The City in Modern Chinese Literature*

and Film: Configurations of Space, Time, and Gender (Stanford: Stanford University Press, 1996), pp. 118–23.

24. Lu Xun (Lu Hsun), *Selected Works of Lu Hsun*, trans. Yang Hsien-yi and Gladys Yang (Peking: Foreign Languages Press, 1959), 3: 115.

25. Suopo Sheng (Bi Yihong) and Bao Tianxiao, *Renjian diyu* (Human hell) (Shanghai: Shanghai guji chubanshe, 1991), vols. 1–2; Bao Tianxiao, *Shanghai chunqiu* (Shanghai chronicles) (Shanghai: Shanghai guji chubanshe, 1991), vols. 1–2.

26. For details, see Dafeng Zhong, Zhen Zhang, and Yingjin Zhang, "From *Wenmingxi* (Civilized Play) to *Yingxi* (Shadowplay): The Foundation of Shanghai Film Industry in the 1920s," *Asian Cinema* 9, no. 1 (Fall 1997): 46–64.

27. See Cheng Jihua, Li Shaobai, and Xing Zuwen, eds., *Zhongguo dianying fazhan shi* (A history of the development of Chinese cinema) (Beijing: Zhongguo dianying chubanshe, 1981), 1: 18–19, 43–45, 64–70.

28. See Tang Chunfa, *Kai yidai xianhe—Zhongguo dianying zhifu Zheng Zhengqiu* (Opening a new road—Zheng Zhengqiu, the father of Chinese cinema) (Beijing: Guoji wenhua chuban gongsi, 1992), pp. 333–38. See also Xuan Jinglin's own recollection, reprinted in Dai Xiaolan, ed., *Zhongguo wusheng dianying* (Chinese silent films) (Beijing: Zhongguo dianying chubanshe, 1996), p. 1485.

29. The plot sheet (*shuoming shu*) distributed by Rongjin Theater describes Lingling as a "new woman" (*xinde nüxing*) who endures the hellish life in Shanghai; see *Zhongguo wusheng dianying juben* (Screenplays of Chinese silent films) (Beijing: Zhongguo dianying chubanshe, 1996), p. 2573.

30. Perhaps more than just an intertextual coincidence, a kind of public fascination with women's charming smiles was reflected in numerous photographic pages—bearing such English titles as "Youth and Pleasure" and "Let's All Smile and [Be] Happy"—in contemporary issues of *Liangyou* (The young companion), reputedly the most attractive and popular magazine in China at the time. For example, see *Liangyou*, no. 63 (Nov. 1931): 29; no. 78 (July 1933): 29; no. 80 (Sept. 1933): 29.

31. Another significant textual detail that links *Daybreak* to *Goddess* is the scene in which Lingling grabs a bottle and hits a factory supervisor on the head, almost killing this evil man who has sneaked into her room and attempted to rape her. In *Goddess*, the prostitute does the same with a bottle and instantly kills the gambler.

32. A 1934 review of *Goddess* praised the film's "skilful techniques" and hailed it as "a unique achievement in Chinese cinema," while another reviewer in 1934, "with greatest enthusiasm," welcomed Wu Yonggang as "a miraculous newcomer;" see Chen Bo, ed., *Zhongguo zuoyi dianying yundong* (The leftist film movement in China) (Beijing: Zhongguo dianying chubanshe, 1993), p. 553–54. For positive evaluations of *Goddess* in later years, see Cheng et al., *Zhongguo dianying*, 1: 344–45; "Bei maimo de dianying dashi?" (A forgotten master of film?), a special section on Wu Yonggang, *Lianhe wenxue* (Unitas) 9, no. 3 (Jan. 1993): 163–74. More recently, William Rothman is convinced that *Goddess* is "a masterpiece, one of the major examples of the worldwide art of silent cinema, worthy of comparison to the greatest American, French, Soviet, German, or Japanese silent films"; see his "*The Goddess*: Reflections on Melodrama East and West," in Wimal Dissanayake, ed., *Melodrama and Asian Cinema* (New York: Cambridge University Press, 1993), p. 60.

33. For more details concerning his early film experience, see Wu Yonggang, *Wode*

tansuo he zhuiqiu (My explorations and quests) (Beijing: Zhongguo dianying chubanshe, 1986), pp. 175–84.

34. Ibid., p. 130.

35. These are the words Wu Yonggang used in his article published in *Lianhua huabao* (Lianhua pictorial) 5, no. 1, in 1935 following the completion of *Goddess*; reprinted in Wu Yonggang, *Wode tansuo*, p. 134.

36. Rothman, "*Goddess*," pp. 65, 68.

37. Ibid., p. 69.

38. Ibid.

39. A different type of conservatism in *Goddess* was noted as early as 1934 by Cheng Wu, who pointed out the "weakness" behind the intellectual's sense of justice—a weakness revealed in the film's lack of solution to pressing social problems (see Chen Bo, *Zhongguo zuoyi dianying*, pp. 551–52).

40. Sharpe, *Unreal Cities*, p. 9.

41. There is a striking resemblance between this sequence in *Goddess* and one in the German silent film *Dirnentragödie* (Tragedy of the whore, 1927), as described by Patrice Petro in *Joyless Streets: Women and Melodramatic Representation in Weimar Germany* (Princeton: Princeton University Press, 1989): "*Dirnentragödie* opens with a series of abstract and elliptical images: the camera tracks a woman's legs as they move cautiously across a cobblestone pavement until they meet a man's legs, at which point both pairs enter a doorway and disappear out of sight" (p. 165). However plausible that Wu Yonggang might have seen the German film in Shanghai, a case of direct borrowing in Chinese cinema is hard to pinpoint due to the lack of specific acknowledgment from the director involved.

42. Rothman, "*Goddess*," pp. 66–67. Rey Chow's observation is also relevant here: "Before the camera eye, the different parts of her body, such as a smile, a leg, an arm, a coiffure, or a beautiful dress, serve as the loci of society's displaced desire"; see her *Primitive Passions: Visuality, Sexuality, Ethnography, and Contemporary Chinese Cinema* (New York: Columbia University Press, 1995), p. 24.

43. Rothman, "*Goddess*," p. 67.

44. A film dealing with Western as well as Chinese prostitutes in China, *Shanghai Express* was judged to be a film that humiliated China (*ruhua pian*). In July 1932, the Nationalist censors not only banned the film in China but also demanded that Paramount destroy all copies of the film. When Paramount objected to the demand, the censors stopped issuing licenses to all Paramount titles. However, Paramount went ahead and screened another film at Guanglu Theater in the same month without obtaining a license; it even threatened to disregard the Chinese authority altogether. This incident was cited in the Chinese media as an example of China's status as a weak country. See Dai Xiaolan, *Zhongguo wusheng dianying*, pp. 1007–1008, 1334.

45. See Bernheimer, *Figures of Ill Repute*, p. 52.

46. For historical information, see Hershatter, *Dangerous Pleasures*, pp. 226–41.

47. See Bo Jing, "Cong changji shuodao minzu jiankang wenti" (Prostitutes and the question of the health of the nation), *Wanying* (The variety fair monthly) no. 7 (Feb. 1937): no pagination. Hershatter provides a survey of the reformers and regulators of urban prostitution in her *Dangerous Pleasures*, pp. 245–303.

48. Ling He, "Shen Xiling lun" (On Shen Xiling), *Zhonghua tuhua zazhi* (China pic-

torial), no. 45 (1936); reprinted in Dai Xiaolan, *Zhongguo wusheng dianying*, pp. 1291–92.

49. See the script in *Zhongguo xinwenxue daxi* (Anthology of modern Chinese literature) (Shanghai: Shanghai wenyi chubanshe, 1984), 18: 244–46.

50. These are Ling He's words, quoted from Dai Xiaolan, *Zhongguo wusheng dianying*, p. 1292.

51. Bernheimer, *Figures of Ill Repute*, p. 22.

52. A still of this film appeared in *Liangyou*, no. 78 (July 1933): 31. For unknown reasons, reference to this Da Changcheng (Great Wall) production is not found in Cheng et al., *Zhongguo dianying*, or other recent books on early Chinese cinema.

53. See *Xiaoshuo daguan*, no. 6 (June 1916), illustration pages.

54. Bao Tianxiao, *Chuanying lou huiyi lu*, 1: 359–61.

55. For a critical reading of *Olympia* and the idea of prostitution, see Bernheimer, *Figures of Ill Repute*, pp. 89–128.

56. See Tang Zhenchang, ed., *Jindai Shanghai fanhuaji* (A pictorial record of the flourishing city of modern Shanghai) (Hong Kong: Shangwu, 1993), p. 232.

57. See *Beiyang huabao*, no. 145 (Dec. 10, 1927). For further discussion of nude modeling and its rendition in Chinese cartoons of the 1930s, see Yingjin Zhang, "The Corporeality of Erotic Imagination: A Study of Shanghai Pictorials and Fan Magazines of the 1930s," paper delivered at the annual meeting of the Association for Asian Studies, Chicago, Mar. 1997.

58. This scene of *Goddess* is both acted out and replayed in Stanley Kwan's *Ruan Lingyu* (Center Stage, 1991), a Hong Kong production.

59. Hershatter, "Modernizing Sex," p. 163.

60. For a discussion of *New Woman*, see Kristine Harris, "*The New Woman*: Image, Subject, and Dissent in 1930s Shanghai Film Culture," *Republican China* 20, no. 2 (Apr. 1995): 55–79; Yingjin Zhang, "Engendering Chinese Filmic Discourse of the 1930s: Configurations of Modern Women in Shanghai in Three Silent Films," *Positions* 2, no. 3 (Winter 1994): 616–24. Yuan Muzhi's *Street Angel* is said to be a Chinese remake of the 1928 Hollywood production of the same title (directed by Frank Borzage); see James Robert Parish, *Prostitution in Hollywood Films: Plots, Critiques, Casts and Credits for 389 Theatrical and Made-for-Television Releases* (Jefferson, N.C.: McFarland, 1992), pp. 422–23.

61. Ruan Lingyu's suicide was top news at the time; tens of thousands of people attended her funeral in Shanghai. See Gongsun Lu, *Zhongguo dianying shihua* (A history of Chinese cinema) (Hong Kong: Nantian shuye gongsi, 1977), 2: 55–56. In the late 1980s, a television drama series about Ruan Lingyu's life was broadcast in mainland China; in 1991, Stanley Kwan's *Central Stage* was released in Hong Kong.

62. See Hershatter, *Dangerous Pleasures*, pp. 327–92; see also Ho, "Selling Smiles," p. 132; Ren, "China," pp. 94–97.

63. For discussions of *Rouge*, see Rey Chow, "A Souvenir of Love," *Modern Chinese Literature* 7, no. 2 (Fall 1993): 59–78; Leo Ou-fan Lee, "Two Films from Hong Kong: Parody and Allegory," in Nick Browne, Paul Pickowicz, Vivian Sobchack, and Esther Yau, eds., *New Chinese Cinemas: Forms, Identities, Politics* (New York: Cambridge University Press, 1994), pp. 202–15. See also Jenny Lau, "*Farewell My Concubine*: History, Melodrama, and Ideology in Contemporary Pan-Chinese Cinema," *Film Quarterly* 49, no. 1 (Fall 1995): 16–27.

64. An earlier example in mainland China is *Zhiyin* (Intimate friends, 1981), which tells of a late Qing courtesan who assisted in the plotting of the Republican Revolution in 1911. Admittedly, there is a noticeable gender difference between cinematic representations of prostitution by the male and the female directors. In *Huahun* (Soul of the painter, 1994) by Huang Shuqin (b. 1939), the glamorous aspect of prostitution receives far less attention than the physical and psychological tortures the prostitutes suffer in the brothel. In *Hongfen* (Blush, 1994) by Li Shaohong (b. 1955), which focuses on the reform of the prostitutes after 1949, the glory of the good old days is evoked through verbal means more than visual images. Like their contemporary male counterparts, however, both Huang Shuqin and Li Shaohong do not approach prostitution exclusively from an ethico-moral point of view (as was customarily done in the 1930s), although their emphasis on female psychology greatly reduces the voyeuristic pleasure their films would have otherwise offered to the male audience. For a brief discussion of *Blush*, see Hershatter, *Dangerous Pleasures*, pp. 396–98; for a survey of women's film in contemporary China, see Dai Jinhua, "Invisible Women: Contemporary Chinese Cinema and Women's Film," *Positions* 3, no. 1 (Spring 1995): 255–80.

65. For a discussion of Hong Kong's nostalgia films such as *Rouge*, see Luo Feng, *Shijimo chengshi: Xianggang de liuxing wenhua* (The fin-de-siècle city: popular culture in Hong Kong) (Hong Kong: Oxford University Press, 1995), pp. 60–75.

66. Gronewold, *Beautiful Merchandise*, p. 87.

67. My argument here dovetails Hershatter's observation that, in literary and cinematic representations of prostitution in post-Mao China, "notably absent was any hint of condemnation" (see her *Dangerous Pleasures*, p. 396).

68. Hendrik De Leeuw, *Cities of Sin* (New York: Harrison Smith and Robert Haas, 1933; reprinted by New York: Garland Publishing, 1979), p. 20. De Leeuw's book was published when the report to the Council of the League of Nations Commission of Enquiry into the Traffic in Women and Children in the East was made available to the public.

69. According to Orville Schell, a longtime China observer, China "has now been reborn as an epicenter of a new Asian hedonism," where wealthy local millionaires and overseas businessmen "no longer troll night-clubs for sex, but keep a 'second wife' in an apartment or hotel room for the sake of convenience" (see his "China—the End of an Era," *The Nation*, July 17–24, 1995: 86). In a sense, prostitution has become once again a "private" practice for these *nouveaux riches*, who have revived the lost tradition of concubinage and are eager to "seek enjoyment" (*zhaole*) in the kind of male fantasy visually delivered to them in such spectacular films as *Dahong denglong gaogao gua* (Raise the red lantern, 1991) and *Yao a yao, yao dao waipo qiao* (Shanghai triad, 1995), both directed by Zhang Yimou (b. 1950). For more details of the cultural scenes in post-Mao China, see Jianying Zha, *China Pop: How Soap Operas, Tabloids, and Bestsellers Are Transforming a Culture* (New York: New Press, 1995).

CHAPTER EIGHT

1. See Julia C. Strauss, "Symbol and Reflection of the Reconstituting State: The Examination Yuan in the 1930s," *Modern China* 20, no. 2 (Apr. 1994): 211–38; Thomas Rawski, *The Economic Growth in Pre-War China* (Berkeley: University of California Press, 1989); Theodore Hsi-en Chen, "Education in China, 1927–1937," in Paul K. Sih, ed.,

The Strenuous Decade: China's Nation-Building Efforts, 1927–1937 (New York: St. John's University, 1970), pp. 289–314; Weh-hsin Yeh, *The Alienated Academy: Culture and Politics in Republican China 1919–1937* (Cambridge, Mass.: Harvard University Press, 1990); and Frederic Wakeman, Jr., *Policing Shanghai 1927–1937* (Berkeley: University of California Press, 1995).

2. For a discussion of the relationship between the NFCC and the CFCC as well as the question of "leftist cinema," see Zhiwei Xiao, "Film Censorship in China, 1927–1937," Ph.D. diss. (University of California–San Diego, 1994).

3. Cheng Jihua, Li Shaobai, and Xing Zuwen, eds., *Zhongguo dianying fazhan shi* (A history of the development of Chinese cinema) (Beijing: Zhongguo dianying chuban she, 1981), 1: 164.

4. Baiyou Heliang, "*Yulihun* yingpian ping" (A review of *Yulihun*), *Dianying zhoukan* (Movie weekly), no. 25 (1924): 5–6.

5. *Dianying jiancha weiyuanhui gongzuo baogao* (The work report of the NFCC) (Nanjing, 1934), pp. 15, 26, 28, 85–86.

6. Yuen Ren Chao, "Some Contractive Aspects of the Chinese National Language Movement," in Anwar S. Dil, ed., *Aspects of Chinese Sociolinguistics: Essays by Yuen Ren Chao* (Stanford: Stanford University Press, 1976), p. 97.

7. Zhu Ge, "Quanhu xiao gongsi chafeng hou zhi biantai" (The closing of smaller studios and its aftermath), *Dianying xinwen* 1, no. 3 (July 20, 1935): 4–5.

8. *Dianying jiancha weiyuan hui gongbao* (The NFCC bulletin) 1, no. 16 (1932): 47.

9. Luo Gang, speech at the meeting with China's major film studio producers, in *Quanguo dianying gongsi fuze ren Tanhua hui ji'nian ce* (Proceedings from the symposium of the Chinese film producers) (Nanjing, 1935), pp. 41–42.

10. *Diansheng* (Movietone) 5, no. 44 (Nov. 1936): 1169.

11. Ibid., no. 49: 1305.

12. By the end of 1936, 90 percent of the films showing in the local theaters were again of foreign origins. See *Diansheng* 5, no. 50 (Dec. 1936): 1351.

13. Ibid., no. 30: 753.   14. Ibid., no. 48: 1283.

15. Ibid., 6, no. 23 (June 1937): 1004.   16. Ibid.

17. Ibid., no. 25 (June 1937): 1079–119. It was also stipulated that during the first year, no less than 10 percent of the total movie production had to be in *guoyu*; during the second year, 20 percent; by the third year, 30 percent.

18. Ibid., no. 29: 1237.

19. Ibid., no. 31: 1317.

20. Ibid., no. 19: 370.

21. *Dianying zhoukan* 1, no. 1 (Sept. 1938): 4–5.

22. Daniel W. Y. Kwok, *Scientism in Chinese Thought, 1900–1950* (New Haven: Yale University Press, 1965).

23. Prasenjit Duara, "Knowledge and Power in the Discourse of Modernity: The Campaign Against Popular Religion in Early Twentieth-Century China," *Journal of Asian Studies* 50, no. 1 (Feb. 1991): 67–83.

24. For the ban on *Ben-Hur*, see the report in *China Weekly Review* Jan. 19, 1929: 347. For *The Ten Commandments*, see *Dianying jiancha weiyuan hui gongbao* 1, no. 5 (1932): 30.

25. Perry Link, *Mandarin Ducks and Butterflies: Popular Fiction in Early Twentieth-Century Chinese Cities* (Berkeley: University of California Press, 1981).

26. Huang Yichuo, "Guochanpian de fuxing wenti" (The question of the revival of Chinese cinema), *Yingxi zazhi* 1, nos. 7–8 (June 1, 1930): 24.

27. "Neizhengbu banbu dianying pian jiancha guize" (The ministry of interior announced regulations on film censorship), *Shen bao* (Sept. 6, 1928).

28. See Zhiwei Xiao, "Film Censorship," pp. 293–94.

29. *Dianying jiancha weiyuanhui gongzuo baogao*, p. 15.

30. See Chen Lifu, *Zhongguo dianying shiye* (The film enterprise in China) (Shanghai: Chenshe, 1933).

31. Ju Lu, "Ying hua" (Some comments about films), *Yingxi zazhi* 1, no. 9 (Aug. 1930): 28.

32. Some people in the film industry even congratulated the establishment of the National Film Censorship Committee. See the editorial in *Dianying yuekan* no. 26 (1933): 3.

33. Wang Baisou, "Yeshi jiaoyu" (It's also educational), *Minguo ribao*, Mar. 7, 1931.

34. Wan Cheng, "Zhonggao dangzhou" (A piece of advice to the authorities), *Yingxi shenghuo* 1, no. 30 (Aug. 1930): 1–2.

35. Mao Dun, "Fengjian de xiaoshimin wenyi" (The culture of the feudalistic philistines), *Dongfang zazhi* 30, no. 3 (Feb. 1, 1933). Reprinted in *Mao Dun quanji* (Beijing: Remin wenxue chuban she, 1991), 19: 368–72.

36. Zhou Jianyun, "Dianying shencha wenti" (The question of film censorship), *Dianying yuebao*, no. 5 (Aug. 1928): 1–3. See also Huang Rongpei, "Heian zhong guopian de shuguang" (The twilight of Chinese films), *Yingxi zazhi* 1, no. 10 (1931): 69.

37. Zhu Ge, "Quanhu xiao gongsi chafeng."

38. See the editorial article in *Diansheng* 4, no. 3 (Jan. 1935): 55.

39. *Yingxi shenghuo* 1, no. 31 (Aug. 1931): 1–3.

40. *Diansheng* 3, no. 25 (July 1934): 495.

41. Ye Baishe, "Suowang yu dianjianhui zhe" (My expectations from the NFCC), *Yingxi shenghuo* 1, no. 11 (Mar. 1931): 1–2.

42. *Diansheng* 5, no. 19 (1936): 466.

43. Gong Tianyi, "Shenguai yingpian kaijin wenti de tantao" (The debate over lifting the ban on magic/ghost movies), *Shehui yuebao* 1, no. 3 (1934): 71–72.

44. *Diansheng* 5, no. 11 (1936): 268; 5, no. 24: 604.

45. B. Y. Lee, "Modernists and Anti-Modernists in China," *China Weekly Review*, May 26, 1934: 498.

46. During my research I encountered many such magazines. For a contemporary testimony, see *China Weekly Review* (Jan. 21, 1933): 354.

47. Su Xiao, "Mingxing shangpin hua" (The commodification of the movie stars), *Dianying xinwen* 1, no. 8 (1935): 2.

48. Zhou Shixun, "Shanghai you wochuo yingpian faxian" (Pornographic movies are found in Shanghai), *Yingxi chunqiu* no. 4 (1925): 10. See also Yi De, "Gongzi ge'er zhengying chungong pian" (The showing of pornographic movies among the dandies), *Yinhai zhoukan* 1, no. 7 (Apr. 1936): 6; Yi De, "Changsha yeyou chungong pian fangying" (Pornographic films are also found in Changsha), *Diansheng* 5, no. 13 (1936): 314.

49. *Dianying jiancha weiyuan hui gongbao* 1, no. 1 (Aug. 1, 1932).

50. Ibid., no. 11 (Nov. 1932).

51. Ibid., no. 12: 16. See also "Xianggang Guangzhou jinying luoti pian" (Nude pictures are prohibited in Hong Kong and Canton), *Diansheng* 3, no. 26 (July 14, 1934): 504.

52. Ibid., no. 2 (1934): 31.

53. Zi Yu, "Duguo dianying guanggao ban zhihou" (After reading the movie ads section), *Chen bao* (Morning post), July 14, 1932.

54. Yu Bingru, "Dianying guanggao de duoluo" (The degeneracy of the movie ads), *Diansheng* 3, no. 23 (1934): 453.

55. One critic complained about the eroticism and nude scenes of *The Spider Queen*; see *Beiyang huabao* 2, no. 65 (1927). Another critic praised the graceful performance of nude dancers in a German film titled *The Oriental Secret*; see ibid., 9, no. 406 (Dec. 1929).

56. Hong Yu, "Jieluo zhang" (A list of nude scenes), *Yingxi shenghuo* 1, no. 39 (Oct. 10, 1932): 7.

57. Feng Xizui, "Rougan yu dianying" (Eroticism and movies), *Dianying yuekan*, nos. 11–12 (1929).

58. See Yan Ciping, "Mingxing men hetong shangde jintiao" (The no's on the studio contracts with stars), *Qingqing dianying* 3, no. 1 (Mar. 1937).

59. *Diansheng* 3, no. 27 (1934).

60. Bian Cinian, "Naizhao cenku yinxiang tai xialiu le" (Bras and panties: the image of obscenity), *Diansheng* 3, no. 41 (1934): 811–12.

61. Ibid., 5, no. 24 (June 19, 1936): 589.

62. "Xiao gongsi rougan pian taitou" (Small studios begin to make racy films), ibid., 4, no. 2 (Jan. 11, 1935): 39.

63. For instance, *Zaihui ba, Shanghai* (Goodbye, Shanghai, 1934) was ordered to delete a kissing scene. See *Zhongyang dianying jiancha weiyuan hui gongbao* (The bulletin of the CFCC) 1, no. 12 (1934): 90.

64. Mei Nu, "Qinzui de laiyuan" (The origins of kissing), *Beiyang huabao* 21, no. 1018 (1933).

65. Ka Er, "Luoti yu jiewen" (Nudity and kissing), *Qingqing dianying* 1, no. 11 (1935).

66. "Kiss manhua" (A few observations about kissing), *Dianying*, no. 14 (1932).

67. For instance, it was reported that Wang Ying's lover was quite unhappy about Wang's kissing scene. See *Diansheng* 3, no. 42 (1934): 824.

68. J. H. Kraus, "Jiewen zhibing de yanjiu" (The study of diseases caused by kissing), translated by Xi Jing, *Beiyang huabao* 2, no. 87 (June 1927).

69. *Diansheng* 4 (end-of-the-year supplement issue, Dec. 1935): 1116.

70. Ibid., 6, no. 6 (1937): 318.

71. Ibid., 4, no. 8 (1935): 157.

72. Liu Xu, "Xiandai nüxing xinmu zhongde yinmu xingxiang" (Modern women's tastes for the screen image), *Furen huabao*, no. 31 (Aug. 1935): 49–50.

73. Lu Gong, "Foluoyite zhuyi zhipei xiade dianying" (The cinema under the Freudian spell), *Chen bao* (Sept. 14, 1932).

74. Until the late 1920s, the male movie stars were very much in accord with the *xiaosheng* types in traditional theaters.

75. Jiang Zhenxin, "Xiandai nü dianxing—Xia Peizhen" (A model of modern beauty—Xia Peizhen), *Yingxi shenghuo* 1, no. 16 (May 1, 1931): 10–11.

76. Huang Jiamo, "Tan nüxing mei" (On female beauty), *Furen huabao*, no. 24 (1934): 19–21.

77. Sha Li nüshi (Lady Sherry), "Wode bu keqi de zhonggao" (My frank advice), *Chen bao*, July 13, 1932.

78. Commenting on American movie stars, a Chinese writer wrote: "Among the American movie actresses, there is no lack of beauties whose physical features vary greatly. But I am a Chinese. As a Chinese I think Lillian Gish satisfies the Chinese ideal of female beauty. She is attractive, but not sensuous; graceful, but not dull (*yan er buye, duan er buzhi*). For westerners, such a beauty is only reserved for angelic roles. In their daily lives they prefer the sensuous and active types." *Dianying zhoukan*, no. 8 (Apr. 25, 1924): 22.

79. Yang Jun, "Huazhuang nüren de mei he shimei" (The use of cosmetics), *Qingqing dianying* 1, no. 6 (1934).

80. Jiang Zhenxin, "Xiandai nü dianxing."

81. *China Weekly Review*, Aug. 25, 1934: 501.

82. Ibid., Oct. 31, 1936: 322.

83. *Beiyang huabao* 25, no. 1242 (May 1935).

84. *China Weekly Review*, Aug. 25, 1934: 501.

85. See Jiang Li, "Zhu Jiaye guanyu jinzhi funü suxiong detian" (Zhu Jiaye's proposal to ban breast binding), *Minguo chunqiu*, no. 1 (Jan., 1990). See also Huanxiangge zhu, "Funü zhuangsu de yige da wenti—xiaosan zhi yingfou baocun" (A big problem regarding women's garment—should the corset be abandoned), *Beiyang huabao*, no. 84 (May 1927).

86. *Shen bao*, Dec. 17, 1929.

87. Paul K. Whang, "Deficiencies of the 'modern Chinese girl,'" *China Weekly Review*, Oct. 5, 1929: 199.

88. It ranges from claiming that modern women are undesirable to ridicule of their unconventional behavior. See "The 'Unmarriageable' Chinese Girl," ibid., Sep. 19, 1931; B. Y. Lee, "Modernists and Anti-Modernists in China," ibid., May 26, 1934.

89. Li Shiwei, "Xing de wenti" (The problem of sex), a transcript of Dr. Mark Seldon's lectures, *Dagong bao*, May 4, 1932.

90. L. T., "Dianying yuan zhong zaji" (Observations from the movie theater), *Beiyang huabao* 1, no. 32 (Oct. 1926).

91. Paul Pickowicz, "The Theme of Spiritual Pollution in Chinese Films of the 1930s," *Modern China* 17, no. 1 (Jan. 1991): 38–75.

CHAPTER NINE

I would like to thank Yingjin Zhang and the members of the panels and of the audience at the 1995 meeting of the Association for Asian Studies for their comments. I also express my thanks to Richard Bauman, Andrew Field, Poshek Fu, Casey Man Kong Lum, Rulan Chao Pian, Ronald R. Smith, and Jeffrey Wasserstrom for reading earlier drafts and for offering invaluable suggestions and references.

1. Claudia Gorbman, *Unheard Melodies: Narrative Film Music* (Bloomington: Indiana University Press, 1987), p. 31.

2. Jay Leyda, *Dianying: An Account of Films and the Film Audience in China* (Cambridge, Mass.: MIT Press, 1972), p. 79.

3. Paul Clark, *Chinese Cinema: Culture and Politics Since 1949* (Cambridge, Eng.: Cambridge University Press, 1987), p. 13.

4. Ma Ning, "The Textual and Critical Difference of Being Radical: Reconstructing Chinese Leftist Films of the 1930s," *Wide Angle* 11 (1989): 24.

5. The violinist and composer Fritz Kreisler (1875–1962) was well known in Chinese music circles and performed in a 1923 concert in Beijing.

6. Shen Xiling, "Dianying yishu de fengong" (Division of work in film art), *Dazhong shenghuo* 1, no. 5 (Dec. 24, 1935), reprinted and distributed by Shanghai shuyinxing (1982), p. 122.

7. Wang Yunjie, "Dianying yinyue" (Film music), in Wang Zhongcheng and Tan Long, eds., *Dianying chuangzuo yu pinglun* (Film production and criticism) (Beijing: Zhongguo dianying chubanshe, 1986), p. 175.

8. Gorbman, *Unheard Melodies*, p. 2.

9. For discussion of the formal and social-cultural significance of the intertextual relations of genre and of processes of contextualization, decontextualization, and recontextualization, see Charles Briggs and Richard Bauman, "Genre, Intertextuality, and Social Power," *Journal of Linguistic Anthropology* 2 (1992): 131–72; and Richard Bauman and Charles Briggs, "Poetics and Performance as Critical Perspectives on Language and Social Life," *Annual Review of Anthropology* 19 (1990): 59–88.

10. Briggs and Bauman, "Genre," pp. 147, 163.

11. Royal S. Brown, "Film Music: The Good, the Bad, and the Ugly," *Cineaste* 21 (1995): 63.

12. Bogumil Jewsiewicki, "The Identity of Memory and the Memory of Identity in the Age of Commodification and Democratization," *Social Identities* 1 (1995): 258. See Clifford Geertz, "After the Revolution: The Fate of Nationalism in the New States," in his *The Interpretation of Cultures: Selected Essays* (New York: Basic Books, 1973), pp. 234–54. He describes processes of "raising settled cultural forms out of their particular contexts, expanding them into general allegiances, and politicizing them" (p. 245). Royal S. Brown's *Overtones and Undertones: Reading Film Music* (Berkeley: University of California Press, 1994) refers to these processes of linking and of the escape "from a causal or historical determination of that moment of time and piece of space" (pp. 8–9).

13. Wang Yunjie, "Dianying yinyue", pp. 174–75.

14. Cheng Jihua, Li Shaobai, and Xung Zuwen, *Zhongguo dianying fazhanshi* (A history of the development of Chinese film) (Beijing: Zhongguo dianying chubanshe, 1963), 2 vols.; 1: 13–15, 1: 33–35. For the influence of silent films on sound films, see Brown, *Overtones*, pp. 12–22; Zhou Chuanji, "Dianying shikong jiegouzhong de shengyin" (Sound in the time-space structure of film), in *Dianying meixue* (Beijing: Zhongguo dianying chubanshe, 1985), reprinted in Luo Yijun, ed., *Zhongguo dianying lilun wenxuan 1920–1989* (Theoretical essays on Chinese cinema) (Beijing: Wenhua yishu chubanshe, 1992), 2: 243–61. Histories of film music, particularly from the United States, can be found in Brown, *Overtones*; Gorbman, *Unheard Melodies*; Charles Merrell Berg, "An Investigation of the Motives for and Realization of Music to Accompany the American Silent Film, 1896–1927," Ph.D. diss. (University of Iowa, 1973).

15. Y. [Yuan] Kao, "Motion Pictures," in Kwei Chungshu, ed., *Chinese Yearbook 1935–36* (Shanghai: Chinese Yearbook Publishing Company, 1935), p. 967; see also Clark, *Chinese Cinema*, p. 7. Marie Cambon describes the role of American films in "The Dream Palaces of Shanghai: American Films in China's Largest Metropolis Prior to 1949," *Asian Cinema* (Winter 1995): 34–45.

16. Ma Ning, "Textual and Critical Difference," p. 25. See also Berg, "American Silent Films;" Fred Steiner, "What Were Musicians Saying about Movie Music during the First Decade of Sound? A Symposium of Selected Writings," in Clifford McCarty, ed., *Film Music 1* (New York: Garland, 1989), pp. 81–104.

17. Si Bai, "Chuangzaozhong de shengpian biaoxian yangshi" (Creating expressive form in sound films), *Min bao: Yingtan* (Aug. 30–Sept. 2, 1934), reprinted in Luo Yijun, *Zhongguo dianying*, 1: 183.

18. Leyda, *Dianying*, p. 65; Cheng Jihua et al., *Zhongguo dianying*, 1: 156–61. Issues that had to be faced with the advent of sound film, and a short history of cinematic sound and equipment, are given in Zhou Chuanji, "Dianying shikong"; Ye Yuan, ed., *Dianyingxue gailun* (An introduction to film studies) (Shanghai: Shanghai shehui kexueyuan chubanshe, 1988), pp. 278–79; Rick Altman, "The Sound of Sound: A Brief History of the Reproduction of Sound in Movie Theaters," *Cineaste* 21 (1995): 68–71.

19. Isabel K. F. Wong, "From Reaction to Synthesis: Chinese Musicology in the Twentieth Century," in Bruno Nettl and Philip V. Bohlman, eds., *Comparative Musicology and Anthropology of Music: Essays on the History of Ethnomusicology* (Chicago: University of Chicago Press, 1991), p. 44; see also Liu Jingzhi, ed., *Zhongguo xinyinyueshi lunji 1920– 1945* (A history of Chinese new music 1920–1945: collected essays) (Hong Kong: University of Hong Kong Press, 1988), vol. 1.

20. Leo Ou-fan Lee, "The Tradition of Modern Chinese Cinema: Some Preliminary Explorations and Hypotheses," in Chris Berry, ed., *Perspectives on Chinese Cinema* (London: British Film Institute, 1991), pp. 6–20.

21. For more detailed descriptions of these trends, see Richard Curt Kraus, *Pianos and Politics in China: Middle-Class Ambitions and the Struggle over Western Music* (New York: Oxford University Press, 1989); Sue Tuohy, "Imagining the Chinese Tradition: The Case of Hua'er Songs, Festivals, and Scholarship," Ph.D. diss. (Indiana University, 1988), pp. 89–101 and 330–35. Excerpts from Nie Er's diary are quoted in Wang Yizhi, *Nie Er Zhuan* (A biography of Nie Er) (Shanghai: Shanghai yinyue chubanshe, 1992), p. 243.

22. See Tang Zhenchang, ed., *Jindai Shanghai fanhuaji* (A pictorial record of the flourishing city of modern Shanghai) (Hong Kong: Shangwu yinshuguan, 1993), for a vivid portrayal of metropolitan Shanghai, the lure of city life and its amusements (pp. 172–73 and 218–19), and photos of film studios and theaters (pp. 221–22, 225), and of a peep show, a form used in *City Scenes,* on a Shanghai street (p. 264). The record companies are discussed in Pekka Gronow, "The Record Industry Comes to the Orient," *Ethnomusicology* 25 (1981): 251–84, esp. pp. 262–67; Tang Zhenchang, p. 277. Frederic Wakeman describes cabarets, movies, and the home-rental business in Victrolas in his *Policing Shanghai: 1927–1937* (Berkeley: University of California Press, 1995).

23. See Zhongguo Shanghai shiwei dangshi ziliao zhengji weiyuanhui, ed., *"Yi'er jiu" yihou Shanghai jiuguohui shiliao xuanji* (An anthology of historical materials from the Shanghai national salvation organizations of the Dec. 9th [1935] movement) (Shanghai: Shanghai shehui kexueyuan chubanshe, 1987), esp. pp. 235–50, for articles on the mass assemblies and on National Salvation music, and pp. 431–33 for Liu Liangmo's reminiscences. See also Zhongguo dabaike quanshu zongbianji weiyuanhui *Yinyue wudao* bianji weiyuanhui, ed., *Zhongguo dabaike quanshu: yinyue Wudao* (Chinese encyclopedia: music and dance) (Beijing: Zhongguo dabaike quanshu chubanshe, 1989), pp. 338–39;

Jeffrey Wasserstrom, *Student Protests in Twentieth-Century China: The View from Shanghai* (Stanford: Stanford University Press, 1992).

24. See Dianying yishu cidian bianji weiyuanhui, ed., *Dianying yishu cidian* (A dictionary of cinematic art) (Beijing: Zhongguo dianying chubanshe, 1986), pp. 95–96; Ye Yuan, *Dianyingxue*, pp. 280–81. For comments about the mythic and exaggerated nature of later commentaries, see Paul Pickowicz, "Melodramatic Representation and the 'May Fourth' Tradition of Chinese Cinema," in Ellen Widmer and David Der-wei Wang, eds., *From May Fourth to June Fourth: Fiction and Film in Twentieth-Century China* (Cambridge, Mass.: Harvard University Press, 1993), p. 304; Paul Clark, *Chinese Cinema*, p. 188.

25. Leyda, *Dianying*, p. 93.

26. Cheng Bugao, *Yingtan yijiu* (Reminiscences of the film circles) (Beijing: Zhongguo dianying chubanshe, 1983), p. 30.

27. Technical terms are covered in *Dianying yishu cidian*, pp. 499–500; *Zhongguo dabaike quanshu*, p. 131. For a discussion of characteristics of film music, see *Dianying yishu cidian*, pp. 488–91; Gorbman, *Unheard Melodies*, p. 15.

28. See Kraus, *Pianos and Politics*, p. viii. Unlike those of today, 1930s film credits did not list the titles of this background music.

29. They are also included in anthologies published in mainland China during the 1940s, 1950s, and 1980s, where they are identified with the films for which they became known.

30. Leyda, *Dianying*, p. 96. The same story is described in Wang Yizhi, *Nie Er zhuan*, p. 265; in Zhongguo yinyuejia xiehui, Sichuan fenhui, ed., *Zhongguo yinyuejia xiaozhuan* (Short biographies of Chinese composers) (Chengdu: Sichuan renmin chubanshe, 1981), p. 79. Ren Guang's song became extremely popular, as did the film itself, which ran for a record-breaking 81 days.

31. Liu Jingzhi, *Zhongguo xinyinyueshi*, 1: 83–84. Liang Mingyue writes that public school songs "reflected the times and were full of revolutionary fervor, propaganda for democracy, freedom and even women's liberation. . . . The melodic ideas . . . were mainly borrowed and revised Western European and American songs most of which came from secondary sources as Japanese military and popular songs." See *Music of the Billion: An Introduction to Chinese Musical Culture* (New York: Heinrichshofen, 1985), pp. 138–39.

32. Bauman and Briggs describe this process of entextualization, "of rendering discourse extractable, of making a stretch of linguistic production into a unit—a *text*—that can be lifted out of its interactional setting. . . . Entextualization may well incorporate aspects of context, such that the resultant text carries elements of its history of use within it" ("Poetics and Performance," p. 73). Today, entire film scores have become detachable from films and are issued as compact disks.

33. Zhongguo Shanghai shiwei, *"Yi'er jiu,"* p. 238. The list of songs "popular during the time" on pp. 247–50, however, was written in 1957.

34. For what are believed to be the original lyrics of "March of the Volunteers," see Cheng Bugao, *Yingtan*, pp. 207–208.

35. Tian Han, in *Nie Er: cong juben dao yingpian* (Nie Er: from script to movie) (Beijing: Zhongguo dianying chubanshe, 1963), p. 396; Lian Kang, ed., *Nie Er huazhuan* (A biography of Nie Er) (Beijing: Yinyue chubanshe, 1958), p. 38. The song later was recontextualized in another genre, as the national anthem of the PRC. The story of the song's composition is repeated: Xia Yan's version in Lian Kang, *Nie Er*, p. 37; Tian Han's version

in Tien Han, "The Composer Nieh Erh," *Chinese Literature* 1959, no. 11: 128. Nie Er, fearing government reprisals, had gone to Japan by that time.

36. Sources on the activities of musicians include *Nie Er: cong juben*; entries under the individual musicians in *Zhongguo dabaike quanshu*; Lian Kang, *Nie Er*; Wang Huihe, *Zhongguo jinxiandai*, esp. pp. 118–70, the chapter on the Left-Wing Music Movement; Liu Jingzhi, *Zhongguo xinyinyueshi*; Zhongguo yinyuejia xiehui, *Zhongguo yinyuejia*. See also Kraus, *Pianos and Politics*, pp. 40–69.

37. Cheng Bugao, *Yingtan*, p. 201; Tian Han, in Lian Kang, *Nie Er*, p. 19.

38. Different explanations for Nie Er's popularity are given in Liu Jingzhi, *Zhongguo xinyinyueshi*, 1: 67. For a script and stories about the movie, see *Nie Er: cong juben*; the movie was shown again on television in 1995 in the series of films commemorating the war years.

39. So many critiques of Li Jinhui were published that his name and his songs became a shorthand reference to "weak and dispirited" music at odds with the goals of saving the nation. For descriptions of Li, see Liu Jingzhi, *Zhongguo xinyinyueshi*, 1: 70–74; Zhongguo yinyuejia xiehui, *Zhongguo yinyuejia*, 1: 46–48. Jonathan Stock discusses the singer Zhou Xuan's performance of Li's songs and her participation in the Bright Moon Opera Troupe in "Reconsidering the Past: Zhou Xuan and the Rehabilitation of Early Twentieth-Century Popular Music," *Asian Music* 26 (Spring/Summer 1995): 120–25.

40. Kraus, *Pianos and Politics*, pp. 103–4.

41. For a discussion of similar trends in musicology in the first few decades of this century, see Wong, "From Reaction to Synthesis."

42. Gorbman, *Unheard Melodies*, p. 6.

43. This theme—of peasants leaving the rural village and the miserable conditions they often encountered in the city—is common in the films and in Shanghai.

44. I express my thanks to Rulan Chao Pian for providing information, along with her English-language translation of the complete original text; see also her preface in Zhao Yuanren, *Zhao Yuanren yinyue lunwenji* (A collection of essays by Zhao Yuanren) (Beijing: Zhongguo yishu chuban gongci, 1994), p. 5. Among those lines left out are the following:

> Of ten miles of foreign concession land, nine miles lay waste;
> of ten able-bodied young men, nine remain idle.
> . . . Of ten shops opened, nine close down.
> . . . When you come to a crossroad, do not stand and wait.
> Let us go forward together, and build a better state.

(adapted from the English-language translation)

45. Quoted in Steiner, "What Were Musicians Saying," pp. 88–89.

46. Through its location in the film, the music accumulates meaning through indexical processes or, as Gorbman writes, "codifies associations" (*Unheard Melodies*, p. 3).

47. The filmmakers seem intrigued by the notion of synchronization of music and image: special music plays as doors are opened and telephones dialed, background drums accompany a visual of the character drumming his fingers, traffic sounds as characters open a shop door and walk out on to the street, and so on throughout the film. An unusual effect is created as musical instruments synchronize with speech (so that the speech can no longer be understood), particularly within scenes of arguments.

48. Xian Xinghai studied with Paul Dukas while in Paris.

49. Other pieces heard in the two films are Wagner's *Der Meistersinger*, symphonic band and big band music (popular in the United States during the same period), a French Impressionist string quartet, waltzes, snatches of traditional Chinese opera, Mendelssohn's *Midsummer Night's Dream* and "Spring Song" (transformed in a popular version), and a Sousa march.

50. For a discussion of dance-hall life, see Andrew Field's essay, Chap. 5 in this volume.

51. This theme is seen in several of the films, such as "New Women," where the female character Wei Ming is a music teacher. Choral forms, concerted singing in unison or in four-part harmony, were common in the musical rhetoric of national unity at the time.

52. Zhongguo Shanghai shiwei, "*Yi'er jiu,*" p. 241. This quote also illustrates the intertextuality of the debate concerning Li Jinhui's songs, many of which were banned by the Shanghai Education Bureau in 1934–36. Even the police in the Foreign Settlement sought to eradicate these songs in entertainment centers (Shanghai Municipal Police Files, Reel 22, D-6383, Dec. 13 and 31, 1934, Jan. 2, 1935, and Feb. 9, 1935).

53. Kraus, *Pianos and Politics*, p. 43; Pickowicz, "Melodramatic Representation," pp. 296, 297.

54. Heinrich Fruehauf, "Urban Exoticism in Modern and Contemporary Chinese Literature," in Widmer and Wang, *From May Fourth to June Fourth*, p. 141.

CHAPTER TEN

The research on which this chapter is based was funded by the U.S. Department of Education / Fulbright-Hays and by the Committee on Scholarly Communication with China. I am grateful to Keith Brown, Prasenjit Duara, Megan Ferry, Miriam Hansen, William Schaefer, and Xiaobing Tang for their careful readings of earlier drafts.

Primary source materials for the chapter were collected at the Shanghai Municipal Library, and through interviews. Foremost among the latter was an interview with Yamaguchi Yoshiko / Li Xianglan in Tokyo on February 19, 1996. In the interview, which lasted several hours, points from Yamaguchi's autobiography were covered, as well as supplementary material concerning the former actress's relationship with Shanghainese fans and the fan press. I am indebted to Sarah Frederick and Melissa Wender for their help in and around the interview.

1. Pei Pei, "*Wanshi liufang* yu Li Xianglan" (*Eternity* and Li Xianglan), *Xin yingtan* 1, no. 7 (May 1943): 31.

2. Yamaguchi Yoshiko and Fujiwara Sakuya, *Ri Koran—Watashi no hansei* (Li Xianglan—My half life) (Tokyo: Shinchosha, 1987), translated into Chinese by Jin Ruojing under the title *Zai Zhongguo de rizi—Li Xianglan: Wode bansheng* (My days in China—Li Xianglan: my half life) (Hong Kong: Baixing wenhua shiye youxian gongsi, 1989). All page references in this chapter are made to the Chinese translation, and all translations into English are my own.

3. Du Yunzhi, *Zhongguo dianying shi* (A history of Chinese cinema) (Taibei: Taiwan shangwu yinshuguan, 1972), 2: 58.

4. I borrow the phrase from Miriam Silverberg, "Remembering Pearl Harbor, For-

getting Charlie Chaplin, and the Case of the Disappearing Western Woman: A Picture Story," *Positions* 1, no. 1 (Spring 1993): 35.

5. Manchukuo refers to the Manchurian puppet state set up by Japan and in existence from 1932 to 1945. As in the above article, the contemporary press most often referred to the area as "Manzhou," which translates as "Manchuria."

6. Shimizu Akira, in interview with the author, Tokyo, Feb. 17, 1995.

7. John Dower, *War Without Mercy: Race and Power in the Pacific War* (New York: Pantheon, 1986), p. 264.

8. Quoted in Joseph L. Anderson and Donald Richie, *The Japanese Film: Art and Industry* (Rutland, Vt.: Charles E. Tuttle, 1959), p. 158. The authors go on to note that, with tightening controls by 1943, Japan's attitude to these industries had changed to one of "a wise parent toward his immature child."

9. In her autobiography, for example, Yamaguchi recounts the story of an unwilling Chen Yunshang's (b. 1919) employment by the Japanese in a public appearance offering flowers to Japanese troops. See Yamaguchi, *Zai Zhongguo*, pp. 226–27. Zhonglian's managing director Zhang Shankun (1905–57) may be cited as another example of a film personality employed publicly for the promotion of Sphere ideology. Perhaps to a greater extent than Li, however, Zhang appears to have used the position for his own ends. See Poshek Fu, "Struggle to Entertain: The Political Ambivalence of Shanghai Film Industry under Japanese Occupation, 1941–1945," in *Cinema of Two Cities: Hong Kong–Shanghai* (Hong Kong: The 18th Hong Kong International Film Festival, 1994), p. 53.

10. Bo Zi, "Sheying riji" (Filming diary), *Xin yingtan* 1, no. 4 (Feb. 1943): 22. In this magazine's previous issue, a similar production diary piece bemoans the fact that Li was forced to leave early, but reassures readers that the set still benefits from the liveliness of her co-stars Gao Zhanfei (1904–1969) and Yuan Meiyun (b. 1917). See Bo Zi, "Sheying riji" (Filming diary), *Xin yingtan* 1, no. 3 (Jan. 1943): 23.

11. Though my emphasis in this chapter is on Li Xianglan's persona as seen through fan magazines, studio publicity, and spectatorship response, consideration of her screen persona is crucial insofar as her total star text is comprised of both filmic and extrafilmic factors.

12. The original Japanese titles for these films, which are available for viewing at the Motion Picture Division of the Library of Congress, and available commercially in Japan, are *Byakuran no uta*, *Shina no yoru*, and *Nessa no chikai*. According to Japanese sources, because of the offensive nature of the term "Shina," *Shina no yoru* was renamed *Shanghai zhi ye* (Night in Shanghai) for Chinese screening. I have found it advertised in period newspapers, however, under either its original title or under the revised title *Chun de meng* (Spring dream). In magazine interviews the actress tended to refer to the film by its original title translated into Chinese, and my informants similarly remember the film by this title. Following their example, then, in this chapter, I refer to the film as *Zhina zhi ye*, or *Night in China*. For a more detailed analysis of the film in terms of its Japanese audience, see Freda Freiberg, "China Nights: The Sustaining Romance of Japan at War" in John Whiteclay Chambers II and David Culbert, eds., *World War II, Film, and History* (New York: Oxford University Press, 1996). For more on the "Continental Series," see Shimizu Akira, "War and Cinema in Japan," in *Media Wars: Then and Now* (Yamagata International Documentary Film Festival, 1991), p. 22.

13. The couplings are, however, only hinted at; each fails to be consummated on

screen. While the rhetoric behind a paternalistically loving relationship between Japanese man and Chinese woman was clearly forceful, Japanese propagandists perhaps wanted to avoid the films being read as promoting literal miscegenation. In this light, it's interesting that many people apparently saw Li Xianglan as the child of a mixed marriage. In her autobiography Yamaguchi recounts a 1978 reunion with some of her Chinese co-stars, in which they reveal that they had assumed one of her parents was Japanese. See Yamaguchi, *Zai Zhongguo*, pp. 84–86. Several of my informants have made the same assumption. If Li Xianglan was indeed thought by many to be a product of miscegenation, this would seem to detract from her effectiveness as an instrument of Japanese ideology since—all rhetoric of Asian assimilationism aside—as Dower points out, "Intermarriage with native peoples was to be avoided at all costs—not merely because mixed-blood children were generally inferior, but also because intermarriage would destroy the psychic solidarity of the Yamato race." See Dower, *War Without Mercy*, p. 275. This is just one example of the impossibility of any easy fit between star and political ideal.

14. Studio publications, for example, capitalized on the welcoming of Li Xianglan into the circle of Chinese stars, with articles describing her enthusiastic reception by Chen Yunshang, then Shanghai's most popular star. See, for example, "Chen Yunshang Li Xianglan niguan huijian" (Chen Yunshang and Li Xianglan meet in a convent), *Zhonglian yingxun* (Zhonglian movie report) no. 23 (Nov. 1942). For more on the significance of this film from the Japanese perspective, see Shimizu Akira, *Shanhai sokai eiga shishi* (A private history of film in the Shanghai concession) (Tokyo: Shinchosha, 1995), pp. 144–49, 298–99.

15. "Yinse lieche" (Silver train), *Shanghai yingtan* 1, no. 1 (Oct. 1943): 31.

16. "Li Xianglan lai Hu youqi!" (There is hope that Li Xianglan will come to Shanghai!), *Shanghai yingtan* 1, no. 2 (Nov. 1943): 27. The modernist metaphor of the elevator resonates with other journalistic representations of the star that highlight her cosmopolitanism.

17. Chen Wei, "Yu Li Xianglan linbieshi de tanhua" (A talk with Li Xianglan prior to her departure), *Xin yingtan* 1, no. 3 (Jan. 1943): 24.

18. *Xin yingtan* 1, no. 2 (Dec. 1943): 12. Remarkably, at least one report of Li Xianglan continues in this vein more than three years following the conclusion of the war. In a December 1948 issue of *Yingju tiandi* (Film and drama world), Li is reported to be back at work singing and acting in her native Japan. But, due perhaps to the fact that Li's "crude Japanese isn't as sweet and agreeable as her Chinese," Japanese fans have been slow to respond to her. For this reason, Li is reportedly longing to return to Shanghai. "But," the writer concludes, "she is in the end a Japanese, and China has prohibited Japanese from coming. So I'm afraid her ideal has no way of being actualized." See Yu Sun, "Li Xianglan zai Riben" (Li Xianglan in Japan), *Yingju tiandi* 1, no. 3 (Dec. 1948).

19. Christine Gledhill, "Signs of Melodrama," in Christine Gledhill, ed., *Stardom: Industry of Desire* (London: Routledge, 1991), p. 213.

20. "Wugui lieche" (Trackless train), *Xin yingtan* 2, no. 6 (May 1944): 38.

21. The first quotation is from Huang Bi, "Li Xianglan pianran lai Hu" (Li Xianglan comes trippingly to Shanghai), *Shanghai yingtan* 1, no. 9 (June 1944): 16; the second from Chen Zuwei's letter to the editor, *Shanghai yingtan* 1, no. 10 (Aug. 1944): 43.

22. "Yingren zhidong" (Movements of the stars), *Xin yingtan* 1, no. 1 (Nov. 1942): 17.

23. The first quotation is from Pei Pei, "*Wanshi liufang* yu Li Xianglan," p. 31; the second from "*Wanshi liufang*" (Eternity), *Xin yingtan* 1, no. 6 (Apr. 1943): 12.

24. "*Wanshi liufang* wancheng!" (*Eternity* is completed!), *Zhonglian yingxun* no. 37 (Mar. 1943): 1. Quotation marks in the original.

25. Fang Mei, "Canzhuobian huijian Li Xianglan" (Meeting with Li Xianglan over a meal), *Nüsheng* 3, no. 2 (June 1944): 13.

26. Gledhill, "Signs of Melodrama," p. 219. See also Christian Metz, *The Imaginary Signifier: Psychoanalysis and the Cinema* (Bloomington: Indiana University Press, 1977).

27. "Li Xianglan bu an yu shi" (Li Xianglan restless in her lodgings), *Shanghai yingtan* 2, no. 7 (July 1945): 23. As suggested with the earlier metaphor of the elevator, descriptions of Li moving throughout distinctively urban settings encouraged fans to identify in her a fluid cosmopolitanism, and explains in part why she should find most support among spectators in China's urban centers of Beijing and Shanghai. This cosmopolitanism, her mobility through time and space, as well as her absent presence all point toward various aspects of modernity, and suggest an interesting contrast to her image as a repository for traditional Chinese femininity—her primary appeal, according to Japanese sources, among the Japanese audience.

28. Lu Ping, "Li Xianglan de gechang—shiye—lianai he jiehun" (Li Xianglan's singing—work—love and marriage), pts. 1 and 2, *Shanghai yingtan* 1, no. 11 (Sept. 1944): 24–25; 1, no. 12 (Oct. 1944): 34–35.

29. *Xin yingtan* 1, no. 4 (Feb. 1943): 21.

30. Yamaguchi, *Zai Zhongguo*, p. 24. There were also, of course, her postwar names and identities. She returned to her birth name when she began to take Japanese film roles after the war. As she hastened to tell me, however, she did this only after her Shanghai colleagues had been safely cleared of war crimes charges. While they were still under suspicion, she could only feel that it was wrong for her to pursue her own acting career and in this, she says, "I guess I must still have been Li Xianglan" (Yamaguchi Yoshiko, in interview with the author, Tokyo, Feb. 19, 1996). She was known as Shirley Yamaguchi during her brief stint in Hollywood; and her married name, Otaka Yoshiko, was the name by which she was known in her capacity as a member of the Japanese Diet. As I observed during several phone conversations and one meeting with her, she still refers to herself in different contexts as Otaka Yoshiko, Yamaguchi Yoshiko, Shirley Yamaguchi, or Li Xianglan.

31. Yamaguchi, *Zai Zhongguo*, p. 99

32. Ibid., p. 230.

33. Ibid., p. 232. She was considered "Beijing's own" due to the fact that she had spent her school years in that city.

34. Yamaguchi, *Zai Zhongguo*, p. 233.

35. Yamaguchi, in interview with the author.

36. Yamaguchi, *Zai Zhongguo*, p. 234.

37. Shimizu, *Shanhai sokai*, pp. 138–40.

38. Sato Tadao, *Kinema to hosei: Nicchu eiga zenshi* (Cinema and gunfire: The prehistory of Japanese and Chinese cinema) (Tokyo: Riburopoto, 1985), p. 85.

39. See, for example, *Nüsheng* 1, no. 11 (Mar. 1943).

40. "Riben yintan de canlan huaduo" (Brilliant flowers of the Japanese silver forum), *Riben yingxun*, no. 1 (Sept. 1943). This publication was discontinued after one issue.

41. "Xing jian" (Study of the stars), *Shanghai yingtan* 2, no. 1 (Nov. 1944): 40–41.

42. Lu Ping, "Li Xianglan de gechang," p. 35.

43. Chen Wei, "Yu Li Xianglan," p. 24.

44. Identification of Li as the Chinese girl she plays on screen is further encouraged in the best known of these films, *Night in China*, by the name of the character she plays: Keiran, phonetically similar to the Japanese version of the (stage) name (Ri) Koran.

45. Originally published as "Naliang huiji" (Record of a cool-night meeting), *Zazhi yuekan* 15, no. 5 (Aug. 1945): 68. Reprinted under the same title in *Lianhe wenxue* (Unitas) 9, no. 5 (July 1993): 101.

46. Tsuji Hisakazu, *Chuka deneishiwa* (A narrative history of Chinese cinema) (Tokyo: Gaifusha, 1987), p. 246. Yamaguchi quotes this passage in her autobiography, p. 229, expressing embarrassment at Tsuji's interpretation. I have relied upon both versions in my translation.

47. Herein, of course, lies the problematic nature of the methodology whereby one attempts to excavate fifty-year-old memories through the process of interviews. It has proven impossible to ascertain to what extent my informants' responses are the result of the intervening years and, particularly, the recent plenitude of media events throughout China commemorating the fiftieth anniversary of the end of Japanese militarism.

48. Yamaguchi, in interview with the author. In fact, she and the Japanese scholars all cite reports that this song, as well as "Maitang ge" (Selling sweets song), were popular even in the Nationalist Chongqing and Communist Yan'an areas. The latter song definitely seems to have made the most impact on one of my informants, who remembers the title of the film not as *Wanshi liufang*, but rather as *Maitang ge*.

49. I have found this film noted elsewhere in the Shanghai press as *Mannü qinghua* (Love flowers of the barbarian girl). See Jin Ling, "Li Xianglan fangwen ji" (Record of an interview with Li Xianglan), *Shanghai yingtan* 1, no. 5 (Feb. 1944): 19. The film is known in Japanese as *Sayon no kane* (Bell of Sayon).

50. "Li Xiaojie shuo: 'Zheiyang de youqing cai zhenshi zhide baogui ne!'" (Miss Li says: "This sort of friendly feeling is really worth valuing!"), *Xin yingtan* 3, no. 1 (June 1944): 23. The original Japanese title for *Harbin genü* is *Watashi no uguisu* (My oriole).

51. Yamaguchi, in interview with the author.

52. Wang Meng, "Ren—lishi—Li Xianglan" (People—history—Li Xianglan), *Dushu* (Nov. 1992): 9–17.

53. Cheng Jihua, Li Shaobai, and Xing Zuwen, eds., *Zhongguo dianying fazhan shi* (A history of the development of Chinese cinema) (Hong Kong: Wenhua ziliao gongying-she, 1978).

54. Wang Meng, "Ren," p. 17.

55. "Chuxia yingxing lianhuanhui" (Movie stars' early summer social gathering), *Xin yingtan* 3, no. 1 (June 1944): 20.

56. "Yingxing jian gechang yiren Li Xianglan" (Li Xianglan, film star and vocal artist), *Nüsheng* 3, no. 4 (Aug. 1944): 22.

57. Chi Qing, "Tan *Wanshi liufang*" (Discussing *Eternity*), *Zazhi yuekan* 11, no. 3 (June 1943): 194. Note again that she is identified with Asia as a totality.

58. See Jin Ling, "Li Xianglan fangwen ji," p. 18. This is one of several instances in which legitimation for Li is framed in Western terms. See also Luo Fu, "*Wanshi liufang* kaipai huaxu" (Stories about the filming of *Eternity*), *Xin yingtan* 1, no. 1 (Nov. 1942): 41.

59. Fang Mei, "Canzhuobian," p. 13.

60. Jin Ling, "Li Xianglan fangwen ji," p. 19.

61. A practice evidenced most (in)famously, perhaps, in the 1930s with Ruan Lingyu (1910–35), and still a major component of the 1940s popular press.

62. "Numingxing de mimi" (Secrets of the female stars), *Shanghai yingtan* 1, no. 10 (Aug. 1944): 23.

63. Richard Dyer, *Stars* (London: British Film Institute, 1979), p. 51.

64. Yamaguchi, *Zai Zhongguo*, pp. 98–99.

65. "Li Xianglan pianran lai Hu!" (Li Xianglan suddenly arrives in Shanghai!), *Huaying zhoukan* (Huaying weekly), no. 49 (June 7, 1944).

66. Chen Wei, "Huijian Li Xianglan" (Meeting Li Xianglan), *Xin yingtan* 1, no. 1 (Nov. 1942): 41.

67. "Wugui lieche," *Xin yingtan* 1, no. 3 (Jan. 1943): 27.

68. Luo Fu, "*Wanshi liufang*," p. 37.

69. See Jin Ling, "Li Xianglan fangwen ji," p. 18; "Li Xiaojie shuo," p. 2; "Chuxia yingxing," p. 24; "Yintan zajin" (Mixed brocade of the screen circle), *Yingwu zhoubao* (Film and dance weekly), no. 1 (Nov. 1942): 7.

70. *Xin yingtan* 3, no. 2 (July 1944): 10.

71. Li Xianglan, "*Wanshi liufang* de hua" (Speaking of *Eternity*), *Xin yingtan* 1, no. 6 (Apr. 1943): 29.

72. Judging from Shanghai's fan magazines, by the following year, 1944, Film Sphere ideology was already on the wane. Decreasing slightly their emphasis on the notion of an assimilated Asian film industry, these publications instead featured more photos and stories on exclusively Japanese stars. The waning of Film Sphere ideology mirrors, by this time, that of the Co-Prosperity Sphere in general, though this is a subject for another project.

73. The fleetingness and dislocation that characterize the star in her movements throughout the Asian theater incarnate as well the way in which Sphere ideology was to be taken up by Japan's new subjects. As a blueprint with hegemonic intent, Sphere ideology was designed to be accepted by them over time. But as with any attempts at hegemony, it is important that the subjects not recognize the ideology for what it is. Rather, just as Li Xianglan moved from place to place, attached to no one location but rather to all, Sphere ideology, to be effective, had to exist everywhere and nowhere. Like the readers of the Shanghai fan magazines who in time grow convinced that Li Xianglan is Shanghai's own star and thus begin to regret her absence, Japan's newest subjects would gradually and unconsciously come to take up the encroaching ideology as their own.

74. Dyer, *Stars*, p. 24.

75. While her reticence here contrasts with all other interviews I have read, it is congruent with her retrospective narrativizing of this period in the autobiography. This late in 1945, she writes, it was clear to many which way the war was going. In her reserve, then (and indeed in her subsequent outburst), we may read not only her continuing reluctance to maintain the persona of Li Xianglan (she had already officially discontinued her Man'ei contract in the fall of 1944), but also a looking forward to Japanese defeat and to a consequent personal insecurity. See Yamaguchi, *Zai Zhongguo*, p. 249.

76. Reorganized in 1943, Zhonglian was henceforth known as Huaying (Zhonghua dianying lianhe gufen youxian gongsi, or China United Film Company, Limited).

77. "Naliang huiji," *Zazhi yuekan*, pp. 67–72; *Lianhe wenxue*, pp. 100–109.

78. One could rightfully argue that any notion of the self is always both relational and in process. But what I wish to focus upon here is the anguish expressed by the star in regards to what she sees as her own lack of a fundamental self.

79. Gledhill, "Signs of Melodrama," p. 217.

Select Bibliography

This bibliography does not include all Chinese articles cited in individual chapters and notes.

A Ling. "Nü mingxing de xingyun" (The lucky female stars). *Dianying yuekan* 26 (1933): 31–32.
A Wei, ed. *Pi yingxi* (Leather-puppet shadowplay). Beijing: Zhaohua meishu chubanshe, 1955.
All About Shanghai: A Standard Guidebook. Shanghai: University Press, 1934–35. Reprinted by Oxford University Press, 1983.
Altman, Rick. "The Sound of Sound: A Brief History of the Reproduction of Sound in Movie Theaters." *Cineaste* 21 (1995): 68–71.
Anderson, Joseph L., and Donald Richie. *The Japanese Film: Art and Industry.* Rutland, Vt.: Charles E. Tuttle, 1959.
Andrew, Julia F. "Judging a Book by Its Cover: Book Cover Design in Shanghai." Paper delivered at the annual meeting of the Association for Asian Studies, Chicago, Mar. 1997.
Anstice, E. H. "Shanghai's White Russians." *Contemporary Review* (Feb. 1937): 215–20.
Baiyou Heliang. "*Yulihun* yingpian ping" (A review of *Yulihun*). *Dianying zhoukan* (Movie weekly) no. 25 (1924): 5–6.
Bakhtin, M. M. *The Dialogic Imagination: Four Essays.* Ed. Michael Holquist. Trans. Caryl Emerson and Michael Holquist. Austin: University of Texas Press, 1981.
Bao Jing, ed. *Lao Shanghai jianwen* (Impressions of old Shanghai). Shanghai: Shanghai guoguang shudian, 1947.
Bao Minglian. *Dongfang Haolaiwu: Zhongguo dianying shiye de jueqi yu fazhan* (The Hollywood of the East: the rise and development of the Chinese film industry). Shanghai: Shanghai renmin chubanshe, 1991.
Bao Shiying. *Shanghai shi hang hao lutu lu* (Shanghai city business road map and record). Vol. 1. Shanghai: Fuli yingye gufen youxian gongsi, 1947.
Bao Tianxiao. *Chuanying lou huiyi lu* (Reminiscences of the Bracelet Shadow Chamber). Hong Kong: Dahua chubanshe, 1971.
———. *Chuanying lou huiyi lu xuji* (Sequel to reminiscences of the Bracelet Shadow Chamber). Hong Kong: Dahua chubanshe, 1973.
———. *Shanghai chunqiu* (Shanghai chronicles). 1924–26. 2 vols. Shanghai: Shanghai guji chubanshe, 1991.
Barrios, Richard. *A Song in the Dark: The Birth of the Musical Film.* New York: Oxford University Press, 1995.

Bauman, Richard, and Charles Briggs. "Poetics and Performance as Critical Perspectives on Language and Social Life." *Annual Review of Anthropology* 19 (1990): 59–88.

Benjamin, Walter. *Illuminations: Essays and Reflections.* Ed. Hannah Arendt. New York: Schocken Books, 1968.

Benson, Carlton. "The Manipulation of *Tanci* in Radio Shanghai During the 1930s." *Republican China* 20, no. 2 (Apr. 1995): 117–46.

Berg, Charles Merrell. "An Investigation of the Motives for and Realization of Music to Accompany the American Silent Film, 1896–1927." Ph.D. diss., University of Iowa, 1973.

Bergeron, Régis. *Le Cinéma chinois, 1905–1949.* Lausanne: Alfred Eibel, 1977.

Bernardi, Joanne R. "The Early Development of the Gendaigeki Screenplay: Kaeriyama Norimasa, Kurihara Tomas, Tanizaki Jun'ichirō and the Pure Film Movement." Ph.D. diss., Columbia University, 1992.

Bernheimer, Charles. *Figures of Ill Repute: Representing Prostitution in Nineteenth-Century France.* Cambridge, Mass.: Harvard University Press, 1989.

Berry, Chris. "Poisonous Weeds or National Treasures: Chinese Left Films in the 30s." *Jump Cut* 34 (Mar. 1989): 87–94.

———. "The Sublime Text: Sex and Revolution in *Big Road.*" *East-West Film Journal* 2, no. 2 (June 1988): 66–86.

Berry, Chris, ed. *Perspectives on Chinese Cinema.* Enlarged edition. London: British Film Institute, 1991.

Bhabha, Homi K. "Signs Taken for Wonders: Questions of Ambivalence and Authority Under a Tree Outside Delhi, May 1817." In Henry Louis Gates, Jr., ed., *"Race," Writing, and Difference,* pp. 163–84. Chicago: University of Chicago Press, 1986.

Bi Yihong. *See* Suopo Sheng.

Bian Cinian. "Naizhao cenku yinxiang tai xialiu le" (Bras and panties: the image of obscenity). *Diansheng* 3, no. 41 (1934): 811–12.

Bickers, Robert A. *Changing Shanghai's "Mind": Publicity, Reform and the British in Shanghai, 1927–1931.* London: China Society, 1992.

Bickers, Robert A., and Jeffrey N. Wasserstrom. "Shanghai's 'Dogs and Chinese Not Admitted' Sign: Legend, History and Contemporary Symbol." *China Quarterly* 142 (June 1995): 444–66.

Bo Jing. "Cong changji shuodao minzu jiankang wenti" (Prostitutes and the question of the health of the nation). *Wanying* (The variety fair monthly) no. 7 (Feb. 1937): np.

Booker, Edna Lee. *News Is My Job: A Correspondent in War-Torn China.* New York: Macmillan, 1940.

Bordwell, David, Janet Staiger, and Kristin Thompson. *The Classical Hollywood Cinema: Film Style and Mode of Production to 1960.* New York: Columbia University Press, 1985.

Braester, Yomi. "Shanghai's Economy of the Spectacle: The Shanghai Race Club in Liu Na'ou's and Mu Shiying's Stories." *Modern Chinese Literature* 9 (1995): 39–56.

Briggs, Charles, and Richard Bauman. "Genre, Intertextuality, and Social Power." *Journal of Linguistic Anthropology* 2 (1992): 131–72.

Brooks, Peter. *The Melodramatic Representation.* New York: Columbia University Press, 1985.

Brown, Royal S. "Film Music: The Good, the Bad, and the Ugly." *Cineaste* 21 (1995): 62–67.

———. *Overtones and Undertones: Reading Film Music*. Berkeley: University of California Press, 1994.

Browne, Nick, Paul G. Pickowicz, Vivian Sobchack, and Esther Yau, eds. *New Chinese Cinemas: Forms, Identities, Politics*. Cambridge: Cambridge University Press, 1994.

Brownlow, Kevin. *Behind the Mask of Innocence—Sex, Violence, Prejudice, Crime: Films of Social Conscience in the Silent Era*. New York: Knopf, 1990.

Burch, Noël. *To the Distant Observer*. Berkeley: University of California Press, 1979.

Burke, Peter. "Reflections on the Origins of Cultural History." In Joan H. Pittock and Andrew Wear, eds., *Interpretation and Cultural History*, pp. 5–24. New York: St. Martin's Press, 1991.

Butler, Judith. *Gender Trouble: Feminism and the Subversion of Identity*. London: Routledge, 1990.

Cai Chusheng. "Bashi siri zhihou—gei *Yukuang qu* de guanzhongmen" (Eighty-four days later—to the audience of *Fisherman's Song*). In Chen Bo, ed., *Zhongguo zuoyi dianying yundong*, pp. 364–65.

———. *Cai Chusheng de chuangzuo daolu* (Cai Chusheng's creative path). Beijing: Wenhua yishu chubanshe, 1982.

———. "Zhaoguang" (Morning light). *Xiandai dianying* 1 (1933).

Cambon, Marie. "The Dream Palaces of Shanghai: American Films in China's Largest Metropolis Prior to 1949." *Asian Cinema* 7, no. 2 (Winter 1995): 34–45.

Cao Maotang and Wu Lun. *Shanghai yingtan huajiu* (Reminiscences of the Shanghai film scene). Shanghai: Shanghai wenyi chubanshe, 1987.

Cao Yongfu. "Shanghai Daguangming dianying yuan gaikuang" (General account of Shanghai's Grand Theater). *Shanghai dianying shiliao* 1 (Oct. 1992): 207–11.

Carlitz, Katherine. "Desire, Danger, and the Body: Stories of Women's Virtue in Late-Ming China." In Christina Gilmartin et al., eds., *Engendering China*, pp. 101–24.

Chai, May-lee. "Urban Divorce and the Divorce Debate in Republican-Era China." M.A. thesis, Yale University, 1992.

Chartier, Roger. *Cultural History: Between Practices and Representations*. Oxford: Polity Press, 1988.

Chen Bo, ed. *Zhongguo zuoyi dianying yundong* (The leftist film movement in China). Beijing: Zhongguo dianying chubanshe, 1993.

Chen Dingshan. *Chunshen jiuwen* (Old tales of Shanghai). 2 vols. Taibei: Chenguang yuekan she, 1964.

Chen Huiyang. *Mengying ji* (Dreaming of movies). Taibei: Yunchen, 1990.

Chen Lifu. *Zhongguo dianying shiye* (The film enterprise in China). Shanghai: Chenshe, 1933.

Chen, Theodore Hsi-en. "Education in China, 1927–1937." In Paul K. Sih, ed., *The Strenuous Decade: China's Nation-Building Efforts, 1927–1937*, pp. 289–314. New York: St. John's University, 1970.

Chen Wei, ed. *Ke Ling dianying wencun* (Ke Ling's film essays). Beijing: Zhongguo dianying chubanshe, 1992.

Chen Wu. "Qingsuan Liu Na'ou de lilun" (Liquidating Liu Na'ou's theory). In Chen Bo, ed., *Zhongguo zuoyi dianying yundong*, pp. 162–67.

Chen, Xihe. "Shadowplay: Chinese Film Aesthetics and Their Philosophical and Cultural Fundamentals." In George Semsel et al., eds., *Chinese Film Theory*, pp. 193–201.

Cheng Bugao. *Yingtan yijiu* (Reminiscences of the film circles). Beijing: Zhongguo dianying chubanshe, 1983.

Cheng Jihua, Li Shaobai, and Xing Zuwen, eds. *Zhongguo dianying fazhanshi* (A history of the development of Chinese cinema). 2 vols. Beijing: Zhongguo dianying chubanshe, 1980 (1963).

Cheng Shu'an, ed. *Zhongguo dianying yanyuan cidian* (Dictionary of Chinese movie actors and actresses). Beijing: Zhongguo guangbo dianshi chubanshe, 1992.

Cheng, Weikun. "The Challenge of the Actresses: Female Performers and Cultural Alternatives in Early Twentieth Century Beijing and Tianjin." *Modern China* 22, no. 2 (Apr. 1996): 197–233.

Chow, Rey. *Primitive Passions: Visuality, Sexuality, Ethnography, and Contemporary Chinese Cinema.* New York: Columbia University Press, 1995.

———. "A Souvenir of Love." *Modern Chinese Literature* 7, no. 2 (Fall 1993): 59–78.

———. *Woman and Chinese Modernity: The Politics of Reading Between West and East.* Minnesota: University of Minnesota Press, 1991.

Chow, Tse-tsung. *The May Fourth Movement: Intellectual Revolution in Modern China.* Cambridge, Mass.: Harvard University Press, 1960.

Cihai (Sea of Words). Vol. 2. Taibei: Taiwan Zhonghua shuju, 1969.

Clark, Paul. *Chinese Cinema: Culture and Politics Since 1949.* Cambridge: Cambridge University Press, 1987.

Clifford, Nicholas. *Spoilt Children of Empire: Westerners in Shanghai and the Chinese Revolution of the 1920s.* Hanover, Conn.: University Press of New England, 1991.

Couzens Hoy, David, ed. *Foucault: A Critical Reader.* New York: Basil Blackwell, 1986.

Dai Jinhua. "Invisible Women: Contemporary Chinese Cinema and Women's Film." *Positions* 3, no. 1 (Spring 1995): 255–80.

Dai Xiaolan, ed. *Zhongguo wusheng dianying* (Chinese silent films). Beijing: Zhongguo dianying chubanshe, 1996.

Davis, Nanette J., ed. *Prostitution: An International Handbook on Trends, Problems, and Policies.* Westport, Conn.: Greenwood Press, 1993.

Day, Ruth. *Shanghai: 1935.* Claremont, Calif.: Saunders Studio Press, 1936.

De Leeuw, Hendrik. *Cities of Sin.* New York: Harrison Smith and Robert Haas, 1933. Reprinted by New York: Garland Publishing, 1979.

Dianying jiancha weiyuanhui gongbao (The bulletin of the National Film Censorship Committee). Nanjing, 1932.

Dianying jiancha weiyuanhui gongzuo baogao (The work report of the National Film Censorship Committee). Nanjing, 1934.

Dianying jiancha weiyuanhui jiancha dianying baogao (Report on film censorship by the National Film Censorship Committee). Nanjing, 1934.

Dianying yishu cidian (A dictionary of cinematic art). Beijing: Zhongguo dianying chubanshe, 1986.

Dil, Anwar S., ed. *Aspects of Chinese Sociolinguistics: Essays by Yuen Ren Chao.* Stanford: Stanford University Press, 1976.

Ding Ling. "Mengke" (Mengke). *Xiaoshuo yuebao* (Short story monthly) 18, no. 12 (Dec. 10, 1927): 11–35.

Dissanayake, Wimal, ed. *Melodrama and Asian Cinema.* Cambridge: Cambridge University Press, 1993.

Doane, Mary Ann. *The Desire to Desire: The Woman's Film of the 1940s*. Bloomington: Indiana University Press, 1987.

Dong Jieyuan. *Master Tung's Western Chamber Romance*. Trans. Li-li Chen. Cambridge: Cambridge University Press, 1976.

———. *Xixiang ji zhugongdiao zhuyi* (The Romance of the Western Chamber, chantefable with annotations). Annotated by Zhu Pingchu. Lanzhou: Gansu renmin chubanshe, 1982.

Dong Jingxin. "Zhongguo yingxi kao" (An examination of Chinese shadowplay). *Juxue yuekan* 3, no. 11 (1934): 1–19.

Dower, John. *War Without Mercy: Race and Power in the Pacific War*. New York: Pantheon, 1986.

Dreyfus, Hubert L., and Paul Rabinow. *Michel Foucault: Beyond Structuralism and Hermeneutics*. 2d edition. Chicago: University of Chicago Press, 1983.

Du Yunzhi. *Zhongguo de dianying* (Film in China). Taibei: Huangguan, 1978.

———. *Zhongguo dianying shi* (A history of Chinese cinema). Taibei: Taiwan Shangwu, 1972.

———. *Zhonghua minguo dianyingshi* (A history of film in the Republic of China). 2 vols. Taibei: Xingzheng yuan wenhua jianshe weiyuan hui, 1988.

Duara, Prasenjit. "Knowledge and Power in the Discourse of Modernity: The Campaign Against Popular Religion in Early Twentieth-Century China." *Journal of Asian Studies* 50, no. 1 (Feb. 1991): 67–83.

Duchesne, Isabelle. "The Chinese Opera Star: Roles and Identity." In John Hay, ed., *Boundaries in China*, pp. 217–42. London: Reaction Books, 1994.

Dyer, Richard. *Stars*. London: British Film Institute, 1979.

Elsaesser, Thomas. "Social Mobility and the Fantastic: German Silent Cinema." In Mike Budd, ed., *The Cabinet of Dr. Caligari: Texts, Contexts, Histories*, pp. 171–89. New Brunswick: Rutgers University Press, 1990.

Elsaesser, Thomas, ed. *Early Cinema: Space, Frame, Narrative*. London: British Film Institute, 1990.

Elvin, Mark. "Tales of *Shen* and *Xin*: Body-Person and Heart-Mind in China During the Last 150 Years." *Zone*, special ed., *Fragments from the History of the Human Body*, no. 2 (1991): 289–315.

Erenberg, Lewis A. *Steppin' Out: New York Nightlife and the Transformation of American Culture, 1890–1930*. Chicago: University of Chicago Press, 1981.

Erhlich, Linda C., and David Desser, eds. *Cinematic Landscapes: Observations on the Visual Arts and Cinema of China and Japan*. Austin: University of Texas Press, 1994.

Feng Ge. "Funü yu dianying zhiye" (Women and the film industry). *Funü zazhi* (The ladies' journal) 13, no. 6 (June 1927): 9–13.

Feng Min, Shao Zhou, and Jin Fenglan. *Zhongguo dianying yishu shigang* (An outline history of Chinese film art). Tianjin: Nankai daxue chubanshe, 1992.

Feng Xizui. "Rougan yu dianying" (Eroticism and movies). *Dianying yuekan*, nos. 11–12 (1929).

Finch, Percy. *Shanghai and Beyond*. New York: Charles Scribner's Sons, 1953.

Foucault, Michel. *The Archaeology of Knowledge and the Discourse on Language*. Trans. A. M. Sheridan Smith. New York: Pantheon Books, 1972.

————. *The Use of Pleasure: Vol. 2 of the History of Sexuality.* Trans. Robert Hurley. New York: Vintage Books, 1990.

Freedman, Maurice. *The Study of Chinese Society: Essays by Maurice Freedman.* Stanford: Stanford University Press, 1979.

Freuhauff, Heinrich. "Urban Exoticism in Modern and Contemporary Chinese Literature." In Ellen Widmer and David Der-Wei Wang, eds., *From May Fourth to June Fourth,* pp. 132–64.

————. "Urban Exoticism in Modern Chinese Literature, 1910–1933." Ph.D. diss., University of Chicago, 1990.

Fu, Po-shek. "Framing History: Popular Film Culture in Wartime Shanghai." Paper delivered at the annual meeting of the Association for Asian Studies, Washington, D.C., Apr. 1995.

————. *Passivity, Resistance, and Collaboration: Intellectual Choices in Occupied Shanghai, 1937–1945.* Stanford: Stanford University Press, 1993.

————. "Projecting Loyalty: The Marginality and Ideological Ambivalence of Occupied Shanghai Cinema." Paper presented at the Luce Seminar on Twentieth-Century Urban Shanghai, University of California–Berkeley, Dec. 1994.

————. "Struggle to Entertain: The Political Ambivalence of Shanghai Film Industry under Japanese Occupation, 1941–1945." In *Cinema of Two Cities: Hong Kong–Shanghai.* Hong Kong: Eighteenth Hong Kong International Film Festival, 1994.

Gan Yazi (Atsu Kann), Cheng Shuren, and Chen Dingxiu (D. S. Chen), eds. *1927 Zhonghua yingye nianjian* (1927 China cinema yearbook). Shanghai: Zhonghua yingye nianjian she, 1927.

Geertz, Clifford. *The Interpretation of Cultures: Selected Essays.* New York: Basic Books, 1973.

Gilmartin, Christina K., Gail Hershatter, Lisa Rofel, and Tyrene White, eds. *Engendering China: Woman, Culture, and the State.* Cambridge, Mass.: Harvard University Press, 1994.

Gledhill, Christine, ed. *Stardom: Industry of Desire.* London: Routledge, 1991.

Gong Jia'nong (Robert Kung). *Gong Jia'nong congying huiyi lu* (Gong Jia'nong's memoirs of his film activities). 3 vols. Taibei: Wenxing shudian, 1967. Reprinted by Taibei: Zhuanji wenxue zazhi she, 1980.

Gong Tianyi. "Shenguai yingpian kaijin wenti de tantao" (The debate over lifting the ban on magic/ghost movies). *Shehui yuebao* 1, no. 3 (1934): 71–72.

Gongsun Lu. *Zhongguo dianying shihua* (A history of Chinese cinema). 2 vols. Hong Kong: Nantian shuye gongsi, 1977.

Gorbman, Claudia. *Unheard Melodies: Narrative Film Music.* Bloomington: Indiana University Press, 1987.

Gould, Randall. "Where Races Mingle but Never Merge." *Christian Science Monitor* (June 24, 1936): 4.

Gronewold, Sue. *Beautiful Merchandise: Prostitution in China, 1860–1936.* New York: Haworth Press, 1982.

Gronow, Pekka. "The Record Industry Comes to the Orient." *Ethnomusicology* 25 (1981): 251–84.

Gu Jianchen. *Jutuan zuzhi ji wutai guanli* (Drama organization and stage management). Changsha: Shangwu, 1940.

————. *Minzhong xiju gailun* (Introduction to popular drama). n.p./n.d.

————. "Zhongguo dianying fada shi" (A history of the development of Chinese cinema). In *Zhongguo dianying nianjian* (Yearbook of Chinese cinema, 1934); reprinted in Dai Xiaolan, ed., *Zhongguo wusheng dianying*, pp. 1349–54.

Guan Wenqing (Moon Kwan). *Zhongguo yintan waishi* (Stories of Chinese film). Hong Kong: Guangjiaojing chubanshe, 1976.

Gunning, Tom. "An Aesthetic of Astonishment: Early Film and the (In)Credulous Spectator." *Art and Text* 34 (Spring 1989): 31–45.

————. "The Cinema of Attractions: Early Film, Its Spectator and the Avant-Garde." *Wide Angle* 8, nos. 3–4 (Fall 1986): 63–70.

————. "Film History and Film Analysis: The Individual Film in the Course of Time." *Wide Angle* 12, no. 3 (July 1990): 4–19.

Guo Moruo. "Geming yu wenxue" (Revolution and literature, 1926). Reprinted in Zhang Ruoying, ed., *Zhongguo xinwenxue yundongshi ziliao* (Sources on the history of China's new literature movement), pp. 363–75. Shanghai: Guangming shuju, 1934; facsimile edition by Shanghai shudian, 1982.

Habermas, Jürgen. *The Structural Transformation of the Public Sphere: An Inquiry into a Category of Bourgeois Society*. Trans. Thomas Burger. Cambridge, Mass.: MIT Press, 1989.

Han Bangqing. *Haishang hua liezhuan* (Sing-song girls of Shanghai). *Zhongguo jindai wenxue daxi* (Anthology of early modern Chinese literature), 3: 153–648. Shanghai: Shanghai shudian, 1991.

Hansen, Miriam. "Adventures of Goldilocks: Spectatorship, Consumerism and Public Life." *Camera Obscura* 22, no. 2 (Jan. 1990): 50–71.

————. *Babel and Babylon: Spectatorship in American Silent Film*. Cambridge, Mass.: Harvard University Press, 1991.

————. "Early Cinema, Late Cinema: Permutations of the Public Sphere." *Screen* 34, no. 3 (Fall 1993): 192–210.

Hao, Dazheng. "Chinese Visual Representations: Painting and Cinema." In Linda Ehrlich and David Desser, eds., *Cinematic Landscapes*, pp. 45–62.

Harris, Kristine. "*The New Woman*: Image, Subject, and Dissent in 1930s Shanghai Film Culture." *Republican China* 20, no. 2 (Apr. 1995): 55–79.

————. "Silent Speech: Envisioning the Nation in Early Chinese Cinema." Ph.D. diss., Columbia University, 1997.

He Ma. *Shanghai jiuhua* (Old stories from Shanghai). Shanghai: Shanghai wenhua chubanshe, 1956.

He Xiujun. "Zhang Shichuan he Mingxing yingpian gongsi" (Zhang Shichuan and Mingxing Film Company). *Wenhua shiliao* 1 (1980): 111–66.

Henriot, Christian. "Chinese Courtesans in Late Qing and Early Republican Shanghai (1849–1925)." *East Asian History* 8 (Dec. 1994): 33–52.

————. "'From a Throne of Glory to a Seat of Ignominy': Shanghai Prostitution Revisited (1848–1949)." *Modern China* 22, no. 2 (Apr. 1996): 132–63.

Hershatter, Gail. "Courtesans and Streetwalkers: The Changing Discourses on Shanghai Prostitution, 1890–1949." *Journal of the History of Sexuality* 3, no. 2 (1992): 245–69.

————. *Dangerous Pleasures: Prostitution and Modernity in Twentieth-Century Shanghai*. Berkeley: University of California Press, 1997.

―――. "The Hierarchy of Shanghai Prostitution, 1870–1949." *Modern China* 15, no. 4 (Oct. 1989): 463–98.

―――. "Modernizing Sex, Sexing Modernity: Prostitution in Early Twentieth-Century Shanghai." In Christina Gilmartin et al., eds., *Engendering China*, pp. 147–74.

―――. "Regulating Sex in Shanghai." In Frederick Wakeman and Wen-hsin Yeh, eds., *Shanghai Sojourners*, pp. 145–85.

―――. "A Response." *Modern China* 22, no. 2 (Apr. 1996): 164–69.

Ho, Virgil Kit-yiu. "Selling Smiles in Canton: Prostitution in the Early Republic." *East Asian History,* no. 5 (June 1993): 107–27.

Hong Shi. "Diyici langchao: mopian qi Zhongguo shangye dianying xianxiang shuping" (The first wave: a discussion of commercial films in the silent era of Chinese cinema). *Dangdai dianying* 1995, no. 2: 5–12.

Hong Shi, et al. "Zhongguo zaoqi gushipian de chuangzuo tansuo" (Explorations on the creation of early Chinese narrative cinema). *Dianying yishu* 1990, no. 1: 54–69.

Hong Yu. "Jieluo zhang" (A list of nude scenes). *Yingxi shenghuo* 1, no. 39 (Oct. 10, 1932): 7.

Honig, Emily. *Sisters and Strangers: Women in the Shanghai Cotton Mills, 1919–1949.* Stanford: Stanford University Press, 1986.

Hou Yao. *Fuhuo de meigui* (Revived rose). Shanghai: Shangwu, 1929 (1924).

―――. *Qifu* (The abandoned wife). Shanghai: Shangwu, 1929 (1925).

Hsia, C. T. *A History of Modern Chinese Fiction.* 2d edition. New Haven: Yale University Press, 1971.

Hsieh Shu-fen. "A Nostalgic Look at Classic Chinese Films." *Sinorama* (Guanghua) 18, no. 5 (May 1993): 44.

Hu Daojing. "Shanghai dianyingyuan de fazhan" (The development of cinemas in Shanghai). In Shanghaitong she (Society of Shanghai experts), ed., *Shanghai yanjiu ziliao xuji* (Sequel to research materials on Shanghai), pp. 532–63. Shanghai: Zhonghua shuju, 1939.

Hu Die. *Ou you zaji* (Miscellaneous notes on a European journey). Shanghai: Liangyou, 1936.

Hu Die, with Liu Huiqin. *Hu Die huiyi lu* (Hu Die's memoirs). Taibei: Lianhe bao chubanshe, 1986. Reprinted by Beijing: Wenhua yishu chubanshe, 1988.

Huang Ailing. "Shilun sanshi niandai Zhongguo dianying danjingtou de xingzhi" (On the nature of the single long take in 1930s Chinese cinema). In *Zhongguo dianying yanjiu* (Hong Kong), no. 1 (Dec. 1983): 31–57.

Huang Jiamo. "Tan nüxing mei" (On female beauty). *Furen huabao* no. 24 (1934): 19–21.

Huang Ren. "Wei Zhongguo wuxia dianying tanyuan" (In search of the origins of Chinese martial arts films). *Dianying xinshang* (Taiwan) 7, no. 4 (1989): 82–83.

Huang Rongpei. "Heian Zhongguopian de shuguang" (The twilight of Chinese films). *Yingxi zazhi* 1, no. 10 (1931): 69.

Huang Shixian. "Zhongguo dianying daoyan 'xingzuo' jiqi yishu puxi" (The "galaxy" of Chinese film directors and their artistic genealogy). *Dangdai dianying* 1992, no. 6: 77–85.

Huang Yichuo. "Guochanpian de fuxing wenti" (The question of the revival of Chinese cinema). *Yingxi zazhi* 1, nos. 7–8 (June 1, 1930): 24.

Huanxiangge zhu. "Funü zhuangsu de yige da wenti—xiaosan zhi yingfou baocun" (A big problem regarding women's garments—should the corset be abandoned). *Beiyang huabao* (The pei-yang pictorial news) no. 84 (May 1927).

Huitu youli Shanghai zaji (An illustrated guidebook to Shanghai with miscellaneous notes). Shanghai: Wenbao shuju, 1906.

Huo Xueyin. "Dianying mingxing" (Movie star). *Xin Shanghai* 1, no. 9 (Jan. 1926): 9–13.

Jelavich, Peter. *Berlin Cabaret*. Cambridge, Mass.: Harvard University Press, 1993.

Jewsiewicki, Bogumil. "The Identity of Memory and the Memory of Identity in the Age of Commodification and Democratization." *Social Identities* 1 (1995): 227–62.

Jia Leilei. "Zhongguo wuxia dianying yuanliu lun" (On the genesis and development of the Chinese martial arts film). *Yingshi wenhua* 5 (Sept. 1992): 204–24.

Jia Ming, ed. *Ruan Lingyu* (Ruan Lingyu). Beijing: Zhongguo dianying chubanshe, 1985.

Jiang Gubai. *Jutuan zuzhi ji wutai guanli* (Drama organization and stage management). Changsha: Shangwu, 1940.

———. *Minzhong xiju gailun* (Introduction to popular drama). n.p./n.d.

———. "Zhongguo yingye guoqu xianzai yu jianglai" (The past, present, and future of the Chinese film industry). In *Lingxing zazhi erzhounian zhuanji* (The second anniversary issue of the *Stars Magazine*), pp. 99–124. Hong Kong: Lingxing, 1933.

Jiang Li. "Zhu Jiaye guanyu jinzhi funü suxiong detian" (Zhu Jiaye's proposal to ban breast binding). *Minguo chunqiu*, no. 1 (Jan. 1990).

Jiang Xingyu. *Xixiang ji kaozheng* (The Romance of the Western Chamber: textual verification). Shanghai: Shanghai guji chubanshe, 1988.

Jiang Zhenxin. "Xiandai nü dianxing—Xia Peizhen" (A model of modern beauty—Xia Peizhen). *Yingxi shenghuo* 1, no. 16 (May 1, 1931): 10–11.

Jin Shan. "Yi wangshi nian wangyou" (Reminiscing about the past, thinking of my deceased friends). *Dazhong dianying*, no. 139 (1956): 25.

Johnson, David, Andrew J. Nathan, and Evelyn S. Rawski, eds. *Popular Culture in Late Imperial China*. Berkeley: University of California Press, 1985.

Jones, Andrew F. *Like a Knife*. Ithaca: Cornell University, East Asia Program, 1992.

Ju Lu. "Ying hua" (Some comments about films). *Yingxi zazhi* 1, no. 9 (Aug. 1930): 28.

Judge, Joan. *Print and Politics: "Shibao" and the Culture of Reform in Late Qing China*. Stanford: Stanford University Press, 1996.

Ka Er. "Luoti yu jiewen" (Nudity and kissing). *Qingqing dianying* (The chin-chin screen) 1, no. 11 (1935).

Kaes, Anton. "German Cultural History and the Study of Film: Ten Theses and a Postcript." *New German Critique* 65 (Spring–Summer 1995): 47–58.

Kao, Y. (Yuan). "Motion Pictures." In Kwei Chungshu, ed., *Chinese Yearbook 1935–36*, pp. 963–86. Shanghai: Chinese Yearbook Publishing Co., 1935.

Ke Zhaoyin and Zhuang Zhenxiang, eds. *Shanghaitan yeshi* (Shanghai unofficial history). Nanjing: Jiangsu wenyi chubanshe, 1993.

Kernan, Alvin. *The Death of Literature*. New Haven: Yale University Press, 1990.

Ko, Dorothy Y. *Teachers of the Inner Chambers: Women and Culture in Seventeenth-Century China*. Stanford: Stanford University Press, 1994.

Kou Tianwu. "Zhongguo dianying shishangde diyi" (The "firsts" in Chinese film history). *Yingshi wenhua* 2 (Nov. 1989): 265–301.

Kracauer, Siegfried. *From Caligari to Hitler: A Psychological History of German Film*. Princeton: Princton University Press, 1947.

Kraus, J. H. "Jiewen zhibing de yanjiu" (The study of diseases caused by kissing). Trans. Xi Jing. *Beiyang huabao*, no. 87 (June 1927).

Kraus, Richard Curt. *Pianos and Politics in China: Middle-Class Ambitions and the Struggle Over Western Music*. New York: Oxford University Press, 1989.

Kwok, Daniel W. Y. *Scientism in Chinese Thought, 1900–1950*. New Haven: Yale University Press, 1965.

Laing, Ellen J. "Commodification of Art Through Exhibition and Advertisement." Paper delivered at the annual meeting of the Association for Asian Studies, Chicago, Mar. 1997.

Landes, Joan B. *Women and the Public Sphere in the Age of the French Revolution*. Ithaca: Cornell University Press, 1988.

Lau, Jenny. "*Farewell My Concubine*: History, Melodrama, and Ideology in Contemporary Pan-Chinese Cinema." *Film Quarterly* 49, no. 1 (Fall 1995): 16–27.

Le Goff, Jacques. "Mentalities: A History of Ambiguities." In Jacques Le Goff and Pierre Nora, eds., *Constructing the Past: Essays in Historical Methodology*, pp. 167–69. Cambridge: Cambridge University Press, 1985.

Le Goff, Jacques, and Pierre Nora, eds. *Faire de l'histoire: nouveaux problèmes*. 3 vols. Paris: Gallimard, 1974.

Le Zheng. *Jindai Shanghairen shehui xintai, 1860–1910* (The social *mentalités* of Shanghai people in the early modern period). Shanghai: Shanghai renmin chubanshe, 1991.

Lee, B. Y. "Modernists and Anti-Modernists in China." *China Weekly Review*, May 26, 1934.

Lee, Leo Ou-fan. "The Cultural Construction of Modernity in Early Republican China." Paper delivered at a conference on "Passages to Modernity in Republican China," University of California–Berkeley, Sept. 1995.

———. "The Tradition of Modern Chinese Cinema: Some Preliminary Explorations and Hypotheses." In Chris Berry, ed., *Perspectives on Chinese Cinema*, pp. 6–20.

———. "Two Films from Hong Kong: Parody and Allegory." In Nick Browne et al., eds., *New Chinese Cinemas*, pp. 202–15.

Lee, Leo Ou-fan, and Andrew J. Nathan. "The Beginnings of Mass Culture: Journalism and Fiction in the Late Ch'ing and Beyond." In David Johnson et al., eds., *Popular Culture in Late Imperial China*, pp. 360–95.

Levenson, Joseph. *Confucian China and Its Modern Fate*. Berkeley: University of California Press, 1965.

Lévi-Strauss, Claude. *The Savage Mind*. Chicago: University of Chicago Press, 1966.

Levine, Lawrence W. *Highbrow/Lowbrow: The Emergence of Cultural Hierarchy in America*. Cambridge, Mass.: Harvard University Press, 1988.

Leyda, Jay. *Dianying / Electric Shadows: An Account of Films and the Film Audience in China*. Cambridge, Mass.: MIT Press, 1972.

Li Baotan, ed. *Wenxue yanjiu hui xiaoshuo xuan* (Selected stories by the Literary Association). Vol. 1. Beijing: Renmin wenxue chubanshe, 1991.

Li, H. C. "Chinese Electric Shadows: A Selected Bibliography of Materials in English." *Modern Chinese Literature* 7, no. 2 (Fall 1993): 117–53.

———. "Chinese Electric Shadows III: And the Ship Sails On." *Modern Chinese Literature* 10, nos. 1–2 (1998): 207–68.

————. "More Chinese Electric Shadows: A Supplementary List." *Modern Chinese Literature* 8 (1994): 237–50.

Li Shaobai. *Dianying lishi ji lilun* (Film history and theory). Beijing: Wenhua yishu chubanshe, 1991.

Li Shiwei. "Xing de wenti" (The problem of sex). Transcripts of Dr. Mark Seldon's lectures. *Dagong bao*, May 4, 1932.

Li Suyuan and Hu Jubin. *Zhongguo wusheng dianying shi* (A history of Chinese silent film). Beijing: Zhongguo dianying chubanshe, 1996.

Li Tuo. "Chang jingtou he dianying de jishixing" (The long take and film's documentary realism). In Zhong Dianfei, ed., *Dianying meixue: 1982* (Film aesthetics: 1982), pp. 94–131. Beijing: Zhongguo wenyi lianhe chuban gongsi, 1983.

Lian Kang, ed. *Nie Er huazhuan* (A biography of Nie Er). Beijing: Yinyue chubanshe, 1958.

Liang, Mingyue. *Music of the Billion: An Introduction to Chinese Musical Culture.* New York: Heinrichshofen, 1985.

Lin Niantong. *Jingyou* (Camera work). Hong Kong: Suye chubanshe, 1985.

————. "Zhongguo dianyingde kongjian yishi" (The sense of space in Chinese cinema). *Zhongguo dianying yanjiu* (Hong Kong), no. 1 (Dec. 1983): 58–78.

Link, Perry. *Mandarin Ducks and Butterflies: Popular Fiction in Early Twentieth-Century Chinese Cities.* Berkeley: University of California Press, 1981.

Liu Guojun. *Cong xiao yatou dao da mingxing: Ruan Lingyu zhuan* (From servant to star: the biography of Ruan Lingyu). Chengdu: Sichuan wenyi chubanshe, 1986.

Liu Jingzhi, ed. *Zhongguo xinyinyueshi lunji 1920–1945* (A history of Chinese new music 1920–1945: collected essays). Vol. 1. Hong Kong: University of Hong Kong Press, 1988.

Liu Na'ou. "Dianying xingshi mei de tanqiu" (The search for the formal aesthetics of film). *Wanxiang* (Kaleidoscope) 1 (1934).

Liu Peiqian, ed. *Da Shanghai zhinan* (A guide for greater Shanghai). Shanghai: Guoguang shudian, 1936.

Liu, Ts'un-yan, ed. *Chinese Middlebrow Fiction: From the Ch'ing and Early Republican Eras.* Hong Kong: Chinese University Press, 1984.

Liu Xu. "Xiandai nüxing xinmu zhongde yinmu xingxiang" (Modern women's tastes for the screen image). *Furen huabao*, no. 31 (Aug. 1935): 49–50.

Lu, David Chi-hsin. "Gems from the Mosquito Press." *T'ien Hsia Monthly* 6, no. 1 (Jan. 1938): 7–17.

Lu Gong. "Foluoyite zhuyi zhipei xiade dianying" (The cinema under the Freudian spell). *Chen bao*, Sept. 14, 1932.

Lu Hanchao. "Away from Nanking Road: Small Stores and Neighborhood Life in Modern Shanghai." *Journal of Asian Studies* 54, no. 1 (1995): 93–123.

Lu Hsun. See Lu Xun.

Lu Mengshu, ed. *Dianying yu wenyi* (Film and the arts). Shanghai: Liangyou, 1928.

Lu, Sheldon Hsiao-peng. "Postmodernity, Popular Culture, and the Intellectual: A Report on Post-Tiananmen China." *Boundary 2* 23, no. 2 (Summer 1996): 139–69.

————, ed. *Transnational Chinese Cinemas: Identity, Nationhood, Gender.* Honolulu: University of Hawaii, 1997.

Lu Si. *Yingping yijiu* (Film criticism in recollection). Beijing: Zhongguo dianying chubanshe, 1962.

Lu Xun (Lu Hsun). *Selected Works of Lu Hsun.* Trans. Yang Hsien-yi and Gladys Yang. 3 vols. Peking: Foreign Languages Press, 1959.

Lu Yiping. "Shanghai xuesheng de minjian xuanchuan" (Shanghai students' propaganda work among the people). *Dazhong shenghuo* 1, no. 13 (Feb. 8, 1936).

Luo Feng. *Shijimo chengshi: Xianggang de liuxing wenhua* (The fin-de-siècle city: popular culture in Hong Kong). Hong Kong: Oxford University Press, 1995.

Luo Yijun. "Wenhua chuantong yu zhongguo dianying lilun" (Cultural tradition and Chinese film theory). *Dianying yishu* 1992, no. 2: 20–30.

———, ed. *Zhongguo dianying lilun wenxuan 1920–1989* (Chinese film theory: an anthology). 2 vols. Beijing: Wenhua yishu chubanshe, 1992.

Ma Junxiang. "Zhongguo dianying qingxiede qipaoxian" (The slanting starting line of Chinese cinema). *Dianying yishu* 1990, no. 1: 6–21.

Ma Ning. "The Textual and Critical Difference of Being Radical: Reconstructing Chinese Leftist Films of the 1930s." *Wide Angle* 11, no. 2 (1989): 22–31.

Ma Yunzeng and Hu Zhichuan, eds. *Zhongguo sheying shi, 1840–1937* (A history of Chinese photography). Beijing: Zhongguo sheying chubanshe, 1987.

Maltin, Leonard, ed. *1979–80 TV Movies.* New York: Signet, 1980.

Mao Dun. "Fengjian de xiaoshimin wenyi" (The culture of the feudalistic philistines). *Dongfang zazhi* 30, no. 3 (Feb. 1, 1933). Reprinted in *Mao Dun quanji* (Collected works of Mao Dun), 19: 368–72. Beijing: Renmin wenxue chubanshe, 1991.

Mao Zipei. "Wei yinghou Hu Die 'jia mian'" (The "crowning" of the movie queen Hu Die). *Shanghai wenshi,* no. 3 (Apr. 1990): 33.

Marchetti, Gina. *Romance and the "Yellow Peril": Race, Sex, and Discursive Strategies in Hollywood Fiction.* Berkeley: University of California Press, 1993.

Marshall, Jim. "Sad Sin in Shanghai." *Collier's,* July 10, 1937: 46–47.

Martin, Brian G. "The Green Gang and the Guomindang State: Du Yuesheng and the Politics of Shanghai, 1927–37." *Journal of Asian Studies* 54, no. 1 (Feb. 1995): 64–92.

———. "'The Pact with the Devil': The Relationship between the Green Gang and the Shanghai French Concession Authorities, 1925–1935." In Frederic Wakeman and Wen-hsin Yeh, eds., *Shanghai Sojourners,* pp. 266–304.

McMahon, Keith. "The Classic 'Beauty-Scholar' Romance and the Superiority of the Talented Woman." In Angela Zito and Tani Barlow, eds., *Body, Subject, and Power in China,* pp. 227–52.

Mei Lanfang. *Wo de dianying shenghuo* (My life in the movies). Beijing: Zhongguo dianying chubanshe, 1984 (1962).

Mei Nu. "Qinzui de laiyuan" (The origins of kissing). *Beiyang huabao,* no. 1018 (Nov. 1933).

Mellencamp, Patricia, ed. *Cinema Histories / Cinema Practices.* Los Angeles: American Film Institute, 1984.

Metz, Christian. *The Imaginary Signifier: Psychoanalysis and the Cinema.* Bloomington: Indiana University Press, 1977.

Miller, E. G. *Shanghai: Paradise of Adventurers.* New York: Stratford Press, 1937.

Mu Shiying. *Hei Mudan* (Black peony). Shanghai: Liangyou, 1934.

Mulvey, Laura. *Visual and Other Pleasures.* Bloomington: Indiana University Press, 1989.

Nie Er: Cong juben dao yingpian (Nie Er: from script to movie). Beijing: Zhongguo dianying chubanshe, 1963.

Nivard, Jacqueline. "Women and the Women's Press: the Case of *The Ladies Journal* (Funü zazhi), 1915–1931." *Republican China* 10, no. 1 (Nov. 1984): 37–56.

Ombre elettriche: Saggi e ricerche sul cinema cinese. Milan: Regione Piemonte/Electa, 1982.

Ombres électriques: Panorama du cinéma chinois 1925–1982. Paris: Centre de Documentation sur le Cinéma Chinois, 1982.

Ouyang Yuqian. *Dianying banlu chujia ji* (Entering the film world in my mid-career). Beijing: Zhongguo dianying chubanshe, 1984.

———. "Tan wenmingxi" (On the civilized play). In *Zhongguo huaju yundong wushinian shiliaoji* (Collection of historical materials on fifty years of Chinese spoken drama movement), 1: 48–108. Beijing: Zhongguo xiju chubanshe, 1958.

Pal, John. *Shanghai Saga*. London: Jarrolds, 1963.

Pan Gongzhan. *Xuesheng de xin shenghuo* (New life of students). Nanjing, 1935.

Pan, Lynn. *Sons of the Yellow Emperor: The Story of the Overseas Chinese*. London: Secker and Warburg, 1990.

Parish, James Robert. *Prostitution in Hollywood Films: Plots, Critiques, Casts and Credits for 389 Theatrical and Made-for-Television Releases*. Jefferson, N.C.: McFarland, 1992.

Petro, Patrice. *Joyless Streets: Women and Melodramatic Representation in Weimar Germany*. Princeton: Princeton University Press, 1989.

Pickowicz, Paul G. "Melodramatic Representation and The 'May Fourth' Tradition of Chinese Cinema." In Ellen Widmer and David Wang, eds., *From May Fourth to June Fourth*, pp. 295–326.

———. "Sinifying and Popularizing Foreign Culture: From Maxim Gorky's *The Lower Depths* to Huang Zuolin's *Ye dian*." *Modern Chinese Literature* 7, no. 2 (Fall 1993): 7–31.

———. "The Theme of Spiritual Pollution in Chinese Films of the 1930's." *Modern China* 17, no. 1 (Jan. 1991): 38–75.

———. "Unpacking China's Wartime Baggage: The Early Postwar Films of Shi Dongshan, Cai Chusheng, and Zheng Junli." Paper delivered at the annual meeting of the Association for Asian Studies, Washington, D. C., Apr. 1995.

Pike, Burton. *The Image of the City in Modern Literature*. Princeton: Princeton University Press, 1981.

Qu Qiubai (Shi Tie'er). "Puluo dazhong wenyi de xianshi wenti" (The problem of reality in proletarian popular art). *Wenxue* (Literature) (1932). Reprinted in *Qu Qiubai wenji: wenyi* (Collected writings of Qu Qiubai: arts and literature), vol. 1. Beijing: Renmin wenxue chubanshe, 1985.

Quanguo dianying gongsi fuze ren tanhua hui ji'nian ce (Proceedings from the symposium of the Chinese film producers). Nanjing, 1935.

Quiquemelle, Marie-Claire, and Jean-Loup Passek, eds. *Le Cinéma Chinois*. Paris: Centre national d'art et de culture Georges Pompidou, 1985.

Rao Yu. *Shi Zhicun, Mu Shiying, Liu Na'ou xiaoshuo xinshang* (Appreciating the fiction of Shi Zhicun, Mu Shiying, and Liu Na'ou). Nanning: Guangxi jiaoyu chubanshe, 1992.

Rawski, Thomas. *The Economic Growth in Pre-War China*. Berkeley: University of California Press, 1989.

Rayns, Tony, and Scott Meek, eds. *Electric Shadows: 45 Years of Chinese Cinema*. Dossier no. 3. London: British Film Institute, 1980.

Reed, Christopher. "Gutenberg in Shanghai: Mechanized Printing, Modern Publishing, and Their Effects on the City, 1876–1937." Ph.D. diss., University of California–Berkeley, 1997.

Roach, Joseph. *Cities of the Dead: Circum-Atlantic Performance*. New York: Columbia University Press, 1996.

Rothman, William. "*The Goddess*: Reflections on Melodrama East and West." In Wimal Dissanayake, ed., *Melodrama and Asian Cinema*, pp. 59–72.

Rowe, William. "The Problem of 'Civil Society' in Late Imperial China." *Modern China* 19, no. 2 (Apr. 1993): 139–57.

Rui Heshi, Fan Boqun, Zheng Xuetao, Xu Sinian, and Yuan Cangzhou, eds. *Yuanyang hudie pai wenxue ziliao* (Research materials on mandarin ducks and butterflies literature). 2 vols. Fuzhou: Fujian renmin chubanshe, 1984.

Sa Mengwu. "Wenhua jinhua lun" (On the evolution of culture). *Dongfang zazhi*, Dec. 10, 1927: 13.

Sang Hu. "Wo xinmu zhong de Hu Die" (Hu Die in my eyes). *Shanghai wenshi* 3 (Apr. 1990): 32–33.

Sato Tadao. *Kinema to hosei: Nicchu eiga zenshi* (Cinema and gunfire: The prehistory of Japanese and Chinese cinema). Tokyo: Riburopoto, 1985.

Schell, Orville. "China—the End of an Era." *The Nation*, July 17–24, 1995: 84–98.

Schwarcz, Vera. *The Chinese Enlightenment: Intellectuals and the Legacy of the May Fourth Movement of 1919*. Berkeley: University of California Press, 1986.

Semsel, George S., Xia Hong, and Hou Jianping, eds. *Chinese Film Theory: A Guide to the New Era*. Westport, Conn.: Praeger, 1990.

Semsel, George S., Chen Xihe, and Xia Hong, eds. *Film in Contemporary China: Critical Debates, 1979–1989*. Westport, Conn.: Praeger, 1993.

Sergeant, Harriet. *Shanghai: Collision Point of Cultures, 1918–1939*. New York: Crown Publishers, 1990.

Sha Li nüshi (Lady Sherry). "Wode bu keqi de zhonggao" (My frank advice). *Chen bao*, July 13, 1932.

Shanghai yanjiu zhongxin (Shanghai research center), ed. *Shanghai qibainian* (Seven hundred years of Shanghai). Shanghai: Shanghai renmin chubanshe, 1991.

Shanghai zhinan (Guide to Shanghai: a Chinese Directory of the Port). 19th edition (revised). Shanghai: Shangwu, 1919 (1909).

Shanghaitong she (Society of Shanghai experts), ed. *Shanghai yanjiu ziliao* (Research materials on Shanghai). Taibei: Zhongguo chubanshe, 1973.

Shao Mujun. "Dianying shouxian shi yimen gongye, qici caishi yimen yishu" (Cinema is primarily an industry and only secondarily an art form). *Dianying yishu* 1996, no. 2: 4–5.

Sharpe, William. *Unreal Cities: Urban Figuration in Wordsworth, Baudelaire, Whitman, Eliot, and Williams*. Baltimore: Johns Hopkins University Press, 1990.

Shaw, Ralph. *Sin City*. London: Futura, 1986.

Shen Feide. "1933 nian Hu Die dangxuan 'Dianying huanghou' shengkuang" (The grand spectacle of Hu Die's election as "Movie Queen"). *Minguo chunqiu* (Mar. 1993): 16–17.

Shen, Kuiyi. "Comics, Illustrations, and the Cartoonist in Republican Shanghai." Paper delivered at the annual meeting of the Association for Asian Studies, Chicago, Mar. 1997.

Shen Xiling. "Dianying yishude fengong" (Division of work in film art). *Dazhong shenghuo* 1, no. 5 (Dec. 24, 1935).

———. "Zenyang zhizuo *Shizi jietou*" (How *Crossroads* was made). In Chen Bo, ed., *Zhongguo zuoyi dianying yundong*, pp. 395–97.

Shi Tie'er. *See* Qu Qiubai.

Shimizu Akira. *Shanhai sokai eiga shishi* (A private history of film in the Shanghai concession). Tokyo: Shinchosha, 1995.

———. "War and Cinema in Japan." In *Media Wars: Then and Now*. Yamagata International Documentary Film Festival, 1991.

Shu Qi, et al. *Ruan Lingyu shenhua* (The legend of Ruan Lingyu). Hong Kong: Chuangjian, 1992.

Shu Yan. "Dianying de 'lunhui'—jinian zuoyi dianying yundong 60 zhounian" (The cycles of film—in commemoration of the sixtieth anniversary of the leftist film movement). *Xin wenxue shiliao* 1994, no. 1: 72–93.

Shu Zi. "Fengyu zhai yingxi tan" (Talking about movies from the Wind-and-Rain Studio), *Banyue* 2, no. 4 (1922): 3–4.

Si Bai. "Chuangzao zhongde shengpian biaoxian yangshi" (Creating expressive form in sound films). *Min bao: Yingtan* (Aug. 30–Sept. 2, 1934). Reprinted in Luo Yijun, ed., *Zhongguo dianying lilun wenxuan*, 1: 182–87.

Silverberg, Miriam. "Remembering Pearl Harbor, Forgetting Charlie Chaplin, and the Case of the Disappearing Western Woman: A Picture Story." *Positions* 1, no. 1 (Spring 1993): 24–76.

Sima Fen (Wang Bin). *Zhongguo dianying wushinian* (Fifty years of Chinese film). Taibei: Huangding wenhua chubanshe, 1983.

Smith, Steve. "Class and Gender: Women's Strikes in St. Petersburg, 1895–1917, and in Shanghai, 1895–1927." *Social History* 19, no. 2 (May 1994): 141–68.

Snow, Edgar. "The Americans in Shanghai." *American Mercury* (Aug. 1930): 437–45.

Spence, Jonathan. *The Search for Modern China*. New York: Norton, 1990.

Steiner, Fred. "What Were Musicians Saying about Movie Music During the First Decade of Sound? A Symposium of Selected Writings." In Clifford McCarty, ed., *Film Music 1*, pp. 81–104. New York: Garland, 1989.

Stock, Jonathan. "Reconsidering the Past: Zhou Xuan and the Rehabilitation of Early Twentieth-Century Popular Music." *Asian Music* 26 (Spring/Summer 1995): 119–35.

Strauss, Julia C. "Symbol and Reflection of the Reconstituting State: The Examination Yuan in the 1930s." *Modern China* 20, no. 2 (Apr. 1994): 211–38.

Su Xiao. "Mingxing shangpin hua" (The commodification of the movie stars). *Dianying xinwen* 1, no. 8 (1935): 2.

Sun Yu. *Yinhai fanzhou—huiyi wode yisheng* (Sailing across the sea of the silver screen—my life in recollection). Shanghai: Shanghai wenyi chubanshe, 1987.

Suopo Sheng (Bi Yihong) and Bao Tianxiao. *Renjian diyu* (Human hell). 1923–24. 2 vols. Shanghai: Shanghai guji chubanshe, 1991.

Tanizaki Jun'ichirō. "Katsudō shashin no genzai to shōrai" (The present and future of the moving pictures). *Shin shōsetsu* (New fiction) (Sept. 1917).

———. *Tanizaki Jun'ichirō zenshū* (Complete works of Tanizaki Jun'ichirō). 14 vols. Tokyo: Chūō kōron sha, 1957–1959.

Tansuo de niandai (Early Chinese cinema: the era of exploration). Program for a festival of films of the 1930s, sponsored by the Hong Kong Arts Center and the Hong Kong Chinese Film Association in 1984.

Tang Bihua. "Huiyi Hu Die ersan shi" (A few memories of Hu Die). *Shanghai wenshi*, no. 3 (Apr. 1990): 35.

Tang Chunfa. *Kai yidai xianhe—Zhongguo dianying zhifu Zheng Zhengqiu* (Opening a new road—Zheng Zhengqiu, the father of Chinese cinema). Beijing: Guoji wenhua chuban gongsi, 1992.

Tang Youfeng, ed. *Xin Shanghai* (New Shanghai). Shanghai Yinshuguan, 1931.

Tang Zhenchang, ed. *Jindai Shanghai fanhuaji* (A pictorial record of the flourishing city of modern Shanghai). Hong Kong: Shangwu, 1993.

Tian Han. "The Composer Nieh Erh." *Chinese Literature* 1959, no. 11: 124–31.

———. "Cong yinse zhi mengli xingzhuan lai" (Awakening from the silvery dream). *Dianying* (May 1, 1930). Reprinted in *Tian Han wenji*, 14: 348–62.

———. *Tian Han wenji* (Collected writings of Tian Han). 14 vols. Beijing: Zhongguo xiju chubanshe, 1987.

———. "Xiju dazhonghua he dazhonghua xiju" (The popularization of theater and the popularized theater). *Beidou* 2, no. 3 (July 20, 1932).

———. *Yingshi zhuihuai lu* (Recollections of film activities). Beijing: Zhongguo dianying chubanshe, 1981.

———. "Yinse de meng" (The silvery dream). *Yinxing*, no. 5 (1927).

Trumbull, Randolph. "The Shanghai Modernists." Ph.D. diss., Stanford University, 1989.

Tsuji Hisakazu. *Chuka deneishiwa* (A narrative history of Chinese cinema). Tokyo: Gaifusha, 1987.

Tu Shiping, ed. *Shanghai chunqiu* (Vicissitudes of Shanghai). Hong Kong: Zhongguo tushu jicheng gongsi, 1968.

Tuohy, Sue. "Imagining the Chinese Tradition: The Case of Hua'er Songs, Festivals, and Scholarship." Ph.D. diss., Indiana University, 1988.

Vuillermoz, Emile. "Chronique Cinematographique." *Le Temps* (Paris), Apr. 28, 1928: 4.

Wakeman, Frederic, Jr. "Licensing Leisure: The Chinese Nationalists' Attempt to Regulate Shanghai, 1927–49." *Journal of Asian Studies* 54, no. 1 (Feb. 1995): 19–42.

———. *Policing Shanghai 1927–1937*. Berkeley: University of California Press, 1995.

Wakeman, Frederic, Jr., and Yeh Wen-hsin, eds. *Shanghai Sojourners*. Berkeley: University of California–Berkeley, Institute of East Asian Studies, 1992.

Wan Cheng. "Zhonggao dangzhou" (A piece of advice to the authorities). *Yingxi shenghuo* 1, no. 30 (Aug. 1930): 1–2.

Wang Baisou. "Yeshi jiaoyu" (It's also educational). *Minguo ribao*, Mar. 7, 1931.

Wang, David Derwei (Wang Dewei). *Cong Liu E dao Wang Zhenhe* (From Liu E to Wang Zhenhe). Taibei: Shibao wenhua chubanshe, 1986.

———. *Fin-de-Siècle Splendor: Repressed Modernities of Late Qing Fiction, 1849–1911*. Stanford: Stanford University Press, 1997.

Wang Dingjiu, ed. *Dangdai nüzuojia sanwen* (Prose essays by contemporary women writers). Shanghai: Zhongyang shuju, 1935.

———, ed. *Dangdai nüzuojia shuxin* (Correspondences by contemporary women writers). Shanghai: Zhongyang shuju, 1935.

———, ed. *Dangdai nüzuojia suibi* (Occasional writings by contemporary women writers). Shanghai: Zhongyang shuju, 1935.

———, ed. *Shanghai menjing* (Guide to Shanghai). 4th edition. Shanghai: Zhongyang shuju, 1935.

Wang Hanlun. "Wo de congying jingguo" (My experience in the film industry). In *Gankai hua dangnian* (Sighing about those years), pp. 50–59. Beijing: Zhongguo dianying chubanshe, 1962.

———. "Yingtan huiyi lu" (Recollections of the film world). *Liangyou* (The young companion), no. 64 (Dec. 1931): 32–33.

Wang Huihe. *Zhongguo jinxiandai yinyueshi* (A history of music in modern China). Beijing: Renmin yinyue chubanshe, 1984.

Wang Meng. "Ren, Lishi, Li Xianglan" (People, history, Li Xianglan). *Dushu* 1992, no. 11: 9–17.

Wang Renmei, with Xie Bo. *Wode chengming yu buxing: Wang Renmei huiyi lu* (My rise to fame and unhappiness: the reminiscences of Wang Renmei). Shanghai: Shanghai wenyi chubanshe, 1985.

Wang Shifu. *The Moon and the Zither: The Story of the Western Wing*. Trans. Stephen H. West and Wilt L. Idema. Berkeley: University of California Press, 1991.

———. *The Romance of the Western Chamber*. Trans. S. I. Hsiung; intro. C. T. Hsia. New York: Columbia University Press, 1968 (1936).

Wang Suping, ed. "Zhongguo dianying tuohuangzhede zuji—zaoqi dianying daoyan tanyilu" (Footprints of the pioneers of Chinese cinema—early film directors on their art). *Yingshi wenhua* 2 (Nov. 1989): 302–15.

Wang Yizhi. *Nie Er Zhuan* (A biography of Nie Er). Shanghai: Shanghai yinyue chubanshe, 1992.

Wang Yunjie. "Dianying yinyue" (Film music). In Wang Zhongcheng and Tan Long, eds., *Dianying chuangzuo yu pinglun* (Film production and criticism), pp. 174–92. Beijing: Zhongguo dianying chubanshe, 1986.

Wang Yunman. *Zhongguo dianying yishu shilüe* (An outline history of Chinese film art). Beijing: Zhongguo guoji guangbo chubanshe, 1989.

Wang Zilong. *Zhongguo yingju shi* (A history of Chinese film theater). Taibei: Jianguo chubanshe, 1960.

Wasserstrom, Jeffrey N. *Student Protests in Twentieth-Century China: The View from Shanghai*. Stanford: Stanford University Press, 1992.

Wei Shaochang. *Yiyuan shiyi* (Recollections from the garden of arts). Shanghai: Sanlian shudian, 1991.

Wei Shaochang, ed. *Wu Jianren yanjiu ziliao* (Sources for research on Wu Jianren). Shanghai: Shanghai guji chubanshe, 1980.

Wei, Betty Pei-t'i. *Old Shanghai*. Hong Kong: Oxford University Press, 1993.

Whang, Paul K. "Deficiencies of the 'modern Chinese girl.'" *China Weekly Review*, Oct. 5, 1929: 199.

White, Hayden. *Tropics of Discourse: Essays in Cultural Criticism*. Baltimore: Johns Hopkins University Press, 1978.

Widmer, Ellen, and David Der-wei Wang, eds. *From May Fourth to June Fourth: Fiction and Film in Twentieth-Century China*. Cambridge, Mass.: Harvard University Press, 1993.

Williams, Alan. *Republic of Images: A History of French Filmmaking.* Cambridge, Mass.: Harvard University Press, 1992.

Wilson, Elizabeth. *The Sphinx in the City: Urban Life, the Control of Disorder, and Women.* Berkeley: University of California Press, 1991.

Witke, Roxane. "Women in Shanghai of the 1930's." In Lionello Lanciotti, ed., *La donna nella Cina imperiale e nella republicana*, pp. 95–122. Firenze: Leo S. Olschki Editore, 1980.

Wong, Isabel K. F. "From Reaction to Synthesis: Chinese Musicology in the Twentieth Century." In Bruno Nettl and Philip V. Bohlman, eds., *Comparative Musicology and Anthropology of Music: Essays on the History of Ethnomusicology*, pp. 37–55. Chicago: University of Chicago Press, 1991.

Wong, Wang-chi. *Politics and Literature in Shanghai: The Chinese League of Left-Wing Writers, 1930–36.* Manchester, Eng.: Manchester University Press, 1991.

Wu Kaisheng. "Die ying huaxiang liu renjian" (The shadow and sweet fragrance of Hu Die lingers). *Shanghai wenshi*, no. 3 (Apr. 1990): 34.

Wu Qiufang, ed. *Shanghai fengwu zhi* (Gazetteer of Shanghai lore). Shanghai: Shanghai wenhua chubanshe, 1982.

Wu Xiwen. "Guochan yingpian yu nanyang wenhua" (Chinese film and nanyang culture). *Zhongnan qingbao* 2, no. 2 (Mar. 1935): 20–22.

Wu Yin. *Huishou yi dangnian* (Remembering the past). Beijing: Zhongguo dianying chubanshe, 1993.

Wu Yonggang. *Wode tansuo he zhuiqiu* (My explorations and quests). Beijing: Zhongguo dianying chubanshe, 1986.

Xi Shen. "Shanghai zhi dianying shiye" (The Shanghai film industry). *Xin Shanghai* 1, no. 1 (May 1925): 71–80.

Xia Yan. *Lanxun jiumeng lu* (Too lazy to seek old dreams). Beijing: Sanlian shudian, 1985.

———. "Zai 'ershi-sishi niandai Zhongguo dianying huigu' kaimu shi shangde jianghua" (Speech at the opening ceremony of "Retrospective of Chinese cinema of the 1920s–1940s"). *Xin wenxue shiliao* 1984, no. 1: 21–29.

Xiao Jianqing. *Manhua Shanghai* (Shanghai cartoons). Shanghai: Jingwei Shuju, 1936.

———. *Shanghai xiangdao* (Shanghai guide). Shanghai: Jingwei Shuju, 1937.

Xiao, Zhiwei. "Film Censorship in China, 1927–1937." Ph.D. diss., University of California–San Diego, 1994.

———. "Wu Yonggang and the Ambivalence in the Chinese Experience of Modernity: A Study of His Three Films of the Mid-1930s." *Asian Cinema* 9, no. 2 (Spring 1998): 3–15.

Xie Echang. "Duiyu yingpian ye zhi qiyou yu qiwang" (Concerns and hopes for the film industry). *Xin Shanghai* 2, no. 6 (Mar. 1927): 35–38.

Xu Changlin. "Zaoqi Zhongguo yinmu shang de minzu tese" (The national characteristic in early Chinese cinema). *Zhongguo dianying yanjiu* (Hong Kong), no. 1 (Dec. 1983): 20–21.

Xu Daoming and Sha Sipeng. *Zhongguo dianying jianshi* (A brief history of Chinese cinema). Beijing: Zhongguo qingnian chubanshe, 1990.

Xu Min. "Shi, chang, you—wan Qing Shanghai shehui shenghuo yipie" (Literatus, prostitute, actor: a glimpse of social life in late Qing Shanghai). *Ershiyi shiji* (Twenty-first century), no. 23 (June 1994): 37–38.

Xun Huisheng. *Xun Huisheng yanchu juben xuan* (Selected scripts of Xun Huisheng's performances). Shanghai: Shanghai wenyi chubanshe, 1982.

Yamaguchi Yoshiko and Fujiwara Sakuya. *Ri Koran—Watashi no hansei* (Li Xianglan—my half life). Tokyo: Shinchosha, 1987.

———. *Zai Zhongguo de rizi—Li Xianglan: wode bansheng* (My days in China—Li Xianglan: my half life). Trans. Jin Ruojing. Hong Kong: Baixing wenhua shiye youxian gongsi, 1989.

Yan Ciping. "Mingxing men hetong shangde jintiao" (The no's on the studio contracts with stars). *Qingqing dianying* 3, no. 1 (Mar. 1937).

Yan Jiayan, ed. *Xinganjue pai xiaoshuo xuan* (A selection of new perceptionist writings). Beijing: Renmin wenxue chubanshe, 1985.

Yang Cun. *Dianying yu dianying yishu* (Film and film art). Hong Kong: Chuangken, 1953.

———. *Zhongguo dianying sanshinian* (Thirty years of Chinese film). Hong Kong: Shijie chubanshe, 1954.

———. *Zhongguo dianying yanyuan cangsang lu* (The vicissitudes of Chinese movie actors and actresses). 2 vols. Hong Kong: Shijie chubanshe, 1954–55.

Yang Jun. "Huazhuang nüren de mei he shimei" (The use of cosmetics). *Qingqing dianying* 1, no. 6 (1934).

Yao Hsin-nung. "When Sing-Song Girls Were Muses." *T'ien-Hsia Monthly* (May 1937): 474–83.

Ye Baishe. "Suowang yu dianjianhui zhe" (My expectations from the National Film Censorship Committee). *Yingxi shenghuo* 1, no. 11 (Mar. 1931): 1–2.

Ye Shuping and Zheng Zu'an, eds. *Bainian Shanghai tan* (A hundred years of Shanghai). Shanghai: Shanghai huabao chubanshe, 1990.

Ye Yuan, ed. *Dianyingxue gailun* (An introduction to film studies). Shanghai: Shanghai shehui kexueyuan chubanshe, 1988.

Yeh, Wen-hsin. *The Alienated Academy: Culture and Politics in Republican China 1919–1937*. Cambridge, Mass.: Harvard University Press, 1990.

———. "Corporate Space, Communal Time: Everyday Life in Shanghai's Bank of China." *American Historical Review* 100, no. 1 (Feb. 1995): 97–122.

Yi De. "Changsha yeyou chungong pian fangying" (Pornographic films are also found in Changsha). *Diansheng* 5, no. 13 (1936): 314.

———. "Gongzi ge'er zhengying chungong pian" (The showing of pornographic movies among the dandies). *Yinhai zhoukan* 1, no. 7 (Apr. 1936): 6.

Yi Ming, ed., *Sanshi niandai Zhongguo dianying pinglun wenxuan* (Selections of Chinese film criticism in the 1930s). Beijing: Zhongguo dianying chubanshe, 1993.

Yin Hong. "Shangpin baiwujiao yu dianying guannian bianxi" (Differentiating commodity fetishism and film concepts). *Dianying yishu* 1996, no. 2: 6–10.

Yiren Ruan Lingyü nüshi rong'ai lu (An elegiac record for the artist Ms. Ruan Lingyü). 1935.

Yong Li. "Woguo diyizuo yingyuan jin hezai?" (Where is China's first movie theater today?). *Shanghai dianying shiliao*, no. 5, n.d.: 99–100.

Yong yanjing kan de Zhongguo dianying shi (A history of Chinese cinema seen through the eyes). Taibei: Longjiang, 1979.

Yu Bingru. "Dianying guanggao de duoluo" (The degeneracy of the movie ads). *Diansheng* 3, no. 23 (1934): 453.

Yu Xingmin. *Shanghai, 1862 nian* (Shanghai, 1862). Shanghai: Shanghai renmin chuban-she, 1991.

Zha, Jianying. *China Pop: How Soap Operas, Tabloids, and Bestsellers Are Transforming a Culture*. New York: New Press, 1995.

Zhang Chengshan. *Zhongguo dianying wenhua toushi* (Cultural perspectives on Chinese film). Shanghai: Xuelin chubanshe, 1989.

Zhang Junxiang and Cheng Jihua, eds. *Zhongguo dianying dacidian* (China cinema encyclopedia). Shanghai: Shanghai cishu chubanshe, 1995.

Zhang Ruogu. *Duhui jiaoxiangqu* (Urban symphonies). Shanghai: Zhenmeishan shudian, 1929.

Zhang Ruoying, ed. *Zhongguo xinwenxue yundongshi ziliao* (Sources on the history of China's new literature movement). Shanghai: Guangming shuju, 1934; facsimile edition by Shanghai shudian, 1982.

Zhang Ruoyu. "Hu Die koushu Ouzhou youzong" (Hu Die recounts her footsteps through Europe). *Shidai huabao* 8, no. 3 (July 20, 1935): 5–6.

Zhang Wei, Ying Xian, and Chen Jing. "Zhongguo xiandai dianying chubanwu zongmu tiyao" (A concise listing of modern Chinese film publications). *Shanghai dianying shiliao* 1 (Oct. 1992): 212–34; 2/3 (May 1993): 289–344.

Zhang Zhenhua. "'Shanghai dianyingde dansheng jiqi meixue tezheng" (The birth of Shanghai cinema and its aesthetic traits). *Dianying yishu* 1992, no. 3: 62–65.

Zhang Zhongli, ed. *Jindai Shanghai chengshi yanjiu* (Urban studies of modern Shanghai). Shanghai: Shanghai renmin chubanshe, 1990.

Zhang, Yingjin. "Chinese Cinema and Transnational Cultural Politics: Reflections on Film Festivals, Film Productions, and Film Studies." *Journal of Modern Literature in Chinese* 2, no. 1 (July 1998): 105–32.

———. *The City in Modern Chinese Literature and Film: Configurations of Space, Time, and Gender*. Stanford: Stanford University Press, 1996.

———. "The Corporeality of Erotic Imagination: A Study of Shanghai Pictorials and Fan Magazines of the 1930s." Paper delivered at the annual meeting of the Association for Asian Studies, Chicago, Mar. 1997.

———. "Engendering Chinese Filmic Discourse of the 1930's: Configurations of Modern Women in Shanghai in Three Silent Films." *Positions* 2, no. 3 (Winter 1994): 603–28.

———. "From 'Minority Film' to 'Minority Discourse': Questions of Nationhood and Ethnicity in Chinese Film Studies." *Cinema Journal* 36, no. 3 (Spring 1997): 73–90.

———. "Review Essay: Screening China—Recent Studies of Chinese Cinema in English." *Bulletin of Concerned Asian Scholars* 29, no. 3 (June–Sep. 1997): 59–66.

———. "The Texture of the Metropolis: Modernist Inscriptions of Shanghai in the 1930s." *Modern Chinese Literature* 9, no. 1 (1995): 11–30.

Zhao Dan. *Diyu zhimen* (The gate of hell). Shanghai: Shanghai wenyi chubanshe, 1980.

Zhao Yuanren. *Zhao Yuanren yinyue lunwenji* (A collection of essays by Zhao Yuanren). Beijing: Zhongguo yishu chuban gongsi, 1994.

Zheng Junli. *Huawai yin* (Off-screen sound). Beijing: Zhongguo dianying chubanshe, 1979.

———. "Xiandai Zhongguo dianying shilüe" (A concise history of modern Chinese film). In *Jindai Zhongguo yishu fazhan shi* (A history of the development of art in modern China). Shanghai: Liangyou, 1936. Reprinted in Dai Xiaolan, ed., *Zhongguo wusheng dianying*, pp. 1385–1432.

Zheng Yimei and Xu Zhuodai. *Shanghai jiuhua* (Reminiscences of old Shanghai). Shanghai: Shanghai wenhua chubanshe, 1986.

Zhibian waishi tekan (A special issue on *Migration to the Borders*). Shanghai: Da Zhonghua Baihe, 1926.

Zhong Dafeng. "Lun 'yingxi'" (On "shadowplay"). *Beijing dianying xueyuan xuebao* 1985, no. 2: 54–92.

————. "Zhongguo dianyingde lishi jiqi gengyuan: zailun 'yingxi'" (The history of Chinese cinema and its sources: again on "shadowplay"). *Dianying yishu* 1994, no. 1: 29–35; 1994, no. 2: 9–14.

Zhong Dafeng and Shu Xiaoming. *Zhongguo dianying shi* (History of Chinese cinema). Beijing: Zhongguo guangbo dianshi chubanshe, 1995.

Zhong Dafeng, Zhen Zhang, and Yingjin Zhang. "From *Wenmingxi* (Civilized Play) to *Yingxi* (Shadowplay): The Foundation of Shanghai Film Industry in the 1920s." *Asian Cinema* 9, no. 1 (Fall 1997): 46–64.

Zhong Lei. *Wushinian laide Zhongguo dianying* (Chinese cinema in the past fifty years). Taibei: Zhengzhong shuju, 1965.

Zhongguo dabaike quanshu: yinyue wudao (China encyclopedia: music and dance). Beijing: Zhongguo dabaike quanshu chubanshe, 1989.

Zhongguo daguan (The living China: a pictorial record). Shanghai: Liangyou, 1930.

Zhongguo dianying dadian (Encyclopedia of Chinese films). 4 vols. Beijing: Zhongguo dianying chubanshe, 1996–98.

Zhongguo dianying haibao yishu jingcui (Selections of poster arts in Chinese film). Guangzhou: Guangzhou chubanshe, 1996.

Zhongguo dianying jia liezhuan (Biographies of Chinese film people). 10 vols. Beijing: Zhongguo dianying chubanshe, 1982–86.

Zhongguo dianying nianjian (Yearbook of Chinese cinema). Shanghai: Zhongguo jiaoyu dianying xiehui, 1934.

Zhongguo dianying tuzhi (Illustrated annals of Chinese film). Guangxi: Zhuhai chubanshe, 1995.

Zhongguo jinxiandai yinyueshi jiaoxue cankao ziliao (Teaching materials for a history of modern Chinese music). Beijing: Renmin yinyue chubanshe, 1987.

Zhongguo wusheng dianying juben (Screen plays of Chinese silent films). 3 vols. Beijing: Zhongguo dianying chubanshe, 1996.

Zhongguo xinwenxue daxi, 1927–1937 (Anthology of modern Chinese literature). Vol. 18. Shanghai: Shanghai wenyi chubanshe, 1984.

Zhongguo yinyue cidian (Chinese music dictionary). Beijing: Renmin yinyue chubanshe, 1984.

Zhongguo yinyue jia xiaozhuan (Short biographies of Chinese composers). Chengdu: Sichuan renmin chubanshe, 1981.

Zhonghua yingxing (Chinese film stars). Nanjing: Xinhua chubanshe, 1997.

Zhou Chuanji. "Dianying shikong jiegouzhong de shengyin" (Sound in the time-space structure of film). Reprinted in Luo Yijun, ed., *Zhongguo dianying lilun*, 1: 243–61.

Zhou Jianyun. "Dianying shencha wenti" (The question of film censorship). *Dianying yuebao*, no. 5 (Aug. 1928): 1–3.

Zhou Shixun. "Shanghai you wochuo yingpian faxian" (Pornographic movies are found in Shanghai). *Yingxi chunqiu*, no. 4 (1925): 10.

Zhou Xiaoming. *Zhongguo xiandai dianying wenxue shi* (A history of film literature in modern China). 2 vols. Beijing: Gaodeng jiaoyu chubanshe, 1985.

Zhu Ge. "Quanhu xiao gongsi chafeng hou zhi biantai" (The closing of smaller studios and its aftermath). *Dianying xinwen* 1, no. 3 (July 20, 1935): 4–5.

Zhu Qiang. "Dianju yuan zhong" (In the movie theater). *Xin Shanghai* 1, no. 8 (Dec. 1925): 95–100.

Zi Yu. "Duguo dianying guanggao ban zhihou" (After reading the movie ads section). *Chen bao*, July 14, 1932.

Zito, Angela, and Tani E. Barlow, eds. *Body, Subject and Power in China*. Chicago: University of Chicago Press, 1994.

Character List

This list includes all directors, films, books, stories, journals, song titles, as well as selected critics, characters, places, and special terms mentioned in the book. Entries are alphabetized letter by letter, ignoring word and syllable breaks.

Ai de xietiao　愛的協調
An E (1905–76)　安娥
Anhui　安徽
Anlian taohuayuan　暗戀桃花源
Aodi'an　奧迪安
A Wei　阿維
A Ying (Qian Xingchun)　阿英

Baidai changpian gongsi　百代唱片公司
Bai Guang (b. 1930)　白光
Baihua Xixiangji　白話西廂記
Bailan zhi ge　白蘭之歌
Bailemen　百樂門
Bainian Shanghaitan　百年上海灘
baixiangren　白相人
Baixing daxiyuan　百星大戲院
Bali　巴黎
Banyue　半月
banzhu　班主
Bao Jing　鮑靖
Bao Minglian　鮑明廉
Bao Shiying　鮑士英
Bao Tianxiao (1876–1973)　包天笑
Bawang bieji　霸王別姬
beibi　卑鄙
Beidou　北斗
Beiping　北平

Beiyang huabao　北洋畫報
benbo　奔波
Bengbu xinwenlan bianjishili yizha fei-gaoshang de gushi　蚌埠新聞欄編輯室里一扎廢稿上的故事
bense (pai)　本色 (派)
Bi Feiyu　畢飛宇
Biye ge　畢業歌
Bi Yihong　畢倚虹
Bo Jing　波靜
Bu Shaotian　卜少天
Bu Wancang (1903–74)　卜萬倉

Cai Chusheng (1906–68)　蔡楚生
Cai Chusheng de chuangzuo daolu　蔡楚生的創作道路
Cai Hongsheng (b. 1940)　蔡洪聲
Cailing ge　采菱歌
Cai Xiaomei　蔡笑梅
caizi jiaren　才子佳人
Cao Xueqin (1715–63)　曹雪芹
Chahuanü　茶花女
chang　娼
Changcheng yingpian gongsi　長城影片公司
Chang Gong　長弓
chang jingtou　長鏡頭
chang pian zheng ju　長片正劇

changsan tangzi　長三堂子
changshi　嘗試
chayuan　茶園
Chen bao　晨報
Chen Bo (b. 1920)　陳播
Chen Boer (1907–51)　陳波兒
Chen Dabei　陳大悲
Chen Dieyi　陳蝶衣
Chen Dingshan　陳定山
Chen Dingxiu (D. S. Chen)　陳定秀
Cheng Bugao (1898–1966)　程步高
chenggong　成功
Chen Guofu (1892–1951)　陳果夫
Cheng Jihua (b. 1921)　程季華
chengming　成名
Cheng Shu'an　程樹安
Cheng Shuren　程樹仁
Chen Huaiai (1920–94)　陳懷皚
Chen Huangmei (b. 1913)　陳荒煤
Chen Huiyang　陳輝揚
Chen Jianyu (b. 1938)　陳劍雨
Chen Kaige (b. 1952)　陳凱歌
Chen Lifu (b. 1890)　陳立夫
Chen Liting (b. 1910)　陳鯉庭
Chen Meizhen　陳美珍
Chen Tiansuo　陳天所
Chen Wei　陳緯
Chen Wu (Wang Chenwu)　塵無
Chen Yanyan (b. 1916)　陳燕燕
Chen Yunshang (b. 1919)　陳雲裳
Chongde nü xuexiao　崇德女學校
Chuangtou riji　床頭日記
Chuangzao she　創造社
Chuanjia nü　船家女
chuanqi　傳奇
Chuanyinglou huiyilu　釧影樓回憶錄
chuchu wei xingqu shi shang, yi ji boren
　　yican　處處惟興趣是尚, 以冀博
　　人一燦
Chuka den'ei shiwa　中華電影史
chugui　出軌
Chumu jingxin de xiaoxi　觸目驚心
　　的消息

Chuncan　春蠶
Chun de meng　春的夢
Chungui duan meng　春閨斷夢
Chungui mengli ren　春閨夢里人
chunqing zhuyi　純情主義
Chunqiu　春秋
Chunshen jiuwen　春申舊聞
chunshui　春睡
chun yishu　純藝術
chusheng shidai　初盛時代
Cihai　辭海
Cong xiao yatou dao da mingxing: Ruan
　　Lingyu zhuan　從小丫頭到大明
　　星: 阮玲玉傳
Cui Yingying　崔鶯鶯

Da changcheng　大長城
Da chenghuang　打城隍
Da dongya dianying quan　大東亞電
　　影圈
Da dongya gongrong quan　大東亞共
　　榮圈
Da duhui　大都會
Dagong bao　大公報
Daguangming　大光明
Dahong denglong gaogao gua　大紅
　　燈籠高高掛
Dahu　大滬
Dahu wuting　大滬舞廳
Daibutsu Jiro　大佛次郎
Dai Jinhua　戴錦華
Dai Sijie　戴思杰
Dai Xiaolan　戴小蘭
dajia douyou fen　大家都有分
dajia guixiu　大家閨秀
Dalu　大路
Dalu ge　大路歌
Danao guai juchang　大鬧怪劇場
Dan Duyu (1897–1972)　旦杜宇
Dangdai　當代
Dangdai dianying　當代電影
Daoma dan　刀馬旦
Dao ziran qu　到自然去

Da Shanghai　大上海
Da Shanghai zhinan　大上海指南
Dashijie　大世界
daxi　大戲
Dazhongdianying　大眾電影
Da Zhongguo yingpian gongsi　大中
　國影片公司
Da Zhonghua-Baihe yingpian gongsi
　大中華百合影片公司
Dianju yuanzhong　電劇院中
Diansheng　電聲
Diantong　電通
Diantong huabao　電通畫報
dianying　電影
Dianying banlu chujia ji　電影半路出
　家記
Dianying chuangzuo　電影創作
Dianying de lunhui　電影的輪回
Dianying de molu　電影的末路
dianying huanghou　電影皇後
Dianying jiancha weiyuanhui gongbao
　電影檢查委員會公報
Dianying jiancha weiyuanhui gongzuo
　baogao　電影檢查委員會工作
　報告
Dianying jiancha weiyuanhui jiancha
　dianying baogao　電影檢查委員
　會檢查電影報告
Dianying lishi ji lilun　電影歷史及
　理論
Dianying meixue 1982　電影美學 1982
Dianying mingxing　電影明星
Dianying nü mingxing　電影女明星
Dianying shencha wenti　電影審查
　問題
dianying shuoming shu　電影說明書
Dianying xinshang　電影欣賞
Dianying yishu　電影藝術
Dianying yu dianying yishu　電影與
　電影藝術
Dianying yuebao　電影月報
Dianying yuekan　電影月刊
Dianying yu wenxue　電影與文學

Dianying zazhi　電影雜志
Dianying zhuankan　電影專刊
Diao Banhua　貂斑華
Ding junshan　定軍山
Ding Ling (1904–86)　丁玲
dingpeng　釘棚
Di Pingzi (Di Baoxian, Chuqing, 1872–
　1940)　狄平子 (狄葆賢, 楚卿)
Diyu zhimen　地獄之門
dong cheng　東城
Dongfang Haolaiwu: Zhongguodian-
　ying shiye de jueqi yu fazhan　東方
　好萊塢: 中國電影事業的崛起與
　發展
Dongfang zazhi　東方雜志
Dong Jieyuan (1189–1208)　董解元
Dong Keyi (1906–78)　董可毅
Dongnan daxue　東南大學
Dong Xixiang zhu gong diao　東西廂
　諸宮調
Dongya nü mingxing　東亞女明星
Dongya wuting　東亞舞廳
Duanwu jie　端五節
Duhui jiaoxiang qu　都會交響曲
duibuqi women Zhongguo ren　對不
　起我們中國人
duoluo　墮落
duoqing ya　多情呀
Dushi fengguang　都市風光
Dushi fengguang huanxiang qu　都市
　風光幻想曲
Dushu　讀書
Du Yuesheng (1888–1951)　杜月笙
Du Yunzhi (b. 1923)　杜雲之
Duzhe laigao: yingmi suibi　讀者來稿:
　影迷隨筆

elie　惡劣
Enpaiya　恩派亞
Erbaiwu baixiang chenghuangmiao
　二百五白相城隍廟
erhu　二胡
Ershiyi shiji　二十一世紀

Facong   法聰
fangdang   放蕩
Fang Peilin (?–1949)   方沛霖
Fan Yanqiao (1894–1967)   范煙橋
feichang   廢娼
Fei Mu (1906–51)   費穆
Feng Jicai (b. 1942)   馮驥才
Feng Mengyun   馮夢雲
Feng Min   封敏
Fengren kuangxiangqu   瘋人狂想曲
Fengshen yanyi   封神演義
Fengtai   豐泰
Fengyue   風月
fengyue pingzhang   風月平章
Fengyun ernü   風雲兒女
Fudan   復旦
Fuhuo de meigui   復活的玫瑰
Funiang qu   浮娘曲
Funü ribao   婦女日報
Funü shibao   婦女時報
Funü zazhi   婦女雜志
Furen huabao   婦人畫報
Fushimitsu Osama   伏水修
Fu Wenhao   傅文毫

gan baba   乾爸爸
Gankai hua dangnian   感慨話當年
Gan Yazi (Atsu Kann)   甘亞子
Gao Qianping   高倩萍
Gao Xinbao   高鑫寶
Gao Zhanfei (1904–69)   高占非
Geguo dianying qudi shencha tiaoli   各國電影取締審查條例
geming hongxian   革命紅線
Geming wenxian dishi erji   革命文獻第十二集
genü   歌女
Genü Hongmudan   歌女紅牡丹
genü qucheng   歌女區城
gewu ke   歌舞科
Gewu shengping   歌舞昇平
gewutuan   歌舞團
Gongan ju   公安局

Gong Jianong (1902–93)   龔稼農
Gong Jianong congying huiyilu   龔稼農從影回憶錄
Gong Li (b. 1966)   鞏俐
Gongsun Lu   公孫魯
Gong wutai   共舞台
guan   觀
Guanghua   光華
Guanglu   光陸
Guan Haifeng   管海峰
Guan Jinpeng (Stanley Kwan, b. 1957)   關錦鵬
Guan Wenqing (Moon Kwan, 1896–1995)   關文清
Guanyin   觀音
Guanying zhinan   觀影指南
Guer jiuzu ji   孤兒救祖記
gudao   孤島
Gu Jianchen (b. 1896)   谷劍塵
Gujing chongbo ji   古井重波記
Gu Lenguan   顧冷觀
guochan   國產
guochan dianying   國產電影
guohuo   國貨
Guoji da fandian   國際大飯店
Guomin ribao   國民日報
Guomindang   國民黨
Guo Moro (1892–1978)   郭沫若
Guotai   國泰
guoyu (wenxue bu)   國語 (文學部)
Guoyu zhuanxiu xuexiao   國語專修學校
guniang   姑娘
gupan   顧盼
gushixing   故事性
Guta qi an   古塔奇案
Gu Wuwei (b. 1892)   顧無為
guzhuang pian   古裝片
guzhuang xi   古裝戲

Haijiao shiren   海角詩人
Haishang hua lizhuan   海上花列傳
Haishang huo diyu   海上活地獄

haiyan 海燕

Han Bangqing (Ziyun, 1856–94) 韓邦慶 (子雲)

Hangzhou yingxi yuan 杭州影戲院

Hanlun meirong yuan 漢倫美容院

Hanlun yingpian gongsi 漢倫影片公司

Han Wudi 漢武帝

Haolaiwu de qinlüe 好來塢的侵略

Harbin genü 哈爾濱歌女

Heideng wu 黑燈舞

Heiji yuanhun 黑藉冤魂

Hei mudan 黑牡丹

Hei tianshi 黑天使

He Luting (b. 1903) 賀綠汀

He Ma 赫馬

Henhai 恨海

Heping zhi shen 和平之神

He Rongrong 何融融

Hongbang 紅幫

hongbao 紅包

Hongfen 紅粉

Hongfen kulou 紅粉骷髏

Hong gaoliang 紅高粱

Hongkou da xiyuan 虹口大戲院

Honglou meng 紅樓夢

Hong meigui 紅玫瑰

Hongniang 紅娘

Hongniang xianxing ji 紅娘現形記

Hong Shen (1894–1955) 洪深

Hong Shi 弘石

Hong xia 紅俠

Hou Yao (1900–1945) 侯曜

Hua 華

huachuan 花船

huaguo 花國

huaguo da zongtong 花國大總統

huaguo huanghou 花國皇後

Huahun 畫魂

Huaji dawang youhua ji 稽大王游華記

huajiu 花酒

huaju 話劇

Huamei yingpian gongsi 華美影片公司

Huang Ailing 黃愛玲

Huang Baiying 黃白英

Huang Chujiu 黃楚九

Huang Jiamo 黃嘉謨

Huang Jichi 黃繼持

Huan Ren (b. 1925) 黃仁

Huang Shaofen (b. 1911) 黃紹芬

Huang Shixian (b. 1935) 黃式憲

Huang Shuqin (b. 1940) 黃蜀芹

Huang Su 黃素

Huang tudi 黃土地

Huang Zi (1904–38) 黃自

Huang Zibu (Xia Yan) 黃子布

Huanhua zai 還花債

Huanxian yingpian gongsi 幻仙影片公司

Huashen guniang 化身姑娘

Huawai yin 畫外音

huayan jian 花煙間

Huaying zhoukan 華影周刊

Huayuan wuting 花園舞廳

Hubian chunmeng 湖邊春夢

Hu Daojing 胡道靜

Hu Die (Ruihua, 1908–89) 胡蝶 (瑞華)

Hu Die huiyi lu 胡蝶回憶錄

Huguang 滬光

Hu Hanmin (1879–1936) 胡漢民

Huiluo gongsi 惠羅公司

Huishou yi dangnian 回首憶當年

Hu Jubin 胡菊彬

huopo 活潑

Huoshan qingxue 火山情血

Huoshao honglian si 火燒紅蓮寺

Huo wuchang 活無常

Huozhe 活著

Hu Ping (b. 1913) 胡萍

Hu Rongrong (b. 1929) 胡蓉蓉

Jia Ming 佳明

jian 見

Jiang Gubai 姜谷白

Jiang Jieshi (Chiang Kai-shek, 1887–1975) 蔣介石

Jiang Xingli 蔣星煜

Jiang Xiuxia 江秀霞

jian jin shidai 漸進時代

jianmei yu mei 健美與媚

jiao tiaozi 叫條子

Jiao yu xue yuekan 教與學月刊

Jieyan ge 戒煙歌

Jincheng 金城

Jindai funü 近代婦女

Jindai Shanghai chengshi yanjiu 近代上海城市研究

Jindai Shanghairen shehui xintai 近代上海人社會心態

Jindai Zhongguo yishu fazhan shi 近代中國藝術發展史

Jin Fenglan 靳風蘭

Jingbao 晶報

Jing Fang 靜芳

Jingyou 鏡游

Jin Shan (1911–82) 金山

jinü 妓女

Jin Yan (1910–83) 金焰

Jinyibu de baolu 進一步的暴露

Jinyibu de jiantao 進一步的檢討

Jinyuan chunnong 禁苑春濃

Jiqiao 技巧

Jiqihua 機器化

jiqi wenming 機器文明

Jishu 技術

Jiucheng 酒鎗

Jiuguo Shibao 救國時報

Jiuwang zhige 救亡之歌

Jutuan zuzhi ji wutai guanli 劇團組織及舞台管理

Ju xue yuekan 劇學月刊

Kaerdeng 卡爾登

kaige 凱歌

kai huabang 開花榜

Kaikuang ge 開礦歌

Kailu xianfeng 開路先鋒

Kaixin 開心影片公司

Kai yidai xianhe—Zhongguo dianying zhifu Zheng Zhengqiu 開一代先河——中國電影之父鄭正秋

kan 看

Kan de menjing 看的門徑

Kang Youwei (1858–1927) 康有為

kaohong 拷紅

kaozheng 考證

Kate 卡特

Kawakita Nagamasa (1903–81) 川喜多長政

Kelian de Qiuxiang 可憐的秋香

Ke Ling (b. 1909) 柯靈

Ke Ling dianying wen cun 柯靈電影文存

Ke Zhaoyin 柯兆銀

Kongbu fenzi 恐怖分子

Konggu lan 空谷蘭

kuaigan 快感

Kuaihuolin 快活林

Kuangliu 狂流

kuangwu dahui 狂舞大會

Kumu fengchun 枯木逢春

kunqu 昆曲

Lai Shengchuan (Stan Lai, b. 1954) 賴聲川

Lang Dang 朗當

Langman shusheng 浪漫書生

Lang tao sha 浪淘沙

Lanxun jiumeng lu 懶尋舊夢錄

Laogong zhi aiqing 勞工之愛情

Lao Shanghai jianwen 老上海見聞

Leguan 樂觀

Lezheng 樂正

Liang Saizhen (b. 1906) 梁賽珍

Liangxin de fuhuo 良心的復活

Liangyou (huabao) 良友畫報

Liangyuan qiaohe 良緣巧合

Lianhe wenxue 聯合文學

Lianhua gewu ban 聯華歌舞班

Lianhua gongzhu 蓮花公主

Lianhua huabao 聯華畫報

Lianhua jiaoxiangqu 聯華交響曲

Lianhuan dianying tuhua 連環電影
圖畫

lianhuanxi 連環戲

Lianhua yingpian gongsi 聯華影片
公司

Libailiu 禮拜六

Libao 立報

Li Baoliang 李葆良

Li Bihua 李碧華

lijiao 禮教

Li Jichun 李際春

Li Jinhui (1891–1967) 黎錦暉

Li Lili (Qian Zhenzhen, b. 1915) 黎莉
莉（錢蓁蓁）

Li Minghui (b. 1906) 黎明暉

Li Minwei (1892–1953) 黎民偉

Li Mo 李某

Lingbo xianzi 凌波仙子

Ling He (Shi Linghe, b. 1906) 凌鶴
（石凌鶴）

linghun de 靈魂的

Linglong (funü tuhua zazhi) 玲瓏婦
女圖畫雜志

Lingrou damen 靈肉大門

Lingxing zazhi er zhounian zhuanji
伶星雜志二周年專集

Lin Niantong (1944–90) 林年同

Lin Shu (1852–1924) 林紓

Lin Xuehuai 林雪懷

Lin Zexu 林則徐

Li Pingqian (1902–84) 李萍倩

Li Shaobai (b. 1931) 李少白

Li Shaohong (b. 1955) 李少紅

Li Shen (?–846) 李紳

Li Suyuan 酈蘇元

Li Tuo 李陀

liu 流

Liu Guojun 劉國君

Liu Liangmo 劉良模

Liu Na'ou (b. 1900–40) 劉吶歐

Liu Peiqian 柳培潛

Li Xianglan (Yamaguchi Yoshiko, b.
1920) 李香蘭

Li Zeyuan 李澤源

longtou 龍頭

Lu Jie (1894–67) 陸潔

Lü Ji 呂驥

Lu Lixia 陸麗霞

Lu Mengshu 盧夢殊

Luo Feng 洛楓

Luo Gang (1901–77) 羅剛

Luo Mingyou (1900–1967) 羅明佑

Luo Yijun 羅藝軍

Lu Si (1912–84) 魯思

Lu Xun (1881–1936) 魯迅

mai linghun 賣靈魂

Maitang ge 賣糖歌

Malu tianshi 馬路天使

Manchu eiga kyokai (Man'ei) 滿州
映畫協會

Manhua 漫畫

Manhua Shanghai 漫畫上海

Mangmu de aiqing 盲目的愛情

Mannü qingge 蠻女情歌

Mannü qinghua 蠻女情花

Manting fang 滿庭芳

Mao Dun (Shen Yanbing, 1896–1981)
茅盾

Maomaoyu 毛毛雨

Mao Zipei 毛子佩

Maqiu dawang 馬球大王

Ma-Xu Weibang (1905–61) 馬徐維邦

Ma Yunzeng 馬運增

mei 美

Mei Lanfang (1894–1961) 梅蘭芳

Mei Lin 梅琳

Mei Lin nüshi de sheying zuopin
梅琳女士的攝影作品

Meimei nüxiao 美美女校

Meiqi 美琪

Mei Xuechou 梅雪儔

Meiyue yingtan 每月影談

mengya shidai　萌芽時代

Mengyingji　夢影集

Mi　咪

Mibao　秘報

minggui　名閨

Minguo chunqiu　民國春秋

mini ting　迷你廳

mingxing　明星

Mingxing tekan　明星特刊

Mingxing yingpian gongsi　明星影片公司

Mingyue gejushe　明月歌劇社

Mingyue gewutuan　明月歌舞團

Mingyue si da tianwang　明月四大天王

Minxin yingpian gongsi　民新影片公司

Minzhong xiju gailun　民眾戲劇概論

minzu pai　民族派

Minzu xingshi　民族形式

modeng　摩登

modeng nülang　摩登女郎

mubiao　幕表

mudan yao　牡丹妖

Mumi　幕咪

Mu Shiying (1912–40)　穆時英

mutouren xi　木頭人戲

Muxing zhiguang　母性之光

Naimei (yingpian gongsi)　耐梅 (影片公司)

Nanfu nanqi　難夫難妻

Nanguo she　南國社

Nanjing　南京

Nanjing gaodeng shifan xuexiao　南京高等師範學校

nannü shoushou buqin　男女授受不親

Nanyang　南洋

Nezha chushi　哪吒出世

Nie Er (1912–35)　聶耳

Ningbo　寧波

Niupeng　牛棚

Ni Zhen (b. 1938)　倪震

nü haizi　女孩子

Nü mingxing de xingyun　女明星的幸運

nüren　女人

Nüsheng　女聲

Nüxing de nahan　女性的吶喊

nü yanyuan　女演員

Ouyang Yuqian (1889–1962)　歐陽予倩

Ou you zaji　歐遊雜記

Pan Gongzhan　潘公展

Pan Shuhua　潘淑華

Pansi dong　盤絲洞

paoma ting　跑馬廳

piejian　瞥見

pinxing　品行

piyingxi　皮影戲

Pujiusi　普救寺

Puzhou　蒲州

Qian Xingchun (A Ying, Zhang Fengwu, 1900–1977)　錢杏邨

Qifu　棄婦

Qichongtian　七重天

Qiekan haiyou shenme xuetou　且看還有什麼噱頭

qing　情

Qingbang　青幫

Qinglian ge　青蓮閣

Qingnian jinzing qu　青年進行曲

Qingniao　青鳥

Qingqing dianying　青青電影

Qing Shi　青矢

Qinhuai　秦淮

Qi nüzi　奇女子

qiong　黥

qipao　旗袍

Qiu Dai Anping (b. 1940)　邱戴安平

Qiu Qixiang　裘芑香

Qiushui yiren　秋水伊人

Quanye julebu 　全夜俱樂部

qun fang hui chang 　群芳會唱

Qu Qiubai (1899–1935) 　瞿秋白

Qu Qiubai wenji—wenyi 　瞿秋白文
　集——文藝

Rao Yu 　饒宇

Ren Guang (1900–1941) 　任光

Ren gui qing 　人鬼情

Renjian diyu 　人間地獄

Ren Pengnian (1894–1968) 　任彭年

rensheng yishu 　人生藝術

renxin zai jishi, miaoshou ke huichun
　仁心在濟世, 妙手可回春

Riben yingxun 　日本影訊

Rougan 　肉感

Ruan Lingyu (Fenggeng, 1910–35) 　阮
　玲玉 (風梗)

Ruan Lingyu shenhua 　阮玲玉神話

ruanxing dianying 　軟性電影

Ruan Yongrong 　阮用榮

ruhua pian 　辱華片

ru yuhou chunshun 　如雨後春筍

San'ge modeng nüxing 　三個摩登女
　性

Sang Hu (b. 1916) 　桑弧

Sanguo zhi Cao Cao bigong 　三國志
　曹操逼宮

Sanguo zhi Meiren ji 　三國志美人計

Sanren xing 　三人行

San wunü 　三舞女

Sata Tadao 　佐騰忠男

Sha Mei 　沙梅

Shamo zhishi 　沙漠之誓

Shangbiao 　商標

Shang fenghua 　傷風化

Shanghai chunqiu 　上海春秋

Shanghai de hubuwu 　上海的狐步舞

Shanghai dianying shiliao 　上海電影
　史料

Shanghai ershisi xiaoshi 　上海二十四
　小時

Shanghai fengwu zhi 　上海風物志

Shanghai huo diyu 　上海活地獄

Shanghai jiuhua 　上海舊話

Shanghai menjing 　上海門徑

Shanghai qibai nian 　上海七百年

Shanghai shenghuo 　上海生活

Shanghai shi hanghao tulu 　上海市行
　號圖錄

Shanghai sokai eiga shishi 　上海租界
　映畫私史

Shanghai tan yeshi 　上海灘野史

Shanghai tan zhi wunü 　上海灘之舞
　女

Shanghaitong she 　上海通社

Shanghai wenshi 　上海文史

Shanghai xiangdao 　上海向導

Shanghai yanjiu zhongxin 　上海研究
　中心

Shanghai yanjiu ziliao (xuji) 　上海研
　究資料 (續集)

Shanghai yi furen 　上海一婦人

Shanghai yingtan 　上海影壇

Shanghai yingtan huajiu 　上海影壇
　話舊

Shanghai zhinan 　上海指南

Shanghai zhiye 　上海之夜

Shanghai 1862 nian 　上海 1862 年

Shangwu yinshu guan 　商務印書館

Shao Chunren (1898–1973) 　邵屯人

Shao Lizi (1882–1967) 　邵力子

Shao Mujun (b. 1928) 　邵牧君

Shaoshi xiongdi 　邵氏兄弟

Shao Zhou 　少舟

Shao Zuiweng (1898–1979) 　邵醉翁

Sha Sipeng 　沙似鵬

Shehui ju 　社會局

Shen 　神

Shen bao 　申報

Sheng Aina 　聖愛娜

Shenghuo 　生活

Shengping 　升平

shengdi mente 　生蒂門特

Shenguai pian 　神怪片

Shengwu　聖五

Shennü　神女

Shen Suyue　沈蘇約

Shen Tu shi　申屠氏

Shen Xiling (1904–40)　沈西苓

Shen Yanbing (Mao Dun)　沈雁冰

She yiyang de nüren cai goude shang Shanghai de nüxing　蛇一樣的女人才夠的上上海的女性

shi　視

shidai xi　時代戲

Shidai huabao　時代畫報

Shi Dongshan (1902–55)　史東山

Shi Hui (1915–57)　石揮

shijian tamen delieyan zhuyi　實踐他們的獵艷主義

Shijie yingtan canguan ji　世界影壇參觀記

Shijie zhishi　世界知識

Shijie zhoukan　世界周刊

Shijimo chengshi: Xianggang de liuxing wenhua　世紀末城市: 香港的流行文化

Shimizu Akira　清水晶

Shi Tier　史鐵兒

Shi Yi　施宜

Shi Zhicun (b. 1905)　施蟄存

Shi Zhicun, Mu Shiying, Liu Na'ou xiaoshuo xinshang　施墊存, 穆時英, 劉呐歐小說欣賞

Shizi jietou　十字街頭

shouling　首領

shu chang　書場

shuoming shu　說明書

shuoshu　說書

Shu Qi (b. 1956)　舒琪

Shu Yan (b. 1914)　舒湮

shuyu　書寓

Si Bai　思白

sige huaidan　四個壞蛋

Sima Fen (Wang Bin)　司馬芬 (王斌)

Siming yanghang　四明洋行

si shenghuo　私生活

Situ Huimin (1910–87)　司徒慧敏

Si Tui　思退

Song Meiling (b. 1902)　宋美齡

Song Zhide　宋之的

suipian dengtai　隨片登台

Sulian zhiyou she　蘇聯之友社

Sun Jiaming　孫家明

Sun Lindi　孫林弟

Sun Shiyi (1904–66)　孫師毅

Sun Xiaohua　孫小華

Sun Yu (1900–1990)　孫瑜

Sun Zhongshan (Sun Yat-sen 1866–1925)　孫中山

Sun Zhou (b. 1954)　孫周

Suo Posheng　娑婆生

suowei de daye gongzi men　所謂的大爺公子們

Tan Chunfa (b. 1938)　譚春發

Tan huang　灘簧

Tang Jishan　唐季珊

Tang Na (1914–88)　唐納

Tang Xiaodan (b. 1910)　湯曉丹

Tang Youfeng　唐幼峰

Tanizaki Jun'ichiro　谷崎潤一朗

Tan shejiao　談社交

Tansuo de niandai　探索的年代

Tanxing nüer　彈性女兒

Tan Xinpei (1846–1917)　譚鑫培

Tan Ying (b. 1915)　談瑛

taobi xianshi　逃避現實

Taohua jiang　桃花江

Taohua qixue ji　桃花泣血記

Taoli jie　桃李劫

Taowang　逃亡

Tebie kuaiche　特別快車

Tiangong wuchang　天宮舞場

Tian Han (1898–1968)　田漢

Tian Han wenji　田漢文集

Tianhua　天華

Tianma　天馬

Tianming   天明

Tiantian ribao   天天日報

Tianyi (yingpian gongsi)   天一 (影片公司)

tianzhen   天真

tianzhen er huopo   天真而活潑

tiaowu shi tade shou   跳舞時他的手

Tiaowu shi yeman canhen   跳舞是野蠻殘痕

Tiaowu tingqian   跳舞廳前

tiaowu xuexiao   跳舞學校

Tieshan gongzhu   鐵扇公主

Tieti xiade genü   鐵騎下的歌女

Tiyu huanghou   體育皇後

Tiyu shijie   體育世界

tongqing   同慶

Tongsu xiju congshu   通俗戲劇叢書

Tuhua ribao   圖畫日報

tuoche   拖車

Tu Shiping   屠詩聘

Wan de menjing   玩的門徑

Wang Chenwu (Chen Wu, 1911–38)   王塵無

Wang Dewei   王德威

Wang Dingjiu   王定九

Wang Hanlun (Peng Jianqing, 1903–78)   王漢倫 (彭劍青)

Wang Jingwei   汪精衛

Wang Lucheng   王鹿城

Wang Meng (b. 1934)   王蒙

Wang Renmei (1914–87)   王人美

Wang Shifu   王實甫

Wang Tao (1828–97)   王韜

Wang Tongzhao (1897–1957)   王統照

Wanguo   萬國

Wang Xianzhai (1900–1942)   王獻齋

Wang Yunman   王雲縵

Wang Zhongxian   汪仲賢

Wang Zilong   王子龍

Wanshi liufang   萬世流芳

Wan tiaowu menjing   玩跳舞門徑

Wanxiang   萬象

Wanying   萬影

Watanabe Kunio   渡邊邦男

Weiduoliya   維多利亞

Wei Qiren   魏啓仁

Wei Shaochang   魏紹昌

wenhua ke   文化科

Wenhua shiliao   文化史料

wenming xi   文明戲

Wenming yaji   文明雅集

wenren dianying   文人電影

Wenrong heqi de   溫容和氣的

Wenxue yanjiu hui   文學研究會

Wenxue yanjiu hui xiaoshuo xuan   文學研究會小說選

Wen Yimin   文逸民

Wode chengming yu buxing: Wang Renmei huiyi lu   我的成名與不幸:王人美回憶錄

Wode dianying shenghuo   我的電影生活

Wode tansuo he zuiqiu   我的探索和追求

Wo hen ji le shishi congbai wai guoren de xinli   我恨極了事事崇拜外國人的心理

women nar   我們那兒

Women xuyao wuru?   我們需要侮辱?

Wo xiang: wo shi renshi le tamen ma?   我想:我是認識了他們嗎?

Wuben nü zhongxue   務本女中學

wuchang   舞場

Wuchang manhua   舞場漫話

Wu Cheng   吳澄

Wu Chengyu   伍澄宇

Wuchou junzi   無愁君子

Wufu linmen   五福臨門

Wu Guiyun   吳貴芸

wuguo   舞國

wuguo huanghou   舞國皇後

Wu Hanyi   吳翰儀

Wu Jianren (1867–1910)   吳趼人

Wu Jianren yanjiu ziliao   吳趼人研究資料

Wuliao yingpian gongsi   無聊影片公司

Wu Nonghua   吳農花

wunü   舞女

wunü lei genü chou   舞女淚歌女愁

Wunü tongda shehuiju   舞女痛打社會局

Wu shi nian lai de Zhongguo dianying   五十年來的中國電影

Wushi xunyou   舞市巡游

Wu Songgao   吳頌皋

Wutai jiemei   舞台姐妹

Wu Tiecheng (1888–1953)   吳鐵城

wuting   舞廳

wuxia pian   武俠片

wuxie de guniang   無邪的姑娘

Wuxie zhige   舞榭之歌

Wu Yin (1909–91)   吳茵

Wu Yonggang (1907–82)   吳永剛

Wu Zhifang   吳芷芳

Xia Chifeng   夏赤鳳

Xialingpeike   夏令配克

Xiandai dianying   現代電影

Xiandai Zhongguo dianying shilüe   現代中國電影史略

Xiangcao meiren   香草美人

Xiangchou   鄉愁

xiannü   仙女

xianrou zhuang   咸肉莊

Xiansheng   賢聲

Xian Xinghai (1905–45)   冼星海

xiaobao   小報

Xiaocheng zhi chun   小城之春

Xiao Hong   小紅

Xiao Jianqing   蕭劍青

xiaoji dianying   消極電影

Xiao Lingzi   小玲子

Xiao Luo   小洛

Xiao pengyou   小朋友

Xiaoshuo daguan   小說大觀

Xiaoshuo shibao   小說時報

Xiaoshuo shijie   小說世界

Xiaoshuo yuebao   小說月報

Xiao tianshi   小天使

Xiao wanyi   小玩藝

Xiao Ye (b. 1951)   小野

Xiao Youmei   蕭友梅

Xia Yan (Huang Zibu, 1900–1995)   夏衍

xichao   西潮

Xicheng   西城

Xie Bo   解波

Xie Jin (b. 1923)   謝晉

Xie Tieli (b. 1925)   謝鐵驪

Xi Naifang (Zheng Boqi)   席耐芳

Xinchao   新潮

xin ganjue pai   新感覺派

Xin ganjue pai xiaoshuo xuan   新感覺派小說選

Xingqi   星期

Xinguang   新光

Xingzhengyuan   行政院

Xinhua huabao   新華畫報

xinju   新劇

Xinmin   新民

Xin nüxing   新女性

xinpai ju   新派劇

Xinren (yingpian gongsi)   新人 (影片公司)

Xin Shanghai   新上海

xin shenghuo yundong   新生活運動

Xinshijie   新世界

Xintu   新土

Xin wenxue shiliao   新文學史料

Xin wutai   新舞台

Xinxiang   心香

Xin Xianlin   新仙林

Xinxin   新新

Xin Yebao   新夜報

Xin yingtan   新影壇

Xin yingxing yu tiyu   新銀星與體育

Xin Zhongyang   新中央

Xiong Shiyi   熊式一

xiren dianying   戲人電影

Xixiang ji　西廂記

Xixiang ji kaozheng　西廂記考證

Xixiangji zhugongdiao zhushi　西廂記諸宮調注釋

xiyangjing　西洋鏡

Xiyangjing ge　西洋鏡歌

xiyang yingxi　西洋影戲

Xiyou ji　西游記

xiyuan　西園

Xiyuan　戲園

xizi　戲子

Xuan Jinglin (1907–92)　宣景琳

Xu Changlin (b. 1916)　徐昌霖

Xu Chi　徐遲

Xu Daoming　許道明

Xu Dishan (1893–1941)　許地山

Xue Juexian (1904–56)　薛覺仙

Xuesheng de xin shenghuo　學生的新生活

Xuetang yuege　學堂樂歌

xuetou　噱頭

Xu Ke (Tsui Hark, b. 1952)　徐克

Xu Min　許敏

Xun Huisheng (1900–1985)　荀慧生

Xun Huisheng yanchu juben xuan　荀慧生演出劇本選

Xu Wenrong　徐文榮

Xu Xingzhi (1904–91)　許幸之

Xu Zhudai (1881–1958)　徐卓呆

Xuyuan　徐園

Yamaguchi Yoshiko (Li Xianglan)　山口淑子

Yan Ciping　嚴次平

Yang Aiyuan　楊愛媛

Yang Cun　楊村

Yang Dechang (Edward Yang, b. 1947)　楊德昌

Yang Hansheng (b. 1902)　陽翰生

Yang Lijuan　楊麗娟

Yang Naimei (1904–60)　楊耐梅

yang wawa　洋娃娃

Yang Xiaozhong (1899–1969)　楊小仲

Yan Hong　焉紅

Yan Jiayan　嚴家炎

Yan Jun (1919–80)　嚴俊

Yan Ruisheng　閻瑞生

Yanzhi kou　胭脂扣

Yao a yao, yao dao waipo qiao　搖啊搖搖到外婆橋

Yaochuan ge　搖船歌

yao de lai　妖得來

yaoqianshu　搖錢樹

Yao Sufeng (1905–74)　姚蘇鳳

Yao Xinnong　姚莘農

Yasui qian　壓歲錢

Ya Tang　亞唐

Yaxiya　亞細亞

Ye　夜

Ye ban gesheng　夜半歌聲

Ye Haisheng　葉海生

Ye huayuan　夜花園

yeji　野雞

Ye Jinfeng　葉勁風

Ye Lingfeng (1904–75)　葉靈鳳

Ye meigui　野玫瑰

Ye Shengtao (Ye Shaojun, 1894–1988)　葉聖陶 (葉紹鈞)

Yezonghui lide wuge ren　夜總會里的五個人

Yichuan zhenzhu　一串珍珠

Yihua (yingpian gongsi)　藝華 (影片公司)

Yingju tiandi　影劇天地

Yingmi de baichi　影迷的白痴

Yingpian shang de guochi　影片上的國恥

Yingpian shang de youse renzhong　影片上的有色人種

yingren dianying　影人電影

yingshi wenhua　影視文化

Yingshi zuihuai lu　影事追懷錄

Yingtan　影壇

Yingtan yijiu　影壇憶舊

Yingwu zhoubao　影舞周報

yingxi　影戲

Yingxi chunqiu　影戲春秋
Yingxi congbao　影戲叢報
Yinxing　銀星
Yingxing biaozhun yiming　影星標準
　譯名
Yingxi zazhi　影戲雜志
Yingying benshi ge　鶯鶯本事歌
Yingying zhuan　鶯鶯傳
Ying Yunwei (1904–67)　應雲衛
Yin hai fan zhou—huiyi wo de yisheng
　銀海泛舟——回憶我的一生
Yin Hong　尹鴻
Yin Min　尹民
Yin Mingzhu　殷明珠
Yiren Ruan Lingyu nüshi rong'ai lu
　藝人阮玲玉女士榮哀錄
yiwu chuanqing　以物傳情
Yiyongjun jinxingqu　義勇軍進行曲
Yiyuan shi yi　藝苑拾憶
Yong an gongsi　永安公司
Yong yanjing kan de Zhongguo dianying
　shi　用眼睛看的中國電影史
Youhun　誘婚
You Jing (Yu Ling)　尤競
Youlian　友聯
you shang fenghua　有傷風化
you shen xiqi jingwu　有甚稀奇景物
Youxi bao　游戲報
yuan　元
Yuan Meiyun (b. 1919)　袁美雲
Yuan Muzhi (1909–78)　袁牧之
Yuan Qiuxia　袁秋霞
Yuan Zhen (779–831)　元縝
yuanyang　鴛鴦
Yuanyang hudiepai wenxu ziliao　鴛鴦
　蝴蝶派文學資料
Yuanyang hudiepai xiaoshuo　鴛鴦蝴
　蝶派小說
Yuanyangzuo　鴛鴦座
Yu Boyan　俞伯岩
Yu Dafu (1896–1945)　郁達夫
Yuguang qu　漁光曲
Yu Hua (b. 1960)　余華

yule shangpin　娛樂商品
Yuli hun　玉梨魂
Yu Ling (You Jing, b. 1907)　于伶
Yu Meiyan　余美顏
yunbin　雲鬢
Yuxianwu　羽仙舞
Yu Xingmin　余醒民
Yuyan　欲焰

Zaihui ba, Shanghai　再會吧, 上海
Zaisheng　再生
Zai Zhongguo de rizi—Li Xianglan: Wode
　banshen　在中國的日子——李香
　蘭: 我的半生
zaju　雜劇
Zazhi yuekan　雜志月刊
Zenyang yu wunü tanqing　怎樣與舞
　女談情
Zenyang zuo ge ren　怎樣作個人
Zhaixing zhi nü　摘星之女
Zhang Ailing (1920–96)　張愛玲
Zhang Chengshan (b. 1947)　張成珊
Zhang Damin　張達民
Zhang Daofan　張道藩
Zhang Fengwu (Qian Xingchun)
　張鳳吾
Zhang Gong　張珙
Zhang Ku　張庫
Zhang Man　張曼
Zhang Minggu　張茗谷
Zhangong　戰功
Zhang Ruogu　張若谷
Zhang Ruoying　張若英
Zhang Shankun (1905–57)　張善琨
Zhang Shichuan (1889–1953)　張石川
Zhang Shu　張曙
Zhang Xinsheng　張欣生
Zhang Xueliang　張學良
Zhang Yimou (b. 1950)　張藝謀
Zhang Zhongli　張仲禮
Zhang Ziliang　張子良
Zhang Zongchang　張宗昌
Zhao Dan (1915–80)　趙丹

zhaole 找樂

Zhaoshang ju 招商局

Zhao Yuanren (Yuen Ren Chao, 1892–1982) 趙元任

zhen 真

Zheng Boqi (Xi Naifang, 1895–1979) 鄭伯奇

Zheng Chaoren 鄭超人

Zheng Heng 鄭恆

Zheng Junli (1911–69) 鄭君里

Zheng Yimei (1895–1992) 鄭逸梅

Zheng Zhenduo (1898–1958) 鄭振鐸

Zheng Zhengqiu (Yaofeng, 1888–1935) 鄭正秋 (藥風)

Zhenzhen 真真

Zhibian waishi tekan 支邊外史特刊

Zhiguo yuan 擲果緣

Zhina zhi ye 支那之夜

zhiqing 知青

Zhiyin 知音

Zhizao ju 製造局

Zhong Dafeng 鐘大豐

Zhong Dianpei (1919–87) 鐘惦棐

Zhongguo daguan 中國大觀

Zhongguo dianying dacidian 中國電影大辭典

Zhongguo dianying fada shi 中國電影發達史

Zhongguo dianying fazhan shi 中國電影發展史

Zhongguo dianying haibao yishu jingcui 中國電影海報藝術精萃

Zhongguo dianying jia liezhuan 中國電影家列傳

Zhongguo dianying jianshi 中國電影簡史

Zhongguo dianying nianjian 中國電影年鑒

Zhongguo dianying sanshinian 中國電影三十年

Zhongguo dianying shi 中國電影史

Zhongguo dianying shihua 中國電影史話

Zhongguo dianying tuzhi 中國電影圖志

Zhongguo dianying wenhua toushi 中國電影文化透視

Zhongguo dianying wushinian 中國電影五十年

Zhonghua dianying xueyuan 中華電影學院

Zhongguo dianying yanjiu 中國電影研究

Zhongguo dianying yanyuan cangsang lu 中國電影演員滄桑錄

Zhongguo dianying yanyuan cidian 中國電影演員詞典

Zhongguo dianying yishu shi 中國電影藝術史

Zhongguo dianying yishu shigang 中國電影藝術史綱

Zhongguo dianying yishu shilüe 中國電影藝術史略

Zhongguo dianying zhi jianglai 中國電影之將來

Zhongguo huaju wushinian yundong shi-liao ji 中國話劇五十此運動史料集

Zhongguo jindai wenxue daxi 中國近代文學大系

Zhongguo nü zuojia 中國女作家

Zhongguo sheying shi, 1840–1937 中國攝影史 1840–1937

Zhongguo wusheng dianying 中國無聲電影

Zhongguo wusheng dianying juben 中國無聲電影劇本

Zhongguo wusheng dianying shi 中國無聲電影史

Zhongguo xiandai dianying wenxue shi 中國現代電影文學史

Zhongguo xin wenxue daxi 中國新文學大系

Zhongguo xin wenxue yundong shi zi-liao 中國新文學運動史資料

Zhongguo xinxing yinyue yanjiuhui 中國新興音樂研究會

Zhongguo xuesheng　中國學生

Zhongguo yingju shi　中國影劇史

Zhongguo yingpian dadian: gushipian, xiqupian　中國影片大典: 故事片, 戲曲片

Zhongguo yingxi yanjiu she　中國影戲研究社

Zhongguo yintan waishi　中國銀壇外史

Zhongguo zuoyi dianying yundong　中國左翼電影運動

Zhongguo zuoyi zuojia lianmeng　中國左翼作家聯盟

Zhonghua dianying lianhe gufen youxian gongsi　中華電影聯合股份有限公司

Zhonghua gewuhui　中華歌舞會

Zhonghua gewutuan　中華歌舞團

Zhonghua gewu zhuanmen xuexiao (Gezhuan)　中華歌舞專門學校 (歌專)

Zhonghua lianhe zhipian gufen gongsi　中華聯合制片股份公司

Zhonghua minguo dianying shi　中華民國電影史

Zhonghua tuhua zazhi　中華圖畫雜誌

Zhonghua shuju　中華書局

Zhonghua yingpian gongsi　中華影片公司

Zhonghua yingye nianjian　中華影業年鑒

Zhong Lei　鐘雷

Zhonglian ying xun　中聯影訊

Zhongnan qingbao　中南情報

Zhongwai wenxue　中外文學

Zhongyang　中央

Zhongyang da xiyuan　中央大戲園

Zhou Jianyun (1893–1967)　周劍雲

Zhou Ruiyun　周蕊雲

Zhou Shixun　周世勛

Zhou Shoujuan (1894–1968)　周瘦鵑

Zhou Xiaoming (b. 1954)　周曉明

Zhou Xuan (1918–57)　周璇

zhuangyuan　狀元

Zhu Pingchu　朱平楚

Zhu Shilin (1899–1967)　朱石麟

Zhu Shouju　朱瘦菊

Zhu Wei　朱偉

Zhu Xuehua　朱血花

Zhu Ziqing (1898–1948)　朱自清

Ziluolan　紫羅蘭

Zimei hua　姊妹花

ziran　自然

Ziye　子夜

Ziyou shen　自由神

Ziyoutan　自由談

Zizhi yingpian de quedian　自制影片的缺點

Zuihou zhi liangxin　最後之良心

zong jicha　總稽查

zuo huaishi　作壞事

zuoqing jiaotiao zhuyi　左傾教條主義

zuoyi dianying　左翼電影

Index

Library of Congress Cataloging-in-Publication Data

Cinema and urban culture in Shanghai, 1922–1943 /
edited and with an introduction by Yingjin Zhang.

p. cm.

Includes bibliographical references and index.

ISBN 0-8047-3188-8 (cloth : alk. paper). —
ISBN 0-8047-3572-7 (pbk. : alk. paper)

1. Motion pictures—China—Shanghai—History.
I. Zhang, Yingjin.

PN1993.5.C4C565   1999

791.43'0951'32—dc21   98-47926

                                                       CIP

♾ This book is printed on acid-free paper.

Original printing 1999

Last figure below indicates year of this printing:
08   07   06   05   04   03   02   01   00   99

Designed by Eleanor Mennick
Typeset in Minion Family and Decotura
Compositor: Ralph Fowler